LIGHT, LIBERTY AND LEARNING:
THE IDEA OF A UNIVERSITY REVISITED

NIGEL F B ALLINGTON

NICHOLAS J O'SHAUGHNESSY

EU NO.1/92

Published by the Education Unit, Warlingham Park School,
Chelsham Common, Warlingham, Surrey, CR6 9PB.

Telephone 0883 626844   Fax 0883 625501

Printed by Parchment (Oxford) Limited, Printworks, Crescent Road,
Cowley, Oxford, OX4 2PB

ISBN 1 873188 10 2

1992

© Nigel F B Allington and Nicholas O'Shaughnessy

Loose cover illustration, "Batchelor of Arts" published May 1st 1803
by R. Harraden, Cambridge, Proprietor of the
"Views of Cambridge", etc.

This book, in common with others published by the Education Unit, is intended to present an informed analysis of particular issues as a contribution to wider understanding. The Education Unit does not express any corporate view on the analysis or conclusions of its authors.

CONTENTS

Preface   1

Acknowledgements   3

Tables   4

Abbreviations   7

Chapter 1
Through the Looking Glass: Prologue.   10

    Introduction   12

    Why universities matter.   14

    The universities and government.   15

    Our Programme   (1) Making the customer pay.   16

    Our Programme   (2) Reject current policy options.   19

    Our Programme   (3) Managerial change.   20

    A call to arms.   21

Chapter 2
The World We Have Lost:
The Development of University Education.   27

    Introduction.   29

    Newman and the Idea of a University: Prologue.   30

    Oxford and Cambridge.   32

    Scottish Universities.   37

    London and Durham Universities.   39

    Civic Universities.   42

University Colleges.	44
The Federal University of Wales.	45
New Universities.	47
The Robbins Report and the final phase of expansion.	49
Buckingham.	50
The early development of state funding.	53
The origins and development of UGC.	58
Universities between the wars.	59
State-UGC-University relations after the second world war.	65
Confrontation between University Grants Committee and Public Accounts Committee.	66
Transfer to Department of Education and Science.	67
Planning and the UGC.	68
The post-1979 position of UGC: the rise of state control.	68

Chapter 3
The Way We Live Now: A Situational Analysis. 75

Introduction.	77
The nineteen eighties and nineties.	78
A: Situation now and 1990/91 to 1992/93 allocation of resources.	82
Bidding and student numbers.	91

B: Future strategy: The 1985 Green Paper and the shift to vocations and technology.	94
Access.	95
Funding.	96
The relevance of university activities.	98
Selectivity.	99
Criteria of selectivity.	100
Trouble in the ranks.	101
C: The attempt at management: Big is beautiful.	103
Exploitability.	105
The 1991 White Paper.	106
Consequences of massification.	107
Role of polytechnics.	108
Research.	109
What's in a name?	109

Chapter 4
To Teach the Senators Wisdom:
the Governance of Universities. 111

Introduction.	112
The role of vice chancellors.	112
Internal agents and agencies.	114
Academic personnel.	116
What of incentives and rewards?	119
Course content.	122

Course flexibility.	124
Local students.	124
National policies: Planning.	125
Targets.	126
Contracts.	126
Massification.	126
Research Councils.	128
Brokerage.	128
Capital equipment.	129
Public relations.	129
A Royal Commission.	129

Chapter 5
The Men in White Suits: University Research.   131

Introduction.	132
Part One: The reduction in research funding.	134
Why is research important?	134
The utility of university research.	136
Part Two: The reduction in research funding.	140
Have universities currently met more official generosity?	149
Research funding from industry.	149
Part Three: Current policy proposals: Selectivity and hierarchy.	154
(A) competition and concentration.	155

(B) contracts.	157
Research Councils.	160
Part Four: Assessment.	165
The 1991 White Paper.	173
Conclusions – the death of research.	174
Exodus.	177
Who Pays?	178
Postscript: How is university research funded?	179
Science.	181

Chapter 6
Deconstructing the Ivory Tower :
International Comparisons of Research Funding. 184

Introduction: Lessons from overseas?	185
German experience.	188
Finnish experience.	189
Danish experience.	189
Dutch experience.	190
Norwegian experience.	190
Greek experience.	192
Spanish experience.	192
United States experience.	193
Australian experience.	195
French experience.	196
Japanese experience.	197

Chapter 7
Athena Disrobed:
International Comparisons of the
Funding of Universities and Students.   200

Introduction.	202
Higher education in United States of America.	205
University revenue sources, private and public.	206
Increase in state and private support.	207
Origins and growth of federal student support.	207
Level of total support, mid-eighties.	210
Higher education in Japan.	211
Cuts.	212
Reform.	213
Public and Private.	213
Student support.	214
Higher education in Germany.	215
Funding.	215
Student support.	216
Research.	218
What of the future?	219
Higher education in France: An overview.	219
Funding.	221
Student support.	222
Higher education in Netherlands.	224
Funding.	225
Student support.	226

Higher education in Denmark.	228
Funding.	228
Student support.	229
The threat to autonomy.	230
Higher education in Norway.	230
Funding.	231
Student support.	232
Higher education in Finland.	233
Funding.	234
Student support.	235
Higher education in Spain.	236
Funding.	237
Student support.	238
Higher education in Greece.	239
Funding.	239
Student support.	240
More recent developments.	241
Conclusions.	243

Chapter 8
The Courtiers of Lilliput :
A Survey of Vice Chancellors and Principals.   254

Introduction.	255
Part One : Financing the system.	255
Impact of 1981 cuts.	255
How much more state support?	257
Endowment income.	258

	Fundraising efforts.	259
	Tax incentives.	260
	Alumni support.	260
	Part Two : Independence.	261
	A mixed economy?	263
	Is the market a threat to standards?	264
	Protecting the weak.	265
	Restraint on freedom.	266
	Part Three : Administration.	267
	Staff conditions.	267
	University government.	268
	Part Four : Future plans.	269
	Tripartite division.	270
	Participation.	270

Chapter 9
Minerva and the Market Place:
A Survey of Industry. 274

	Introduction.	276
	Industry support for basic research.	278
	Research funding.	279
	On the UK science base.	281
	Who pays?	282
	Is independence an option?	283
	Independence.	283
	Business and the science base.	288
	Personnel : Staff training.	289
	Graduate demand.	290

	Participation.	292
	Conclusion.	292

Chapter 10
Prometheus Unbound : A New Funding Mechanism. 296

	Introduction.	297
	The new charge mechanism.	299
	The charge mechanism and repayment scenarios.	301
	Some illustrative costings.	304
	Why a voucher?	320
	Grants and loans.	321
	The graduate tax and ideological rectitude.	326
	Conclusion.	328

Chapter 11
The Ruins Are Inhabited : Epilogue. 330

	Introduction	331
	The role of government.	331
	Our mechanism.	332
	Our defence.	334
	The future and how to avoid it.	335

Select Bibliography	338
Name Index	346
Subject Index	347

Preface

This is an impertinent book. The authors have not, after all, had to manage a university, or even a department. What, therefore, do they offer? Part of the answer lies in the fact that as lecturers we have an immediacy of tutorial experience which the oligarchs lack, and, therefore, some appreciation of what the changes in higher education are meaning where they matter most. Moreover, this book has a dual purpose, and those who reject its policy proposals on management, research and student funding may still approve its other function as a work of reference on international practice, history, industrial and vice-chancellor opinion and such.

A second part of the answer is that such a book, a book about universities, is urgently needed, and since none has been forthcoming these authors have sought (however incompletely) to fill the gap. For our universities are to become a monolithic system, charged with educating one third of the nation's youth, but the achievement of this will for most of them mean the surrender of what they see as the core meaning of their title, that is academic research. How can the competing claims of national interest and professional élan be reconciled? What kind of system do we need and how should we fund it? What kind of research do we want, and at what price?

While the policy formulae offered in this book may be controversial, its real contribution is to condense and clarify the complex of strategic issues in higher education and, above all, to begin by asking those elementary questions so ignored by pontificating commissions and circumlocutory civil service reports over the past decade. That is, what is the mission of a university as illuminated by history and amplified by modern need, how is this defined, and what objectives flow from this? Without such a sense of superordinate goals, all attempts to formulate a public policy would reduce to a mechanical and aimless tinkering, as, indeed, has proved to be the case.

Our original intention, at the behest of our commissioning editor Stuart Sexton, was to produce an IEA Hobart Paper on the funding of higher education. However, two chapters for IEA conference books and several articles later, we have produced a book with a much wider and, hopefully, provocative coverage. We owe a particular debt to Stuart for his advice and constant enthusiasm for the project through its long gestation period. Debts are also acknowledged without any implications for sins of omission or commission to: John Evans (research assistant); John Barnes (LSE); Nick Barr (LSE); Michael Barrett (University of Buckingham); Robert Jones; (Welsh Office); John Kelly (Surrey University); Robin Marris (Birkbeck College); John O'Shaughnessy (Columbia University); Patrick O'Sullivan (Cardiff University); Bryan Taylor (Bath University); Jim Taylor (Lancaster University); Ian Thomson (Cardiff University); Stephen Watson (Cambridge University); Gareth Williams (London University); Maureen Woodall (London University); Cathy Colgan; Jan Richards; Heather Rowlands; Mark Goode; Barry Jones; Carl Miller; and the Librarians of Cardiff and Cambridge Universities. Special thanks goes to the un-named managing directors, vice-chancellors and college masters who answered written and verbal questions and gave much useful advice and information, some of which is yet to be used. Finally, financial assistance is acknowledged from the IEA Education Unit and the Esmé Fairbairn Trust.

Nigel Allington
Nicholas O'Shaughnessy
Cambridge, January 1992.

To our parents:

The magnitude of our debt to whom we only fully realise with the passage of time. Their example of integrity and industry is a constant inspiration.

TABLES

Table 1:1	Funding Universities and Other Major Developments: A Chronology.	23-26
Table 2:1	The Development of the New Universities and Proposed Student Numbers Up to 1966-67.	48
Table 2:2	Local Authority Provision for the New Universities.	49
Table 2:3	Annual Distribution of Grant 1889-1894.	56
Table 2:4	Distribution of Grant 1897.	56
Table 2:5	Grants and Local Income for Universities 1895-96.	57
Table 2:6	University Income Accounts 1895-96.	57-8
Table 2:7	Sources of University Income 1913/14 to 1989/90.	60-3
Table 2:8	Grant and Student Number Reductions Announced 1st July 1981.	69-70
Table 3:1	1990/91 Allocation of Resources Including Teaching Component.	83-85
Table 3:2	1991/92 Allocation of Resources.	85-87
Table 3:3	Allocation of Student Numbers by Subject Group.	87
Table 3:4.1	Teaching and Research Funding Increase 1992/93.	88-90
Table 3:4.2	Funding Subject by Subject.	90
Chart 3:1	Allocation of Additional Funded Student Numbers for 1992/93.	92
Table 3:5	UFC Subject Group Guide Prices.	93
Table 3:6	Sources of University Funding in the UK.	97
Table 5:1	Global Balances for British Universities 1977/78 to 1987/88.	142-3
Table 5:2	Financial Forecasts to 1992/93.	144
Table 5:3	Universities' Deficit or Surplus as a Percentage of Recurrent Grant, 1990.	145-6
Table 5:4	Comparative University Salaries in Units of Purchasing Power.	147
Table 5:5.1	University Research Incoming from Industry.	151

Table 5:5.2	University External Research Income.	151
Table 5:5.3	Industry Expenditure on Research.	151
Table 5:6	Annual Review of Government Funded Research and Development.	152
Table 5:7	Overheads Recovery by University Research Departments.	163
Table 5:8	1989 Selectivity Exercise by Cost Centre.	167
Table 5:9	1989 Selectivity Exercise by Unit of Assessment.	167-8
Table 5:10	Institutional and Subject Ranking 1989.	169
Table 5:11	Subject Group Best Departments 1989 – University Respondents.	169-70
Table 5:12	1986 University Research Rankings.	171-2
Table 5:13	Science Budget: Recommended Allocations for 1989/90 and Planning Figures for 1990/91 and 1991/92.	182
Table 5:14	DES Science Provision 1991/92 to 1994/95.	182
Table 6:1	General Expenditure on R and D as a Percentage of GDP.	186
Table 6:2	Government Funding of R and D by Socio-Economic Objective.	187
Table 6:3	Government and EC Funded Civil Research and Development.	188
Table 7:1	Higher Education in Europe in 1989.	203
Table 7:2	Tuition at State Universities, Tuition Plus Fees 1989-1990.	208
Table 7:3	United States Student Aid Packages.	209
Table 7:4	Annual Student Loan Default Costs.	211
Table 7:5	Summary Statistics of International Comparisons.	244
Table 7:5.1	Percentage of GNP Devoted to Higher Education.	244-5
Table 7:5.2	Annual Rate of Growth of Current Expenditure on Higher Education Institutions.	246

Table 7:5.3	Average Current Institutional Expenditure Per Student.	247-9
Table 7:5.4	Sources of Income of Higher Education Institutions.	250-1
Table 7:5.5	Percentage of Income from Industry and Commerce and from Medical Services (other than tuition fees).	251-2
Table 7:5.6	Student Financial Aid.	252-3
Table 9:1.1	Research and Development Performed by British Industry.	294
Table 9:1.2	R and D Performed in Manufacturing Industry.	294-5
Table 9:1.3	Sources of Funds for Industrially Performed R and D.	295
Table 10:1	The Higher Education User Payment Scheme in Outline.	302-3
Chart 10:1	Geography of the HEUP Scheme.	304
Table 10:2	Projected University Student Numbers to 2000 AD.	306
Table 10:3	Total Enrolment and Home Students 1988-1989.	306-7
Table 10:4	Student Number Projections by Cost Centre to 2000 A.D.	307-9
Table 10:5	Cost of Courses and Maintenance at 1990 Prices.	310
Table 10:6	Cost to Exchequer.	311-313
Table 10:7	Numbers Graduating, Continuing and Entering Universities 1990/91 – 1999/2000.	314
Table 10:8	Possible Repayment Scenarios.	315-17
Table 10:9	Revenue Generated From Two Possible Scenarios.	318
Table 10:10	Revenue if 20% Pay Up-Front.	319
Table 10:11	Revenue if 10% Pay Up-Front.	319
Table 10:12	Mandatory Students Awards, England and Wales: Real Terms Changes 1962/63 to 1987/8.	323
Table 10:13	Department of Education Plans for Student Awards.	324

ABBREVIATIONS

ABRC	Advisory Board for the Research Councils.
ACOST	Advisory Council on Science and Technology.
ARC	Agriculture Research Council.
AURC	Australian Research Council.
ASI	Adam Smith Institute.
BOA	Board of Agriculture.
BOE	Board of Education.
BTG	British Technology Group.
CAG	Comptroller and Auditor General.
CAT	Colleges of Advanced Technology.
CBI	Confederation of British Industry.
CERN	European Particle Physics Laboratory.
CHEI	Council for Higher Education and Industry.
CPS	Centre for Policy Studies.
CVCP	Committee of Vice Chancellors and Principals.
DES	Department of Education and Science.
DHSS	Department of Health and Social Security.
DSIR	Department of Scientific and Industrial Research.
EEC	European Economic Community.
ESRC	Economic and Social Research Council.
ETP	Engineering and Technology Programme.
FE	Fellowship of Engineering.
GDP	Gross Domestic Product.
GNP	Gross National Product (GDP plus net property income from abroad).

HEUPS	Higher Education User Payment Scheme.
IEA	Institute of Economic Affairs.
IOD	Institute of Directors.
LEA	Local Education Authorities.
MIT	Massachusetts Institute of Technology.
MRC	Medical Research Committee.
MSEP	Manufacturing System Engineering Programmes.
NAAS	New Academics Appointments Scheme.
NAO	National Audit Office.
NERC	Natural Environment Research Council.
NIC	National Insurance Contributions.
NSF	National Science Foundation.
NUS	National Union of Students.
OECD	Organisation for Economic Co-operation and Development.
OTRR	Office for Transfer of Research Results.
PAC	Public Accounts Committee.
PCFC	Polytechnic and Colleges Funding Council.
PESC	Public Expenditure Select Committee.
RC	Research Councils.
RCn	Royal Commission.
RS	Royal Society.
SBS	Save British Science.
SCE	Select Committee on Estimates.
SEPSU	Science and Engineering Policy Studies Unit.
SERC	Science and Engineering Research Council.
THES	*Times Higher Educational Supplement.*

UCCA	Universities Central Council for Admissions.
UFC	Universities Funding Council.
UGC	University Grants Committee.
VC	Vice Chancellor.

CHAPTER ONE
THROUGH THE LOOKING GLASS: PROLOGUE

"It is education which gives a man a clear conscious view of his own opinions and judgements, a truth in developing them, an eloquence in expressing them, and a force in urging them. It teaches him to see things as they are, to go right to the point, to disentangle a skein of thought, to detect what is sophisticated, and to discard what is irrelevant. It prepares him to fill any post with credit, and to master any subject with facility".
J.H. Newman,
The Idea of a University, New York, 1959.

"But the intellect, which has been disciplined to the perfection of its powers, which knows, and thinks while it knows, which has learned to leaven the dense mass of facts and events with the elastic force of reason, such an intellect cannot be partial, cannot be exclusive, cannot be impetuous, cannot be at a loss, cannot but be patient, collected, and majestically calm, because it discerns the end in every beginning, the origin in every end, the law in every interruption, the limit in each delay; because it ever knows where it stands, and how its path lies from one point to another".
J.H. Newman,
The Idea of a University, New York, 1959.

"If then I am arguing, and shall argue, against Professional or Scientific knowledge as the sufficient end of a University Education, let me not be supposed, Gentlemen, to be disrespectful towards particular studies, or arts, or vocations, and those who are engaged in them. In saying that Law or Medicine is not the end of a University course, I do not mean to imply that the University does not teach Law or Medicine. What indeed can it teach at all, if it does not teach something particular? It teaches all knowledge by teaching all. I do but say that there will be this distinction as regards a Professor of Law, or of Medicine, or of Geology, or of Political Economy, in a University and out of it, that out of a University he is in danger of being

absorbed and narrowed by his pursuit, and of giving Lectures which are the Lectures of nothing more than a lawyer, physician, geologist, or political economist; whereas in a University he will just know where he and his science stand, he has come to it, as it were from a height, he has taken a survey of all knowledge, he is kept from extravagance by the very rivalry of other studies, he has gained from them a special illumination and largeness of mind and freedom and self-possession, and he treats his own in consequence with a philosophy and a resource, which belongs not to the study itself, but to his liberal education''.
J.H. Newman,
The Idea of a University, New York, 1959.

"The universities are now being engulfed in the long and general trend in British society which entrenches the past, slows down innovation and destroys individual institutions and responsibility; the growth of bureaucratic state control; the impairment of the state as leader and the development of the state as housekeeper and administrator; the universalising of the committee system so that everyone can refer everything to everyone else''.
Professor Fearns,
How Much Freedom for Universities, I.E.A. Occasional Paper 65, 1970.

"At least in the upper reaches of higher education where training and research go hand in hand, the hand of official regulation may be deadening.... I have no doubt that the general advancement of learning flourishes best in an atmosphere of liberty''.
Lord Robbins,
Higher Education (Robbins Report) 1963.

INTRODUCTION

Disraeli thought a university ought to be a place of light, liberty and learning, Sean O'Casey said they polished pebbles and dimmed diamonds. The Irish radical was describing what he thought they were actually like, the brilliant Jew what he felt they should aspire to be.[1] Today, in 1992, it is O'Casey's cynicism that would appear to have triumphed. You thought that these places should hum with the delights of intellectual exploration, of old truths reaffirmed and new ones discovered, yet, were you to step in from the teeming street, and visit here, you would not find it so.

You are struck by the monolithic ugliness: these tombstones of glass and concrete, of windswept walkways and fortress-like halls, of tunnels, harsh corners and menacing heights, without ornament, without resonance back to three thousand years of human building, set not in the present but within the ideological exactitude of the age in which they were constructed rather than created. They represent the aesthetic equivalent of foul language. They are as faceless as any inner-city housing estate.

This is what you notice first. Secondly you notice the mediocrity, not poverty, of nearly everything. The students unlike their European peers dress rather badly. Buildings are dowdy. Occasionally there is a reminder of the bold age we are in: evidence of life: a new annexe here, perhaps with the name of its corporate sponsor stuck to it, a troupe of smooth businessmen there, attending the university's new management programmes. Overall though the atmosphere is one of motion without meaning. The structures themselves speak of a discredited idea of the public aesthetic. Within them, their academics wonder at how much they believed in has been uprooted from society. There is nothing the government could not do to them and each, losing the will for corporate struggle, inhabits a world of individual survival which he tries to make as comfortable as he may.

If such men and women, their skills and labours, were of little relevance to society, this would not matter. It would be immoral, but it would not matter. A policy report, however, must necessarily concern itself with efficiency and effectiveness, and leave ethical ruminations to others.

---

[1] B. Disraeli, Speech in the House of Commons, 11 March, 1873; S. O'Casey, *Autobiography One*, Carroll and Graf, 1988, p.149.

But it might be that they do matter. What is discovered, refined and created and explored has every relevance to the ability of our industry to generate new products, to innovate, and for us to have at least the promise of controlling the various threats to our life on earth, whether from disease or in the environment. None of us can ignore what universities are doing, for within these awful monoliths may be conducted work that can change forever our lives, those of our families and of our friends.

But even to define the contribution thus is to neglect the key function, education. A nation must compete: our more successful rivals believe that they must educate more people more thoroughly than we do, for they see a linkage between higher education and economic success that still, in 1992, apparently eludes many senior people in our society, or is perceived so myopically that they refuse to resource it. The proof of education is faster growth, greater competitiveness and a more flexible workforce.

In his recent book demonstrating why some nations prosper and some do not, Michael Porter places at the core of his 'factors', his structural enhancers of competitive advantage, the pursuit of excellence in state education; quality universities; research which stresses the applied as well as the theoretic; and skills training which includes the theoretic as well as the applied. However much of a truism, the exhortation cannot be rehearsed too often, less it eludes the deaf ears and myopic vision of policy makers in Britain. It is a necessary condition for commercial success.

It is linkages with universities and university research that Porter particularly extols. Thus in Germany academics enjoy high prestige. Generally the higher education system of universities and Fachchoschulon (practical technical colleges) is extensive in Germany. Individual universities specialise in fields relating to the needs of local industries via specialised university research institutes, for example, the packaging machinery institute of the University of Dortmund. There are also many semi-private research institutes funded jointly by government and industry. German companies themselves engage in active research.

Switzerland also has a strong tradition of university research and links with companies: "world-leading capabilities in chemistry helped give rise to the Swiss pharmaceuticals industry". Swiss companies are committed to research, with research centres throughout the world. In Sweden also university research contributes to the local scientific and technical base.

While most research is highly applied and takes place within the large Swedish companies, it is often done in some type of collaboration with universities (R & D spending as a percentage of GDP in Sweden was the highest of any nation in 1987). And in Japan, some 180 universities and colleges have robotics laboratories (the AIST has a seven year research programme to develop intelligent robots).[2]

WHY UNIVERSITIES MATTER

Firstly there is the strategic value of higher education in the United Kingdom. No macro economic policy can make sense without an attempt to build up both the industrial and the educational resources of the country, and yet, as our survey of industry will indicate, industry fears for the future because of the decline in the universities' science base.[3] Universities are also important in other ways. They generate new knowledge and review old knowledge, and thus invigorate education throughout the system: what schools and colleges teach often has its genesis in what universities themselves have researched and disseminated.

The vigour of higher education has cultural as well as economic ramifications. What after all are the aims of civilisation – the endless accumulation of goods, like a drug addict and his narcotic? Anyone who has known the ennui of the well-heeled will recognise the banality of this vision, and could a traveller from a past time visit us today he would judge us shallow, our culture celebrated by the perpetual strum of the electronic guitar that anaesthetises thought. If we believe mass values are the standard of truth and that what is right is exclusively what most people want, then this book has nothing more to communicate, but education at least softens the coarseness of our life and challenges our mediocrity, makes us review some at least of our assumptions. The critical faculty is more important than ever. Perhaps indeed even the universities have failed to give cultural breadth, perhaps they have produced narrow technologists and useless poets for the convenience of their teachers. This would not we would hope be the case if the vision of universities which we wish to resurrect came to pass. But universities and their research do minister to man's basic curiosity: they help turn a culture into a civilisation.[4]

---

[2] M. Porter, *The Competitive Advantage of Nations*, Harvard University Press, 1990.
[3] See Chapter Nine below, p.281.
[4] J. Newman's, *The Idea of a University*, personifies this view (All references in this volume are to the New York, 1959 Edition).

THE UNIVERSITIES AND THE GOVERNMENT

Part of the sadness of the current crisis is that both parties entertain caricatures about each other. Universities doubt the government's basic sense of educational mission, they believe that it is anti-intellectual and actively despises that avocation, and the government perceives universities as part of a liberal totalitarianism, inefficient, lazy, and perpetuating left wing values. Thus both sides seem to argue from two fixed and mutually uncomprehending positions. Perhaps there is even an element of truth in these caricatures.

But there has surely been a naivety to much government thinking about universities. They entertain inflated hopes as to what industry and private individuals may be willing or yet able to do. They compare our system and its funding invidiously to that in the United States. But, increased fund-raising from private sources is a matter of the dynamics of cultural change and will therefore take time, and in addition we still lack in the United Kingdom the kind of extravagantly wealthy people that the United States offers in profusion. And other claims are now being made on our industry, which also has responsibility to shareholders: what if it simply does not want to assume the burden the government asks of it, even though the politicians think it should?[5] Fundraising is not only affected by the state of the economy, but by the location of the university and the individual academics' need for funds.

One has a sense that the government is dealing with an ethos very alien to it, for only a few MP's after all have made any significant research contribution (for example Mr Robert Rhodes James and Mr Stuart Holland) and that is in the arts, not science or technology. Therefore there exists a genuine difficulty of understanding. Many MP's have been businessmen, accountants, lawyers and so on: but few were research academics. To the House it is a foreign culture. The universities' tribulation is an inevitable concomitant of their being part of a state system subject to politicians' control. Universities have also been easy and frequent targets for ministerial abuse. Listen to Robert Jackson "Academics are failing to understand the challenge to their assumptions posed by government policies on higher education. They should stop cowering in the secret

---

[5] In some areas the climate is changing, for example law firms were reluctant to sponsor chairs but since 1988 the position has changed: S. Bright and M. Sunkin, "Sponsoring Law Schools", *New Law Journal*, November 1991, pp.1491-2.

garden of knowledge and get to grips with the real world... knowledge for its own sake is no longer the prime concern".[6] The minister had also advised university academics to moonlight.[7]

Even those responsible for running the system have on occasion given forth much anti-intellectual cant. Thus Sir Peter Swinnerton Dyer, former chief executive of the University Funding Council (UFC), said that the government is not thinking in terms of grants but of buying certain services: "it will use the power which this situation gives it to press for higher quality and greater efficiency just as Marks and Spencer for example does in similar circumstances".[8] Herein is an argument of false analogy on at least two counts. Firstly, suppliers to Marks and Spencer, since they have alternative customers, enjoy some bargaining power: in the absence of this the relationship becomes simply a coercive one, and under conditions of state monopoly the universities cannot simply turn to alternative 'customers', and their views on what is important necessarily becomes subordinate to those of the government of the day. Secondly, those who run Marks and Spencer know about the products they sell and the nature of the business. The government knows neither of these and should therefore refrain from seeing higher education only as a market. 'Market' is a convenient metaphor which helps conceptualise the process but it is not the process itself, thus the best universities in the land could sell their services exclusively to foreign students and close their doors to non-fee paying U.K. undergraduates. This would accord with market processes, but it would not be serving the broader goals of society. It is equally as erroneous for the government to demand more output from universities without increasing spending. Universities are free not because they are corporate invalids who crave the elixir of state subsidy but rather to guarantee meritocracy, in fact some could even be privatised: but they accept subsidy in order to guarantee equality of access to higher education.

OUR PROGRAMME: (1) MAKING THE CUSTOMER PAY

The central platform of our programme is, controversially, a proposal to adopt and adapt the Australian system of financing higher education, where

---

[6] *Times Higher Education Supplement*, 17 June 1988; Cf.J. Griffith, "The Threat to Higher Education", *The Political Quarterly*, 1989, pp. 50-63.
[7] Andrew Smith M.P., *Hansard*, March, 1988.
[8] Speech to Committee of Vice Chancellors and Principals, Manchester, 23 September, 1987.

students pay some of the tuition costs of their degree in the form of taxation or as an up-front charge.[9]

Their living costs would be, similarly, paid for out of future taxation. Our current system of tuition support was feasible when universities were conceived as being for a small élite, but there has been a fourfold increase in the number of students since the publication of the Robbins report in 1963. Universities are now ripe for administrative revolution, and Australia provides a bold example of what can be done through the medium of its new graduate tax. This may very well require a change to the existing statutes and ordinances of universities, that presently prevent the imposition of fees (unilaterally or otherwise) and also disallow borrowing, investing and other commercial activities.

There is in fact a deceit at the heart of our system, for it is not generally known that 20% of qualified students have in the recent past been turned away from universities. Such arrangements gives the appearance of meritocracy since their costs, at least as far as tuition is concerned, are free to the student, but the high per capita charge thus accrued leads to a severe rationing of places and entry becomes almost hereditary. We propose therefore to confiscate the enhanced earnings that a university education brings, a charge on future affluence, not a debt on present penury, for the total subsidy of students is at the core of the current malaise in universities and if we are to have better conditions this totality must diminish, and significantly; unless it does, we cannot expect government amongst others to invest new resources into higher education.

For in the debate on higher education the government does, curious though it may seem, have a case. That is why it should never seek refuge in fibs and half truths, since our spending on higher education relative to other countries is indeed high (even if this seems incredible to the researcher using dated equipment and such), because of the exorbitant unit costs imposed by a commitment to entirely free tuition and subsidised living. This subsidy is greater than anywhere else in the world. Therefore a Conservative government is anxious not to increase it, otherwise it could not obtain its objective of educating more, and anyway it has an ideologically fixed aversion to increasing state spending.

---

[9] Report of the Committee on Higher Education Funding (Wran Report), Australian Government Publishing Service, Canberra, 1988. Cf. *Times Higher Educational Supplement*, November 18, 1988.

Thus according to a *Times* leader of May 26th 1987 "paying the living costs of half a million students in higher education costs nearly £700 million a year".[10] When grants were first introduced in 1962, 98,000 students benefited, yet last year 468,000 university and polytechnic students were on a grant. But the maintenance grant is only a third of total university spending. All of the tuition costs for 350,000 students at fifty one universities has to be met by the British state. Clearly there is a return to the state, in the form of enhanced future taxes, and we certainly do not propose that most of the tuition costs are placed on the student: it is the proper business of the state to fund universities, as in all civilised countries.

It is possible to become paternalistic about students. But their prospects are different from their predecessors in the nineteen fifties and sixties, being soon propelled into material affluence, and we find it difficult to understand why there is such reluctance to seek payment from those who are in a limited sense customers. In spite of the propaganda of the National Union of Students (NUS), the modern campus is more redolent of California than of Kant.

There is of course the counter argument that students will pay high taxes anyway. But not all their future affluence is readily attributable to their university degree, and they are taxed highly on grounds of redistributive social equity rather than services they have consumed. Why should other earners, high and otherwise, who have not gone to the university, subsidise completely its products?

Vice chancellors and senior academics have therefore been culpable in failing to point up the error of a system of free tuition, the victims of which are their own staffs and the research capacities of their own institutions.[11] We wish to coax academics into seeing the intimate connection between their own tawdry conditions, and the imperative of free tuition to all irrespective of means both actual and potential, for academic support for this arrangement, and refusal to look to alternatives, may seal their fate as a professional group and lead to their marginalisation; as it is they have been blamed for, and sustain the burden of, ills attributable not to them but to the system of which they are the inheritors. In order to preserve this

---

[10] *The Times*, 26 May, 1987.
[11] There are exceptions: Cf.J. Kelly and G. Hills, "An Alternative Funding Scheme for Higher Education", Unpublished, 1989; A. Peacock, "Education Voucher Schemes – Strong or Weak?", *Journal of Economic Affairs*, January 1983, pp.113-6.

edifice of free tuition, that is, not to offend key political constituents, many a university will eventually be forced to cease as a university and become a teaching-only institution. We cannot allow the part-extinction of intellectual life in this country: for universities are a main support. If the government fails to impose tuition taxes, then universities should unilaterally impose fees.

Indeed, the government is not following its own interdict, that the 'customer' pays, when it comes to the universities. We are cynical because academics are castigated for ignoring the values of the market-place, but when it comes to students the government does precisely that, by giving a hundred percent tuition subsidy to the consumer because it knows their parents are its most loyal supporters. The other source of subsidy is university personnel themselves: 70% of university costs are salary costs and academics subsidise the students, professions and commerce by their level of remuneration. Ministers have not forgotten the back bench revolt launched against Keith Joseph for trying to increase the means tested parental contribution. Therefore their talk about universities charging fees for tuition has been sotto voce. They will not say so volubly. One may, or one may not, admire the government's bulldozing of class interests in other spheres, but it is strange how university free tuition has become sacrosanct. Well it might be. At Harvard University in the United States for example tuition fees amount to $50,000 for a B.A. degree course.[12] America's middle class have to sustain such costs.

OUR PROGRAMME: (2) REJECT CURRENT POLICY OPTIONS

Of the policy options now being imposed or considered, the following are of particular importance. Firstly contracts. That is to say the government becomes a buyer of services from the universities on a contractual basis, and secondly competitive bidding for funds between institutions, that is, universities try and bid against each other for research funds. Thirdly, merged funding of universities and polytechnics and indeed now, merged identities. Fourthly, a split between the research and teaching function so that the appropriations targeted for teaching go only to teaching, not to research. Next, the evolution of teaching-only universities, and the 'massification' of higher education. Another suggestion, typical of the

---

[12] *Daily Mail*, 11th August, 1989.

forces for cheapening universities, is that we create two-year degree schemes.

Now all of these proposals are interrelated. But the notion of competition underlying them is fallacious, for academic research is driven by inherent intellectual curiosity, and while competition does arise it is disciplinary rather than institutional, so these authors are therefore against any attempt to classify institutions in terms of a hierarchy of universities. While an informal and fluid hierarchy exists, a formal hierarchy would condemn some universities to perpetual mediocrity. We are also sceptical about the separate funding of teaching and research, and of the government's assertion (through Edwin Appleyard, financial secretary to the funding councils) that it wishes to double student numbers in the system for roughly the same amount of money.[13]

OUR PROGRAMME: (3) MANAGERIAL CHANGE

In addition to the advocacy of new directions in broad public policy, the authors also seek managerial change in the governance of universities: there is an obvious interdependency between policy and operational levels.

Thus we wish to address the serious problem of the 'lost generation' of academics. Major vacancies will arise in the late 1990's, to be filled by cohorts all drawn from the same generation, in other words the cycle of mediocrity created in the nineteen sixties will perpetuate itself. Therefore we urge that the government do all in its power to spread recruitment, temporally, over the next few years. The 'new-blood' scheme was too little and too late.

Another area of concern is the quality of university governance. The senate bodies and the committee systems represent a form of pseudo-democracy that is really an oligarchy, that is to say the least efficient form of government, a recipe for inertia, evasion and rancour, neither enabling strategic decision making, since power is vested in obstreperous interests, nor giving the staff proletariat adequate expression. And the bureaucracy also leaves something to be desired. Universities do not seem to have experts, only administrators who have learnt by experience, that is, they continue to repeat the same errors and bequeath them to their successors.

---

[13] Edwin Appleyard, quoted in *The Times*, 14 June, 1989.

The salaries structure is overly rigid and fails to provide realistic incentives. Therefore the government should employ the ill manners it is so adept at using to demolish a system that demotivates the most talented members of a profession. There should be regional variations in salary, and extra increments for tangible achievement rather than merely automatic increases according to age, for currently there is scant distinction between institutions in terms of pay, whether they are good or not. And tenure should not be abolished but modified so that it becomes a reward for achievement and service, as in the United States of America.[14] But as long as the public demands, and the state accepts, that free higher education tuition is a matter of public right, then low academic salaries are inevitable (the government is nevertheless claiming that academic salaries have risen on average 35% in real terms over the past 10 years: an assertion that is about as true as the proposition that Elvis Presley still lives).[15]

More generally there should be a use of symbolic rewards to provide better non-monetary incentives, for example, importing the title of 'associate professor'. At the moment universities discriminate little between "the underpaid originality, creativity and dedication of the few, and the overpaid humbug and inertia of the many". The function of government is not to run universities or any other organisation. It is, however, to create enabling conditions for the more efficient operation of those institutions, in other words to create the right form of social context. And the goodwill of university teachers is important if the government is to implement its programmes for university reform, otherwise they will be sabotaged. Finally, whilst performance indicators, teaching quality assurance and academic audit are, in their own right, all desirable checks and balances, academics need to guard against their becoming a covert way for government to manage the university machine in addition to purely financial controls.

A CALL TO ARMS

We chose to write a book whose subject matter lay outside the parameters of our customary research because we perceived, with no little unease, that the debate on universities was expressed in arcane bureaucratic formulae,

---

[14] G. Williams, et al., *The Academic Labour Market*, Elsevier, Amsterdam, 1974, p.217.
[15] "Higher Education", *Politics Today*, November, 1989. See below p. for the actual position (real rise of 6% between 1969/89 when average earnings rose 49%).

arid and technical in its focus. It did not ask deeper questions about the mission of higher education. Vision is not often talked about in public policy documents, yet, without it, policy making becomes myopic, a sterile exercise in rational deduction, both ignorant of the legacy of the past and failing to illuminate the broad contours of the future.

No public policy critique could ever be entirely beyond the influence of ideology, but we have tried to avoid the lure of transitory dogma, to be idealists, not ideologues. The icons of partisan political debate, whether free market or state control, are relevant only where their associated ideas enhance the vision of a lively and profound intellectual and research culture in the United Kingdom, and a well educated, humane public. Our stance is one of scepticism both towards the government and to those who administer British universities; neither, we believe, emerge creditably from the past 10 years, and incremental cuts and snide abuse on the part of the government have been no substitute for a coherent policy: "if government is seen largely as an arena for cultural counter-revolution rather than as an exercise in rational public administration, sensible policies are difficult to sustain".[16]

What is the prognosis for the universities in the absence of a significant change in public policy? Some universities will in the years ahead face the abolition of what they see as their raison d'etre, namely research. It is, therefore, time for university men and women to abandon their inertia and actively create policies for their own governance that will not invariably demand of the state, given the other commitments it is insistent upon honouring, high increase of funding in the longer term.

However the danger with all reforms, and all reformers, as Burke observed of the French Revolution, is their failure to perceive any good in the Ancien Régime. It would be easy to be merely destructive. There is much good in the existing system that the government has apparently failed to recognise. For compared to Europe and elsewhere we are efficient (Australia for example has a 40% drop out rate and France a rate of 50%), and all of our universities have some departments of national, and many have some departments of international, standing. This strong academic tradition includes a closer superintendence on an individual basis to students than

---

[16] M. Kogan and D. Kogan, *The Attack on Higher Education*, London, 1983. Cf.M. Warnock, *Universities: Knowing our Minds*, Chatto and Windus, London, 1989.

overseas universities give, while the universities are also now reforming: assessment of teaching is being implemented, tenure is ending for better or worse, and there are significant strides in the search for private funding (Cambridge university for example is attempting to raise £250 million from private sources). Table 1.1 gives a chronology of major developments affecting universities after 1705.

TABLE 1:1 FUNDING OF UNIVERSITIES AND OTHER MAJOR DEVELOPMENTS: A CHRONOLOGY

Year	Development
1705	*Act of Scottish Parliament* establishes principle of public and/or royal support of Scottish universities.
1827	*Proprietors of the University of London* joint stock company formed.
1831	Scottish universities endowments placed on annual Parliamentary vote.
1836	Government makes grants to cover administrative expenses of London University.
1839	First government grants to English university, University of London.
1848	*Select Committee on Miscellaneous Expenditure* – Treasury defends grants.
1858	*Universities (Scotland) Act.*
1861	*University of Durham Act.*
1867	*Schools Enquiry Commission on Technical Instruction.*
1871	*University Test Act* – abolishes religious tests at Oxbridge.
1882	Aberdare Committee appointed to investigate Welsh education.
	Aberystwyth and then Cardiff (1883) and Bangor (1884) colleges receive government grants.
1889	Board of Agriculture makes grants for practical and scientific instruction.
	Grant of £15,000 made by the Treasury and distributed by an *ad hoc* Committee on Grants to University Colleges in Great Britain.

1889	*Technical Instruction Act* passed.
1889/1904	Various Committees examine universities' work.
1904	Grant doubled.
1905	Haldane Committee.
1905/1906	Grants double again.
1906	Advisory Committee on Grants to University Colleges appointed, reporting to Treasury.
	Ad hoc Committee on Grants formalised.
1907	Triennial grant allocations.
1908	Informal quinquennial system of grants.
1910	Committee transferred to the Board of Education's jurisdiction.
1911	Advisory Committee reports to Board of Education.
	Welsh Colleges remain with Treasury.
1912	Universities Bureau of British Empire established as secretariat of Congress of Universities and Committee of Vice Chancellors and Principals, an informal organisation with no constitution.
1919	Standing Committee (UGC) on financial need within universities appointed. Now reports to Treasury once again.
1919	UGC created.
1922	Oxford and Cambridge join grant list.
1923	*Oxford and Cambridge Act* passed.
1925	Start of Quinquennial funding.
1928	Quinquennial system resumes after interruption of war.
1930	Committee of Vice Chancellors and Principals formed.
1936	Full-time chairman of the UGC appointed.
1944	Education Act passed, potential student numbers increased.
1945	The CVCP and UGC plan for university expansion.
1946	Barlow Committee on Scientific Manpower reports and UGC's terms of reference altered to incorporate notion of 'national need' in financial arrangements.

1946/47	Exchequer grants reach 50% of universities' income.
1947/52	Earmarked grants deployed.
1952	Earmarked grants terminated but detailed guide-lines on expenditure instituted.
1957-67	Student numbers increase enormously, CAT's and new universities added to the system.
1960	Anderson Report – maintenance grants available for qualified university students.
1963	Robbins Report – university education for all that are qualified and would benefit from it.
1964	UGC under the jurisdiction of the DES.
1965	Anthony Crosland introduces binary policy.
1967	UGC issues letters of guidance.
1966/1967	Comptroller and Auditor General receives access to UGC and university accounts.
1968	Crosland reduces student fees.
1972	DES White Paper signals fall in grants.
1973	World economic crisis.
1974/75	No supplementary grants despite inflation rate of 20%.
	Grants for the final two years of the quinquennium not available until six months before their commencement.
1975	Quinquennial system of funding suspended, triennial funding starts.
	CVCP/UGC Report recommends fees be set at 10% of university income.
1978	*Higher Education into the 1990s* published by the DES.
1979	Thatcher Government.
	The UGC warns DES that reductions in university funding in excess of 2.5% would be disastrous.
1979/80	Subsidy to overseas students ends, full cost fees instituted.
	Level funding for home students.

1981-84	Planned cuts in the real recurrent grant of 8.5%. CVCP estimated that cuts would amount to 15%.
1982	Merrison Report (ABRC/UGC) – recommends higher and selective research funding.
1984	*A Strategy for Higher Education into the 1990's* published by the UGC.
	Selective funding to be instituted.
1985	CVCP publishes Jarratt Report.
	DES Green Paper *The Development of Higher Education into the 1990's* published.
1985/86	UGC introduces new allocative mechanism for distribution of 1986/87 grant.
1987	DES publishes Croham Report.
	DES White Paper *Higher Education: Meeting the Challenge* published.
	ABRC publishes *A Strategy for the Science Base*.
	The Education Reform Bill published.
	DES publishes *Changes in the Structure and National Planning for Higher Education*.
	UGC publishes Oxburgh Report.
1988	UGC publishes *Next Research Selectivity Exercise* paper.
	UFC established.
1989	Higginson Report published.
	DES consultation paper announces intention to shift to greater emphasis on fees.
	Education Reform Act on statute book.
	Final Report of Working Group on Powers and Functions, Daniels Report, (University of Wales).
	UFC assumes responsibilities of UGC.
1990	Public Accounts Committee, 36th Report, Restructuring and *Finances of Universities*.
1991	White Paper, *Higher Education: A New Framework*.

CHAPTER TWO

THE WORLD WE HAVE LOST: THE DEVELOPMENT OF UNIVERSITY EDUCATION.

"The state should not treat the universities as if they were higher classical schools or schools of special sciences. On the whole the State should not look to them at all for anything that directly concerns its own interest, but should rather cherish a conviction that, in fulfilling their real destiny, they will not only serve its own purposes, but serve them on an infinitely higher plane, commanding a much wider field of operation, and affording room to set in motion much more efficient springs and forces than are at the disposal of the state itself".
W. von Humboldt,
Ideen zu eniem Versuch die Grenzen der Wirksamkeit des Staats zu bestimmen, Berlin, 1854.

"(The university) is not a place of professional education. Universities are not intended to teach the knowledge required to fit men for some special mode of gaining their livelihood... Men are men before they are lawyers, or physicians, or merchants, or manufacturers; and if you make them capable and sensible men, they make themselves capable and sensible lawyers or physicians".
John Stuart Mill,
In F.A. Cavenagh, *James and John Stuart Mill on Education*, Cambridge, 1931, p.133.

"There is no doubt that an academic (Wissenschaftlich) course of study is still expected to influence significantly the general personal development of the students, particularly their rational and critical faculties and their ability to act responsibly".
H. Peisart and G. Framheim,
System of Higher Education, Federal Republic of German, New York, 1978, p.6.

"That idea must have a substance in it, which has maintained its ground amid these conflicts and changes, which has ever served as a standard to measure things withal, which has passed from mind to mind unchanged, when there was so much to colour, so much to influence any notion or thought whatever, which was not founded in our nature".

J.H. Newman,
The Idea of a University, New York, 1959.

INTRODUCTION

In order to bring developments in the funding and management of universities in the late twentieth century into sharper focus, this chapter analyses the evolution of the whole system: ancient, English, civic and university colleges. The contrasts between early foundations in England and Scotland are examined; the failure of Oxbridge to embrace science and thus the establishment of civic universities; the London extension movement and the formation of university colleges; the University of Wales. Such a survey demonstrates the importance of endowments from numerous benefactors before the Second World War: individual, church, monarchy, industrial entrepreneurs and as provincial rivalry increases, local government too. The war is a conspicuous watershed, for expansion thereafter – including the addition of the 'new' universities and the regrading of the Colleges of Advanced Technology – is dependent upon planning by the University Grants Committee and funding from central government. Presaging these developments are: inflation; scientific advancement and opportunities for new research; the erosion of industrial competitive advantage; the demand both for more graduates and more residential accommodation. The independent University of Buckingham, the newest foundation, is given special attention in view of the possibility that it could be a model for future development of the university system.

Having followed through university foundations, attention shifts to relations with the state. The states's early tentative steps in funding are charted until the sclerosis in independent funding necessitates greater state support and leads to the formation of the University Grants Committee. A further section examines the role of the UGC as buffer between the state and the universities and its effectiveness as a funding body, including its early investigation by the Public Accounts Committee. Tensions between the Barlow Committee position, requiring greater planning by the state of university expansion and the Gates Committee, warning against over-dependence on the state, are examined. With the Treasury assuming responsibility for the UGC in 1919, the government itself warned of the dangers of reliance on a single source of revenue, although the universities were seduced by the illusion of easy money. But, the CVCP and the government reached the conclusion that consolidation and expansion of the system were only possible with substantial state support. Subsequent sections deal with the quinquennial funding mechanism and its effectiveness, the shift in responsibility for the UGC to the Department of Education and Science (1964) which was initially an effective advocate for universities, but later became a distinct liability. Finally, the reduction in financial support from the state and its more dirigiste role post-1979 receives detailed attention. Capital expenditure rather than student numbers now determines expansion and the distribution of resources: the UGC rewards initiative, but neglects efficiency and effectiveness as it operates a policy of equal misery following the 1981 cuts. In the planning process the UGC had been marginalised, but as it proved its pro-government credentials and implemented the required cuts, it moved back into favour, and as the UFC now takes a proactive role.

NEWMAN AND THE IDEA OF A UNIVERSITY: PROLOGUE[1]

The image Newman gives of the man who passed through a university institution is certainly florid: and this sanitised image should be seen for what it is, propaganda: his graduate is humane, sober, informed, mature in his judgements, broadly cultured and free of all prejudice. Of course, few such paragons have ever existed. Newman is really describing the ideal, but the exercise is not voided because of that. He refers to "the gentleness and effeminacy of feeling, which is the attendant of civilisation".

But universities are not crucibles of genii: their training is "the great ordinary means to a great but ordinary end; it aims at raising the intellectual tone of society... at purifying the national taste". Their aim is social: they have a cultural mission that will be implemented by their cadres, one defined very grandly as enobling and refining the public atmosphere. Of the philosophy of utility he has nothing but contempt: "The philosophy of utility, you will say, Gentlemen, has at least done its work, and I grant it – it aimed low, but it has fulfilled its aim". For Newman "any kind of knowledge... is its own reward", it is something beyond the individual. A cultivated intellect brings power and grace to every work it undertakes. Thus he castigates the prejudice that all education should be directly instrumental, speaking of "two methods of Education; the end of the one is to be philosophical, of the other to be mechanical; the one rises towards general ideas, the other is exhausted upon what is particular and external".

---

[1] All references are to the New York edition published in 1959.

But Newman is at pains to state that he does not disparage useful, scientific or vocational studies at a university; indeed, a university "teaches all knowledge by teaching all". Outside the university environment a vocational tutor would indeed be narrowed by what he taught and his lectures would have no breadth or resonance.

The pursuit of knowledge is morally uplifting and draws the mind off from things which will harm it. There is a beauty in perfection of the intellect as there is in physical beauty or moral beauty. The intellect is "majestically calm", it has "learned to leven the dense mass of facts and events with the elastic force of reason", it "discovers the end in every beginning, the origin in every end, the law in every interruption, the limit in each delay". The core of intellectual development is the idea of system: what is acquired is hence related to what is already known. Knowledge enables us to interpret and systemise what we perceive: it "sees more than the senses convey; which reasons upon what is sees, and while it sees; which invests it with an idea". Knowledge is an "acquired illumination", a permanent intellectual endowment.

For the uneducated man, a seafarer for example, forms and events stand alone as phenomena, without interconnectedness: they can describe but they cannot integrate. Intellectual growth resides in the recognition of systems, relative values and interrelationships. He seeks to evoke the process of intellectual development: it is evolution to a newness; the student "has a new centre, and a range of thoughts to which he was before a stranger". University education enables a man to develop and articulate his ideas with eloquence, focus and clarity, as against the ill focussed, blundering aggression of less educated opponents, to grasp the core of the matter and tear through the skein of sophistry and redundancy. He is thus equipped to master any subject.

The cultivation of the mind brings with it a stability; the mind reposes in a settled state, not nagged by superstitions, fetishes, exaggerated faiths on the one hand, and confused vacuity on the other. His perception is of the permanency of ideas, which must imply their substance having stood the test of time: a university communicates them.

But in education, depth is everything; he criticises the notion "that a smattering in a dozen branches of study is not shallowness, which it really is, but enlargement, which it is not". America would shock him! But the life of the intellect is not to be confuted with mere pedantry: "How many commentators... from whom we rise up wondering at the learning which has passed before us, and wondering why it passed!" Coherence of intellectual design is critical: "How many writers are there ... who, breaking up their subject into details, destroy its life, and defraud us of the whole in their anxiety about the parts".

OXFORD AND CAMBRIDGE

There is no government statute or report defining a university, but the legal concept refers to a body incorporated for the purposes of learning, and possessing endowments and privileges.[2] This corporate status has been enshrined in one of several ways: common law, papal bull, royal charter or Act of Parliament.

The modern university dates back to the Middle Ages and the twelfth century models of Paris, Bologna, Salerno and Oxford, during a period frequently referred to as the Latin Renaissance. These schools, or *stadium generale*, were created as a result of individual endeavour or through the agency of an ecclesiastical body, whereby distinguished teachers attracted disciples who would jointly admit, teach, examine and license apprentices. Civil or ecclesiastical recognition of these bodies would be enshrined in law or edict to prevent other cities enticing them away. As the wealth of benefactors and host cities increased, so the endowments of these schools were enlarged.

Developments in Britain are surrounded by mystery and controversy. One authority, Rashdall, argues that the *stadium generale* at Oxford resulted from a dispute between Henry II and Thomas à Beckett, Archbishop of Canterbury, in 1167, when the King banned English clergymen from attending the University of Paris, a declaration that precipitated the King of France to take retaliatory action and expel all remaining English scholars from France.[3] Expelled scholars gathered in Oxford, a geographically well located city which in addition was patronised by royalty.

---

[2] W. A. Robson, "las universidades britanicas y el estado", Nuestro Tienipo, Vol 3, 1956, p.3; quoted in R. O. Berdahl, *British Universities and the State*, Cambridge University Press, 1959, p.189. Cf. Bertrand Russell, *History of Western Philosophy*, Allen and Unwin, London, 1961, p.474.

[3] H. Rashdal, *Universities of Europe in the Middle Ages*, 3 Vols, Oxford, 1936, especially volume three.

The dispute between town and gown in Oxford in 1209, a not uncommon occurrence, but this time one in which students were hanged, led to a migration of scholars to Cambridge (as well as Reading and Paris) and the foundation of a further *stadium generale* there, although the reason for that particular location is unclear. Hence in those days 'private' initiative was important, although it was almost entirely clerical, and since the church could be more powerful than the state and monarch 'private' is something of a misnomer.[4]

At both universities groups of students rented houses and these lodgings eventually came under university control. Endowed hostels were established by wealthy benefactors to support poor students and these eventually developed into the colleges that are so prominent today. William of Durham endowed Great University Hall that in 1280 became University College, Oxford. In 1264 Walter de Merton founded Merton College and in 1266 Sir John de Balliol founded Balliol College Oxford as a penance for his sins. Cambridge colleges developed in similar fashion: Hugh de Balsham, Bishop of Ely, founded the House of Peter that became Peterhouse College in 1254; Michaelhouse, later Trinity College, was founded in 1324. In every case the colleges had separate buildings, endowments, administration, fellows and heads, created by statutes, and thus enjoyed independence from external pressures.

The expenses of the students were high: food, clothing, books and fees for the degrees themselves. Instruction focussed on the seven liberal arts, divided into the trivium of grammar, rhetoric and logic and the quadrivium of geometry, arithmetic, astronomy and music. Teaching was based on the *lectis*, the reading and comprehension of a textbook, and the *quaestio*, a disputation between lecturer and student based on the earlier lecture. Modern syllabi and pedagogic methods thus have clear ancestry. It is indeed curious how these foundation subjects, once the only study of the university, have suffered in the retrenchments of the nineteen eighties.

During the Reformation and its aftermath, different monarchs tried to impose their religion upon the universities. Henry VIII, having become exasperated with the lack of support from the universities for his divorce and break with Rome, sanctioned major political interference. *A Royal*

---

[4] A.B. Cobham, *The Medieval Universities: Their Development and Organisation*, Methuen, London, 1975.

Injunction of 1525 called for an oath of loyalty from lecturers, set conditions for lecturing, banned the study of Canon Law and of Duns Scotus' philosophy and demanded further that divinity lectures be based on the Scriptures.[5] The *Second Act of Uniformity* and the issue of the Second Prayer Book in 1552, led to the appointment of a Royal Commission to remove the last vestiges of popery from the universities: during this period there were acts of vandalism committed against buildings and libraries, with the expulsion of students and lecturers. The accession of Mary in 1553 posed a major threat to the Protestants and led to the martyrdom of Cranmer, Latimer and Ridley: the inquisition only halted with Mary's death in 1558. Thus there never was a primitive academic freedom. Powerful groups, especially the church and above all the state and monarch, always threatened it. Today's perils are tame by comparison: early retirement, not beheading.

Lay rather than clerical beneficence secured the post-Reformation foundations: St John's (1555), Trinity (1554/5), Wadham (1612) and Pembroke (1628) all at Oxford and Magdalene (1542), Emmanuel (1584) and Sidney Sussex (1596) at Cambridge. Dr Price's endowment for Jesus College, Oxford, was accepted on the basis that Elizabeth I be regarded as the founder of the College: education remained a much sort after investment by the clergy, but progressively more so by the mercantile and professional classes.

Oxford sided with the monarch in the Civil War and Cambridge found itself occupied by Cromwell. Then in 1647 a parliamentary commission reformed both universities, and the commitment of the parliamentarians to learning and scholarship, particularly in science and mathematics, meant that a period of intellectual prosperity ensued prior to the Restoration. With the Restoration, there followed an exodus of undesirable lecturers from the universities after the *1662 Act of Uniformity* that demanded conformity to the revised Liturgy and submission to the parliamentary and religious *status quo*. Note, again, the fitful political control of the syllabus as well as of the religion, ethos and loyalty of universities – a pattern evident throughout English history.

---

[5] Despite these considerable changes, Henry VIII recognised at the same time the need for a greater supply of trained men for the royal and national administration and founded Christ Church College, Oxford and Trinity College, Cambridge, endowing five regius professorships at each university.

The Glorious Revolution put an end to attempts by James II to intervene in university affairs, although the power invested in the heads of colleges acted as an effective impediment to his worst excesses.

With the beginning of the Hanoverian dynasty, there were renewed calls for university reform since inertia was endemic in Oxford and Cambridge, and both universities narrowly missed being totally dominated by the Crown, with administration of their revenues and centralised appointments at the Lord Chancellor's diktat. But the accession of George III meant that both universities enjoyed a further lease of decadence that led to moribundity in scholarship, upon which Gibbon and Smith commented in harsh terms.[6] The sloth consequent upon vaguely defined duties, certain streams of income, and lack of connection between input and reward has periodically plagued us in times since: Ministers today draw on this in their attempts to justify financial reductions.

Gibbon referred to his Magdalen College tutors as "monks... easy men, who supinely enjoyed the gifts of the founder" whilst his own tutor: "remembered he had a salary to receive and only forgot he had a duty to perform", so that Gibbon regarded his period at Oxford as "the most idle and unprofitable of my whole life".[7] Smith's barbed comments are often quoted, and writing of Balliol he said "the greater part of the public professors have for these many years, given up altogether even the pretence of teaching", whilst the older universities in general had become "sanctuaries in which exploded systems and obsolete prejudices found shelter and protection" so that "improvements were more easily introduced into some of the poorer universities, in which the teachers, depending upon their reputation for the greater part of their subsistence, were obliged to pay more attention to the current opinions of the world".[8]

Decadence derives from the loss of a sense mission. There arises a frivolity where social and economic status and not merit is the exclusive criterion of entry. A university is defined by the intelligence and motivation of its

---

[6] D.A. Winstanley, *The University of Cambridge in the Eighteenth Century*, Cambridge University Press, 1922.
[7] Edward Gibbon, *Memoirs of My Life*, edited by G.A. Bernard, Nelson, 1966, pp.52 and 56-57.
[8] Adam Smith, *An Inquiry into the Nature and Cause of The Wealth of Nations*, edited by R. H. Campbell and A. S. Skinner, Glasgow Edition, Oxford, 1976, Vol 2, pp.761 and 772/3. Cf. *Correspondence of Adam Smith*, edited by E C Mossner and I S Ross Oxford, 1987, Letter 143 addressed to William Cullen, pp.173-179.

student body, and this is what the state subsidy latterly enabled, for when Oxbridge was indeed 'private' sclerosis was the consequence.

Reform came in the first half of the nineteenth century, when written examinations where added to the oral and the curriculum changed. In 1807 the classics and mathematics courses were divided at Oxford and two honours schools with high reputations emerged: industry and ability were rewarded by first or second class honours. Cambridge added a second Tripos in classics to that already established in mathematics. The curriculum became extended to include scientific subjects, so that by 1851 there were Triposes in moral and natural sciences and the Oxford honours schools were extended to include mathematics, natural science, law, modern history and theology. Religious tests were removed from Oxford in 1854 and Cambridge in 1856, with complete removal following the passage of the 1871 *University Test Act*.[9]

More reforms followed with the 1877 Oxford and Cambridge Act, thereby transforming the formerly clerical institutions into modern universities. As a consequence of numerous legislative enactments, the power of the university over the colleges increased and administration devolved to representative bodies, further weakening the position of the Heads of Colleges, and college revenues were partly diverted to the university. Fellowships and scholarships were revised and became more competitive. With the final abolition of religious tests, encouragement was given to applications from the more meritorious of the working classes. But however worthy this might be, whilst attainment rather than aptitude remained the test for admission, open competition favoured the rich over the poor. Attempts by Bishop Gore of Birmingham to widen access were frustrated by the outbreak of the First World War.

Both universities were disrupted by the War, but made a substantial contribution to the advance of scientific knowledge – useful during the war and capable of further refinement and exploitation afterwards. In 1918 it became essential for Oxford and Cambridge to receive state aid, not only to cope with the influx of students from the War, but also to establish new scientific disciplines. A sum of £30,000 was voted by the government, but both universities were forced to submit to a further Royal Commission to establish the extent of their resources – both at the college and university

---

[9] D.A. Winstanley, *Early Victorian Cambridge*, Cambridge University Press, 1940, p.411.

level. The subsequent Report gave rise to the 1923 *Oxford and Cambridge Act* and the need for regular approval for grant purposes.

State aid can be seen to be intimately correlated with the growth of scientific knowledge, the state's perception of its importance, especially in defence, and the inability of private finance to sustain it. The growth of dependence on the state was gradual and incremental, and due to a lack of private sources. We might compare the situation with that in the USA, where mighty fortunes had been made from steel and the like and were ripened by the existence of a homogeneous internal market, while Britain, challenged by foreign competition, its rich made leaner by death duties and higher taxes, never remotely possessed the same cohorts of private wealth with which to endow universities.

Direct state interference of the kind envisaged by Sir William Hamilton in the case of Oxford and Cambridge was essentially concluded with the inception of the University Grants Committee, which assumed responsibility for administering government grants in 1919. Oxbridge did not, however, join the university list until 1922.

SCOTTISH UNIVERSITIES

Historically the Scottish system was more meritocratic and advanced. Developments in Scotland had more in common with Europe than England with its Oxbridge collegiate system.[10] The continental system was more open and flexible and students occupied a more powerful position in the university hierarchy. Students were free to live where they chose and were not subjected therefore to internal university discipline. The lecture represented the major vehicle for instruction (as opposed to the tutorial) and although the interchange of staff did not permit a sense of community to become established, there was nevertheless a fertile exchange of ideas quite uncommon in Oxbridge until the late nineteenth century. The major differences between England and Scotland can be summarised as follows:

(1)　Scottish universities were non-residential;

(2)　Whereas endowments at Oxbridge went to Colleges, in Scotland they went to professorial chairs and teaching;

---

[10] John Kerr, *Scottish Education, School and University from Early Times to 1908*, 1910.

(3) Universities in the civic centres of Edinburgh, Glasgow and Aberdeen were closely associated with the local community with the latter taking a proactive role; the Court comprised academic and civic leaders;

(4) Scottish national development and institutions made universities both democratic and popular. Further, a short academic year, from October to May, meant that the cost of education remained low in comparison with Oxbridge;

(5) Enrolments were spread across a wide spectrum of society, aided by a better system of secondary education than England.[11]

As there were no universities in Scotland in the Middle Ages, students were forced to seek education on the continent of Europe where there was, for example, a Scots College at the University of Paris, founded by the Bishop in 1326: there were also Scottish students at Bologna and Padua universities, and Balliol College Oxford was founded primarily to educate poor Scottish students. However, the risks associated with overseas travel and the periodic disputes with England paved the way for the development of indigenous Scottish higher education. Students expelled from the University of Paris after its split with the Pope in 1408, congregated at the seat of the grandest Bishopric in Scotland, St Andrews, where lectures were organised for them.[12] Bishop Wardlaw founded a university there in 1412 and the grant of a charter came from Pope Benedict and then later from James I. The University of Paris was the model for this foundation and its members were divided into four nations, the names of which were derived from the districts they emanated from: Fife, Lothian, Angus and Alban.[13] A rector presided over the university as head and private benefactors endowed a number of buildings despite the fact that in the early days there were few students and insufficient staff. The three colleges of St Salvator's, St Leonard's and St Mary's each owe their existence to the Bishops of St Andrews.

The church also took a hand in the foundation of Glasgow, where Bishop Turnbull petitioned James II in 1450 in order to seek a charter of incorporation from Pope Nicholas V. Initially ecclesiastical buildings were used for lectures, but Lord Hamilton granted land and provided

---

[11] J. Kerr, *Ibid*.
[12] R. G. Gant, *The University of St Andrew's*, Edinburgh, 1946.
[13] R. G. Gant, *Ibid*.

endowments for new buildings. Aberdeen university followed in 1494, Bishop Elphinstone took responsibility for ensuring there were adequate endowments and it subsequently prospered more than either St Andrew's or Glasgow, essentially through his foresight and early guidance.

Thus in Scotland the church played a major part in the foundation of the universities and through much of their history. In the case of Edinburgh, though, we see the role of the municipality in the formation and early sustenance of the college and the role of civic pride, a theme that will recur many times. The University of Edinburgh, founded in 1582, owes its existence in fact to the efforts of the Town Council that retained control of the institution until the *Universities (Scotland) Act* of 1858.

All the universities drew their students from a wider range of schools than their English counterparts did, so that they were less élitist, but populist and popular. Teaching and research in theology, law, science and medicine prospered, particularly the latter. Frequent interchange between mercantile society and academe took place, and this had no counterpart in Oxford or Cambridge and gave Scottish education a distinctive flavour. Confessions of allegiance to the faith of the Kirk were never demanded, so that relations between church and the universities remained enlightened: the climate secular and liberal. The ideas of Bacon, Newton and Locke were widely taught and Dutch influence on the universities of Scotland became significant.

LONDON AND DURHAM UNIVERSITIES

Religious considerations lay behind the growth of English universities in the early nineteenth century. There was not such a well developed system of primary and secondary education in England and Wales as there was in Scotland, but the increase in the population, and availability of suitably qualified Dissenters wanting a university education but debarred by religious tests under existing arrangements, called for new university institutions to be established. Between 1826 and 1836 University College and King's College London and Durham were founded, the two former colleges being affiliated to London University, chartered in 1836. Whereas Durham, like Oxford and Cambridge, was residential, the London colleges catered for a commuting population comprising mainly the professional and industrial middle classes.

The movement to create London University began with the poet Thomas Campbell's letter to *The Times* in 1825 which received support from several leading dissenters, including Jeremy Bentham, Francis Place, Dr Birkbeck, Henry Brougham and Joseph Hume "'a combination (of) Scotch lawyers, English utilitarians and philanthropists, Jewish financiers and dissenters of all complexions".[14] Interested parties formed a joint-stock company in 1827, the *Proprietors of the University of London*, and an appeal for funds followed to provide non-sectarian education in the arts, history, political economy, law, languages, sciences, physics, mathematics and finally medicine. Theology did not feature in the subject list and there was no religious test, signifying a radical departure from the position at the ancient universities. Inevitably in such a climate, demands for a rival pro-church institution where heard. The new college took the name King's College, receiving a charter in 1829. In 1836, the University of London came into being to grant degrees, but with no teaching function, and the 'University of London' converted to University College. Note the role of private finance, but also the religious nature of its giving: not a source we can tap today. Of particular significance for university funding in terms of relations with the state, the merger brought with it the first national grant to an English university in 1839 and the government also assumed responsibility for providing central administrative headquarters. Formal state support therefore can be dated to the very beginning of Victoria's reign (taking the 'state' also to include the important local government finance).

From about 1850 many other institutions became affiliated to the University of London: 50 medical schools and 29 arts colleges, many of which were outside London. A new charter of 1857 made it possible for candidates to enter themselves for examinations of the University without attending a course at an affiliated institution. Thus the University of London external degree was born and the Board of Examiners for the Empire created.

Another feature of developments in the 1850s centred upon the creation of a science faculty, so that London became the first university in Britain to offer a degree in science.

---

[14] T. L. Humberstone, *University Reform in London*, 1926, p.27.

New administration offices and a library were provided in Bloomsbury, supported by the Government (£212,000) and local authority grants, grants from city companies, banks, businesses and most importantly, the American Rockefeller Foundation (£400,000). The external degree system flourished and enabled the University Colleges of Exeter, Southampton, Leicester and Hull to undertake degree work in England as well as numerous Commonwealth Universities. The University of London had reached its majority. These non-traditional devices, external degrees, greatly increased the franchise of university participation: would that our own age showed such imagination and flexibility. Here, as elsewhere in the nineteenth century, there was direct state intervention – not only in the structure but also in the curriculum. So there never was an age of aboriginal academic independence. Underlying this university expansion was society's need for professional cadres (usually clergy in the early days).

Plans for a university for the North of England date back to the sixteenth century. Cromwell finally allowed a college to be established in Durham in 1656 after the Revolution. However, following the Restoration, the college was dissolved and the University of Durham lay dormant until an Act of Parliament of 1832 revived it to provide clergy for the church. A charter permitting the award of degrees followed in 1836 and the curriculum accepted closely followed that at Oxford and Cambridge. Funding arrangements provided by the Durham Chapter were generous, but this was partly to enable them to avoid the confiscation of church funds by a zealous and reforming government.

Government intervention at Durham came in the form of statutory commissioners appointed in 1861 under the terms of the *Durham University Act*. The conclusion of this investigation brought a reformed curriculum and general expansion to shake the university out of the sloth into which it had sunk, and then in 1871, following the passage of the *Universities Test Act*, Durham like Oxford and Cambridge abandoned religious tests for all entrants except those reading theology. Again like Oxford and Cambridge, Durham developed a residential college system and did not follow London with its fluid population. Such a pattern of residential accommodation is a very specific feature of the United Kingdom and American systems. It simply appears to have evolved over time – influenced perhaps by the institution of the 'public' boarding school.

We should also observe here that the growth of university education was strongly influenced by the improvements in state secondary education.

CIVIC UNIVERSITIES

Critics were keen to point out the deficiencies that existed at Oxford and Cambridge in the first half of the nineteenth century (and in particular their failure to embrace science):

> "We must get out of our heads all notion of making the mass of students come and reside... at Oxford or Cambridge, which neither suit their circumstances nor offer them the instruction they want. We must plant facilities in the eight or ten principal seats of population, and let the students follow lectures there from their own homes with whatever arrangements for their living they and their parents choose. It would be everything for the great seats of population to be thus made intellectual centres as well as mere places of business".[15]

Indeed technical education of all kinds remained underdeveloped and this state of affairs was acknowledged by the *Schools Enquiry Commission on Technical Instruction* of 1867.

A further impetus to new development in higher education came with the 1870 *Education Act* that required areas not served by voluntary societies to set up local school boards to manage elementary schools. In 1902, the Bryce Commission gave rise to the Education Act that made Local Education Authorities responsible for all education below university level: free and compulsory education had been established.

The civic universities, that owe their existence to a combination of liberal benefactors and provincial rivalry, made university education more widely available and although initially serving local needs they soon developed into national institutions. H.C. Dent described their development in the following terms:

> "the foundation, through the generosity of one or more private benefactors, of a college designed to teach chiefly scientific and technical subjects to the people of a great industrial town; the expansion of this into a university college by the addition of 'faculties' in the humane subjects and a department for the training of teachers; and finally, the securing of a Royal Charter".[16]

John Owen provided funds for Owen's College which opened in Manchester in 1851 where students read for London University external

---

[15] M. Arnold, *School and Universities on the Continent*, 1868, p.276, quoted in Berdahl, *Ibid.*, p.41.
[16] H. C. Dent, *British Education*, 1949, p.28.

degrees. The college only prospered after considerable improvements had taken place in secondary education, since in the early days there were too few suitable candidates presenting themselves for matriculation. By 1874 new buildings had been provided through generous donations and student numbers passed the thousand mark. Thereafter the College went from strength to strength and engaged in first class scholarship over a wide range of subjects.

In 1874 the Yorkshire College of Science came into existence at Leeds, largely through the demand for scientific and technical education, but with improved secondary education providing an additional impetus. And private benefaction and the generosity of Liverpool Corporation had led to the foundation of University College, Liverpool, in 1881. Mark Firth, a Sheffield steel maker, endowed a College in 1879 to accommodate the Cambridge University Extension Movement and in 1897 this merged with the Sheffield Medical School to form the University College, Sheffield. Funds were raised for new buildings and the university received a charter in 1905.

The lack of scientific education in Birmingham, when its industrial transformation required more highly trained manpower, led Joseph Mason, a manufacturer of steel pins and electro plate, to endow a college in 1860 called Mason Science College. Rather perversely in the circumstances of its birth, the Science in its title was excised owing to the inclusion of liberal subjects in the curriculum demanded by London for the award of external degrees. Mason subsequently launched an appeal for funds and after receiving extremely generous support a charter was granted in 1900 in the name of Birmingham University, making it the first provincial university with degree granting powers.

A successful triumvirate of west country businessmen, W.Carpenter, W. Baker and L.Fry established a College of Science for the West of England in 1876, although culture formed an equally important part of the curriculum. These private donations, combined with ones from Jowett of Balliol and New College Oxford and generous civic support, led to the creation of University College Bristol in 1876. The University received its charter in 1909. The significance of such private and municipal benefaction lay in the provision of initial endowments, buildings and so on, but only a small sized operation would be sustainable on this basis, a college and not a university as such. Therefore state aid, diminutive though it originally was, goes back to the very beginnings of our modern system: the principle was early established and therefore indivisible from the concept of a British university.

The threat of German and American industrial competition served to emphasise the need for an expansion of technical education and the so-called 'civic universities' were from their very inception a response to these developments. The National Association for the Promotion of Technical Education came into being to campaign for state aid to assist with the development of indigenous technical education. Thus in 1889 the government responded with the *Technical Instruction Act*, empowering local authorities to levy a rate to support technical education. Furthermore, in 1889, the first distribution of treasury funds to university colleges (excluding Oxford, Cambridge and London) took place, through the precursor of the University Grants Committee (1919), and it offered advice on the allocation of the £15,000 involved. In the following year a far more substantial sum of £75,000, destined originally as compensation to publicans losing their licenses, was diverted to the colleges to assist with technical education. Another lucrative source of revenue derived from state subsidised candidates for the teaching profession, where numbers were swelled by the vacancies created in the wake of the 1870 and 1902 Education Acts. Thus a steady progress down the path towards majority state support had begun.

THE UNIVERSITY COLLEGES

A combination of initiatives started by the University Extension Movement, and civic pride, saw the establishment of a number of university colleges initially offering University of London external degrees until such time as they were chartered as full independent universities. Reading emerged as the first of these, although unlike the others it drew students from all over the country like the colleges of the University of London, primarily because it did not develop in a large industrial conurbation. Consequently Reading built a complex of residential halls, contributing significantly towards community life, and unknowingly very much a harbinger of future university developments. The college opened in 1892 and received its own charter in 1926.

Nottingham emerged out of the extension movement too, University College being founded in 1881. Its finances were sound but its future progress became assured in the early years of this century, when Sir Jesse Boot, founder of a highly successful pharmaceutical business, provided substantial funds for new buildings. The University received its charter in 1948. Exeter, Southampton, Leicester and Hull University Colleges followed in 1901, 1902, 1918 and 1927 respectively, with charters in 1952, 1957, 1955 and 1954.

The last new establishment before the post Second World War expansion was the foundation of an experimental college, University College of North Staffordshire, eventually chartered in 1948. To avoid what were perceived to be the over-rigid specialisations at other universities, four year multi-disciplinary degrees were to be offered, not of the University of London, but sanctioned by three sponsoring universities, Oxford, Manchester and Birmingham. No generous private benefaction was involved either, for the University Grants Committee provided significant financial assistance from the very beginning.[17] This was a foretaste of what was to come, an abandonment of the principle of the integrality of the private benefactor. The college became Keele University in 1962 and suffered badly in the 1981 cuts.

THE FEDERAL UNIVERSITY OF WALES

The early developments in Welsh higher education are also linked to the inability of the Anglican church to find enough candidates for holy orders. Bishop Burgess of St David's consequently organised the establishment of St David's College Lampeter, a charter being granted in 1828.[18] Parliament received a petition for a Welsh university in 1852 and in 1863 a committee was formed to campaign for this, led by Sir Hugh Owen, G. Morgan and E. Salisbury. However, the first tangible steps were not taken until 1872, when the Castle Hotel Aberystwyth became available following its bankruptcy, providing accommodation for the residential University College of Aberystwyth and offering external London degrees. The College struggled against financial hardship and without any government support despite several petitions during the 1870's, until the Welsh Members of Parliament argued successfully that financial support represented the only hope for its continued existence. The 1882 Aberdare

---

[17] See R. O. Berdahl, *Ibid.*, pp.142-3.
[18] J.G. Williams, "The Historical Background of the University of Wales", *Final Report of the Working Group on Powers and Functions*, (Daniels Report), June 1989, pp.1(1)-1(10).

Committee, appointed to investigate Welsh education generally, recommended national grants to establish sound secondary and university education: initially Aberystwyth received a small grant of £4,000 and when Cardiff (1883) and Bangor (1884) were established, similar sums were made available to them. As elsewhere, private sources seem to have been unable or unwilling to build up a vigorous foundation on their own, without state or municipal help. A campaign in the late 1880's led to the establishment of the federal University of Wales in 1893, with the power to confer its own degrees, despite the independence of the three founder members. Before the Second World War two further independent institutions, Swansea Technical College (1920) and the Welsh National School of Medicine (1931) joined the federation, now one of the key national institutions in Wales.[19]

Individual colleges did not enjoy any degree of financial liberation after 1893 any more than they did before and state grants remained low. However, after the Liberal victory of 1906, a Departmental Committee chaired by Sir Thomas Raleigh was set up in the following year to examine the finances of the University and the individual colleges. As a result of its recommendations higher grants were obtained. This continuous process of enlarging state support for British universities was due to the demands of science; increasing numbers; and the breadth and depth of subjects. The state became much the senior partner; the private donor less important and eventually almost invisible.

In Wales the growth of the individual colleges weakened the federal structure over time and this reached a new climax in 1988 with the amalgamation of University College, Cardiff and the University of Wales Institute of Science and Technology to form the University of Wales, College of Cardiff.[20] As the largest single college, it exerts a distorting pressure upon the University, since it dominates the whole federation and will probably be less tolerant of its idiosyncrasies. Indeed it is exerting pressure for independence for some of the colleges from the University and an independent funding body for Welsh higher education can only presage

---

[19] The University of Wales Institute of Science and Technology joined the federation in 1967 and St David's College Lampeter in 1969.

[20] Reported in J. G. Williams, "The Historical Background", Appendix I of the *Final Report of the Working Group on Powers and Functions, Daniels Report*, 1989. During the 1960's and 1970's the University of Wales became a rubber stamp for the plans of the individual colleges. With annual grants from 1981, the UGC strengthened to links directly with the Colleges.

this development. Such a development will save an entirely unnecessary administrative bill, for the University of Wales Registry costs some £4m and this can be redirected towards research and better facilities in Wales.

THE NEW UNIVERSITIES

This phase in the development of British universities marks the beginning of state domination of events, since whilst the initiative for new foundations might rest with interested local authorities, state sanction and finance were both imperative.

The need for expansion and the upgrading of existing facilities had been acknowledged by the University Grants Committee and the Committee of Vice Chancellors and Principals immediately after the Second World War. Sir Ernest Simon, in a pamphlet entitled *The Development of British Universities* published in 1944, called for expansion to match that taking place in the United States of America if Britain wished to succeed industrially and commercially, on the a priori grounds that there was a causal relationship involved.[21] Part of the post-war governments' enthusiasm for state planning embraced university education, although (it should be stressed) without affecting university autonomy, and led to numerous official enquiries into developments in professional fields from agriculture to technological education and to the consequences for student numbers and university expansion. Also, the 1944 *Education Act* held the promise of larger numbers of students reaching matriculation standard, requiring greater co-ordination of university activities.

Certain reports provided official supplementary evidence of the need to expand higher education that would of necessity involve state financial support, since the private sector had long since run out of steam. In particular, the *Barlow Committee* called for the output of scientists and technologists to be doubled within a period of ten years, a proposal that reached fruition five years earlier than planned.[22] Also, providing sufficient employment could be found for them, the numbers studying arts and social science subjects were to be expanded significantly. As we have already noted above, developments between 1857 and 1927 had done much to

---

[21] For the contrary view in the case of British science, see T. Kealey, "Science Fiction: and the true way to save British Science", *Centre for Policy Studies*, 1989.
[22] *Committee on Scientific Manpower*, (The Barlow Report), London, HMSO, Cmnd. 6824, 1946.

increase the status of science and technology in British universities, but after Barlow activity in these areas quickened.[23]

In the late 1950's and the 1960's the need for new institutions could no longer be resisted, and as early as 1947 local authorities in Norwich, York and Brighton petitioned the University Grants Committee (UGC) for universities and were the strongest candidates amongst several others to do so. In 1955 Brighton revived its plan and no fewer than five local authorities offered financial assistance, enabling the UGC to support the establishment of a University College of Sussex. Herein was a recognition that a university lent status to a region. The government approved the capital expenditure.

By 1959 the UGC envisaged an expansion of between 35 and 40,000 places and awaited Treasury approval for the necessary capital expanditure. To meet the 1970 student projections from the 1960 base, some £175m of capital expenditure would be required, of which 50% represented arrears of building work or the need to counter obsolescence in the capital stock.

TABLE 2:1: THE DEVELOPMENT OF THE NEW UNIVERSITIES AND PROPOSED STUDENT NUMBERS UP TO 1966-67

UNIVERSITY	GOVERNMENT ANNOUNCEMENT	PROPOSED STUDENT NUMBERS 1966-67
SUSSEX	FEBRUARY 1958	1,700
YORK	APRIL 1960	1,070
EAST ANGLIA	APRIL 1960	1,225
ESSEX	MAY 1961	600
KENT	MAY 1961	700
WARWICK	MAY 1961	670
LANCASTER	NOVEMBER 1961	600

Source: *UGC, University Development 1962-1967,* 1968.

---

[23] A. Flexner, *Universities American, English, German*, Oxford University Press, 1930.

In 1960, York and Norwich were advised to proceed with plans for universities and in the following year detailed discussions took place with Kent, Essex and Warwick local authorities. A seventh university was to be located in the North of England at Lancaster, to strengthen the provision in the area and attract graduates into local employment. Table 2:1 indicates the governments' announcement of the new foundations and the proposed student numbers for the academic year 1966/67.

Any further university developments were to await the outcome of the *Robbins Report*. Thus seven new universities had been established *before Robbins reported*, with experimental syllabi and the power to award their own degrees, thereby guaranteeing academic self-determination. They were not the product of a single benefactor's whim and were not founded in opposition to Oxford and Cambridge, but rather to supplement them.

TABLE 2:2: LOCAL AUTHORITY PROVISION FOR THE NEW UNIVERSITIES.

	£
University of Sussex	39,000
University of York	36,000
University of East Anglia	60,000
University of Essex	122,000
University of Kent	55,000
University of Warwick	55,000
University of Lancaster	82,000

Source: UGC, *University Development 1962-1967*, 1968.

Capital appeals in the locality were also successful, with the following sums raised: Sussex £830,000; York £1,420,000; East Anglia £1,339,000. Table 2:2 indicates local authority provision for the new institutions.

THE ROBBINS REPORT AND THE FINAL PHASE OF EXPANSION

Robbins provided the first comprehensive and definitive analysis of British higher education and focussed particularly on the need for further expansion in student numbers. This followed directly on the heels of the establishment of seven new universities that *pre-date Robbins:* "It is no disrespect to the Robbins Committee to say that their Report did not inhibit the process of expansion in the universities, or in other sectors of higher education. What their Report did was to establish, publicly and authoritatively, ten principles which should govern the scale and pattern of higher education in (Britain)".[24] The UGC had planned for an increase in numbers from 113,000 in 1962 to 170,000 in 1973/74, but under Robbins courses were to be made available to all those "qualified by ability and attainment to pursue them and who wished to do so", hence the new target of 218,000 by 1973/74. This adjustment required a further expansion in the number of universities, since only part could be met within the constraint of existing facilities, and Robbins proposed raising the ten Colleges of Advanced Technology (CAT's) to university status, plus the Scottish College of Commerce, Glasgow and the Heriot-Watt College, Edinburgh. The government in turn undertook to make available the necessary non-recurrent and recurrent resources and the universities responded by more than meeting the student targets detailed in Robbins.

Whether the universities had the staff to serve the expansion remained at the time unclear and in retrospect it emerged that a great many mediocre minds were recruited.

Robbins estimated that the demand for student places by 1980 would reach 350,000, whereas the capability of the existing universities would fall short of the target by some 50,000 places. Thus the creation of a further six universities formed part of the Robbins proposals, with at least one being located in Scotland. By mid-1964 Stirling had emerged as the favoured site and government approval followed swiftly. No decisions were taken on the other institutions proposed, but plans would proceed further once the existing one had been consolidated.

BUCKINGHAM

Buckingham provides a salutory case for anyone interested in university freedom, for here indeed is Britain's one university that is genuinely independent of the state. But Buckingham is highly vocational. It is largely concerned with business and law, and very largely foreign. The question arises, what is the point of it? It serves neither the nation nor academic

---

[24] *Higher Education*, (Report of the Committee appointed by the Prime Minister under the Chairmanship of Lord Robbins, 1961-63), London, HMSO, Cmnd. 2154, 1963.

research, save in a narrow band of professional training, since as usual teaching posts are dictated by student demand.[25]

Buckingham is highly dependent on fee income and has found difficulty in raising significant amounts from private sector corporations compared with the U.S.: in Britain therefore the state will always be the dominant partner in higher education.

However, other U.K. universities have as it were inherited wealth: their facilities already in place, they have not had to sustain Buckingham's start-up costs. Rightly, Buckingham would point out that the ground of play is not even, as a private institute they have to compete with larger standing public institutions with much more extensive facilities and range of academic choice, and, above all else, complete freedom from tuition fees. How indeed could Buckingham compete with a subsidised monopolist?

Still Buckingham, which epitomises what a consumer demand-led university might look like, disappoints. One doubts whether something so narrowly focussed should properly be called a university. Perhaps it is only right that students should pay for business and law. The concept underlying Buckingham is a pedestrian one, and no insight or vision has animated the organism. But it will survive.

Buckingham received its first students, 66 of them, in 1976; rapidly they encountered huge deficits – £270,000 in 1976; by 1980 the accumulated revenue deficit was £686,000 and they were faced with closure. Donations to the revenue account enabled the operation to survive (by 1988 cumulative donations to revenue stood at nearly £2 million; over 4 million pounds have been donated to capital, and such donations were recently running at £430,000 per annum). Expansion of student numbers and increasing official recognition followed: the fragile enterprise took root, and proved hardy. By 1988 the university enjoyed a £250,000 surplus.

Buckingham has been a pioneer in a number of areas since it is free of the usual bureaucratic constraints. Its students do their degree in two years, four terms a year. Staff have no tenure: reward accords with performance or need, students are expected to take a language course and courses in two schools of study over and above that of registration. There are many mature students, 25% of the total. There is a higher staff student ratio (1:13.3). And

---

[25] M. Barratt, "The Buckingham Experience," *Funding and Management of Higher Education*, edited S. Sexton, Institute of Economic Affairs, 1989, pp.104-24.

students mostly pay all of the costs: state help constitutes a moiety of Buckingham's finances.

The university is small, 314 of its compliment of 700 study law, 209 business and accountancy. By 1994 it is expecting 950 students. The future plan is to expand the school of accounting, business and economics; and provide more taught masters in law, business, fisheries and biology. The aim is also to raise capital benefactions to £600,000 per annum (and remember there is no significant alumni badge). This seems a rather prosaic future that will not change Buckingham's role as a trade school for rich overseas students (who account for 3/5 of the total). Nevertheless standards are not lax, with external examiners and a 10% failure rate in finals.

Fees for tuition are £6,184 per annum and a full degree is £12,368, while there is no specific extra charge for science. State universities charge a similar rate for the overseas market. Student's other costs are estimated at £1,000 per term, and those who pay their fees beforehand receive a discount. Buckingham also has a loan operation with its bank: repayments are made over a five year period, the loan is seldom more than £1,500 and has to be spent on tuition fees. According to the vice-chancellor, about 3/4 of the student body is involved in personal fundraising and scholarships are also available.

What of the involvement of the state in the support of Buckingham? Mandatory awards for U.K. students were accepted in 1981, and the university received its Royal Charter in 1983. Now, U.K. students receive a tuition award (26% of full fee) and may get a maintenance allowance. Only one L.E.A. pays full tuition: but "The total income to Buckingham via LEA awards paid to 178 students in 1987 was circa £272,000".[26]

How efficient is Buckingham relative to the state sector? Comparisons with similarly-sized Lampeter are interesting. But Lampeter has only 18 overseas students. Its cost per graduate is nearly £2,000 higher than Buckingham though this is a cost for three years not two. Both universities at £2.8 million have the same income. Nor does Lampeter have the 'vocational' emphasis of Buckingham.

Comparisons with the U.S. also merit attention. About 83% of Buckingham's turnover comes from tuition fees compared to 38.8% in U.S.

---

[26] M. Barrett, *op cit.*

private institutions. The American institutions derive 18.2% of their income from government, 5.2% from endowments, and donations can be much higher, each constituting 30% of revenue. Buckingham is and will remain 'tuition driven': future sources of non-government finance for U.K. universities must therefore lie with the actual or potential wealth of the consumer of university education rather than with industry, alumni, rich benefactors and the like.

THE EARLY DEVELOPMENT OF STATE FUNDING

Unlike its European counterparts, British higher education did not witness state intervention beyond Royal Commissions and these often at the behest of the universities themselves. Indeed British experience before the first world war has been well summarised by Ernest Barker in the following terms:

> "[The British genius] prefers, whenever it can, to act in the same sphere of 'society' – the sphere of voluntary action – and not to depend on the State for every initiative and impulse. But that is not all, even while scope is demanded for the play of voluntary action, the demand is also made that the State should aid such action, and aid it without impeding or seeking to control its freedom. This may seem paradoxical – indeed it is paradoxical – and yet it is true".[27]

When the state did intervene, it concentrated upon financial assistance, although before 1889 this was of an extremely limited kind. The earliest examples of state aid followed the passage of the 1705 *Act of Scottish Parliament*, that guaranteed the Scottish universities in perpetuity to secure the Protestant religion and Presbyterian Church Government in Scotland. Endowments to these universities came from church sources initially, but later from Royal or public revenues, Scottish hereditary revenues and Crown land revenues. Then in 1831 the endowments were placed on an annual Parliamentary vote and there followed some involvement by Parliament in the minutiae of academic planning too. The sums involved however were very small, amounting for example to only £5,077 in 1832.

As a result of the chartering arrangements relating to London University, whereby institutions in Britain and the Empire prepared students for external London degrees, the Government undertook to make grants available to cover administrative expenses as well as accommodation. Any short-fall from fees, with regard to the cost of examinations and the award

---

[27] E. Barker. *The British University*, London, 1949, p.8.

of prizes and honours, were also covered. The Secretary of State for Home Affairs recommended the necessary payments and to a limited extent involved himself in academic affairs.[28]

The Universities of Oxford, Cambridge and Durham did not receive any Parliamentary support. But Owen's College Manchester in the 1850's and again in the 1870's, joined this time by Aberystwyth College Wales, called for government assistance to stave off financial disaster. Significantly neither came under the aegis of the Church of England to serve its purposes. So the survival of universities in infancy was due to state aid. Our current system has its origins in the nineteenth century and has had organic evolution since then. Although these colleges were informed that the government did not have a policy to provide financial assistance to promote higher education, the Treasury significantly had responded to the 1848 *Select Committee on Miscellaneous Expenditure* in terms that defended the existing grant system, whilst at the same time emphasising the need for universities to retain their independence: "universities, as representing the highest intellect of the nation, should not be dependent on its politics. The normal condition of a flourishing university should be one of independence and stability".[29]

Following the Report of the *Aberdare Committee*, appointed in 1880 to investigate Welsh education, Aberystwyth received a grant of £4,000 with the Cardiff and Bangor colleges receiving similar sums upon their foundation. As a result of this development, the English colleges increased their pressure for assistance, particularly for scientific laboratories, libraries and hostels, highlighting the total exhaustion of funds from local benefactors: science and residences were both factors impelling state support. The country recognised science's importance for its economic competitiveness against Germany and America.

Attempts were made to co-ordinate the campaign for government support in 1887, and finally the technological superiority of Germany and America alleged in government reports, the most recent being the 1884 *Royal Commission on Technical Education*, plus nagging from the national press,

---

[28] In 1841 the Chancellor of the Exchequer returned the estimates for grants to the University Senate since they were regarded as too high by the House of Commons. The Senate declined to make any adjustment, so that Chancellor Goulbourn was forced to impose a 20% cut himself, having sought expert opinion first of an impartial, but informed, kind. The first university 'cuts' were in 1841.

[29] *Select Committee on Miscellaneous Expenditure*, 1848.

convinced the authorities of the urgent need for action. Hence a grant of £15,000 was agreed in 1889 and the Chancellor of the Exchequer established an *ad hoc* Committee on Grants to University Colleges in Great Britain, to determine the colleges to be assisted and to oversee its distribution. The state had thus assumed some responsibility for technological and scientific education that could no longer be sustained by donations and endowments. Its aim had been to strengthen the finances of the poorer colleges and provide pump-priming monies in the hope that further benefactions would be forthcoming.

Hence eleven colleges received support in the form of deficiency payments ranging from £700 to £1,800; and the advisory committee recommended, and the Treasury accepted, a five year grant period with inspection of the colleges by seperate committee, and the publication of financial accounts by the colleges themselves. Quinquennial funding had thus been created, to aid continuity and prevent uncertainty over funding arrangements without the risk of complacency through a system of monitoring.

Table 2:3 gives the annual breakdown for the first quinquennial distribution of Parliamentary grant. This covers the colleges and, excluding Bedford, the distribution is fairly even. Table 2:4 gives the figures for 1897 in the middle of the second quinquennium and here the distribution is more uneven, with Manchester receiving three times as much as Bristol, Sheffield, Nottingham, King's and Dundee. Twelve colleges now received awards. Table 2:5 indicates the relative status of local income and Parliamentary grants for 1895/96. Grants may vary between 5.5 and 30% of local income, but in most cases are less than 15%. Finally, Table 2:6 gives total income accounts for 1895/96: Treasury grants inexplicably do not agree with Table 2:5.

TABLE 2:3
ANNUAL DISTRIBUTION OF GRANT 1889-1894*

Owen's College, Manchester	1,800
Liverpool University College	1,700
Mason College, Birmingham	1,500
Yorkshire College, Leeds	1,400
Nottingham University College	1,400
Bristol University College	1,200
Durham College of Science (Newcastle upon Tyne)	1,200
Firth College, Sheffield	1,200
Bedford College, London	700
	£13,300
King's College, London (if denominational test removed)	1,700
Total	£15,000

* Source: *Accounts and Papers (Education)* Vol LXVI.

TABLE 2:4
DISTRIBUTION OF GRANT 1897*

Owen's College, Manchester	3,500
Liverpool University College	3,000
Mason College, Birmingham	2,700
Yorkshire College, Leeds	2,200
Nottingham University College	1,500
Bristol University College	1,200
Durham College of Science (Newcastle upon Tyne)	2,200
Firth College, Sheffield	1,300
Bedford College, London	1,200
King's College, London	2,200
Dundee	1,000
University College London	3,000
Total	£25,000

* Source: *Accounts and Papers (Education)* Vol LXVIII

TABLE 2:5
GRANTS AND LOCAL INCOME FOR UNIVERSITIES 1895/96*

	Grant	Local Income	Grant as Percent of Local Income
Owen's College, Manchester	1,800	32,301	5.5
University College, London	1,700	16,150	10.5
Liverpool University College	1,700	10,743	15.1
Mason College, Birmingham	1,500	13,990	10.7
King's College, London	1,400	10,718	13.0
Durham College of Science	1,400	8,608	16.2
Yorkshire College, Leeds	1,200	8,671	13.8
Nottingham University College	1,200	6,374	18.8
Firth College, Sheffield	1,200	4,106	29.2
Bristol University College	1,200	3,642	32.9
Bedford College, London	700	5,840	12.0
Dundee	500	4,918	10.1
Reading Extension College	-	2,018	-
Exeter Extension College	-	604	-
Total	£15,500	£128,683	

* Source: *Accounts and Papers (Education)* Vol LXVIII

TABLE 2:6
UNIVERSITY INCOME ACCOUNTS 1895-96

	Fees	Endowments	Subscription	Scholarships	Treasury	Deficit	Total
Owen's College Manchester	13,442	12,276	5,095	2,488	1,920	2,074	36,295
University College London	8,259	5,907	988	996	1,812	361	18,323
King's College, London	8,079	344	1,654	666	1,275	1,268	13,286
University College, Liverpool	6,094	5,565	1,857	474	1,601	794	16,385
Mason College, Birmingham	5,342	4,459	250	667	1,462	1,104	13,284
Yorkshire College, Leeds	6,126	1,099	722	661	1,494	2,769	12,871
Nottingham University College	2,396	400	3,225	353	1,310	448	8,132
Bristol University College	2,713	75	716	138	1,255	810	5,707

TABLE 2:6
UNIVERSITY INCOME ACCOUNTS 1895-96 (Cont'd)

	Fees	Endowments	Subscription	Scholarships	Treasury	Deficit	Total
Durham College of Science	5,320	1,470	1,700	181	1,282	428	10,381
Firth College, Sheffield	1,503	1,039	1,393	171	1,310	19	5,435
Bedford College, London	4,836	36	501	467	749	-	6,589
Dundee	460	4,288	75	95	500	373	5,791
Reading	528	-	1,490	-	-	370	2,388
Exeter	204	4	396	-	-	16	620
Total	65,302	36,692	19,062	7,357	15,970	10,834	155,487

Five committees reported between 1889 and 1904, none of which were standing committees, and two Commissioners were appointed in 1896 to survey the work carried out in the universities. The vote was subsequently raised to £25,000 in 1897/98.[30] By 1904 it had risen further to £54,000 in the wake of a vigorous campaign for greater state support from national figures, including Joseph Chamberlain and Sidney Webb. The grant doubled again in 1905/6 and a University Colleges Committee was appointed the year before under R B Haldane's chairmanship to arrange for the appropriate allocations. A close relationship had developed between the various Committees, and the universities and colleges regarded the distribution of the grant as objective and impartial whilst being free to deploy them as they saw fit. The Treasury accepted the Committee's recommendations, although retaining the right to determine the global total, and the quinquennial system looked to be firmly established. Note here particularly the lack of government direction of the grant: it was for universities themselves to decide. Even with Edwardians, there was no accountability of a rigid kind.

THE ORIGINS AND DEVELOPMENT OF THE UGC

The ad hoc committee, of which Haldane was chairman, placed the whole issue of state support for the universities on a new footing in its *Third*

---

[30] University Grants Committee, *University Development 1957-62*, London, HMSO, Cmnd. 2267, 1962, Chapter 8, p.174.

Report. Haldane called for a permanent and independent advisory body that would receive and distribute the grant, make annual reports to the Treasury and arrange quinquennial visitations to the universities.[31]

The first Advisory Committee on Grants to University Colleges was appointed in 1906. A three year allocation of grant was agreed in 1907 to cover what became a transitional phase, but in actual fact only the academic years 1907/8 and 1908/9. Allocations split into a 90% block grant and a 10% ear-marked grant.

Between 1913 and 1931 the universities received support from newly established research bodies, mainly funded by the government. These were:

1913	Medical Research Committee;
1915	Department of Scientific and Industrial Research (DSIR);
1931	Agricultural Research Council.

UNIVERSITIES BETWEEN THE WARS

After the first world war the universities were faced with many difficulties: inflation had eroded the real value of university endowments, whilst at the same time all cost categories had increased. Fee income also fell because of the drop in student numbers, although the demand for student places very quickly accelerated. As a result of neglect during the war there was an enormous backlog of repairs and maintenance work. Finally, the large strides made in scientific knowledge opened up numerous avenues for further research and development, plus important industrial applications that would enhance the country's industrial base and balance of trade. A meeting of interested university and government parties in 1918 argued, therefore, that as a result of all of these developments the need for an increase in the level of state funding of universities was of paramount importance, with the usual caveat of no state interference in its distribution. The Advisory Committee on University Grants prepared to receive the list of requests and the President of the Board of Education made clear his position when tackling the government:

---

[31] Tom Owen, "The University Grants Committee", *Oxford Review of Education*, 1980, pp.255-78.

TABLE 2:7
SOURCES OF UNIVERSITY INCOME

ANALYSIS BY SOURCE IN PERCENT OF TOTAL INCOME

YEAR	TOTAL INCOME OF UNIVERSITIES '000	PARLIAMENTARY GRANTS	LOCAL AUTHORITY GRANTS	FEES TUITION EXAMIN-ATIONS	ENDOWMENTS TOTAL	ENDOWMENTS LOW	ENDOWMENTS HIGH	DONATIONS AND SUBSCRIP-TIONS	OTHER SOURCES[1]
1913/14	971	34.7	15.3	30.7	11.9	-	-	3.3	.1
1914/15	NOT								
1915/16	PUBLISHED								
1916/17	DURING								
1917/18	FIRST								
1918/19	WORLD								
1919/20	WAR								
1920/21	3,020	33.6	9.3	32.2	11.2	1.6^2	30.9^2	2.7	9.2
1921/22	3,578	35.3	11.7	28.9	10.3	1.3^2	44.3^4	2.7	9.5
1922/23	3,582	35.6	11.9	27.8	10.9	1.6^2	43.7^5	2.2	4.8
1923/24	3,587	35.5	12.0	26.6	11.6	2.7^2	43.5^4	2.5	4.8
1924/25	3,635	35.9	13.5	25.4	11.4	2.0^2	38.1^5	2.6	4.9
1925/26	3,942	39.5	13.1	23.4	10.7	2.0^6	29.4^9	2.7	4.6
1926/27	4,948	36.9	10.5	22.5	11.1	1.8^6	31.1^9	2.2	6.6
1927/28	5,038	36.6	10.0	22.7	13.5	2.2^6	26.7^7	2.5	6.9
1928/29	5,174	35.9	10.1	23.0	13.9	2.4^8	29.5^9	2.4	6.9
1929/30	5,338	36.1	9.7	22.9	13.9	2.3^8	29.8^9	2.3	7.1
1930/31	5,830	36.3	9.7	23.7	13.7	3.9^6	31.6^9	2.1	6.9
1931/32	5,874	36.0	9.4	23.8	13.6	4.5^6	29.9^9	2.4	7.0
1932/33	5,919	35.4	9.1	24.5	13.7	3.7^6	30.0^9	2.5	6.8
1933/34	5,953	35.1	9.2	24.7	13.7	4.1^6	31.2^9	2.4	6.8
1934/35	6,072	33.9	9.9	24.6	13.9	2.0^2	32.6^9	2.7	7.1
1935/36	6,060	34.3	8.7	24.6	14.5	3.0^2	33.5^4	2.5	7.5
1936/37	6,410	36.1	8.5	30.6	14.8	2.3^2	32.7^4	2.4	7.6
1937/38	6,545	36.2	8.7	29.9	15.2	2.9^2	37.3^9	2.7	7.3
1938/39	6,712	35.8	9.0	29.8	15.4	2.8^2	29.9^9	2.6	7.4

TABLE 2:7 (Continued)
ANALYSIS BY SOURCE IN PERCENT OF TOTAL INCOME

YEAR	TOTAL INCOME OF UNIVERSITIES '000	PARLIAMENTARY GRANTS	LOCAL AUTHORITY GRANTS	FEES TUITION EXAMIN- ATIONS	ENDOWMENTS TOTAL	ENDOWMENTS LOW	ENDOWMENTS HIGH	DONATIONS AND SUBSCRIP- TIONS	OTHER SOURCES[1]	RESEARCH
1939/40	NOT									
1940/41	PUBLISHED									
1941/42	DURING									
1942/43	SECOND									
1943/44	WORLD WAR									
1944/45	7,600	38.9	8.3	24.2	14.0	2.3^2	44.3^9	2.2	12.4	
1945/46	10,280	49.3	6.9	22.5	11.2	1.9^2	36.3^9	1.9	8.2	
1946/47	13,043	52.7	5.6	23.2	9.3	1.4^2	30.8^9	2.2	7.0	
1947/48	16,276	57.8	4.8	21.4	7.6	0.9^2	25.1^9	2.0	6.4	
1948/49	18,156	59.2	5.0	20.6	6.7	0.8^2	20.6^9	1.9	6.6	
1949/50	22,009	63.9	4.6	17.7	5.7	-	-	1.7	6.4	
1950/51	24,268	64.9	4.3	16.5	5.5	0.8^2	17.9^9	1.8	7.0	
1951/52	25,747	66.5	4.1	14.8	5.2	0.8^2	16.3^9	1.9	7.5	
1952/53	29,698	69.6	3.6	12.7	4.4	0.8^2	11.6^1	1.6	7.7	
1953/54	31,112	70.5	3.6	12.0	4.3	0.7^2	10.2^9	1.6	8.0	
1954/55	35,600	70.4	3.2	10.7	4.1	0.6^2	10.3^1	1.1	5.0	3.4
1955/56	36,894	72.7	3.1	10.8	3.8	-	-	0.9	8.7	4.1
1956/57	41,595	69.6	3.1	10.8	4.0	-	-	1.2	11.0	6.1
1957/58	49,418	70.7	2.8	11.5	3.6	-	-	1.1	4.2	6.1
1958/59	52,273	69.7	2.9	11.0	3.4	0.5^2	9.4^0	0.9	5.0	7.0
1959/60	59,800	72.2	2.6	10.0	2.9	0.4^2	7.5^9	0.7	3.6	7.9
1960/61	68,706	72.2	2.3	9.1	2.9	0.4^2	7.8^{10}	0.7	3.6	9.1
1961/62	74,112	69.5	2.1	9.0	2.7	0.4^2	7.2^{10}	0.8	3.7	11.1
1962/63	86,402	70.1	1.9	9.9	2.4	0.3^2	7.3^{10}	0.6	3.2	11.0
1963/64	104,411	71.3	1.7	8.8	2.1	-	-	0.5	4.1	11.5
1964/65	124,161	71.7	1.4	8.1	1.9	-	-	0.6	4.9	11.4

TABLE 2:7 (Continued)
ANALYSIS BY SOURCE IN PERCENT OF TOTAL INCOME

YEAR	TOTAL INCOME OF UNIVERSITIES '000	PARLIAMENTARY GRANTS	LOCAL AUTHORITY GRANTS	FEES TUITION EXAMIN- ATIONS	ENDOWMENTS TOTAL	ENDOWMENTS LOW	ENDOWMENTS HIGH	DONATIONS AND SUBSCRIP- TIONS	OTHER SOURCES[1]
1965/66	164,733	74.1	1.1	7.4	1.5	-	-	0.4	3.2	10.8
1966/67	192,245	72.5	1.0	6.9	1.4[11]	-	-	-	5.4	11.2
1967/68	216,624	72.7	0.9	7.4	1.7	-	-	-	6.3	11.0
1968/69	240,815	71.0	1.0	7.0	2.0	-	-	-	8.0	11.0
1969/70	275,041	72.0	1.0	7.0	1.0	-	-	-	9.0	12.0
1970/71	322,337	71.0	0.52	6.0	2.0	-	-	-	8.0	13.0
1971/72	361,984	74.0	1.0	6.0	1.0	-	-	-	6.0	12.0
1972/73	422,681	77.0	0.28	5.0	1.0	-	-	-	5.0	11.0
1973/74	479,833	78.0	0.23	5.0	1.0	-	-	-	5.0	11.0
1974/75	572,299	78.0	0.15	5.0	1.0	-	-	-	5.0	12.0
1975/76	726,573	76.0	0.07	6.0	1.0	-	-	-	5.0	12.0
1976/77	829,623	75.0	0.05	7.0	1.0	-	-	-	5.0	11.0
1977/78	904,304	64.0	0.03	18.0	1.0	-	-	-	6.0	11.0
1978/79	1,028,827	66.7	0.03	17.5	0.96	0.1^{12}	0.25^9	-	2.6	12.5
1979/80	1,298,580	63.3	0.02	15.9	0.93	0.1^{12}	0.27^9	-	2.7	13.4
1980/81	1,604,055	62.9	-	17.0	0.9	0.1^{13}	6.3^9	-	6.2	12.7
1981/82	1,764,612	59.3	-	19.4	0.9	0.1^{14}	5.9^9	-	7.5	12.8
1982/83	1,927,336	64.4	-	12.9	1.0	0.1^{15}	5.7^9	-	7.8	13.8
1983/84	2,034,768	62.1	-	12.8	1.1	0.1^{16}	5.5^9	-	8.6	15.0
1984/85	2,190,482	59.8	-	13.0	1.0	0.1^{15}	4.5^9	-	9.7	16.1
1985/86	2,379,064	57.8	-	13.4	1.2	0.1^{15}	6.0^9	-	9.2	17.5
1986/87	2,573,353	55.6	-	13.3	1.3	0.1^{15}	6.1^9	-	10.5	19.0
1987/88	2,807,127	55.3	-	13.1	1.3	0.1^{18}	5.7^9	-	10.7	19.2
1988/89	3,193,331	53.0	-	12.8	1.5	0.1^{17}	5.5^9	-	10.8	20.0
1989/90	4,040,217	44.4	-	13.9	3.3	-	-	-	5.6	18.9

Source: *Returns from Universities and University Colleges in Receipt of Treasury Grant, UGC,* **HMSO**, *Various Issues; University Statistical Record, Volume 3 Finance.*

KEY

1. Includes: examination fees; surplus from subsidiary accounts; hostels etc.,
2. Southampton University
3. Royal Holloway College
4. Durham University
5. London School of Tropical Medicine
6. Exeter University
7. St. Andrews University
8. Birbeck College
9. Oxford University
10. Cambridge University
11. Donations incorporated with endowments
12. University of East Anglia
13. University of Surrey
14. Stirling University
15. Strathclyde University
16. Sussex University
17. Aston University
18. University College Swansea

63

"I will... say just two things with respect to the principles by which I shall make those recommendations. I am convinced of the necessity of very much more liberal assistance from the state to higher learning in this country. And I am equally convinced from my long connection with the universities of the great value of preserving university autonomy".[32]

Both aspects of this statement were answered in 1919, firstly by the announcement of a large increase in grants and secondly by the decision of the Chancellor of the Exchequer to appoint a Standing Committee "to enquire into the financial needs of university education in the United Kingdom and to advise the Government as to the application of any grants that may be made by Parliament to meet them".[33] To ensure impartiality in the distribution of the grant, the University Grants Committee, as the standing committee was called, was transferred to the Treasury from the Board of Education. Another factor in the transfer is of importance, and that is the fact that the writ of the Treasury extended over the whole of the United Kingdom, not just England and Wales, which had been the position of the Board of Education. Quoting a later chairman of the UGC Sir Keith Murray, Berdahl records the satisfaction this move provided:

"[This placement] was deliberate and one which has been the source of much confidence which the universities have placed in the Committee, [for] they have no fears that a Minister, or his officials, who is likely to have theories or special interest in educational matters, may question the objective advice of the Committee and exert an undue influence on university affairs".[34]

This principle of inviolability was a constant feature of university life until the nineteen eighties.

To put these developments into some kind of perspective it should be recognised that government grants at this stage did not represent any more than 30% of an institution's recurrent income. For example, between 1923 and 1929 £500,000 in grant should be judged against £3,320,000 from endowments. Table 2:7 shows the development of university funding from 1913/14 to 1989/90 and demonstrates the watershed of the Second World War. After the war the state assumed the role of major financier, although parliamentary grants fell to 44.4% of university income in 1989/90 – a level comparable with the inter-war period. In 1919 the government offered increased funding as conditions allowed, but the Chancellor of the

---

[32] University Grants Committee, *Ibid.*, p.177.
[33] Treasury Minute, 14 July 1919.
[34] R. Berdahl, Ibid., p.58, quoting Sir Keith Murray, "The Work of the University Grants Committee in Great Britain", *Universitut en Hogeschool*, 1, 1955, p.251.

Exchequer, Austen Chamberlain, made it clear that other sources of finance should not be neglected either:

> "To require generous treatment....expenditure would grow as they (the Government) could afford it. They all (that is the members of the Government) recognised that science must play a large part in our national life, that knowledge was one of our national assets and that we (have) to cultivate both...the Government would do its share, but it would do it on one condition only – that towns and districts around them did their share also... *It will be an evil day if universities look only to the Government*".[35]

This was a prescient remark, but one that fell on almost deaf ears.

Voices of dissent were heard though, and the Chancellor of Cambridge University, the Earl Balfour, feared that growing dependence upon Government funding would lead to the expansion of applied science at the expense of the pure sciences that were in his view the forte of the universities, at the behest of the government and the public interest. The UGC itself stressed several times that the function of the university remained the pursuit of knowledge, although this enlightened view evaporated in the utilitarian days of the 1970's and 1980's.[36]

STATE-UGC-UNIVERSITY RELATIONS AFTER THE SECOND WORLD WAR

During the Second World War, student numbers fell less dramatically than they had done in the first war, down from 50,000 to 36,000, because of the more careful deployment of their services. However, buildings were requisitioned and the London Colleges relocated. The combination of inflation, the need to reinstate and improve facilities in the light of scientific advances and so on, placed an enormous additional burden on university finances. The UGC and Committee of Vice Chancellors and Principals together recognised that consolidation and further expansion could only be achieved with substantial government support. Hence in 1945 the grant effectively doubled and this increase applied for two years, whilst specialist committees reported on post-war needs and priorities (again see Table 2:7).

---

[35] A. Chamberlain "Centenary Commemoration of James Watt", *The Times*, 18 September, 1919, italics added.

[36] The Lloyd George government announced its policy as: (a) increased grants; (b) a single advisory body; and (c) a method of distribution "*which would safeguard the legitimate interests of university autonomy*", *The Times*, 23 June 1919, italics added. The article also announced that the annual sums would be fixed for a period of years and be expended at the discretion of the governing bodies.

The government of the day moved towards greater measures of state planning and inaugurated the apparatus of the welfare state; and there arose an enormous increase in the demand for university education, the professions, civil service and education itself all needing many more graduates. The 1944 *Education Act* guaranteed a larger supply of qualified students for university entrance in subsequent years. Official reports on agriculture, veterinary medicine, medicine, social and economic research, scientific research and languages, all presaged an expansion in university education. As a result of these enquiries, the government grant to the universities increased – over the quinquennium 1947-52, the grant rose from £13m to £24m.

In consequence of the *Barlow Committee's* report on scientific manpower, the terms of reference of the UGC were modified. Barlow commented that:

> "We must here record that we are unanimously opposed to any infringement of the cherished independence of the universities, even if it could be justified on the ground that it would facilitate the execution of [our recommended] expansion programme [for scientific manpower]. We do not, however, believe that the maintenance of the universities' independence is in any way incompatible with the extension and improvement of the machinery for adjusting their policy to the needs of the country... the State has perhaps been over-concerned lest there should be even a suggestion of interference with the independence of the universities... *we think that circumstances demand that it should increasingly concern itself with positive university policy*. It may be desirable for this purpose to revise terms of reference and strengthen its machinery".[37]

A period of genuine partnership between the UGC and the universities had dawned, with the former now assuming, at least formally, a more proactive role.

CONFRONTATION BETWEEN THE UNIVERSITY GRANTS COMMITTEE AND THE PUBLIC ACCOUNTS COMMITTEE

The Public Accounts Committee (PAC) and its sister committee the Select Committee on Estimates (SCE), questioned the statutory position of the UGC in 1947 on the ground that it had become a significant charge on public funds. In its 1948 *Report*, the PAC demanded statutory authority for the continued funding of the UGC and questioned the whole administrative arrangements for funding universities. At the time, the Treasury resisted moves for a change on the grounds that university autonomy and possibly

---

[37] *Committee on Scientific Manpower*, (Barlow Committee), 1946, London, HMSO, Cmnd. 6824, p.21, italics added.

even academic freedom might be infringed and further that existing procedures ensured maximum flexibility in the allocation of the grants, particularly at a time of expansion. In 1949 the PAC accepted the arguments put forward by the Treasury, but still wanted further information on funding to ensure economy in its application. All the Treasury was prepared to concede at this juncture was more detailed financial statements so that comparisons could be made between different years.

The SCE took a fresh look at the subject in the early 1950's and required justification for increases in recurrent grant and an analysis of estimates alongside actual expenditure. The Treasury applied the same defence strategy and the principle at stake found defenders in the press and bodies outside the universities as well as inside. The Gates Committee reported to the Treasury that it could find no evidence of abuse in the operation of the UGC, but did question the degree to which universities were becoming dependent upon the State, although it offered no tangible alternatives.

Temporarily the PAC accepted the new position whilst its operation was monitored, but the first marker in State control, once funding from the state became significant, had been laid down. In retrospect one can only marvel at the Treasury's Commitment to university autonomy, something the DES has been incapable of emulating.

TRANSFER TO THE DEPARTMENT OF EDUCATION AND SCIENCE

Treasury responsibility for the UGC ceased in 1964, although all official pronouncements make it clear that the universities lost neither support, autonomy nor money whilst under its umbrella. The key reason for the transfer appears to lie in concern about the separation of ministerial responsibility for the universities from the rest of education. In effect this meant that the government had minimum impact on the universities either to exhort them to greater effort or to limit their growth. Even the UGC recognised the need for a change.

The UGC did not feel aggrieved by these changes: "Our connection with a policy Department has in no sense introduced politics, still less party politics, into our activities" and again "appointments to the Committee... remain... non-political" and "no single one of the responsible Ministers or Permanent Under Secretaries since 1963 has shown the slightest inclination to reduce the independence of the Committee or of the universities" and finally "the link with the Department of Education and Science has seemed.... to interpose another link between Committee and Government".[38] The DES proved in the first instance to be an effective advocate for the UGC during this expansionary phase in university activity. Student numbers and their projection seemed to be the major preoccupation of the DES in the years following their assumption of responsibility, until cost assumed centre stage around 1972.

PLANNING AND THE UGC

The quinquennial system worked well until its demise in 1975, and there are those who have campaigned vigorously for its reinstatement or something like it. Its weaknesses are many: its inability to address major and expensive needs that cannot be predicted; its inability to cope efficiently with inflation, particularly the high levels experienced in the 1970's; and finally its failure to provide some continuity between succeeding quinquenniums. If anything the Committee wanted to extend, not shorten, the planning period. Following on from Robbins, the UGC assumed a more proactive, centralised and strategic planning role, rather than the buffer role it had before, to prevent more direct control of university affairs by the government.

In 1977, faced with unprecedented economic difficulties, the UGC abrogated all planning functions, so that any new developments hinged upon savings being made in other areas of a particular university's activities. Discipline based sub-committees assumed greater importance over this whole period and rationalisation of subjects became an issue of growing concern. Nevertheless, the UGC essentially retained a directive rather than a dictatorial function, recommending the closure of three departments of agriculture as a result of the findings of the *Northumberland Committee*. But there is little evidence to suggest that any of these recommendations were followed through and monitored in their execution by the UGC.

THE POST-1979 POSITION OF THE UGC: THE RISE OF STATE CONTROL

In its defence against these criticisms, the UGC could argue that the

---

[38] University Grants Committee, *Ibid.*, 1962, p.185.

initiative rested firmly with the universities and that in the post-1972 period, with increasing economic difficulties nationally, its function became that of preserving the existing structure. Planning represented a marginal activity and after the 1981 cuts a policy of equal misery was preferred to a more imaginative one of building on academic strengths in individual universities and academic departments. The failure to be innovative left the UGC open to the charge by the government that both it and the university system had not responded to national needs. Table 2:8 details the cuts showing Salford suffering greatest misery at -44%, Keele -34%, Bradford -33%, Aston -31% down to York at -6%.

TABLE 2:8 GRANT AND STUDENT NUMBER REDUCTIONS ANNOUNCED 1ST JULY 1981

Universities ranked according to % loss of home students	Home and EEC Students			Grant £m			% overseas students 1979-80
	1979-80	1983-84 or 1984-1985	% change	1980-81 (est.)[39]	1983-1984	approx. % change	
Salford	3,940	2,750	-30	15.31	8.59	-44	14
Aston	4.670	3,640	-22	14.39	9.86	-31	17
Bradford	4,360	3,530	-19	14.45	9.64	-33	13
Stirling	2,470	2,020	-18	6.99	5.08	-27	8
Keele	2,680	2,230	-17	8.57	5.64	-34	5
Hull	5,070	4,200	-17	11.44	9.19	-20	7
Surrey	2,880	2,470	-14	11.81	8.78	-26	12
Heriot-Watt	2,430	2,120	-13	8.16	7.09	-13	12
Kent	3,430	3,180	-7	8.44	6.64	-21	10
St. Andrews	3,110	2,880	-7	9.24	7.51	-19	9
Lancaster	4,210	3,920	-7	10.32	8.68	-16	9
Sussex	3,890	3,710	-5	11.67	9.21	-21	12
City	2,130	2,020	-5	10.31	8.24	-20	20
Reading	5,030	4,770	-5	15.00	12.66	-16	12
Aberdeen	5,140	4,940	-4	19.75	15.19	-23	7
Essex	2,240	2,150	-4	6.88	5.47	-20	22
Strathclyde	5,790	5,540	-4	17.90	14.69	-18	12
London	33,510	32,220	-4	200	165.03	-17	16
Bristol	6,650	6,390	-4	23.05	19.43	-16	4
Nottingham	6,380	6,150	-4	21.39	18.36	-14	7
Newcastle	6,880	6,600	-4	23.97	20.85	-13	11
Durham	4,530	4,360	-4	12.93	11.60	-10	4

[39] 1980/80 Grant figures are updated to current prices, and are only estimates.

TABLE 2:8 GRANT AND STUDENT NUMBER REDUCTIONS ANNOUNCED 1ST JULY 1981 (Cont'd)

Universities ranked according to % loss of home students	Home and EEC Students			Grant £m			% overseas students 1979-80
	1979-80	1983-84 or 1984-1985	% change	1980-81 (est.)	approx. 1983-1984	% change	
Oxford	10,700	10,410	−3	34.00	29.74	−13	10
Glasgow	9,100	8,810	−3	33.08	29.56	−11	6
East Anglia	3,760	3,640	−3	11.25	10.28	−9	8
Leicester	4,340	4,200	−3	13.12	11.95	−9	4
Loughborough	4,670	4,550	−3	13.06	11.98	−8	10
Exeter	4,690	4,600	−2	12.21	9.69	−2	16
Manchester	9,930	9,710	−2	38.20	31.93	−16	11
Liverpool	7,060	6,910	−2	31.18	26.13	−16	6
Leeds	9,430	9,270	−2	33.93	28.72	−15	12
Cambridge	10,490	10,280	−2	32.27	28.91	−10	8
Warwick	4,600	4,550	−1	13.17	11.23	−15	6
Brunel	2,460	2,470	0	11.14	8.99	−19	11
Birmingham	7,750	7,770	0	30.18	25.69	−17	13
Univ. of Wales	17,330	16,130	0	57.20	47.67	−17	12
Dundee	2,490	2,480	0	12.64	10.53	−17	11
Sheffield	6,860	6,860	0	25.40	21.72	−14	11
Southampton	5,690	5,660	0	18.91	16.60	−12	9
Edinburgh	8,830	8,840	0	33.81	30.20	−11	7
York	3,100	3,090	0	7.48	7.02	−6	5
Bath	3,190	3,260	+2	9.38	8.69	−7	8
UMIST	2,790	2,980	+7	15.94	11.08	−30	27
Manchester Bus. School.	120	170	+42	1.14	0.87	−2	421
London Bus. School.	170	290	+70	1.13	1.49	+11	26
TOTAL GB	260,970	248,720	−4.7	971.85	808.07	−17	11

This was an epoch of increasing state control of the universities and the waning of the UGC as an independant influence.[40] As government power became more centralised, so the relative autonomy of the UGC went into decline, but not it should be stressed as a result of DES contrivance. The old and direct relationship with the Treasury gave the UGC political protection and direct access to the financial decision making process.

---

[40] M. Shattock and R. Berdahl, "The British University Grants Committee 1919-83: Changing Relationships with Government and the Universities", *Higher Education*, 1984, pp.471-99.

Under the DES we noted the initial claim that there was no loss of autonomy or finance, but with the creation of the Public Expenditure Select Committee (PESC) and reform of the Government's resource allocation mechanism, the transfer began to appear as a distinct liability. Now, the UGC had to submit its plans to the DES and negotiate with them, before these were forwarded as financial plans to the PESC. Each July the Cabinet fixed the level of public expenditure on the basis of a global report produced by the PESC, and with the introduction of cash limits after 1979, the isolation of the UGC from the decision-making process became distressingly obvious. The universities were no longer well represented in the DES either, as a result of changes there: the Labour party abolished the Permanent Secretary Post for higher education and the Heath Government down-graded higher education from representation by a Minister of State to a Parliamentary Under Secretary. By the early 1970's most of the Treasury staff within the DES had left and their valuable expertise and experience in the area of higher education and finance was lost. Finally in 1982 the UGC Secretaryship was down-graded from Deputy Under-Secretary, and as part of the 1981/83 cuts the UGC staff compliment suffered reductions. Hence, even though the budget for the universities is the single largest expenditure category within the DES, disproportionately more time is spent on what are regarded as the more politically sensitive areas of secondary education that lie outside higher education.

Throughout this period the state was tightening its grip on its universities. Financial decision making depended upon student unit costs and this formed the basis of the recurrent grant awards. Until 1972 the UGC did not restrict the expansion of numbers, but after that date the DES wanted to achieve parity between the university and the public sector. In the academic year 1976/77 student targets were reduced by the DES and the UGC requested that universities did not attempt to preserve postgraduate student numbers at the expense of undergraduate places. In effect the DES now assumed control over student forecasts, the science/arts balance and also the postgraduate/undergraduate balance. Undergraduate entry in 1980 was limited to 94% of the 1979 level at the behest of the UGC, although this plan was later dropped, but in 1981/82 universities were fined if they exceeded UGC student targets.

When the universities were expanding, capital expenditure driven by student numbers became the crucial determining factor in the rate of change, but from 1973 it became obvious that the DES used capital expenditure to determine the science/arts balance and consequently the level of overall expansion within the system. Excess capacity had to be utilised, so that new developments at the popular over-subscribed universities became virtually impossible.

Another manifestation of increasing public control was the abandonment of the quinquennial system. Instituted in 1908 in an informal way and regularised in 1924/29, it had worked well to preserve university autonomy. The universities could plan and the government could review developments at five yearly intervals. However, the size and the complexity of the system after the 1972/77 quinquennium, meant that submissions to the DES could not be based on regular visits or on a detailed analysis of plans submitted by the universities. Rather, they had to be based on the UGC's own assessment of global needs. The system had never been accepted uncritically, of course, and the break finally occurred in 1974/75 as a result of the combination of rapid inflation, economic restraint and the termination of the university building programme and thus targets for student numbers. Thereafter, a series of one year allocations were made and after 1981 what looked like a system of three year projections: university activity became closely aligned with government economic policy.

The loss of UGC autonomy can be seen, therefore, to have much more to do with politics and Treasury constraints on the DES, than with DES policy making per se. The DES did take a more proactive stance though, particularly with regard to equal treatment of the university and public sector. Parliament exercised far more control over the executive as a result of the all pervasive role of the Public Accounts Committee, which expected the DES to pursue the same financial strategy as every other government department.

The next decade witnessed a dreary saga of reduction and rationalisation. Estimates prepared by the UGC suggested that the unit of resource available to universities had already fallen 10% in the 1970's, even though overseas student fees were raised in order to preserve the unit of resource available for home students. As a result of these changes and a cut of £100 million in the university budget, the UGC announced that in future it would assume a more *dirigiste* role. In October 1979 it embarked on a planning exercise, seeking university responses to three possible future scenarios:

2% expansion in resources (model E), level funding or a 5% cut. In order that new developments might be undertaken, reviews of subject provision were set in hand with a view to rationalisation and cost savings.

The UGC began to act autocratically, a victim of necessity. By coping with the cuts, amounting to a further 8.5% between 1981/82 and 1983/84 (a total of 11-15% since 1979) the prestige accorded the UGC by the government increased. Evidence of this change in attitude came with the establishment of a three year cycle of grant announcements. However, as the cuts continued, the closure of departments became necessary and only selective developments could be entertained. Student numbers were reduced, temporary appointments expanded, expansion of medical schools dropped and there were reductions in the arts and social sciences, whilst engineering and the physical sciences increased, producing a arts/science ratio of 48:52. New allocations were accompanied by detailed interpretative advice, although the variable effectiveness of the UGC's subject committees rendered this exercise less than satisfactory and the tendency was to consider subjects rather than institutions, thus ignoring regional factors and subject balance. The message from the UGC at the time was harsh and presaged much greater involvement with university developments in the future:

> "There is going to be in the future a somewhat greater degree of direct intervention by the UGC in the affairs of individual universities than has been customary or necessary in the past. Before your hackles rise and you start running to a council for civil liberties for protection, I should add that the Committee is quite as staunch a defender of university autonomy as any of you are, and that it views the prospect of getting more involved in the minutiae of the university world with reluctance – partly as a matter of principle and partly because of the work loads which must ensue".[41]

The UGC attempted to react creatively to the oppressive circumstances. By retaining some funds back from distribution, the UGC was able to reward initiative amongst the universities and remain a vehicle for change if only to a limited degree. It did obtain some funding to deal with the cuts in overseas student numbers (via the Foreign Office), successfully campaigned for a longer planning horizon, initiated an early retirement scheme, even if misconceived in terms of some of its ramifications for small departments and the humanities in particular, and introduced a

---

[41] Address by the Chairman of the UGC (E. Parkes) to the Committee of Vice Chancellors and Principals, October 1980.

'new-blood' scheme of new appointments, plus developments and recruitment in the field of information technology. Clearly the government found the UGC approach acceptable and its initiatives satisfactory, and its judgements appeared to be considerably enhanced, even if unscientifically based. On the negative side of the balance sheet, however, in their efforts to retain and safeguard university autonomy the UGC had largely abandoned the important areas of university effectiveness and efficiency. By encouraging an air of optimism after the 1978 planning document, *Higher Education into the 1990's* appeared, both the DES and the UGC, who supported the planning model E (expand the system to cope with demographic change and then maintain numbers as the relevant cohort declines by encouraging greater working class and mature student participation in higher education) lulled the universities into a false sense of security that rapidly evaporated in 1981.[42]

---

[42] Department of Education and Science/Scottish Education Department, *Higher Education into the 1990's*, A Discussion Document, DES, 1978.

CHAPTER THREE

THE WAY WE LIVE NOW: A SITUATIONAL ANALYSIS

The minister's "advocacy of university teachers moonlighting....was ill judged and insulting".
Andrew Smith,
Hansard, March 1989.

Warning that weak shoots had become vulnerable the minister added "like the good gardener who wants to see his plants flourish, we know that pruning is necessary if the strongest shoots are to grow to their full potential". And... Anything thereby that does not lend itself to the market principles is treated with suspicion and regarded as a suitable case for (state) treatment.
The Chronicle of Higher Education, November 18, 1987.

"Every time he (the minister) opens his mouth, the Government's prestige in the universities suffers a further blow".
Lord Beloff,
House of Lords debate on *Education Reform Bill*, 1988.

"And from the cultural point of view I would argue the familiar case for forms of engagement with the real world, countervailing tendencies to hermeticism, introversion, and evasive radicalism".

"Academics just keep trotting out sacred cows and shibboleths".

"The apparatus and ethos of the self regarding academic producer-monopoly must be dismantled".

"What the government needed to discover, he said, were those elements of the humanities courses' useful to graduates and also to society and which could provide a more reasonable return to the tax-payer".
Robert Jackson,
The Independent, 10 November, 1988.

"The government's words call for expansion and excellence – but their actions lead to catastrophic decline. Such a combination in industry would lead to a change of management".
Dr. Roberts,
Provost of University College London,
Annual Report, University College London, 1989.

"It may clarify things if I look at the figures in a little more detail. If you take the curve from year to year in real terms, it is a bit jagged. If you move from 1979 to 1989 there is an eight per cent increase; however there is a 9.5 per cent increase between 1979 and 1980. From 1980 to 1985 there is something between a one and two per cent decrease per year in real terms. Between 1986 and 1987 there was a five per cent increase and a further one per cent increase in each of the two subsequent years. On the other hand, that does take into account the £50 million a year which the Secretary of State provided for restructuring, which cannot be viewed as an altogether straightforward recurrent grant. All these figures are to some extent conditioned by the amount of money the Secretary of State provided for pay increases, which have gone up 10 per cent in real terms over this decade. Does that help?"

(It does very considerably, but it demonstrates the difficulties the universities must have had in dealing with the oscillations).
Sir Peter Swinnerton-Dyer,
Committee of Public Accounts 36th Report, *Restructuring and Finances of Universities*, 1990, p.16.

INTRODUCTION

This chapter examines the position of the universities in the 1980's and 1990's and pays considerable attention to the 1985 Green Paper, *The Development of Higher Education into the 1990's*. During the decade, real income came under severe pressure as a series of unimaginative cuts and changes were forced on the system. But the universities themselves responded with an equal lack of imagination and instituted panic measures and mergers, with no coherent plan for rationalisation and the solicitation of alternative sources of funding other than industry and the research councils. The 1990/91 allocation of resources reveals the differential funding of teaching and research with most institutions receiving increases below inflation. 1991/92 is shown to be a repeat performance with an efficiency gain of 1.5% expected. Finally, the 1992/93 distribution which incorporates the shift to judgemental criteria in determining research allocations is shown to produce a funding league table that can only be reinforced in future years. Only seven universities out of fifty one received increases of more than 10% under the teaching and research headings: City, Dundee, Durham, Essex, Leicester, Newcastle and Glasgow.

Next the bidding fiasco is considered and the attempt thereby to force down unit costs in universities. A further attempt at this exercise is the incentive of extra funding if universities take fees-only students without allowing the quality of education to fall simultaneously. To gauge what the rest of the 1990's might look like, the argument and analysis returns to the 1985 Green Paper.

Firstly it espouses a shift to science and technology (although the White Paper *Higher Education: A New Framework* expects expansion in the cheaper arts and social sciences), and the development of the economy. Secondly, increased access is acknowledged as a prerequisite for a more highly trained technocracy. The difficulty of course is to achieve this without diluting standards and here the implementation of the Higginson reforms of A levels is important (this involves a switch to an examination of five subjects). Thirdly, funding is shown to be dominated by the state, even if the exchequer grant did fall to less than 50% of total university income in 1989/90, with no prospect of a radical change. Next, the importance to be placed in future on applied or developmental research receives attention, but the fact that industry often ignores universities when commissioning research demonstrates the double edge of such a switch in activities. The opposing pressures of state planning and free market economics again come to the fore, no more so than in the pressure to apply research funds selectively with judgements informed by a rolling programme of peer review. It is accepted, however, that some hierarchy is necessary on the grounds that assessment encourages competition, self-criticism and dispells complacency.

A further section deals with the attempt to create larger and supposedly more dynamic departments following Oxburgh. The ABRC advocated a three tier system with research concentrated at the top with American style liberal arts colleges at the bottom. ABRC also promulgated new criteria for evaluating scientific priorities – essentially a quick and certain pay-back. Finally, the 1991 White Paper is examined, the end of the binary line in higher education, massification and its implications for standards, all to be achieved without any extra funding and probably less. The distinctive ethos of polytechnics receives reaffirmation and is shown to be highly desirable in the future. The dangers inherent in spreading research funding throughout an enlarged university system are shown to be more real than apparent.

THE NINETEEN EIGHTIES AND NINETIES

The history of university education in recent years has been dominated by the idea of more for less: the theme has been reduced inputs and increased outputs. By the end of 1985 the Department of Education and Science was hoping for an annual reduction of 3% in the number of lecturers, and looking for staff/student ratios of 9:1.[1] Soon after, a 50,000 rise in student numbers was being predicted for 1990, and already 153,000 more full and part time students had entered higher education since 1979.[2] But real income was constantly falling: in 1986 universities were promised grant reductions of about 11% over the following four years and in the preceding financial year had already experienced a contraction of 3.5% on grant as against costs, given that university costs rise about 1.5% more than the rate of inflation.[3]

---

[1] *The Development of Higher Education into the 1990's*, London, HMSO, Cmnd. 9524, 1985.
[2] *Ibid.* Cf. *University Statistics*, Universities Statistical Office, Vol.3, 1987.
[3] These extra costs are associated with building maintenance, purchase of equipment and pensions.

Between 1984 and 1985, the 1985 Green Paper tells us, public expenditure on universities was estimated at £1,668 million, excluding research activity and postgraduate awards funded through Research Councils,[4] and student maintenance, £700 million for that period, should be added to this sum. The Green Paper admits that those figures represent a reduction in real terms of 3.5% from 1980-81, while overall student numbers had now risen "substantially".[5]

The theme of falling recurrent state support is typically illustrated by the UGC circular of May 9 1985 dealing with funding over the next four years: "The figures given (that) provide for increases in universities' costs are on average 1.5% below the Government's own assumption about general inflation over the 3 years (5%, 4.5% and 3.5% respectively)".[6] It pointed out that in the previous year the government had simply removed £36 million of the planned provision over the next few years "on the basis that universities would be expected to operate with increased economy". Condemning government rejection of level funding, the report went on to say: "Meanwhile *all* universities must prepare for support from public funds (that is recurrent grant and home tuition fees) to decline in real terms

---

[4] *The Development of Higher Education into the 1990's, Ibid.*
[5] *Ibid.*
[6] UGC Circular, 9 May, 1985.

year by year: universities which suffer less than the average can only do so at the expense of other universities".[7]

The universities certainly responded by carving the joint – innumerable retirements, closure of departments, a virtual freeze on appointments in many areas especially the humanities, and short-term contracts. Whole disciplines were pummelled, the travails of philosophy for example being well known. Sadly the universities demonstrated none of the imaginative flair and competence that might have softened the impact of retrenchment

---

[7] UGC, Circular, *Ibid*. The fall in recurrent income is now subject to doubt given recalculation.

	Total Recurrent Income	Exchequer Grant	Fees & Other Income	Specific Income
1980/81	£1,604,055	£1,008,254	£345,993	£249,806
In 1986/87 Prices	£2,277,758	£1,431,721	£491,310	£354,725

	Total Recurrent Income	Total General	Exchequer Grant	Fees & Other Income	Specific Income
1986/7	£2,573,353	£1,929,246	£143,762	£497,485	£644,108

All in £'000s.

Source: *University Statistics*, 1980, vol.3 and 1986/87 vol.3.

Replying to a question from Radice in the House of Commons, requesting clarification of the position, the Secretary of State for Education and Science replied that in terms of the exclusions mentioned in the question, real income had fallen by 6.3% in 1985/86 prices. The question and answer are:

> Mr. Radice asked the Secretary of State for Education and Science what has been the change in the funding of universities in cash and constant 1985-86 prices between 1980-81 and 1986-87, excluding those amounts representing compensation for changes in home student fees, for redundancy and for early retirement, changes to take account of minor capital works from the recurrent grant, changes in local authority rates and additions made for the information technology and new blood programmes.
>
> Mr. Kenneth Baker: Between 1980-81 and 1986-87 public funding of universities has increased by 28.8% in cash terms, which is a fall of 6.3% in constant 1985-86 prices (using the GDP deflator). Excluding the funding elements selectively listed by the Hon. Member, there was an increase over the same period of 13.1% in cash terms equivalent to a reduction of 17.8% in 1985-86 prices. Such exclusions are unrealistic; payment of items such as local authority rates and compensation for redundancies and early retirement are part and parcel of the cost of running large institutions. Since 1980-81, universities' income from private sources has increased substantially.

Source: *House of Commons Hansard*, 30 June, 1988.

though they have shown initiative in recruiting overseas postgraduate students, sometimes making a mockery of their traditional academic standards. What we did not witness in any useful measure was computer targeted alumni fundraising, the professional solicitation of business and the well-heeled, the drive for more efficiency in the work of administrators and secretarial staff, the substitution of some student labour for the armies of porters and other attendants. Nor was the potential of the campus fully utilised; most of it is idle during vacations, evenings and weekends, even in strategic locations like London; and fittings and such are often too sub-standard to attract business.

Such creative impoverishment was more than matched by the inflexibility of the state. Universities' power of decision making is shackled by the bureaucracy. The number of undergraduates they can take has until comparatively recently been firmly limited. They cannot plan, since they are subject to no certainties in the area of funding. There is, in fact, no policy towards them but to cut their income in the hope that they will generate it privately: since they do not possess the will to do this, or have not a product for which there is an exorbitant private demand, their response was also to cut commensurately from the fat down to the muscle.

Philip Augur comments that the consequences of short-changing the universities can, by its nature, only become clear in the distant future. He points out how misleading it is to view universities in the same light as inefficient nationalised industries, noting the falseness of the analogy: "But an essential feature of the recovery of nationalised industries is that they have a product to sell. State support of the balance sheet has therefore been able to be phased out" and "Reduction in state support has a more serious effect on universities because, unlike the former nationalised industries, it hits their income in addition to their debt level". Finally, "Unlike industry, the effect of lower running costs is not to improve competitiveness.... The determination of the largest customer to pay less for nearly the same, places a considerable burden on other potential sources of revenue".[8]

Peter Scott points to the volatility of government plans for the future of higher education. There is, he says, an elemental conflict in the government's thinking: "Do ministers want higher education to serve the

---

[8] Phillip Augur, "Funding the Universities", *The Cambridge Review*, March, 1989, p.16.

nation more exactingly... or do they wish it to respond more accurately to the demands of the market, which would follow from the new Tory preference for the atomism of individual choice in place of an expression of the 'public interest'... This fundamental strategic choice appears not yet to have been made.... The result is an unresolved tension between different methods of funding higher education (i.e. between contracts and vouchers)". Ministers feel a "... conflict between their present command of the state and their anti-state beliefs".[9]

This author anticipates conditions of eventual 'massification' and 'open access' in higher education. And he adds: "Some cumbersome theory has to be constructed about the need first to use the state's power to overcome the vested interests of the dons' cartels of capitalist monopolists in order to overcome the dazzling inconsistency...". Sadly he concludes: "... the reshaping of higher education in order to live within its reduced means is unlikely to be tackled coherently and purposefully. Indeed it will be left to the 'market', in this sense a dishonest description of an inevitable series of panicky and politicized proposals to merge weaker institutions and predatory raids by the stronger".[10]

An example of the drastic nature of the response to reduced resources comes from the London School of Economics, whose academic board is considering a switch to student fees to avoid losses of £3 million a year in teaching income. They aim to offset the estimated annual 5% erosion of the unit of resource for teaching to improve quality and provide for expansion. Alternatives to this scheme include: changes to the range and type of courses; adjustments to the home/EC and overseas student mix; top-up fees; partial privatisation or recruiting extra students. If privatised, LSE would not differentiate between home and overseas students and all would be charged fees of £6,000 per annum.

A: SITUATION NOW AND 1990/91 TO 1992/93 ALLOCATION OF RESOURCES

Following on from the 1989 research selectivity exercise university funding arrangements for the academic year 1990/91 reveal the differential support for research and teaching. Variations in grant plus fees, the new global category, reflect research ratings, changes in student numbers, new

---

[9] Peter Scott, "The Government and Universities", *The Cambridge Review*, March, 1989, p.4.
[10] Peter Scott, *op cit.*, p.7.

initiatives such as the expansion of biotechnology and the new academic appointments scheme. The figures show Oxford receives 55% of its grant allocation for teaching, followed by Cambridge with 56%, London 60%, UMIST 60%, Essex 62%, Sussex 62%, Warwick 62% and Edinburgh 62%. At the other end of the spectrum come Ulster 76%, Queen's Belfast 73%, Lampeter 74% and Manchester Business School 72%. Table 3:1 gives the breakdown and the average teaching figure is 66%.

Given that inflation reached double figures over the following twelve months, many universities received increases below the rate in 1990/91. Sussex received 5.3%, UMIST 5.7%, Cardiff 6%, Bristol 6.2% and Leeds 6.5%. UMIST, Leeds, Kent, St. Andrew's, Salford, London Business School and four London University Colleges all benefited from the safety net device that prevents funding falling more than 2% below average funding. The safety net will not operate, however, in future years, and arts-based institutions receiving little in the way of research grant or contract work will undoubtedly suffer as a consequence. The two un-named institutions that sustained losses were given no special assistance. Only thirteen institutions received increases at or above 10%: Cambridge 10%, Essex 13.2%, Loughborough* 11.4%, Newcastle 10.4%, Nottingham 10%, Sheffield* 10.7%, Surrey 11.1%, Aberystwyth* 19.6%, Swansea* 14.7%, UWCM 19.5%, Aberdeen* 11.4%, Stirling* 12.0% and Ulster* 10.23%. More than half of these had a teaching allotment above the average of 66% (those starred).

TABLE 3:1 1990/91 ALLOCATION OF RESOURCES INCLUDING TEACHING COMPONENT

£000s	Grants and fees 1990/91	Allocation 1989/90	Percent increase	New academic appointments schemes £m	Teaching percent
Aston	21,510	19,587	9.8	0.000	69
Bath	23,236	21,423	8.5	0.290	67
Birmingham	54,131	50,286	7.6	0.621	65
Bradford	21,911	20,384	7.5	0.324	70
Bristol	46,168	43,478	6.2	0.490	63
Brunel	19,761	18,203	8.6	0.174	70
Cambridge	68,279	62,042	10.0	0.745	56
City	17,193	16,024	7.3	0.196	70
Durham	24,835	22,614	9.8	0.358	67

TABLE 3:1 1990/91 ALLOCATION OF RESOURCES INCLUDING TEACHING COMPONENT (Cont'd)

£000s	Grants and fees 1990/91	Allocation 1989/90	Percent increase	New academic appointments schemes £m	Teaching percent
East Anglia	19,952	18,466	8.0	0.300	65
Essex	13,848	12,232	13.2	0.157	62
Exeter	26,000	23,662	9.9	0.379	69
Hull	21,580	19,757	9.2	0.360	71
Keele	12,345	11,254	9.7	0.200	69
Kent	17,695	16,572	6.8	0.196	65
Lancaster	20,715	19,397	6.8	0.329	66
Leeds	60,642	56,956	6.5	0.694	67
Leicester	27,221	25,477	6.8	0.330	67
Liverpool	53,982	49,495	9.1	0.510	66
LBS	2,803	2,624	6.8	0.028	61
London (inc. Imperial)	360,362	329,037	9.5	3.047	60
Loughborough	30,441	27,326	11.4	0.390	69
MBS	1,693	1,561	8.5	0.007	72
Manchester	73,143	67,070	9.0	0.630	66
UMIST	23,697	22,677	5.7	0.290	60
Newcastle	46,240	41,901	10.4	0.510	65
Nottingham	42,778	38,896	10.0	0.471	65
Oxford	69,112	63,759	8.4	0.890	55
Reading	28,094	26,078	7.7	0.389	65
Salford	19,223	18,003	6.8	0.256	69
Sheffield	47,333	42,773	10.7	0.540	67
Southampton	40,993	37,861	8.3	0.382	63
Surrey	19,888	17,898	11.1	0.144	65
Sussex	22,261	21,135	5.3	0.284	62
Warwick	31,601	29,295	7.9	0.335	62
York	19,484	17,861	9.1	0.260	64
Aberystwyth	16,554	13,842	19.6	0.210	68
Bangor	14,295	13,738	8.6	0.207	69
Cardiff	37,367	35,237	6.0	0.549	66
St David's	3,061	2,869	6.7	0.050	74
Swansea	20,268	17,677	14.7	0.281	69
UWCM	10,864	9,091	19.5	0.020	65
Welsh Registry	3,226	2,699	19.5	0.000	0
Aberdeen	30,305	27,196	11.4	0.233	68
Dundee	19,090	17,465	9.3	0.180	69
Edinburgh	63,577	59,144	7.5	0.564	62
Glasgow	64,878	60,245	7.7	0.710	65
Heriot-Watt	16,109	15,060	7.0	0.223	67
St. Andrews	16,468	15,422	6.8	0.240	66
Stirling	12,125	10,826	12.0	0.204	70

TABLE 3:1 1990/91 ALLOCATION OF RESOURCES INCLUDING TEACHING COMPONENT (Cont'd)

£000s	Grants and fees 1990/91	Allocation 1989/90	Percent increase	New academic appointments schemes £m	Teaching percent
Strathclyde	36,397	33,198	7.3	0.500	66
Queens Belfast	41,834	38,097	9.81	0.542	73
Ulster	50,229	45,568	10.23	0.425	76

Although the global increase in funding amounted to a much vaunted 10%, universities faced increased costs for 1991. In addition to any salary adjustment they had to sustain the addition of VAT charges to fuel and power, the loss of £6m for their equipment grant to pay for part of the previous year's salary award, and the costs of administering the Access fund linked to top-up student loans.

Much the same has happened in 1991/1992 as Table 3:2 demonstrates. Universities are expected to recruit an extra 30,000 students and the recurrent grant has increased by a paltry 7.6%. Resource allocations vary enormously, a gain of 19.62% for Sheffield and 19.05% for Bristol but only 0.28% for Aston that is safety-netted along with City, Loughborough, Salford, and the London Business School. The impact of inflation, as is so often the case, and the cost of educating extra students are ignored. Only those institutions that have been able to convince the UFC that they have planned for growth, have received the funding to implement it. Once again the UFC expects an efficiency gain of 1.5%.

TABLE 3:2 1991/92 ALLOCATION OF RESOURCES

	Resources 1990/91	£000's 1991/92	% rise	Extra Students in 1991/92
1 Sheffield	48,249	57,717	19.62	1,116
2 Bristol	47,932	57,066	19.05	955
3 Swansea	20,921	24,675	17.94	422
4 Hull	22,509	26,542	17.91	444
5 Warwick	33,902	39,662	17.34	708
6 Nottingham	44,067	51,539	16.95	661
7 Newcastle	46,900	54,678	16.58	853
8 York	20,394	23,757	16.49	508

TABLE 3:2 1991/92 ALLOCATION OF RESOURCES (Cont'd)

	Resources 1990/91	£000's 1991/92	% rise	Extra Students in 1991/92
9 Dundee	19,530	22,708	16.27	398
10 Stirling	12,286	14,273	16.17	247
11 Queen's	42,240	48.862	15.7	1,122
12 Welsh Reg.	3,226	3,725	15.47	0
13 St.Andrews	16,817	19,398	15.35	234
14 Sussex	22,765	26,243	15.28	415
15 Leicester	28,196	32,451	15.09	336
16 Lancaster	21,369	24,549	14.88	339
17 St.Davids	3,122	3,561	14.06	71
18 Surrey	20,986	23,933	14.04	211
19 East Anglia	20,761	23,579	13.57	356
20 Birmingham	56,260	63,706	13.23	639
21 Aberdeen	30,368	34,353	13.12	450
22 Glasgow	67,133	75,885	13.04	779
23 Exeter	26,137	29,418	12.55	331
24 Cambridge	70,254	78,963	12.4	725
25 University of Wales College of Medicine	10,891	12,241	12.39	102
26 Kent	18,358	20,559	11.99	289
27 Bangor	15,719	17,598	11.95	157
28 Southampton	43,130	48,227	11.81	450
29 Heriot-Watt	16,576	18,431	11.19	245
30 Reading	33,449	37,046	10.75	374
31 UMIST	24,518	27,151	10.73	261
32 Oxford	71,479	78,876	10.35	543
33 Bradford	22,708	24,825	9.32	194
34 Durham	26,504	28,950	9.23	196
35 Keele	12,959	14,136	9.08	145
36 Edinburgh	66,742	72,607	8.79	344
37 Bath	23,585	25,494	8.09	143
38 London	384,775	415,620	8.02	593
39 Essex	14,155	15,288	8	194
40 Liverpool	55,404	59,700	7.75	458
41 Aberystwyth	17,324	18,628	7.53	182
42 Cardiff	38,540	41,383	7.38	295
43 Leeds	62,725	67,140	7.04	471
44 Strathclyde	38,520	41,166	6.87	346
45 Ulster	50,613	53,920	6.5	524
46 Manchester	75,846	80,030	5.51	168
47 Brunel	20,301	21,276	4.8	207
48 MBS	1,789	1,870	4.53	0
49 =LBS	2,828	2,955	4.5*	19

TABLE 3:2 1991/92 ALLOCATION OF RESOURCES (Cont'd)

	Resources 1990/91	£000's 1991/92	% rise	Extra Students in 1991/92
49 =Salford	21,125	22,076	4.5*	410
49 =Loughborough	30,976	32,370	4.5*	307
49 =City	17,585	18,376	4.5*	52
53 Aston	21,960	22,022	0.28*	0

* Safety-netted

In terms of subject expansion (or contraction), mass communication, architecture, business studies, humanities and biological sciences gain in excess of 14% extra students. Agriculture loses 10.3%, clinical dentistry 8.9% and engineering/technology 2.8%: increases are low for mathematics, physical sciences and computer studies – averaging less than 6%. The figures are given in Table 3:3.

TABLE 3:3 ALLOCATION OF STUDENT NUMBERS BY SUBJECT GROUP

ACADEMIC SUBJECT GROUPS	1990/91	1991/92	PERCENTAGE +/-
Pre-clinical Dentistry	877	1,240	41.4
Mass Communication	404	549	35.9
Architecture,Build.& Plan.	2,756	3,228	17.1
Business & Administrative	11,578	13,540	16.9
Humanities	18,988	21,793	14.8
Biological Sciences	17,605	20,082	14.1
Languages	30,256	34,032	12.5
Subjects Allied to Medicine	6,521	7,333	12.5
Economics...Geography	21,684	23,998	10.7
Politics & Law	14,931	16,425	10.0
Mathematics & Statistics	10,812	11,737	8.6
Creative Arts	4,083	4,397	7.7
Physical Sciences	23,397	24,658	5.4
Computer Studies	7,091	7,334	3.4
Education	5,016	5,124	2.2
Clinical Medicine	10,729	10,749	0.2
Pre-Clinical Medicine	8,027	8,036	0.1
Engineering & Technology	32,900	31,991	-2.8
Clinical Dentistry	2,495	2,273	-8.9
Agriculture	4,676	4,194	-10.3

Table 3:4.1 indicates the most recent (1992/93) changes in the funding of teaching and research and provides an early indication of the emergence of a funding league table. Those universities proving more popular to students receive extra money to fund growth: Brunel 13.8%; City 14.6%; Durham 11.5%; Essex 25.6%; Keele 32.2%; Leeds 12.2%; Leicester 12.4%; Liverpool 13.1%; Loughborough 12.1%; Newcastle 12.3%; Salford 15.3%; Sussex 14.0%; Bangor 19.2%; Cardiff 13.7%; St. David's 23.2%; Swansea 28.6%; Dundee 20.6%; Heriot-Watt 14.4%; Sterling 19.7%; Strathclyde 16.8%. All do well, given a UK average of 11.8%. On the research front, Bristol, Cambridge, City, Durham, East Anglia, Essex, Exeter, Leicester, LBS, London, MBS, Newcastle, Nottingham, Oxford, Sussex, York, Dundee, Edinburgh, Glasgow all receive more than a 11% increase with Ulster, Belfast and Brunel actually losing funding -12.1%, -0.3% and -3.0% respectively. Eleven others receive increases of less than the rate of inflation. Only the universities of City, Dundee, Durham, Essex, Leicester, Newcastle and Glasgow receive increases under both headings of more than 10% and thus enjoy a mixed economy. Those losing most under both headings are: Aston, Bradford and Reading. Overall efficiency gains are expected to be 1.5% on the teaching side. In this year, universities will now be unable to switch funds between teaching and research, lessening still further their room for autonomy. From 1993/94 the amount of research money allocated on the basis of selectivity will double, a process that will eventually see the elimination of distributions based on staff and student numbers. At present £430m of the total of £695m available for research goes to the top fourteen institutions. This includes £38m to Oxford, £37m to Cambridge and £134m to London, with Imperial College receiving £23m of that total.

TABLE 3:4.1 TEACHING AND RESEARCH FUNDING INCREASE 1992/93

UNIVERSITIES	% CHANGE FUNDED NUMBERS	% CHANGE FEES-ONLY STUDENTS	% CHANGE TEACHING	% CHANGE RESEARCH	%CHANGE TOTAL RESOURCES
Aston	-0.5	2.1	2.5	2.0	2.4
Bath	0.0	7.5	3.0	8.8	4.8
Birmingham	1.9	16.4	5.1	9.2	6.5
Bradford	3.6	16.5	6.9	3.0	5.8
Bristol	0.3	11.4	4.0	15.4	8.0
Brunel	12.0	22.7	13.8	-3.0	9.3

TABLE 3:4.1 TEACHING AND RESEARCH FUNDING INCREASE 1992/93 (Cont'd)

UNIVERSITIES	% CHANGE FUNDED NUMBERS	% CHANGE FEES-ONLY STUDENTS	% CHANGE TEACHING	% CHANGE RESEARCH	%CHANGE TOTAL RESOURCES
Cambridge	-0.8	2.7		18.9	9.6
City	14.1	36.8	14.6	12.5	14.0
Durham	8.5	19.5	11.5	11.6	11.5
East Anglia	0.6	9.9	3.9	14.5	7.5
Essex	23.7	26.9	25.6	16.8	22.4
Exeter	3.8	16.5	6.9	11.7	8.2
Hull	4.3	20.3	8.9	4.3	7.6
Keele	29.8	48.0	32.2	2.52	3.4
Kent	3.5	23.7	8.0	8.1	8.0
Lancaster	1.5	18.0	5.3	10.9	7.1
Leeds	10.6	25.2	12.2	8.7	11.1
Leicester	9.2	33.7	12.4	13.1	2.6
Liverpool	12.2	32.2	13.1	9.4	11.9
LBS	0.3	5.6	3.3	27.6	13.7
London	4.0	17.4	6.1	13.7	9.1
of which Imperial	0.1	6.4	3.2	19.9	11.0
Loughborough	9.9	24.9	12.1	3.5	9.5
Manchester	2.5	13.9	4.8	9.5	6.4
of which MBS	-5.8	-3.3	-2.5	13.4	2.2
UMIST	4.6	14.9	7.8	10.6	8.9
Newcastle	10.8	23.8	12.3	12.4	12.3
Nottingham	4.6	19.5	8.5	11.6	9.6
Oxford	0.4	4.6	3.8	18.2	10.2
Reading	2.2	18.2	6.0	6.8	6.3
Salford	11.8	22.4	15.3	0.8	11.4
Sheffield	0.5	17.4	3.6	10.5	5.8
Southampton	0.2	9.3	3.2	10.2	5.6
Surrey	2.9	12.4	5.2	9.7	6.7
Sussex	9.6	23.1	14.0	9.7	12.4
Warwick	0.5	14.1	3.5	17.0	8.2
York	-0.2	9.7	2.9	13.7	6.5
ENGLAND	4.7	17.2	7.4	12.1	9.0
Aberystwyth	1.2	9.2	4.3	8.8	5.6
Bangor	15.7	27.3	19.2	3.8	14.5
Cardiff	12.3	30.9	13.7	1.8	10.2
St. Davids	20.4	31.5	23.2	1.11	8.2
Swansea	28.6	40.6	28.6	4.7	21.5
UWCM	-4.8	-17.5	0.8	8.9	3.4
WALES	13.8	27.9	15.1	4.6	12.0

TABLE 3:4.1 TEACHING AND RESEARCH FUNDING INCREASE 1992/93 (Cont'd)

UNIVERSITIES	% CHANGE FUNDED NUMBERS	% CHANGE FEES-ONLY STUDENTS	% CHANGE TEACHING	% CHANGE RESEARCH	%CHANGE TOTAL RESOURCES
Aberdeen	9.6	23.3	11.9	8.1	10.8
Dundee	21.7	40.7	20.6	12.1	18.0
Edinburgh	2.6	17.9	5.9	17.0	9.8
Glasgow	7.3	17.7	10.1	13.9	11.4
Heriot-Watt	12.8	25.3	14.4	6.4	11.7
St. Andrew's	2.6	15.4	5.1	10.0	6.6
Stirling	16.1	35.2	19.7	9.0	16.7
Strathclyde	15.0	25.6	16.8	6.0	13.4
SCOTLAND	9.3	22.6	11.6	12.0	11.7
GREAT BRITAIN	6.0	18.7	8.5	11.7	9.6
Belfast	6.8	18.0	10.6	-0.3	7.8
Ulster	6.3	14.9	10.4	-12.1	5.1
N IRELAND	6.6	16.2	10.5	-6.2	6.3

Table 3:4.2 shows the funding breakdown by subject, demonstrating that the cheaper arts and social science subjects are spearheading expansion. The method of funding adopted actually discriminates against those areas that the government wishes to expand, science and engineering, simply because fees-only recruitment in those areas is neglible. In 1992/93 fees-only students will be funded as follows: classroom based subjects £1,855 (+£80 on 1991/92); laboratory based subjects £2,770 (+£120); post-graduate courses £2,200 (+£96).

TABLE 3:4.2 FUNDING SUBJECT BY SUBJECT

	Baseline funded numbers under-graduate	Additional pool allocation under-graduate	Additional pool allocation post-graduate research	Teaching unit of resource £	% Increase funded student numbers 1991/92-1992/93
Medicine	24,068	-	-	8,273	-
Science	54,615	3,812	530	5,027	16.2
Engineering & technology	35,221	1,256	106	5,266	2.1
Mathematics	19,049	1,044	82	3,448	2.8
Social sciences	54,471	4,946	128	2,996	23.2
Humanities	59,780	5,942	154	3,344	9.3
Education	5,313	-	-	3,938	-
TOTALS	252,517	17,000	1,000	-	-

From 1992/93 onwards, additional student numbers will be allocated on a competitive basis, where competition means success in recruiting fees-only students. Universities must decide on a subject by subject basis their preferred mix of funded and fees-only students and thus their preferred weighted unit costs. Such a system produces an explicit bidding arrangement, whereby, weighted unit cost determines the 'offer' price. The allocation of additional *funded* student numbers will then be determined according to the parameters of Chart 3:1, providing quality is not threatened. The Academic Audit Unit will ensure both quality audit and quality assessment of teaching.

BIDDING FOR STUDENT NUMBERS

Bidding for student places took place in June 1990 to cover the period 1991/1992 to 1994/1995, in an attempt to make universities compete for numbers by reducing unit costs, thereby educating more at less cost to the government.

To help universities determine their bid prices, the UFC published average prices for teaching in cost centres excluding research, Table 3:5 gives the averages. The UFC expected to receive different bid prices for each subject in every university. It did not obtain them, and the attempted reform degenerated into a farce.

The object of this exercise was to force down unit costs, not by rationalisation or letting universities compete for students directly in the market place but by threatening to withhold funding. More expensive institutions, with higher costs because they are highly geared to research and biased towards engineering and science, would undoubtedly have suffered the most.

CHART 3:1 ALLOCATION OF ADDITIONAL FUNDED STUDENT NUMBERS FOR 1992-93

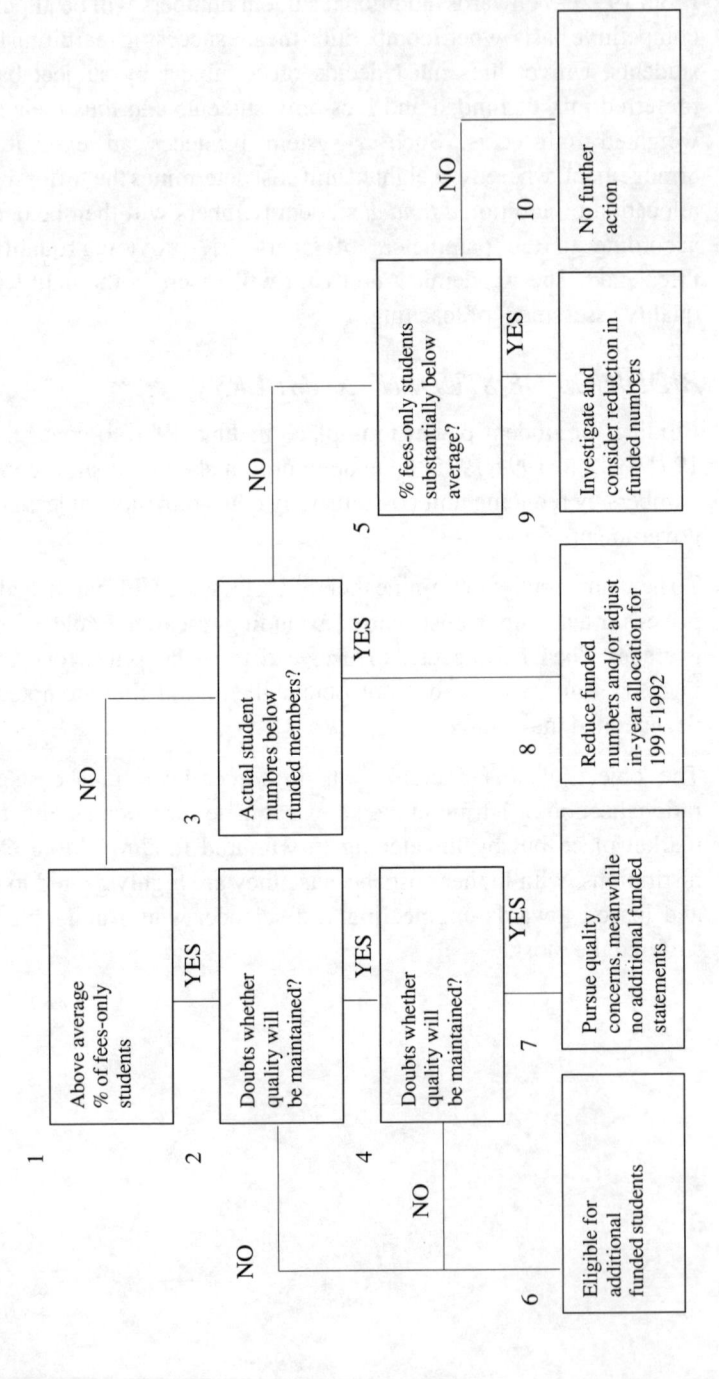

1. Above average % of fees-only students
- NO → **3.** Actual student numbers below funded members?
  - YES → **8.** Reduce funded numbers and/or adjust in-year allocation for 1991-1992
  - NO → **5.** % fees-only students substantially below average?
    - YES → **9.** Investigate and consider reduction in funded numbers
    - NO → **10.** No further action
- YES → **2.** Doubts whether quality will be maintained?
  - NO → **4.** Doubts whether quality will be maintained?
    - NO → **6.** Eligible for additional funded students
    - YES → **7.** Pursue quality concerns, meanwhile no additional funded statements

92

TABLE 3:5 UFC SUBJECT GROUP GUIDE PRICES

Academic subject groups	£
Pre-clinical medicine	4,600
Pre-clinical dentistry	5,200
Clinical medicine	5,500
Clinical dentistry	9,400
Subjects allied to medicine	4,000
Biological sciences	4,300
Veterinary science	8,100
Agriculture	4,200
Physical sciences	4,600
Mathematics & statistics, etc	2,700
Computer studies	3,500
Metallurgy	5,400
Engineering & technology	4,600
Architecture building & planning	3,700
Applied social work	3,400
Economics, sociology, etc	2,700
Politics, law & other social studies	2,200
Business & administrative studies	2,800
Mass communication & documentation	2,900
Languages & related disciplines	2,900
Archaeology	3,400
Humanities excluding Archaeology	2,800
Creative arts	3,300
Education	3,500

In the final UFC allocations, and based on the research selectivity exercise, a sum for research was added to the global revenue from bidding for each institution. A university could therefore have been forced to take students on a fees only basis (£1,675 in 1990/91 and differential fees thereafter of £1,675 for the arts and £2,200 for science), without the provision of a research component. The result could only be a further step towards the division of universities into teaching and research establishments.[11] But the question that has yet to be answered is: what does it cost to conduct first class teaching? Progressively reducing teaching costs tells us nothing about this important question – fails even to address the issue.

So far in this chapter we have considered the immediate, and gloomy, past. Is there a brighter tomorrow? What has the future in store for the universities?

---

[11] This looks even more likely following the White Paper, *Higher Education : A New Framework*, London, HMSO, Cmnd. 1541, 1991.

Some insight into the government's thinking may be gleaned from the 1985 Green Paper.[12] This is as important for its ideological ruminations as for its policy proposals. It is deserving of our attention, for in it are worked out the dogmas that will guide all future state university planning.

B: FUTURE STRATEGY: THE 1985 GREEN PAPER AND THE SHIFT TO VOCATIONS AND TECHNOLOGY

The 1985 Green Paper, *The Development of Higher Education into the 1990's*, must be read as a depressing document by anyone concerned with the traditional values of education. The humanities merit scarcely a mention; marketability rather than intellectual depth is the criterion.

Rightly the paper emphasises the need for a better trained technocracy: "The Government is particularly concerned by the evidence that our competitors are producing, and plan in the future to produce, more qualified scientists, engineers, technologists and technicians than the United Kingdom. A thriving economy needs more skills both to develop the talents of entrepreneurs and to support their achievements".[13] It speaks of "the achievement of the necessary shift towards science, engineering and vocational courses, to produce the balance of skills which the nation requires".[14]

The paper further goes on to pronounce that higher education establishments need to be concerned with attitudes to the world outside higher education, especially to industry and commerce, and beware of anti-business snobbery. It pontificates on the essentiality of the entrepreneurial spirit, the need to foster positive attitudes to work, and for students to be able to work co-operatively in groups. It rehearses therefore just about every tired anti-university cliché that might, once, have been heard in the lounge bar or boardroom. Students today are preoccupied to the point of obsession with the 'world of work': a frequent criticism is that they have become boring to teach since they regard learning as instrumental, and not fascinating for its intrinsic richness. Many students today also plan to run their own businesses.

---

[12] *The Development of Higher Education Into the 1990's*, London, HMSO, Cmnd. 9524, 1985.
[13] *The Development of Higher Education Into the 1990's, Ibid.*
[14] *Ibid.*

The Green Paper however appears to have in mind Mr Gradgrind's industrious pupil, Bitzer, as the new Beau Ideal. Its pronouncements reveal an image of universities as merely an anti-chamber to the commercial world, and the purpose of learning as not to develop the individual but to develop the economy. Such a view is not however new: it is the attitude against which Newman rebelled in the nineteenth century with *The Idea of a University*.[15] Such a view is impregnated with a utilitarianism that would see no use for history, literature and any branch of learning which did not have a commercial significance. In this it is strictly contemporary, with that homage to 'relevance', that infatuation with the current, which mark an instant-gratification culture, for it has no kinship with Toryism as history has revealed it, concerned with the rootedness of value and the organic evolution of things. It is base and it is sinister. Its aim is to create a generation of shoving, street smart persons; not the scholar and the sage, but the graceless spiv, is to be the universities' stock-in-trade.

It can be well doubted whether the things demanded by the Green Paper can be inculcated pedagogically: they are culturally transmitted, that is to say via all the signals from youth's environment, and in prescribing so fully what the values of universities ought to be, the Green Paper betrays a dangerous authoritarianism which should further alarm those who see little good in the state monopoly of university education.

ACCESS

With some justice, the Green Paper emphasises the importance of increased access to higher education, partly to satisfy the demand of business for graduates in the nineteen nineties. 18/19 year olds participating in higher education will increase from 14% to 18.5% by 2000, (now forecast to rise to 30%) and the paper speaks of the need for "commitment by universities, polytechnics and colleges to opening up higher education to more mature entrants, and to more who do not possess traditional entry qualifications".[16] The paper is concerned to include students with a wider set of practical and academic experience, stressing the importance of admitting students with vocational qualifications and the necessity of re-thinking teaching methods to cope with such 'practical background'

---

[15] J.H. Newman, *The Idea of a University*, New York, 1959, p.129.
[16] *The Development of Higher Education Into the 1990's, Ibid. Cf. Higher Education: A New Framework*, London, HMSO, Cmnd. 1541, 1991.

entrants. However, the paper claims to see no evidence that the admission of such non-traditional students, that is, students who do not possess a compatible previous record of examination success, must in general lower overall standards. The Green Paper's deviousness on this point should not necessarily lead us to dismiss it. While we must have the intellectual honesty to admit that more will mean somewhat worse, the integrity of standards cannot be the exclusive consideration even if they must rank high. The needs of commerce for highly trained personnel must signify: and also the matter of whether more people could benefit from higher education in terms of leading rich and more fulfilled lives. The question is, could standards be stretched sufficiently to accommodate them without being stressed to the point where they cease meaningfully to exist, and given that the increase projected by the government is based on universities' and polytechnics' own offers, we may assume that the system can accommodate them without reaching a destructive level.

However, it is regretted that the Green Paper does not also advocate the more demanding concomitant, namely the improvement of secondary education such that dilution of university standards is not necessary.[17] The weakness of British secondary education, created more with a view to social engineering than with the needs of end-customers in mind, is generally acknowledged: universities along with other institutions of national life will continue to suffer because of it.

FUNDING

On the question of funding, the Green Paper points out that the typical U.K. university receives over 90% of its total income from government funds in the early 1980's, funnelled largely through the UFC and previously the UGC. Money also comes from fees, largely via Local Education Authorities (LEA's) who have a 90% grant from the Exchequer. Research Councils, publicly funded, also contribute. In addition to being given the full cost of their tuition, British students also receive a means-tested grant. Table 3:6 shows the sources of university funding for three years, 1960, 1980 and 1988: whilst the Exchequer grant falls, research funding rises.

---

[17] The Higginson Report for example has not been acted upon; *Advancing A Levels, Report of Committee Appointed by the Secretary of State for Education and Science and Secretary of State for Wales*, The Higginson Report, London, HMSO, 1989. The national curriculum is too little and too late.

Since the Green Paper was published, the Exchequer grant fell dramatically in 1989/90 to less than 50% of total university income.

TABLE 3:6 SOURCES OF UNIVERSITY FUNDING IN THE UK

	1988	1980	1960
"Exchequer" revenue from Government.	55%	63%	72%
Fees.	13%	17%	9%
Donations.	1%	1%	4%
Research contracts, grants.	20%	3%	9%
Services.	7%	13%	2%
Other.	4%	4%	4%

Rightly the Green Paper is sceptical about such a maintenance system. It asserts that "certainly the National Defence Student Loan Program in the U.S.A. demonstrates a willingness by low-income students to borrow", and "all countries that operate loan schemes do so in conjunction with other measures of student support".[18]

The Green Paper adds: "the Government concludes, with regret, that no substantial part of established public funding responsibilities can by shed".[19] So it is prepared to preside over a badly run monopoly in obeisance to some dogma which says that universities must be free and public to preserve standards.[20] A broader conception of 'standards' might include such elements as the simple continuity of scholarship in certain now threatened areas.

THE RELEVANCE OF UNIVERSITY ACTIVITIES

The Green Paper expounds a belief that industrial applicability should be the prime aim in all research: "Researchers should be more aware of the importance of commercial exploitation and of their responsibilities for its promotion".[21] In particular, institutions should in applied fields take consultancy and other industrial work fully into account when assessing candidates for promotion, they should resort more to part-time contracts, joint appointments with industry and so on: postgraduate work should have a closer industrial orientation, and employer involvement is particularly important in this sphere.

It is perhaps extraordinary that the state should feel it can prescribe and re-define academic values so precisely, and such insolence is comprehensible only in the light of the absolute monopoly of higher education possessed by the state. In a democracy, rules cannot simply be laid down centrally, to be accepted they have to gain at least the passive acquiescence of the recipient. Moreover it is important for civil servants to realise that academic values are international and not part of some eccentric English provincial cult.

Therefore to all true lovers of intellectual liberty, strengthening of universities' independence must be deemed desirable even though it may

---

[18] *The Development of Higher Education Into the 1990's, Ibid.*
[19] *Ibid.*
[20] Harold Perkins, "The Academic Profession in the United Kingdom", in B.R. Clarke, *The Academic Profession: National Disciplinary and Institutional Setting*, University of California Press, 1987, pp.13-59.
[21] *The Development of Higher Education Into the 1990's, Ibid.*

not be perceived as feasible. Extraordinary too is the locus of blame: universities are seen as the offending party in their relationship with industry, never once is business castigated for myopia in failing to draw ideas from universities or to help them in their work: the behaviour of that which is private must invariably be right, even though, as Corelli Barnett so memorably demonstrated, the 'pragmatic' bias of British industrialists had often given them a mindless contempt for abstracted and theoretic reasoning, and a consequent impoverishment of their competitive effectiveness.[22]

Other moves in this period anticipated or reflected the tone and policies of the Green Paper. The new thinking was summarised in the notions of concentration, selection and hierarchy. A university would cease to be universal, if it ever was. Now they were to be demoted or promoted, truncated, labelled, and calls for the decapitation of their research mandate became ever more vociferous. The core idea was that the entire febrile system would be managed centrally, the thoughts of the ministers made flesh through the national directives of the various bureaux. Devolved management, the letting of an institution make its own decision, became an anachronism. This was because, as in the case of local councils, the government trusted neither the competence nor the governing ethos of the institution.

And so the ideology found itself standing on its head. Conservatives believe passionately in individualism: the bureaucratic corollary of this is to reduce state planning and increase parochial initiative, yet there they now were, creating monstrous, bloated central plans. Their ideological discord emanates from cross pressures – the animosity to bureaucratic central planning versus a commitment to value for money.[23]

SELECTIVITY

The Green Paper points out that the total research expenditure derived from general income in higher education institutions is thought to be around £600 million annually. It comments; "both quality and economy argue for some concentration of research activity – particularly when expensive

---

[22] C. Barnett, *The Audit of War*, London, 1987.
[23] Professor Griffith makes a similar charge, *Universities and the State: the Next Steps*, Council for Academic Freedom, 1989.

equipment is needed and concentration implies selectivity," and "there is no evidence that all academic staff must engage in research".[24]

This questions the very essence of what a university is, and what distinguishes it from a mere training factory. Subtract the research and you cease to have a university. A university is moreover a corporate entity: to eliminate the research capability of one department is to change the overall climate and devalue the research, especially in the arts and social sciences, that need little in the way of equipment. One suspects that in the selectivity exercises the motivation is by no means altruistic: the attempt of large players to gain a monopoly of resources by characterising the smaller departments as inefficient, therefore disposable, merits intellectual scepticism.[25] Moreover a research reputation helps to attract students nationally and internationally for the reason we have stated: that it describes the essence of a university. Students like to receive knowledge from those who are actively adding to it.

The Green Paper also adds that greater concentration and selectivity may mean that whole universities, as well as entire departments, will lose research funding from the UGC. Note, again, the tone of veiled menace that runs through so many official pronouncements on the subject of universities.

CRITERIA OF SELECTIVITY

Selectivity implies judgement, and the Green Paper is therefore much exercised by the need for judgemental criteria. The indices it chooses are particularly maladroit, and embody fallacious reasoning. Thus: external judgements about quality can be attempted by comparing the success of students in obtaining jobs, their relative salaries and their reported performance in employment, and the international standing of qualifications. The Green Paper also welcomes the Jarratt Report's suggestions for developing reliable and consistent performance indicators designed for use both within individual universities and for making comparisons between them.[26]

---

[24] *The Development of Higher Education Into the 1990's, Ibid.*
[25] R. Marris, "The Problem of Research", Paper given at St. George's House Conference, 1989.
[26] *The Development of Higher Education Into the 1990's, Ibid.* Cf. Committee of Vice Chancellors and Principals, *Report of the Steering Committee for Efficiency Studies in Universities*, Jarratt Report, London, 1985.

Use of subsequent student performance contains serious flaws: it measures, first, only success in the first few years. Any student with an 'applied' qualification is bound for early success, but what is of interest surely is how far they eventually progress: is it far-fetched to suggest that those from an exclusively 'applied' background sometimes lack both the political sophistication and intellectual depth necessary for success in its higher forms? Such measures would also encourage universities to steer students away from British industry towards the more lucrative areas of financial and professional activity. As for applying the measurement formulae of the Jarratt Report, its 'mechanical' approach is not invalid, but must be supplemented by interpretative and qualitative judgements: otherwise an apparently scientific approach can give rise to a misleading picture.[27]

TROUBLE IN THE RANKS

The 1985 Green Paper's demand for ranking was a prerequisite of its vision of concentrated resources in superior research universities, to be distinguished from a congeries of pedagogic academies. But if universities and departments are to be ranked, a mechanism would have to be found for so doing.[28] The UGC subsequently tried this in a notorious first exercise that provoked several academics to characterise it thus:

> "The rankings are based on a mixture of data in unstated proportions, apparently giving great weight to grants won from a limited range of sources such as the Medical Research Council (MRC) and the Science and Engineering Research Council (SERC). It is astonishing that the cost of production should largely determine perceived excellence: this has not been the Government's approach to other nationalized industries".

And: "By introducing a heavy reliance on conspicuous expenditure and on personal judgements of the worth of particular types of research, the UGC has substituted a complicated, hidden process".[29]

Not surprisingly therefore, the various rankings were hotly disputed. In Electronics and Electrical Engineering for example, the UGC had rated

---

[27] J. Taylor and I. Johnes, *Measuring the Performance of Universities*, London, 1991. Cf. *Report to ABRC from the Working Group on Peer Review*, and the Science and Engineering Policy Study Units survey of academics' views on *Quantitative Assessment of Departmental Research*. Both reports express mistrust of quantitative measures, particularly citation counts.

[28] *The Development of Higher Education Into the 1990's, Ibid.* Cf. University Grants Committee, "Planning for the Late 1980's", Circular Letter 12/85, 1985 and Circular Letter 22/91 from the UFC, on peer review.

[29] J. Griffith, *Ibid*, 1989.

Imperial College only as "above average": a peer review by Heads of Department rated it second. Glasgow, starred by the UGC, was below 'above average' in the peer review. There are innumerable similar instances. The Institute of Chemical Engineers subsequently produced its own criteria for evaluating research.

A particular source of concern was the use of research income in the evaluations. Income from industrial sources seems ironically to have been ignored by the UGC, and that from the Research Councils given great weight.

Moreover, "A low level of research income does not necessarily mean a low level (or low quality) of research (for instance in the humanities)". The size of the grant is quite unrelated to the quality and profundity of a piece of research, but very closely related to the cost of performing it. In science this is reflected in the cost of equipment, and in the social sciences the social survey is expensive and may simply generate information rather than knowledge. But this criteria "now plays a major role in the UGC allocation of research funds". Of the CVCP's performance indicators, only one was directly connected with research and none with teaching, and 303 indicators dealt with spending, provoking one commentator to bewail... "the insistent and unreasonable demands of a Government that cares little about academic values".[30]

Because evaluation exercises are invariably flawed does not mean they should not be attempted. Some hierarchy is better than no hierarchy. Assessments reduce complacency, encourage self-criticism, they create a climate of competition rather than listless co-existence, but their limitations must be clearly understood: qualitative and impressionistic factors should be recorded, as well as mathematical weightings, otherwise the process becomes mechanical and, since the sum is rarely the total of the parts, deeply misleading. They could act as a disincentive as well as an incentive. They may give disproportionate weight to factors of a fleeting, contemporary interest. Therefore, their usage in allocating resources, as distinct from simply providing feedback, must be circumscribed by a process of discussion and consultation.

It should also be recognised that different institutions will quite legitimately have different purposes. Therefore each university must define

---

[30] UFC, *Report on the 1989 Research Assessment Exercise*, 1989.

its own standards in relation to specific strategic objectives thereby adopting performance indicators that are appropriate to their mission. Universities have applied precisely this argument to teaching assessment, setting and monitoring their own standards, but there seems to be some reluctance to apply this thinking to research. If it were though, the construction of league tables of good and bad research performers would be fundamentally flawed, as the function and type of research undertaken would vary between institutions. Despite such an important caveat, however, research selectivity exercises will continue.

C: THE ATTEMPT AT MANAGEMENT:

BIG IS BEAUTIFUL

If universities are to have a caste system – as the Green Paper seemed to imply – then the extinction of the small department is one inevitable result. The UGC seemed to be at one with the anonymous author of the Green Paper on this point. The UGC continued to stress the importance of rationalising small departments (Strategy Advice 1984) even to the extent of advising on the minimum size of departments: this was but one of its late blooming fetishes, with 'rationalisations' in pharmacy, agriculture, oceanography and Scandinavian studies, reviews in thirteen other subjects (including Celtic studies, Oriental and African studies, Dutch, Hispanic, classics, economic and social history, drama) and some reviews promised in history, philosophy of science, dentistry, archaeology, small accountancy departments, small physics and chemistry departments.[31]

The Oxburgh Report of 1987, a review of the earth sciences, was the UGC's first attempt to 'rationalise' a science, and the harbinger of more: it advocated the closure of small departments and concentration of research in 10 or 12 centres of international standing. Level 2 would be the MSc level, and not be given costly equipment; Level 3 would merely do first or second year undergraduate teaching and probably not maintain separate science departments.[32] The report articulates the concept of a 'satellite campus' on one main site, with lecturers commuting between sites to fulfil their teaching commitments. The chairman of the Advisory Board for the

---

[31] University Grants Committee, *A Strategy for Higher Education in the 1990's*, 1984. There is some evidence to suggest that the UFC proposes to reinstitute subject reviews in the mid 1990's.

[32] University Grants Committee, *Strengthening University Earth Sciences*, The Oxburgh Report, 1987.

Research Councils (ABRC) pointed out that only a few departments could be properly supported for top research. Chemistry, Physics and Bio-medical Sciences were to be given similar reviews; Sir Christopher Ball had also promoted proposals similar to the Oxburgh ideology.[33]

The notion of concentrating money in top institutions has something to recommend it: the criticism is surely that, in these parsimonious days, it is seen as only achievable at the cost of depriving other universities of their departments, or downgrading them into pedagogic academies, and the menace of such an argument is that it does not conceive a university as an organism whose components reinforce each other, which draws its life from its variety, but rather a mechanical feeder into some vast, abstracted research machine. Therefore the closure of a department diminishes the vitality of the entire institution and makes it even less the classical conception of a university. Downgrading a department to teaching status deprives students of the excitement of a direct connection to the frontiers of knowledge: the moribundity of such departments would be unimaginable, their ability to attract students doubtful. The plans are a formula for educational apartheid, British university education as we know it will cease to exist, creating a condescending élite and a demoralised proletariat: for one can happily assume that certain universities will top the list of a rationalised system, whether it is done on a university basis, or piecemeal on a departmental basis.

The Green Paper and the UGC did not however advocate a formalised hierarchy, they conceived an understated English class system rather than some overblown foreign caste system. But the ABRC went much further. It demanded a rigid, branded status. It promulgated a three tier strategy for Britain's science base: thus Type R would be teaching and research; Type T would be for undergraduate teaching and MSc work, with non-advanced research facilities, and Type X would be primarily teaching, with research only in particular fields.[34] The ABRC argued that whole institutions should be so designated, not just individual departments in the UGC's on-going review process, and they echoed Oxburgh in claiming that on the basis of American experience large centres were more effective research performers.[35] They cited the American liberal arts colleges to back the

---

[33] C. Ball, "The Problem of Research", *Higher Education Quarterly*, 1989, pp. 205-215.
[34] ABRC, *A Strategy for the Science Base*, 1987.
[35] UGC, Oxburgh Report, *Ibid*.

notion that good undergraduate teaching could be had without research. But as one commentator has pointed out, the vogue for universities developing specialisations contains the danger of everyone stressing the same fashionable areas to expand into.[36]

Even success with the scheme will still create rather odd institutions, with several bloated 'specialisations', and myriad prosaic, lack-lustre departments. Other factors ignored in formulating such proposals are: the difficulties posed by assessment and the tendency of assessment to promote the *status quo*;[37] the danger of creating inflexible, bureaucratic monoliths instead of the prestigious research centres envisaged; the ability of small departments to foster individualism and human intimacy achieved through smaller departments, and the consequent benefit to our consumers, the students; the well known problems of inducing creative thought in the large, centrally managed institution. None of this is an argument against creating great international research centres, merely against impoverishing the whole system to do so.

EXPLOITABILITY

The ABRC sang in harmony with the government's Green Paper on other points as well. It was interested in utility and commercial exploitability. Subsequently the ABRC enumerated its current criteria for evaluating research: in general, external factors were to be given a heightened role. It asserts that it ought to be possible to give some prediction as to the possibility of "useful findings" emerging, and quotes the Kendrew report on particle physics: "it is not meaningless to assert that research on black holes is less likely to provide utility by the turn of the century than research on self-organising systems".[38] The new ABRC criteria for evaluating scientific priorities are enumerated thus: timeliness, the expectation of quick results (between 5 and 20 years); persuasiveness, that is connections with other research; commercial exploitability; social and other benefits.

We must assume that the ABRC will seek actively to apply these criteria. If this is to be the case, any serious defender of intellectual liberty must be

---

[36] A. Bloom, *The Closing of the American Mind*, London, 1988.
[37] Taylor and Johnes demonstrate that once the peculiar features of a university are taken into account, ranking differences are much diminished, *Measuring the Performance of Universities*, 1991.
[38] ABRC, *A Strategy for the Science Base*, 1987.

alarmed. It is important that scientific research should feed into economic growth. But precisely which line of research will eventually do this is a difficult matter to judge: moreover, research has other objectives besides the British economy. Scientists wish to extend their knowledge of man, matter and the universe, to dive to the causes of things and disinter the wellsprings of being, and to subordinate this noble aspiration to the nagging demand for 'relevance' is to bondage the soul of scientific curiosity: it recalls Tenniel's cartoons in which Political Economy is featured as a wizened, nagging old school-marm.[39]

The state, in its relationship with universities, is increasingly seeking the role of investor and consumer. It demands clear and quantifiable returns, and this would be the movement whatever party was in power. Such a development is inimical to the spirit of intellectual curiosity, an emotion which those who advocate it have presumably never experienced.

Therefore it is not only the libertarian thinker who might dream of more independent universities. Academics who would otherwise applaud a welfare state ought to judge with increasing scepticism the British state's total monopoly of their work, their institutions, their livelihood. That they have failed to do so points up a provincial conservatism, a devotion to archaic modes which causes them to lose every argument they conduct with the state, because they have no new ideas to offer it.

THE 1991 WHITE PAPER

Recently the Conservative government has revealed a plan to comprehensivise Britain's universities.[40] Now the 34 or so polytechnics will be able to call themselves universities. The scheme has been accepted without a murmur. The government is resolved to pull down all distinction between academic and vocational, polytechnics and university, by downgrading their status through a universalisation of the nomenclature. In the words of the Prime Minister: "At the heart of our reforms is the determination to break down the artificial barrier which has far too long divided an academic education from a vocational one".[41] It apparently believes that skill and learning can be achieved by decree, by levelling

---

[39] Tenniel published in *Punch Magazine*.
[40] *Higher Education: A New Framework*, London, HMSO, Cmnd. 1541, 1991.
[41] *The Times*, 3 May, 1991.

institutions, by simplifying exams, by declaring that academic and vocational skills are equal.

The aim is not intellectual or cultural but sociological – the aspiration to accreditise vast sectors of society, more therefore a political slogan, to do with the rhetoric of social justice, than an attempt to confront real economic needs. Such confusion as to ends and purposes creates waste. Here is the fabrication of policy 'on the hoof' with no real thought for consequences, a politics of expedience done when government is in a panic. The changes are probably irreversible and any ruminations on their inefficiency are probably simply 'academic'.

What young people chiefly need is vocational training: expansion should therefore be in distinct polytechnics and technical colleges. The need is for more didactic instruction at a lower level: university lecturers, whose traditions are theoretic, do not have talent for the kind of pedagoguery the new cohorts seek.

CONSEQUENCES OF MASSIFICATION

Now, one third of eighteen year olds will go to university, 200,000 extra students over eight years. Nor is any new money promised to effect this transformation. None of these consequences have been really thought through. Infrastructure will be strained to breaking point, unless the new intake is to be entirely local. For example, library facilities are already universally overstretched, as are accommodation facilities.

The Times, in particular, has celebrated the move. Mr. Major, it says, "can claim to have landed a blow for classlessness more effectively than in any other area of public policy".[42] This is certainly the revolutionary change intended by the system's political masters. But will it have the consequences they desire: indeed, have they defined the consequences they desire? But it is idle – an égalitarian pretence – to maintain that such a large cohort can be admitted without lowering standards. The new intakes will not want the traditional staples of universities but multi-disciplinary degrees and matter with a contemporary bearing and consumerist approach. Less intellectually curious entrants will expect a more paternalist teaching régime and there will be higher failure rates and drop-out rates will rise considerably. The campus itself will be very crowded.

---

[42] *The Times, loc. cit.*

So the consequence of change is that, as in the United States, much of the expensive structure of higher education will become remedial. Because we have lost the ability to control standards in secondary schools, we use universities to make up for it, an extravagant piece of social incompetence. Inevitably also there will be mergers into hyper-universities: soulless bureaucratic monoliths. The abandonment of seminars, tutorials and other aspects of hand tailoring will be a necessary consequence of unfunded expansion and will lead to a decline in teaching standards, in as much as these are facilitated by a more intimate setting; bereft of such intimacies of context, personal knowledge of students will disappear: teaching, deprived of association, will be a boring job.

ROLE OF THE POLYTECHNICS

Polytechnics – with the help of markedly increased government funding – were the education success story of the eighties. They educated many young people in vital technical and applied areas. Their role in the economy is crucial, and they have executed it efficiently and professionally. Why, therefore, change a winning formula? Industry has welcomed their contribution.[43] They have, now, a broad social mix of students. The old snobberies have largely gone. In Germany the 24 polytechnics (Fachhoch Schulen) and 51 universities exist happily alongside each other. No one worries about relative status.[44]

But what, exactly, does a polytechnic do? Much of it is sub-degree or general degree work. Many of the subjects are of great practical utility, though scarcely academic. Currently they teach for example catering management, health visiting; food and beverage management; photographic practice; hotel management; travel and tourism; animation. Now however all these areas will develop thoroughly bogus academic superstructures, with their own unread journals, research and such. But other subjects they teach are non-academic, yet also non-vocational: professional studies: community studies; communication studies; leisure studies; equal opportunities policies; media studies theory and practice;

---

[43] Cf. Evidence of National Advisory Body for Public Sector Higher Education to House of Lords Select Committee on Science and Technology, *Civil Research and Development*, Volume 3, Written Evidence, London, HMSO, Cmnd. HL20-III, 1986, p.199. Also evidence from Plymouth Polytechnic, *Ibid*, p.215.

[44] Zurich Polytechnic does not suffer from an identity crisis and ambitious parents strive to obtain a place at France's École Polytechnic for their offspring.

cultural aspects of sport. And, although polytechnics were never originally conceived to teach philosophy and such, they have also assumed these functions as well. North London Polytechnic employs 8 lecturers in philosophy, 4 less than the University of Cambridge.

RESEARCH

What of academic research under the new order? Research is a tradition. It cannot be simply created and then dissolved on the basis of open competition for an ad hoc grant. We are now putting this culture at risk, since the same research fund may be spread over many more institutions. The applied bias of modern funding policy may even favour polytechnics over universities.[45] The problem is definitional; there is an ethos and aura to the term university which has a limited amount in common with what polytechnics do, but now polytechnics will wish to incorporate that. While it is true that an individual research project may be won by a polytechnic rather than a university, such a competitive system ignores the importance of climate and continuity: it is not therefore inadmissible, but funding policy should always consider the vitality of the overall institution and the extent to which sudden piecemeal funding confiscations can cripple that, and possibly permanently.

The inevitable consequence is that universities will receive much less funding for research. *The Times* is under no illusions: "Universities may begin to lose research money and their more glamorous departments".[46] We will multiply the research output of ex-polytechnics and debauch it in the universities. The government state in the White Paper that universities' entitlement to research funds will remain. It will do no such thing. Questions will be raised about why unit costs are so much lower in the 'new' universities, and how can the excess be justified (it cannot, since the judgement is a value and not an economic one).

WHAT'S IN A NAME?

What is the purpose of a university, and why patent the label? The need is for a definition of what a university is; the importance of defining the name

---

[45] Although Kenneth Clarke when Secretary of State for Education announced that he expected the research mission of the polytechnics to remain the same, ruling out competition for scarce research funds outside the research councils. See below chapter 5, p.173.
[46] *The Times*, 3 May, 1991.

is that it defines the function, so a simple change of name is more revolutionary that it appears. The problem now becomes confusion as to the mission of a university, as in America; is it to become primarily an agency of training? Nor is it possible to distinguish the change in label from the intended massification – both doctrines are interlinked in the same White Paper. It may be that the ex-polytechnics and not the traditional universities will come to carry the definition of what a university is. Such will be the looking-glass world; polytechnics will be called universities, universities will become polytechnic in function, increasingly teaching polytechnic subjects in the polytechnic way.

Yet universities are also part of an international system. The name has universal connotations – for example the practice of research both 'pure' and applied. Because the name has a specific meaning, the newly enfranchised institutions will quite understandably sense a need to perform the functions that their name implies. It is silly to pretend otherwise, silly of government to say no, they will only engage in applied research. They will not; they will demand and adopt practices commensurate with their status. The focus of polytechnics should remain in the applied, technical and vocational areas; to give them a greater research mission would be to dilute their valuable teaching function. The eventual cost to the Exchequer will be incalculable.

However, universities need not necessarily stay at their present number, as if by a divine fiat. If Buckingham were to be the last university foundation in the United Kingdom we might conclude that the system was indeed moribund. A case could be made for some polytechnics to become universities – or for universities to become polytechnics. Privilege has to be earned. We want a class system, not a caste system. And 'Polytechnic', like 'comprehensive', is an ugly word, 'Technical Universities' would still imply that all-important differentiation of function, without making polytechnic students and staff feel alienated.[47]

---

[47] Cf. *THES*, 28 February, 1992, where David Roberts of the Higher Education Information Services Trust reported that existing polytechnic names are more attractive to potential students than the proposed new ones: "Polytechnics were set up to provide education for a different sort of client including many for whom the title university has negative connotations".

CHAPTER FOUR
TO TEACH THE SENATORS WISDOM: THE GOVERNANCE OF UNIVERSITIES

"You see then, here are two methods of Education; the end of the one is to be philosophical, of the other to be mechanical; the one rises towards general ideas, the other is exhausted upon what is particular and external".
J.H. Newman,
The Idea of a University, New York, 1959.

"And so as regards intellectual culture, I am far from denying utility in this large sense as the end of Education, when I lay it down, that the culture of the intellect is a good in itself and its own end; I do not exclude from the idea of intellectual culture what it cannot but be, from the very nature of things; I only deny that we must be able to point out, before we have any right to call it useful, some art, or business, or profession, or trade, or work, as resulting from it, and as its real and complete end".
J.H. Newman,
The Idea of a University, New York, 1959.

"Now this is what some great men are very slow to allow; they insist that Education should be confined to some particular and narrow end, and should issue in some definite work, which can be weighed and measured. They argued as if everything as well as every person had its price; and that where there has been a great outlay, they have a right to expect a return in kind. This they call making Education and Instruction 'useful' and 'Utility' becomes their watchword. With a fundamental principle of this nature, they very naturally go on to ask, what there is to show for the expense of a University; what is the real worth in the market of the article called 'a Liberal Education', on the supposition that it does not teach us definitely how to advance our manufactures, or to improve our lands, or to better our civil economy".
J.H. Newman,
The Idea of a University, New York, 1959.

INTRODUCTION

This book is not merely concerned with the level of the grand strategy of public policy. We also seek detailed recommendations for the better governance of the university system. Now managerial policy can only be meaningfully worked out in relation to a set of objectives, themselves defined by the mission that universities implicitly enunciate, namely the furtherance of intellectual civilization through teaching and original publication, so that managerial initiatives are only relevant in as much as they help further such a mission.

Such a somewhat pettifogging chapter is necessary because there is much that is wrong with the managerial practices and organisation of universities – errors which will not be corrected by some splendid new pan-national system of university finance. These wrongs are endemic. Their immediate consequence is the waste of a lot of public money. Their subtler effects lie in the de-motivating of students, the inertia of academics and undermining of the universities' intellectual mandate. They must be righted.

This chapter is divided into six sections. The first looks at the role of vice chancellors; then internal administration; academic personnel; course content; course flexibility; and national policies.

THE ROLE OF VICE CHANCELLORS

Our analysis at this point must begin at the top. The vigour of the corporation derives in part from the personality and competence of its chief officer, and it is our belief that vice-chancellors often do not meet the measure we would expect in such a responsible position.

Our central criticisms are:

(1) Until the past few years, alarming ignorance about techniques such as alumni fundraising, benefactor solicitation, marketing and the like, although financial imperatives have been a remarkable educating influence in the recent past.

(2) Limited ability to communicate both with the public and with their staffs.

(3) The adoption simply of cost-cutting rather than proactive initiatives in dealing with diminished state funding.

(4) A bureaucratically hidebound administrative style that, sheltering behind lugubrious committees, ensures that decisions are made too little, too late.

(5) Their assumption that the benefits conveyed by universities are self-evident to everyone.

(6) The central problem of graduating from scholarship, often an isolated task, to corporate leadership, requiring talents of personality which are not readily fostered by a life spent in research.[1]

(7) Their apparent appointment exclusively from within the ranks of a 'charmed circle'.

(8) Their selection largely from scientists, 80% of the total, on the fallacious assumption that scientific effectiveness and managerial efficiency are synonymous.[2]

We believe that such mediocrity of leadership has deeply harmed our universities, and we suggest:

(1) The abolition of all academic tenure for vice-chancellors, and its substitution by five year contracts. There can be no justification for a period in high office of ten or even twenty years.

(2) The appointment of some vice-chancellors from outside academic life, with the proviso that they have had some high level involvement with universities previously, on governing bodies, as doctoral candidates and the like. University College London demonstrates the vigour such appointments can engender. We believe this would bring much needed areas of expertise to the top of the university system, in management, enterprise, human relations skills, a degree of vision born of involvement in the wider world. But we do not see industrialists as the only candidates; other areas, including the top ranks of the civil service, would be sources.[3]

---

[1] For the view of the vice-chancellors on this issue see chapter 8 below pp.268-9.
[2] Specialisms of present vice-chancellors are:
Engineering 14; Biological Science 7; Chemistry 5; Physics 3; History 3; Law 2; Education 2; Civil Service 2; Computer Science 2; Philosophy 1; French Linguistics 1; Mathematics 1; Metallurgy 1; Vacancy 1.
[3] L. Southwick, "The University as a Firm", *Carnegie Review*, 1967.

(3) A six month-training period for all new vice-chancellors, possibly through the medium of a staff college, to acquaint them with skills of personnel, fundraising, marketing, public relations and such. Existing vice-chancellors would be encouraged to go on a shortened version of such a high profile, carefully organised programme. The University of Surrey has such a course in embryo and Sheffield has a staff training capability.

There should be established a staff college to train new, and retrain existing, administrators up to the top level.[4] It would inculcate a thorough training, including techniques for the development of external sources of income and the reduction of internal waste. The idea behind it would be a process of re-acculturation to diminish universities' self-concept as a branch of the civil service, and to import a technical knowledge base without which all exhortation to initiative, enterprise and independence is bound to fail, because leadership needs the skill as well as the will.

INTERNAL AGENTS AND AGENCIES

Within the structure of the university one would also look for reform: again the emphasis will be on the import of new skills and the creation of new internal agencies to direct them. We therefore recommend:

(1) Every university must have a properly staffed alumni office. The prime function will be fundraising, but this cannot be done crudely. Parties, dinners, magazines and other functions for alumni will be arranged as part of the permanent appeals process: esoteric but worthwhile departments will be particular targets of support in order to preserve them. Focus will be on maintaining up-to-date lists of where graduates are, and the more progressive universities such as Edinburgh have adopted this approach.[5]

---

[4] K. Baker, "Higher Education: The Next 25 Years", University of Lancaster, 1987. Reprinted in *Policy Studies*, 1989, No. 4, pp.4-10. Since 1988 Sheffield University has had a Universities Staff Development and Training Unit offering training across Britain.

[5] The Campaign for Oxford, organised by Henry Drucker, used the 'solicitation procedure' first developed by Stamford University and refined at Princton. £200m has been raised in less than four years, including 25 contributions of £1m or more, the largest being £10m from the Hong Kong magnet Sir Run Run Shaw, to found the Institute of Modern Chinese Studies. Drucker is evangelical about the campaign: "What we are doing is offering people the opportunity to participate in the growth and development of one of the most valuable institutions in the country. There is something very special about the pursuit of truth, knowledge and learning. People somehow respond to this magic. They are lit up by the notion that they can help humanity progress by increasing the sum of human knowledge".

(2) Each university will have a marketing department, charged with the task of attracting candidates and producing agreeable literature, with some focus on the overseas markets. Marketing will also promote the facilities and services of the campus to business and other potential clients, and run an effective public relations campaign both in the local and national media, publicising for example interesting research results. In particular it will liaise with local industry. Its aim must be to increase the participation of overseas students, with particular reference to Europe and America, who are under-represented on British campuses. One attractive idea would be to encourage American students to read one year at a British university by arranging the appropriate credit transfers.

Senior administrators in universities would also sometimes be chosen from other areas, especially business, to provide a broader array of talents and executive experience.[6] Focus would be on the reduction of work in non-academic areas such as over-staffed administrations, and existing administrators would be encouraged to have some re-training, particularly through the medium of the staff college we have outlined. Vacation administration would become an important job in liaison with the marketing department, and every university would have a vacation strategy for the use of its facilities, thus also creating an extra source of income for its under-paid academic staff. It goes without saying that to obtain top expertise from outside each university must pay for it: here in the short term the government could help, as universities seek to change their internal culture.

The administrative structures of universities must be streamlined: their organizational clumsiness makes for endless delay and inflexibility. The theory – that power derives from staff via their committees and senates – does not conform to practice, and it is important to break the oligarchy because of the inertia created by the vested interests of the oligarchs, though this is also a consequence of attempting academic democracy, an ideal which must not be lost; however, in practice such democracy is often an excuse for inertia and the evasion of decision and action.

---

[6] See R. Middlehurst, "Management and Leadership Development in Universities: What's Happening and Where Are We Going?", in H. Eggins (editor), *Restructuring Higher Education*, 1987, pp.137-150.

Each department must also be subject to the occasional efficiency audit by the university. Are secretarial staff fully occupied throughout the year, and properly paid? Are PhD students well supervised? What is the department's programme for generating external income? Are workloads in the department disproportional, with some of its members having developed a talent to elude? If the vice-chancellor is to exert executive control he must have a clear picture of all activities, and not entrust everything to the delegated authority of the professor.

ACADEMIC PERSONNEL

There should be substantial changes in the incentive and career structure open to the British university academic, for currently an outside observer would see little logic in the way academics are rewarded. The structure really represents an attempt to transfer the Oxbridge conception of cloistered livelihood to a mass profession, to repeat on a large scale the prerequisites of an élite order, but today that attempt seems increasingly anachronistic: lecturers, and equally important those who want to be, continue to suffer for this.

The central problems are:

(1) Entry. The academic profession is inert in non-vocational areas since there are few jobs, and the best the aspirant can hope for is the occasional one-year, or if he or she is lucky, three-year contract, so the profession has an age problem: the average age of university lecturers is 45. In 1980/81 24% were under 35: in 87/88 the figure was 15%. The average reduction in staff 1983/84 - 1988/89 was 2.8%. Between now and the year 2000 30% of the profession will retire.

(2) Pay. The lecturer's scale ranges from £12,000 to £24,000: people progress up it incrementally reaching the top by middle age, so that a 34 year old nuclear physicist is thus paid the same salary as a prison warder. Increments occur almost irrespective of performance: apparently nothing extra is given to those who are

producing work of distinction, have higher teaching loads and so on. The entire profession is thus infused with a lethargy.[7]

(3) Rank. Most academics are certain to stay at the rank of lecturer, probably promoted to senior lecturer when nearing retirement. Financial problems have made promotion increasingly rare, so we have now the position where, whatever the talent and effort, reward is arbitrary if it comes at all. No one would dream of preserving army officers at the rank of lieutenant, on the grounds that this would cause idleness and incompetence, as such practices did in the Victorian army, and the vices of many academics are directly attributable to this perceived hierarchical blockage.

(4) Tasks. All academics are expected to achieve equally at teaching, administration and research. This is a nonsense: these are separate competences with limited relationship to each other.

The structure of the profession is in need of fundamental reform to reward the able and motivate the more languid, but this is better done by positive

---

[7] Comparative median and mid-career salaries are:
Dentists £40,000; General Practitioners £50,000; Senior Civil Servants £35,000; Solicitors (private practice) £60,000; University Lecturers £23,000.

THE AGEING PROFESSION

	Wholly university-funded teaching and research staff	Percent aged 35 or under	Percent aged 36-54	Percent aged 55 or over	Average age
		%	%	%	%
1980/81	33,329	23.8	62.1	14.1	39.2
1981/82	32,755	21.1	64.0	14.9	40.9
1982/83	30,663	18.1	68.3	13.6	41.6
1983/84	30,120	17.4	69.2	13.4	42.3
1984/85	29,626	17.4	69.6	13.0	43.3
1985/86	29,990	17.0	69.2	13.8	43.7
1986/87	30,005	16.2	69.0	14.8	44.1
1987/88	29,856	15.3	69.1	15.6	44.6

Robert Jackson argued that from 1970 to 1979 lecturers pay in 1970 prices fell 8% but rose 15% from 1979 to 1989. The real increase over 20 years is in fact 6%, whilst average earnings rose 49%.

incentives rather than negative sanctions, since the popularly perceived languor of the profession is attributable to the lack of any close relationship between input and reward.[8]

Then there is the question of tenure, a practice that the government finds decadent and incomprehensible. Tenure should be modified rather than abolished in the fashion of the 1988 *Education Act*.[9] It might conform to the American model, where it is given as a reward not a right, often after a period of perhaps eight years of teaching, and this period could be longer here so that people were awarded it in their late thirties.[10]

Its complete abolition would be nefarious, since such a projected move is based on a false analogy between business and academe. A businessman usually becomes more valuable with age as he builds up a bank of experience, but mature teaching skill is not valued so that the temptation to replace a lecturer with someone half his age is strong; while research may decline with age, and publications are the key to the success of any department. Unlike the businessman, the academic does not have the assurance of an external market for his skills should he resign. And the abolition of tenure may lead to purges, often on internal political grounds, so dutiful academics could find themselves unemployed and unemployable in their forties and fifties (though there is some protection for academic freedom due to Jenkins' intervention in the debate on the 1988 Act).[11] No other profession would face such conditions since in other areas there is some form of tenure, the civil service for example, and even in business, people can only be made redundant with good reason.[12] Besides, the academic earns only half what these other groups generally receive and commits himself to seven years' higher education before his earnings begin: tenure is a way of balancing this inequality.[13]

---

[8] To remedy the situation, the UFC has inaugurated performance related incremental salary increases.
[9] *Education Reform Act*, London, HMSO, 1988.
[10] A.A. Alchian, "Private Property and the Relative Cost of Tenure", in P.D. Bradley, (editor), *The Public Stake in Union Power*, University of Virginia Press, 1959, p.370.
[11] House of Lords debate on 1988 Education Act, reported in *Times Higher Educational Supplement*, 27 May, 1988.
[12] See A. Morris, "Flexibility and the Tenured Academic", *Higher Education Review*, 1974, pp.3-25.
[13] J.E. Schuitz, "Academic Employment as Day Labour: The Dual Labour Market in Higher Education", *Journal of Higher Education*, 1982, pp.514-31.

In fact the government have abolished tenure for all promotions and all new appointments: thus the most able and mobile are penalised, precisely the opposite effect to what a thoughtful reward system would enact.[14]

Next, we believe there is, possibly, a case for suggesting that some academics should elect to specialise in teaching and administration.

Currently the fiction that all can do all tasks equally well – note again the sham egalitarianism – leads to inefficiency and distortion. It is wrong that professors, who obtained that rank through research skill, should have to invest most of their time in administration – a kind of misdirection of resources that marks the entire system. The universities as currently operated yield a major hostage to their critics. It is the perception that too many, though thankfully not a majority, of lecturers simply do their lectures and some administration *and nothing else*, and as long as this abuse remains unreformed, universities will continue to be the target of every vulgarian lounge bar critic who finds a crutch for his own enfeebled loathing of intellectual talent in wagging his finger at the universities' ostensible amateurism. What we propose may not be a just solution to the 'part-time' problem. But something radical must be done.

Then there is the related matter of the evaluation of academic performance. The authors welcome it, but with the proviso that there be qualitative as well as quantitative measures of academic performance, always with right of appeal.[15] Measures must be taken to permit and defend the long-term, late yield research project, for example a historical biography.

WHAT OF INCENTIVES AND REWARDS?

Academic pay has not, contrary to the belief of many academics, actually fallen in real terms since 1979. In April 1990 salaries were the same in real value relative to the retail price index as they were in 1979, but in this period they had also fallen 14% relative to public sector salaries; they had dropped 25% in relation to average earnings and 50% relative to average non-manual earnings.[16] The consequences of this are obvious, and in 1988 20% of all new lecturers under the age of 30 left the profession; the evolution of the European market can only increase this leakage. There has

---

[14] *Education Reform Act, Ibid.,* pp.194-99.
[15] See below, chapter 5, pp.165-73.
[16] AUT, "Academic Pay: An International Perspective", *AUT Bulletin*, February, 1991.

been no increase in resources for universities (70% of their costs are salary) while demand has risen, and the government is now proposing to double demand while leaving resources the same.[17]

Therefore academics must be paid substantially more, and the average increase might be around 25% to compensate for historical relative erosion.[18] Moreover, there should be sharper geographic and institutional differences in pay rates, and universities should have freedom to pay above the odds for a top performer.[19] Currently there is conflict between DES determined pay scales and free collective bargaining, but universities must be at liberty to decide their own rates of pay. Clearly the government would be reluctant to fund this: we believe however that, by bringing into play the alternative sources of funding we have described, such a rise will eventually be possible.

An increase would be beneficial in many ways. It would invigorate morale after many years' attrition, it would attract better candidates to academic posts. There seems an extraordinary view current that academics are immune from the material promptings of their fellow men, yet a professional interest in literature or a lively historical mind is often accompanied by a more general cultural awareness and a wish to gratify it, indeed, it would be odd if this were not so. Thus many of the most able enter commerce, finding the vow of poverty intolerable, and this represents a wasteful use of resources, exchanging an area of distinguished performance for one where they perhaps exhibit no special talent. Moreover a salary increase would have important symbolic effects, demonstrating that the Conservative Party had tired of its philistine caricature and was determined to re-awaken academic life through the new medium of diversified funding, while the increase would also encourage academics to accept other less palatable aspects of our programme since the government had given tangible earnest of its good faith.

However, long-term the DES should look into accelerated pay scales for high performers, and higher rates of pay for vocational areas. The absence of both is a prop to mediocrity, and our premise is that the university system

---

[17] The evidence for this is contained in the table in chapter 3, p.80.
[18] AUT, *op cit*.
[19] Even when flexibility is allowed, as in the case of performance pay since 1987, some universities choose not to use it. This applies in Cambridge, where every Professor is paid the sum of £27,800, when the 'scale' is from £23,000 to £34,260.

could become excellent if such artificial structures were removed. The reply is often that such reforms would stimulate envy, would be – the liberals' favourite phrase – divisive. A profession where this can become an issue deserves to be left to its inbred despondency and is not worthy of greater rewards. Too many academics have an amateur's compensation for an amateur task. This must go if they are to be paid justly.[20]

Professional rewards do not have to be monetary. Symbolic measures can be warmly valued and they cost less, their creation merely demands imagination. One discovery the Americans have made is that titles cost nothing, and we advocate the introduction of the titles 'assistant professor' and 'associate professor' and for more promotions between these ranks: no specific salary scale would attach to them, the measures would be costless and, though they would inflate the currency of rank, more in academic life would feel that their skills had been recognised.[21] Moreover, the new titles are actually used throughout much of the rest of the world.

There is the additional problem of entry blockage to the academic profession, a feature that has endured throughout the life of this government. As has been said, the problem posed by recruiting most academics from one generation is that it dooms us to repeating the cycle when they retire at the end of this century. No one however gifted has much of a chance in the intervening space, deferring to men and women of limited ability in the favoured generation. This the government must try to avoid, for it is inconceivable that any other area of national life would persist for a decade with negligible recruitment, the situation leads to the stagnation of broad areas of scholarship and the malaise of talented people as they adjust to careers not of their choosing.

Lastly, academic freedom. This we regard as no small matter and if tenure is further modified there should be stronger legislation guaranteeing liberties under law. The government might reflect that some university departments constitute a liberal totalitarianism, that the politically conservative might suffer if academic freedom had no official status, for academics cannot always be trusted with observing intellectual tolerance, and such is their emotional commitment that as well as vigorous defenders they can be able persecutors. Not least, advances often come from

---

[20] A.J. Culyer, "A Maximising View of Universities", *Scottish Journal of Political Economy*, pp.349-68.
[21] London Business School has, in fact, introduced all of the American nomenclatures.

challenging orthodoxy, yet those in power may owe their position to perpetuating that orthodoxy so that fresh thinking is perceived as a threat: how easy then to extinguish the careers of its advocates and light upon some pseudo-intellectual justification.

COURSE CONTENT

The universities' current inflexibility can be seen as impoverishing the quality of undergraduate intellectual life. There must be more opportunity to pursue several subject areas in a degree course, interdisciplinary combinations, minor options and so forth, though it would be absurd to take this democratic ideal to the American extreme, where diversity is such that often students seem to develop no meaningful core in the pursuit of a bizarre multi-subject, multi-cultural goulash, so that the medium is weakened as a source of intellectual training. Still it seems wrong that undergraduates are so often restricted to a three or four year diet of one subject; but, right or wrong, the 'consumer' (including industry and commerce as legitimate shareholders) should have some choice in the matter and not allow inter-departmental resentments to prevent it. Courses of cultural content might be encouraged for scientists and engineers, given the cultural illiteracy of some graduates who subsequently assume influential positions in society. Arts men and women emerge similarly narrowed by their learning and the existence of two cultural nations has long been the subject of exhortation, not least by the late C.P. Snow, but still in the late twentieth century our indolence prevents action. It is a scandal that unnecessarily polarises students.

Then there is the highly contentious issue of what is taught, of subject content. The humanities and social sciences are alike menaced by the pressure of relevance and contemporanity, and the problem with a consumerist approach to university education is that it will magnify these pressures: the art, not of Samuel Johnson but of Bruce Springsteen, is what English literature students may want to study. The worst kind of academics actively pander to this sort of reasoning, such as that fabled American professor who claimed that the difference between Shakespeare and Mickey Mouse was the difference between a hoagy and a pizza, though the British campus is still far from the fantasy place evoked by Bloom in *The*

Closing of the American Mind, and no British campus yet has, like Yale, a Gay Studies Centre, though Sussex now has an M.A. in gay studies.[22] But the graduates of the pop epoch will become the dominant force on campuses, and we may legitimately fear how far commitment to teach what Gertrude Himmelfarb described as the "the best that there is" will be eroded.[23] *If universities cease to transmit high culture there is absolutely no point in their public funding.* Subjects can also be vulnerable to dogmatists who seek to place them within a rigid ideological framework. Then again there is the growth of bogus subjects such as Peace Studies at Bradford or women's studies: these are not academic since they are founded on an ideology not a discipline, and universities should be free to teach them but government should be under no obligation to fund them.

How then to defend 'the best there is' from the *trahaison des clerks*? One day perhaps there may even be a case for each discipline having its own advisory body on content and standards, not acting as an obtrusive intellectual policeman nor conserving a mummified corpse, but making a critique public if the integrity of disciplines are consistently violated. There is a fine balance between academic freedom and academic degeneracy. Responsible academic policy cannot therefore advocate an entirely consumerist approach since this would spurn the didactic element integral to a good education, the pursuit of that higher learning which will mentally better the student whether or not he or she entirely recognises this, and the understanding that mature choices cannot be made on the basis of ignorance. That is why some disciplines will need special protection under a voucher system, and why 'academic freedom' must not be camouflage for the corruption of standards.

Finally, some element of student assessment of academics should be built into degree schemes: their main merit would be as a guide to teachers themselves, for their status as a mode of evaluating academics is somewhat dubious and every course should be assessed. But without such an instrument there really is no incentive, over and above conscience and professional élan, for an academic to develop as an effective teacher, to update lectures and so on. Systems ought to reinforce the will to be good. That said, clearly teaching ability is not as important as it is in schools since students are self-motivated and can acquire information independently.

---

[22] A. Bloom, *The Closing of the American Mind*, London, 1988.
[23] G. Himmelfarb, *New History and the Old*, Boston, 1987, p.20.

However it is important that they should feel fondness for the subject, and that is something a dud lecturer can extinguish.

COURSE FLEXIBILITY

The universities are often accused of inflexibility. The charge is not altogether a fair one, since cash constraints help to make the ideal of responsiveness a rather difficult one. But with greater variety of funding, universities could do much: for example, many more mature students could be accommodated, and universities could also improve their distance learning programmes rather than preserving this as the exclusive domain of the Open University: that restricts choice and applies one particular institutional and ideological stamp. The possibility ought also to exist in most degree schemes of doing them part-time.

Four year degree schemes with a 'year out' in Europe ought to become increasingly popular, while there could be more passage between universities: the first two years of a four year course for example could be spent in a different part of the country. In certain circumstances eight term, two year degrees may even make sense: but they must never become the norm. Four term years are another idea that is worth considering: they would increase flexibility and enable universities to utilise fully campus facilities and expand somewhat.[24]

LOCAL STUDENTS

Nevertheless, if the state seeks to raise significantly student numbers, it will almost certainly have to find ways of lowering the high cost to the tax-payer of a university degree. It can, of course, attempt to push universities further down the road to efficiency, but it can also seek to recoup costs from the students by giving them a lower level of service or by making them or their subsequent employers pay more towards their education.

A changed culture, with students paying for their degrees via future taxation, might also tempt more to go to the local university. Government must ask why nearly all student participation in university education is of the 'boarding school' variety, for Britain is *unique* in going for a system

---

[24] N.F.B. Allington, "Funding Arrangements for Universities and Students in the European Community." *European Access*, 1991, pp.10-13.

that is accommodation-oriented, its costs to the Exchequer are high, and if student numbers are raised they should be drawn from the local region.[25] Of course this is not ideal, and most would still like, and deserve, to live away from home.

There is also some scope for criticism of the Universities Central Council for Admissions (UCCA). Universities in America do not 'rig' the market in this way, nor do they suffer from the absence of a bureaucratic central admissions system, for UCCA may be seen as representing an artificial restriction on freedom of choice that hampers competition between universities and leads to the inequity of universities rejecting students if they do not put them high on their lists. However it does afford greater certainty of a student enrolling by thus limiting choice. Complete freedom may be chaotic so that reformers should advocate UCCA's modification not its abolition.

NATIONAL POLICIES:

PLANNING

The universities are frustrated in their ability to deal with their crisis by factors beyond their control, not of their making but of state manufacture, and with which no independent enterprise would ever have to deal.

Nowhere is this truer than in the planning process. Every organisation must plan, in order to deploy and invest existing resources most effectively and prepare for tomorrow's likely challenges, but a university cannot plan: it is subject to a government financial commitment that does not extend much beyond the next year. In fact, government has explicitly rejected the Croham Report's advocacy of triennial funding.[26] No enterprise faces this deadening hand, it can analyse existing trends and resources and assess likely cash flows over the next years.

Therefore government must, if it is honest in its desire to make universities more efficient, inform them as to the minimum amounts they are likely to receive over the next five years (sums which may be improved if it feels in a mood of largesse). While long-term financial commitments are rather

---

[25] K. Baker, "Higher Education – 25 Years On", *Policy Studies*, 1989, pp.4-23.
[26] *Review of the University Grants Committee*, The Croham Report, London, HMSO, Cmnd. 81, 1987.

alien to the political process, to discount them is to consign universities to a perpetual cycle of inefficiency.

TARGETS

Universities must continue to be encouraged to seek external support, but a concomitant of this is that they be given the relevant marketing and other forms of expertise and trained personnel. Funding aspirations would be smaller for liberal arts campuses, higher for technological universities. Failure to achieve targets would neither mean cuts nor closures; however the vice-chancellor and senior staffs might be held accountable and those who suffered would be at the top of the system, not the footsoldiers, the lumpen proletariat of lecturers, who up till now have borne the consequences of managerial incompetence.

CONTRACTS

Contracts are irrelevant if it is wished to achieve some sort of market system in higher education. There is no real competitive bidding from universities and the CVCP. The object of contracts is to educate more students at the same or lower global cost, which might be acceptable in social science and the arts. But the science and engineering infrastructure places a limit on numbers there, so that expansion becomes lop-sided. So there are good grounds for opposing a contract system: though theoretically it encourages competition, in practice this is not possible.

Standards in higher education must be jealousy guarded. Movement to a more commercially pressurised system will inevitably mean that they are compromised: to pretend otherwise is merely to deceive ourselves.

MASSIFICATION

The government's proposals for the future of universities cannot be considered without reference to the most important of them all, that is, massification, the influx of cohorts of new students into universities over the ensuing years. Already many universities are planning increases of 20-30% in the immediate future. This projected increase in the proportion of the relevant age group going to university will have an effect on all the proposals the government have raised. Universities will have to teach far more students, and at the expense of basic research.

Should one therefore condone such a policy that both parties, using different mechanisms, endorse, namely this 'massified' system of higher education? Will more mean worse? Would the extra students – an eventual doubling of numbers – tangibly benefit from the rarefied atmosphere of higher education?

What is certainly clear is that many of the new entrants would need higher education that was different in kind, if not in quality. Their inclination or ability to sustain the three year traditional degree in one exclusive subject area is doubtful, they would want a more vocationally relevant input, breadth rather than depth, and flexibility – to enter at a later age, or to complete their degree between blocks of work experience. So the style of degree for them would contain elements of languages and managerial training, as well as exposure to several areas of cultural study. Or they might for example do the traditional course for two years and receive a pass degree. But the customary degree would leave them alienated.

Nor should we ignore the crisis of expectations which more liberal entry may lead to, as graduates fail to gain the kind of jobs which were their usual preserve. Many countries, for example Spain and Egypt, have negative experience of this.[27] And there is the issue of cost. A massified system could not, as the government apparently believes, be achieved under current levels of funding. Such a mandate ignores for example the higher fixed and structural costs massification implies – lecture theatres, halls of residence and such.

In the opinion of these authors, albeit perhaps a minority one, many of the new entrants should be diverted towards an expanded polytechnic system, though future expansion should also occur at certain universities whose research profile has never been high. Universities may lack the will or the flexibility to cope, but more importantly, it is not part of their mission or ethos: training, which is what a massified system essentially implies, is better done by other agencies. Much of the university system should remain relatively small: otherwise standards – the distinctive feature of UK universities – will disappear.

---

[27] OECD, *Changing Patterns of Finance in Higher Education, Country Study Spain*, 1989.

RESEARCH COUNCILS

The Research Councils occupy a key strategic role, especially in scientific and social research. But they should be obligated to supply a full critique as to why an application for funding has been rejected, as this would give researchers immeasurably useful guidance and critical external feedback. They must act speedily so that researchers can turn to alternative sources of funding if rejected; re-submission should also be allowed. Academic personnel on the councils should change regularly so that no individual school of thought or professional network begins to gain a monopoly of ideas, and, during their period of service, some of such personnel might be full time so that the other needs we advocate can be satisfied. Moreover, the Research Councils themselves should seek some element of private support: given their key role in research that is beneficial to the larger society this should be possible.[28] Currently the government has directed cash away from universities to enrich the research councils, no bad thing provided adequate safeguards are maintained, and they might also be buttressed with money from our graduate levy. In particular, they should never have to reject alpha rated projects.

BROKERAGE

Next, we urge the build up of the Council for Higher Education and Industry (CHEI) and the British Technology Group (BTG) as national brokerage organizations to mediate more fully between universities and industry.[29] Their task would be to market university research more effectively to the relevant businesses and communicate from business to the appropriate university departments; to further build up computerised information banks, and publish bulletins on current university research targeted at particular industrial sectors. These organisations would be continued in conjunction with the private sector.

---

[28] Our survey of the research councils (not included in this study) indicated some movement in this direction.
[29] In our industrial survey, a number of firms berated the lack of an agency to link university and industry on the research and teaching front at a national level, although the Council for Industry and Higher Education has made some impact in this area. The Link scheme has been criticised as too long winded in assembling bids, but new procedures, changes in property rights and the involvement of new companies may change this.

CAPITAL EQUIPMENT

There is also need for much new capital expenditure on buildings and equipment. The graduate levy (see chapter ten) would help here: as would taxation incentives for companies to donate used, but still useful, equipment.

PUBLIC RELATIONS

A well funded public relations organisation could be founded to promote the collective image of the universities. They must articulate themselves to their alternate founders, the tax-payers, who have little understanding of what they do, perceive no benefit for themselves, and resent funding the more successful progeny of the middle class. So universities must become popular though not populist. Their inventions must be paraded in the press, their social returns emphasised and their contribution to the welfare and the culture of society trumpeted. Currently they are seen as remote, populated by the precious and the precocious, with a faint odour of jejune nihilism and the memories of worse. Universities carry negative clutter, but nothing which effective public relations cannot dispel. Will professors ever become popular heroes? If they themselves did not scorn the idea, they could.

A ROYAL COMMISSION

Finally we advocate the creation of a Royal Commission to investigate the state and future of Britain's universities. Protracted crisis has made such a commission necessary: moreover, the many ideas on the improvement both of the quality and the efficiency of the system need more thorough investigation, and debate so far has been a declamatory recitative of slogan and half truth from static positions, without interchange, without humility. We admit that many of our ideas are tentative and need rigorous scrutiny and a commission would be the right forum for doing this; the wisdom, the lucid vision which Robbins brought to his report must be the qualities too of his inheritors.[30] It would clear the air. It would allow universities, and government, a full and formal expression of their case. *It would signify that government took universities seriously, and recognised that all was not well.*

---

[30] *Higher Education*, (Robbins Report), *Ibid*.

We believe government strategy for the universities, which has been the negative one of incremental cost-cutting, should become more thoughtful and also more proactive. The aim will be efficiency, but more than that: to leave the objective there is to accept a nagging philistinism that will leave the administration charmless in the pages of history. So the aim is efficiency plus. Plus a sense of mission, a desire to re-awaken intellectual morale and the many somnolent academic disciplines in Britain today: to make universities feel they are worthwhile, to give them a sense not of satisfaction but of hope, and the awareness that industry, achievement, and style, will be equitably rewarded.

CHAPTER FIVE

THE MEN IN WHITE SUITS: UNIVERSITY RESEARCH

"The United Kingdom's declining scientific influence is especially visible in medicine and the physical sciences, including physics, chemistry and earth sciences".
The Institute for Scientific Information,
Science Watch, 26 May, 1991.

"R and D expenditure (is) now a main determinant of economic growth... these downward trends (of R and D expenditure as a fraction of national wealth) must be reversed.... government will have to fund much of the seed-corn exploration".
Michael Heseltine,
The Challenge of Europe, London, 1990.

"Why shouldn't the UK free-load? What would happen if a major developed country decided to give up its research effort altogether? The best known example, of course, is post-war Japan which seems not to have developed a major fundamental research programme until after it had become a very wealthy country. Research seems to be the result, not the cause of wealth in Japan. Korea is an even more remarkable example of a country achieving major economic advancement without a research effort of its own to exploit. The Pacific rim countries provide an interesting challenge to the view that a fundamental research effort is a necessary prerequisite for economic success".
Sir Christopher Ball,
"The Problem of Research", *Higher Education Quarterly*, 3, 1989, p.207.

"Knowledge is capable of being its own end. Such is the constitution of the human mind, that any kind of knowledge if it be really such, is its own reward".

And:

"The philosophy of Utility, you will say, Gentlemen, has at least done its work; and I grant it, – it aimed low, but it has fulfilled its aim".
J.H. Newman,
The Idea of a University, New York, 1959.

INTRODUCTION

The chapter begins by posing a crucial question – Why is research important? – and answers by demonstrating the philosophical and utilitarian benefits to be derived from research in the universities. It stresses the need for the man in the street to be made fully aware of these achievements and their impact on his life and the society in which he lives. A further section on the utility of research stresses its unpredictability and therefore the need to support basic or 'blue sky' research, since its ramifications are never apparent at the time, but have proved to be highly significant at a future date on many occasions.[1] The fall in Britain's contribution to basic research is well demonstrated by the fall in citations in leading scientific journals and the decline in the number of patents registered in the U.S.A.

Part two examines the reduction in research funding when universities' costs are rising faster than inflation for a number of reasons. Consequently a recent UFC report finds that twelve universities are expected to experience serious financial difficulties up to 1993 and probably beyond: every 1% of unfunded pay increase, for example, will raise the global deficit by £51m. Only increased income from research contracts, services provided for industry and more full-cost students can offer any amelioration in the position. Staff numbers have fallen, worsening staff-student ratios, contract workers as a proportion of total staff numbers have risen: researchers financed by the universities have fallen marginally, but those financed externally have risen a massive 71% between 1976 and 1985. Because of the deterioration in pay, retaining and recruiting staff has become, and will continue to be, difficult. Research income per capita had reached £16,500 in 1989 demonstrating the vigorous efforts to raise income.

Given the decline in government funding, the next section attempts to assess the willingness of industry to shoulder some of the burden of research funding. This is the expectation of the government and whilst there are some conspicuous examples of individual genorosity, mass giving on a scale necessary to sustain and then expand existing activities appears unlikely. This is borne out by the findings of the House of Lords Select

---

[1] Cf. Evidence submitted to the House of Lords Select Committee on Science and Technology, *Ibid.*, 1986.

Committee on Science and Technology, *Civil Research and Development*. Industry spends far more on in-house research than it does on commissioning research from the universities. Overseas funding of industrial research and development by multinationals favours industry rather then the universities. ABRC advocated as long ago as 1983 that industry/university collaboration must be increased and several reports have made precisely the same point and yet significant progress has still to be made.

Part three considers current policy proposals: contracts, the separation of teaching and research, bidding, a three tier university system, polytechnics' admission to university ranks, the role of the research councils and the 1991 White Paper. The emphasis in recent pronouncements has been on market forces and accountability and the inevitable division of institutions into mainly research or mainly teaching. The consequences of such a change are explored in depth and the DES's predeliction for a system of contracts to enforce the division: central to contracts are performance indicators, direction and control. The conflict between the state's *dirigiste* instinct and theoretical belief in the free market becomes obvious.

Next, research councils receive attention – specifically, creating a single council; the preference of SERC for supporting large science; the benefits from funding scientists rather than science; the switch of funds from the UFC to the research councils so that they become responsible for overhead costs, although the size of the transfer is subject to dispute given the underestimate of overhead costs; co-operation between research council institutes and the universities and, finally, the distribution of research grants.

Taking contracts as a reference point, part four examines assessment following the more selective allocation of funds for the universities post 1981. The 1986 and 1989 selectivity exercises are analysed and their merits and demerits considered. Following this, the 1991 White Paper and its implications for the funding of research in the universities and polytechnics, *qua* universities, comes under scrutiny. Selectivity and the establishment of judgemental criteria for the distribution of research funds by the combined funding council for higher education are confirmed, with universities determining their own research priorities.

The chapter concludes by extrapolating from the present position of underfunding to discover what the implications might be in the absence of any new funding arrangements. Of special concern here is industrial support that favours applied research, and the so-called brain drain. The implication is that the present government seems to forget that excellence in research is a tradition and not a product. Taking on board the appraisal of Britain's research base by Save British Science, the AUT's seven point action plan – a science strategy for the 1990's – shows what most urgently needs to be done. In a postscript, the allocation of research funds is laid bare.

PART ONE: THE REDUCTION IN RESEARCH FUNDING

WHY IS RESEARCH IMPORTANT?

It is perhaps worth asking the simplest and most basic of questions: why is university research important? The retort is obvious – important for what? – and the answer must be given at several levels.

The temptation is first to say that universities are useful in an instrumentalist way, for that answer will most impress our funders, the British public. But we are convinced that such a utilitarian answer is not the central core of the justification for universities and their research, though it is a very important one. The pursuit of knowledge is valuable for its own sake, since the wish to discover and to interpret is as much a part of human civilisation as the wish to sing or to write poetry: they raise us above the dross of the trivial and everyday; they address the larger questions of our being: they enoble us, raising us beyond coarse appetite and instincts for survival. Sparta, a society bereft of all civilised fripperies, defeated its Athenian neighbour, but what do we remember of the Spartans – that they ate, procreated and quarrelled? What legacy did they hand down? And what indeed would a Britain where universities have atrophied, really give to the future? That they have stagnated in the past is a matter of historical record, as Gibbon testified;[2] but there existed in those days an alternative intellectual culture, a curious admixture of scholarly clergy, noble patrons, educated gentlemen and such, out of whom early science, literature and the arts first flourished.

---

[2] Edward Gibbon, *Memoirs of My Life*, edited by G.A. Bonnard, Nelson, 1966.

Universities are pools of intellectual concentration, where all the matters of humanity are considered reflectively and investigated methodically; the possession of such islands of stillness is to be valued amidst the roar and energy, the preoccupation with the immediate, of commercial civilization. In an era of the instant image and the transient pleasure, universities are one of the few instruments we have for the creation of enduring worth.

Yet universities can also make a very useful contribution. Such utility will help us solve current problems, and universities are the institutions most suited to examine the 'big' questions, since industry with its annual reports and shareholders must inevitably be short-term and narrow in its focus. Thus, the environment, the 'greenhouse' effect and climatic changes, cleaner fuel and substitute fuels and the like; transportation problems (the geographers); change in Eastern Europe, Russia and China; medical matters, Aids, the problems of ageing and senility, new drugs and machines for dealing with illness, cancer, heart disease and the like, in fact, in all of the current litany of public concern, universities are doing important work and the list is almost endless. Even social science, popularly derided on the right, could potentially offer insight through its methods of investigating social phenomena, enriching our understanding of the bonds that make us a society, helping us towards better control of the manifold social threats, drugs, family breakdown and the like. This is the kind of area in which, as a glance at any prospectus will show, universities are doing vital work. To dismiss them as frivolous is mere ignorance. We never know when we might owe our well being or our life to their industry. And of the future agenda, whatever it might be, we can be confident that universities will contribute a great deal to its exploitation and evolution. Indeed over the last twenty years scientific research in Britain has been responsible for twice as many radical breakthroughs as research in the US: the flaw here though is that the US is six times more successful in exploiting such developments and this issue needs to be addressed. Isis Innovation Ltd., established by Oxford University to exploit its research and other such examples, shows the way forward.

But universities are an easy target of satire and scepticism. Nor should academics place too much hope in the benevolence of the Labour Party, whose sense of academic worth was illuminated by a recent House of Lords debate in which a Labour peer advocated using university campuses as housing for the homeless during vacations. Certainly Labour would be committed to more students, but the party demonstrates its own form of anti-intellectualism, a tendency to view educational institutions as vehicles for social engineering. What of their commitment to research? To academic salaries? All public policy is in the end related to the prejudices of the man in the street. Universities are a mystery to him. He really cannot see the point of people studying history or English literature, and any explanation merely makes him sceptical.

Every university achievement, discovery and major insight should therefore be loudly trumpeted. In the aggressive, boorish atmosphere of Britain in this decade, universities must learn to brag; painted courtesans, they should join the audacious throng; not to speak loudly about achievements is to have them ignored.

THE UTILITY OF UNIVERSITY RESEARCH

The University Grants Committee's (UGC) strategic advice quoted the Committee of Vice Chancellors and Principals' (CVCP) 1980 report, *Research in the Universities* and noted that:

> "Many mathematical techniques which seemed esoteric and academic at the time have later proved to be of crucial value for solving problems in engineering. Fundamental studies in solid state physics in universities pointed the way to the development of the whole of the micro-electronics industry which is expanding so rapidly today. The discovery of the genetic code in a Medical Research Council unit in Cambridge University has opened up the possibility of a major new industry concerned with biotechnology. The whole organic chemicals industry, including the synthesis of dyes, drugs and pharmaceuticals, pesticides and many other chemical preparations we now take for granted, has its roots in fundamental studies by organic chemists, mainly in universities, of the structures of the molecules of natural materials and of methods of synthesizing them. The fundamental work on polymerisation and the properties of macro-molecules by Staudinger which eventually led to the polymer industry we have today was started in a university laboratory. The powerful physical analytical techniques such as x-ray crystallography, spectroscopy, mass spectrometry and nuclear magnetic resonance which are now indispensable tools in most large industrial research and development laboratories, were all developed from academic and basic research programmes, mainly in universities; and the universities of the United Kingdom have played a very prominent role in all these developments".[3]

---

[3] University Grants Committee, *A Strategy for Higher Education in the 1990's*, 1984, quoting the Committee of Vice Chancellors and Principals, *Research in the Universities*, 1980.

The Advisory Board to the Research Councils (ABRC) has stressed a very significant aspect of research: its unpredictability.[4]

Chadwick's discovery of the neutron, the discovery and subsequent analytical work on penicillin, the synthesis of physical and biological techniques that led to molecular biology – are but a few of the 'accidental' discoveries. They add that it is vital that support be available for such work even though it may be impossible to describe it in the form properly required by the funding body. And, over the past three decades, over 20,000 public sector inventions have been proffered to the British Technology Group and those organisations that preceded it.[5]

The UGC cogently justified basic research thus:

> "It is a necessary condition for the emergence and exploitation of the new technologies that will be of such importance to the nation's future prosperity. Second, the cost of basic research is small compared with the cost of applied research and development. Third, because basic research takes time to work through to industrial applications, the damage caused by under-investment will not show itself at once, but eventually it will reduce the nation's ability to remain at the forefront of technical innovation. It will also delay the solution of complex problems which depend on the interpretation and integration of the findings of fundamental research in several different disciplines. Finally, the level of research activity determines whether this country retains effective membership of the international community".[6]

They summarised the contribution of universities to basic research thus: "In basic research, we have shown that the universities play the leading part. In the natural sciences and engineering, though much applied work is carried out in specialised research institutes or industry, its roots can always be traced to basic research carried out in universities".[7]

And they lucidly defended the concentration of research in universities:

> "First, they offer the best setting for inter-disciplinary and multi-disciplinary research, because they cover a far wider range of subjects than do other research establishments. This range also facilitates shifts of research, whereas specialised institutes can be left without a useful role as knowledge advances. Second, the findings of university staff are usually disseminated rapidly to a wide variety of users and, unlike some comparable work undertaken in Government

---

[4] Advisory Board to the Research Councils, *Report of Joint Working Party on the Support of University Scientific Research*, 1982, London, HMSO, Cmnd. 8567, 1982.

[5] The British Technology Group, 1983, quoted in ABRC Report, *Improving Research Links Between Higher Education and Industry*, London, HMSO, 1983, p.39. A major function of BTG is to undertake the commercial exploitation of academic inventions.

[6] UGC, *Ibid.*, 1980.

[7] UGC, *Ibid.*, 1980.

departments, have the advantage of being subjected to competitive criticism from other research workers. Third, it is well established that the research ability of staff varies throughout their career, and may tail off as they grow older. In universities this does not usually cause a problem because academic staff can take on more teaching and administration as they do less research. Fourth, the fullest possible use can be made of library and other facilities because they are needed for both teaching and research. Finally, the close association of teaching and research gives a special strength and vitality to the universities. Able young people receive a unique stimulus from being taught by those engaged in extending the frontiers of their disciplines".[8]

The reductions in support for university research have significant implications for the quality of life in Britain. According to one press report: "British science is so starved of funds that research on breast cancer, whooping cough vaccine, and why so many old people die in the winter, might have to be abandoned, (according to the Government's science advisers).... Scientists are so hamstrung by financial shortages that they are unable to play a proper role in research into the greenhouse effect, according to the Advisory Board for the Research Council (ABRC)".[9] Recently the ABRC published a long list of research projects that are threatened by insufficient government funding including: research into viruses that are endemic in Britain; the mechanism of the immune system – which fights disease and is compromised in people who have Aids; into the genetics of inherited diseases; into the way that crops 'fix' nitrogen – essential for reducing the need for artificial fertiliser; and into the ability of the oceans to absorb carbon dioxide – the most important greenhouse gas. "Britain will have to accept an even smaller role than at present in the European Space Agency and may have to close at least one large astronomical telescope......".[10] The single European market in 1992 may create further problems, and the board concludes that "British science is insufficiently resourced to grasp the opportunities for increased co-operation in research. In materials science, chemistry, physics and the medical and biological sciences, Britain is lagging well behind public funding of research in France and West Germany".[11] This view is confirmed by America's Institute for Scientific Information, which records declining influence from British medicine, physical sciences, including physics, chemistry and earth sciences. During the 1980's, Britain showed

---

[8] UGC, *Ibid.*, 1980.
[9] P. Wilsher, "Putting the Punch into Research", *The Sunday Times*, 2 August, 1987.
[10] DES, *Science and Public Expenditure, A Report to the Secretary of State for Education and Science from ABRC*, 1987.
[11] DES, *Science and Public Expenditure, Ibid.*

the largest fall in the number of citations in 3,000 leading scientific journals with the only increase (8.2%) recorded in applied sciences (including engineering). Although the publication of papers in clinical medicine rose 31% in the 1980's many more areas are no longer attracting citations. Some consolation can be derived from the fact that British citations are still above average, according to the same report, but our future influence must be in serious doubt.[12]

Patents are possibly the most accurate measure of inventiveness and innovation as a result of research. The *Annual Review of Government Funded R and D*, certainly reports a significant link between patenting activity and the level of investment in industrial research and development. To compare Britain's performance with other countries, patents per head of population taken out in a third country, the United States, are considered. Whilst patents have increased in absolute terms in the pharmacutical and chemical industries as well as the telecommunications business, there has been a decline in the areas of electrical and mechanical engineering. Britain's patenting activity is below the European average, and less than half that in West Germany and Japan per capita.

So without "basic" research what will happen? Nothing, initially, and ideas will still be circulated for industry to develop, but they will come from abroad, where indigenous companies with closer proximity to the research institute will benefit: if we are to entertain a concept of Great Britain Ltd, universities must become part of the infrastructure which in turn helps the universities themselves.

But does underfunding of arts research, as distinct from the sciences, really matter? If we mainly recycle the critical theories of earlier generations, so what? But there is a contradiction in teaching knowledge if it is to all purposes dead. And such ossification must affect teaching in schools, since many teachers are university graduates: everyone will be drawing on a body of moribund knowledge and there will be no new ideas and interpretation. The best academics will emigrate, a possibility that is made more probable by the re-directing of U.S. immigration laws to discriminate in favour of skilled immigrants. Frank Kermode in English Literature, Amartya Sen in Economics, Paul Kennedy in History – have now left these shores.

---

[12] OECD, *Changing Patterns of Finance in Higher Education, Country Study America*, 1989.

The implications of all this will, however, transcend the secret garden of knowledge. What will be the effect on companies' research and development if the supply of doctoral students dries up, which it may, especially when there are no longer people sufficiently qualified to teach them? Then there are also implications for industry from students being trained on obsolescent equipment: the head of one university production engineering department noted when visiting a polytechnic in Singapore how much superior the equipment was there, and according to a 1982 ABRC report only 14% of university science equipment is "state of the art"; and about 50% of equipment is a decade old or more.[13] It is surprising that the government does not see the business implications of this. And, without a research base, university teaching will lose something of its distinctive flavour; as Albert Sloman, former vice chancellor of Essex University has said: "The distinctive feature of a university is that teaching is done in the context of research. That does not mean it is better teaching, but it is of a different kind".[14]

Long term, the death of basic research will translate into the death of applied research. There will be significant consequences in 'smart' industries like electronics, information technology and computers, biotechnology, aeronautical and machine engineering, especially since many new product concepts have their genesis in fresh scientific thinking, biotechnology being an obvious example. Government is not in the business of running industry: but it is most definately in the business of creating contexts in which industry will flourish, a strategic imperative it has hitherto interpreted narrowly.

PART TWO: THE REDUCTION IN RESEARCH FUNDING

Universities carry out more than 50% of Britain's basic research. The cost of this is a small percentage of the total of applied research and development. According to 1969/70 studies, about one third of university staff time is spent on research or its supervision. As for income, the Research Councils provide half of the externally generated funds; the rest is from industry, charities, and so on. And despite changes, general university funds are still a crucial source of research income. Currently, under what is known as the dual funding system, the core of British

---

[13] ABRC, *Support of University Scientific Research, Ibid.*, 1982.
[14] N. Crequer, "Lifting the Cloud Over Essex", *THES*, 1989.

university financial policy, the Research Councils have received £815 million to distribute and the University Funding Council has been given £860 million to finance university research. Overwhelmingly, such expenditures go on science.

In 1989, the government spent a total of £5.4 billion on research. This was divided into £2.4 billion for the Ministry of Defence and £3.0 billion on the civilian research programme. Of this sum of £5.4 billion, 25% is spent by government departments and devoted to the science base with a further 45% going to military research. And the comparison with our major competitors in terms of percentage of GDP spent on research is not impressive. In 1988/89, the world research league was : United States 2.9%; Germany 2.8% (or £5.5 billion); Japan 2.7%; France 2.45% (or £6.3 billion); United Kingdom 2.3% (or £4.5 billion): if military research is excluded from the UK figure, Italy assumes fifth place and UK is relegated to sixth. Although the government argues spending on basic research has outstripped inflation between 1980 and 1990, Save British Science maintains that it has fallen from 0.35 to 0.3% of GDP, so that £17 billion extra spending would be required over ten years to make up for the short-fall. The cost of science they argue rises 1.5 to 2% faster than the rate of inflation as measured by the retail price index.[15]

Institutions of higher education and the Research Councils account for some 95% of the government's total expenditure on basic research, which has no immediate application. 60% of 'strategic' research is also channelled through the same avenues, and this is defined as research with developmental potential in the near, but not the immediate future.

Currently universities face an extraordinary set of costs that must be set against income. Thus, essential building costs are increasing by 18%, while "Pension costs almost doubled as a result of £29 million of early retirement payments, associated with restructuring and rationalisation of courses".[16] Finances are under pressure from the growing level of maintenance, the building programme, premature retirements, voluntary severance schemes, retraining, temporary part-time posts and library consolidations. And reductions in library provision affect research. The Royal Society warned

---

[15] This arises from the costs of unfunded pay increases, equipment, building costs, pensions, restructuring departments and general rationalisation.
[16] J. Sandback, "The Universities Funding Inheritance", *Public Finance and Accountancy*, April 1989.

some years ago about instability in the scientific information system, since publishers could not publish if libraries were unable to buy journals. In many key areas, income in real terms was constantly reduced. Thus, the equipment grant was only to increase 2% between 1988/89 and 1991/2: "the cost of additional equipment needed to support current research was estimated at £259 million with further items needed for new research being valued at £200 million".[17] Moreover, universities have been hurt by unpredictable Government decisions. For example, in July 1983, £23.5 million was clawed back from the UGC grant for 1983-4.

And in 1988-89 income from tuition fees continued to fall as a percentage of total income, in spite of income from overseas student fees continuing to grow by £16 million, or some 10%. There is certainly room for discussion as to the morality of a monopsony customer, the British state, continually demanding and enforcing price reductions. This is not a 'market' mechanism in any sense.

A report by the UFC shows that as a result of studying 18 institutions' expected progress up to 1993, five are predicted to have severe financial problems and eight others serious problems. In 1986/87 six universities had losses of between £1 and £5 million, and the Committee of Public Accounts (CPE) estimated that by July 1990 the total deficit in the university sector would rise to £44m, with Bristol and Edinburgh universities announcing large and mainly unexpected deficits last year. The position from 1977/78 to 1987/88 is shown in Table 5:1; deficits appeared in 1984/85, fell back for a couple of years, but accelerated again 1987/88.

TABLE 5:1 GLOBAL BALANCES FOR BRITISH UNIVERSITIES 1977/78 TO 1987/88

	1977/78	1978/79	1979/80	1980/81	1981/82	1982/83
TOTAL RECURRENT INCOME (£'000)	881,982	1,003,373	1,266,564	1,563,036	1,719,743	1,879,197
TOTAL RECURRENT EXPENDITURE (£'000)	875,500	1,025,604	1,257,122	1,555,551	1,686,629	1,847,021
BALANCE (£'000)	+6,842	-22,231	+9,442	+7,485	+33,114	+32,176

---

[17] UGC, *A Strategy for Higher Education in the 1990's*, 1984.

TABLE 5:1 GLOBAL BALANCES FOR BRITISH UNIVERSITIES 1977/78 TO 1987/88 (Cont'd)

	1983/84	1984/85	1985/86	1986/87	1987/88
TOTAL RECURRENT INCOME (£'000)	1,982,782	2,119,647	2,295,133	2,483,813	2,707,799
TOTAL RECURRENT EXPENDITURE (£'000)	1,975,957	2,139,721	2,300,715	2,488,014	2,721,909
BALANCE (£'000)	+6,825	-20,074	-5,582	-4,201	-14,110

General funds will fall by £76 million and yet student numbers will rise by 30,000 between 1987/88 and 1992/93, while staff numbers will fall by 3,000, worsening student/staff ratios from 10.8:1 to 11.8:1. Increasing deficits therefore appear to be inevitable following the decision to let institutions fund nearly 27% of restructuring costs as well as most of any pay increases: every 1% of unfunded pay increases raise the deficit by £51 million.

The real problem here, as in the 1970's, is that of inflation: block grant and student fees (home and EEC) are projected to rise by a factor of 1.196, but pay is to increase by a factor of 1.252 between 1987/88 and 1992/93. Increased efficiency would not be sufficient to make up the difference, since there is no longer considered to be any slack in the system. Changes in fees for home or overseas students will do little to ameliorate the situation – investment income is falling and block grant increases are not even nominal: the balance of block grant falls from 72.3% in 1987/88 to 70.6% in 1992/93 and fees rise from 9.8% to 10.5% over the same period. Income from research as already indicated is not expected to rise very much, so that an improved rate of recovery of monies from research contracts, plus increased services provided for industry and more full-cost students, represent the only viable alternatives. Table 5:2 shows the financial forecasts on favourable and then more pessimistic premises for academic years 1989/90 to 1992/93 and Table 5:3 indicates individual university deficits or surpluses as a percentage of recurrent income excluding earmarked grants. Eighteen are in deficit, varying between -0.16% and -6.09%. Thirty four in surplus, varying between 0.05% and 8.37%.

TABLE 5:2

FINANCIAL FORECASTS

	1989/90 £'000	1990/91 £'000	1991/92 £'000	1992/93 £'000
1. Surplus/(Deficit) After Transfers	- 5,607	- 13,201	-19,012	-26,026
2. Overseas fees				
Favourable	7,157	11,641	15,908	19,577
Pessimistic	10,059	14,653		
3. Investment income				
Favourable	4,258	6,597	7,383	8,188
Pessimistic	3,564	5,065	5,754	7,753
4. Research grants and contracts				
Favourable	5,189	8,251	10,591	12,542
Pessimistic	2.399	3,801	5,330	7,544
5. Other service rendered				
Favourable	2,445	4,045	5,407	6,979
Pessimistic	1,499	2,203	2,994	3,736
6. Pay				
Favourable	5,557	11,251	16,407	19,934
Pessimistic	11,324	25,504	38,254	51,421
7. Long-term maintenance				
Favourable	1,005	2,248	2,466	2,605
Pessimistic	8,834	12,397	14,207	13,798
8. Other non-pay				
Favourable	2,748	4,213	5,781	7,219
Pessimistic	7,021	11,636	16,411	21,463
9. Revised Surplus (Deficit) Favourable	23,042	35,045	44,931	51,018
10. Revised Surplus (Deficit) Pessimistic	-52,803	-91,574	-124.821	-159,305

Finely balanced: unexpected shifts in pay, overseas student fees, long-term maintenance and non-pay expenditure can add millions of pounds to universities' spending bills. Line 9 and 10 of the table show how relatively small changes can tip the surplus and deficit scales.

TABLE 5:3

UNIVERSITIES' DEFICIT OR SURPLUS AS PERCENTAGE OF RECURRENT GRANT 1990

	Income	Expenditure	% Deficit/Surplus
KEELE	20,290	21,526	-6.09
LANCASTER	31,931	32,698	-2.4
MANCHESTER	109,953	112,524	-2.34
LAMPETER	3,737	3,819	-2.19
SALFORD	31,201	31,687	-1.56
BRISTOL	72,201	73,783	-1.52
ABERDEEN	49,502	50,226	-1.46
SOUTHAMPTON	67,739	68,709	-1.43
EDINBURGH	113,954	115,572	-1.42
NEWCASTLE	71,708	72,718	-1.41
ABERYSTWYTH	20,733	20,922	-0.91
STRATHCLYDE	63,569	64,045	-0.75
HERIOT-WATT	31,492	31,715	-0.71
ESSEX	21,833	21,953	-O.55
GLASGOW	106,997	107,564	-0.53
UMIST	45,999	46.195	-0.43
NOTTINGHAM	65,535	65,770	-0.36
CAMBRIDGE	114,448	114,632	-0.16
UNIV WALES COLL.OF MEDICINE	22,172	22,160	0.05
EXETER	33,169	33.129	0.12
SUSSEX	34,921	34,856	0.19
DUNDEE	34,690	34,610	0.23
SHEFFIELD	75,525	72,359	0.23
BANGOR	25,091	24,985	0.42
DURHAM	37,619	37,418	0.53
LONDON BUSINESS SCHOOL	9,611	9,558	0.55
SWANSEA	30,238	30,070	0.56
SURREY	37,020	36,665	0.96
STIRLING	22,899	22,662	1.03
WARWICK	56,354	55,750	1.09
LEEDS	96,117	94,551	1.63
HULL	31,671	31,151	1.64
READING	49,129	48,324	1.64
OXFORD	132,034	129,835	1.67
MANCHESTER BUSINESS SCHOOL	6,281	6,174	1.7
LIVERPOOL	83,706	82,215	1.78
EAST ANGLIA	29,82	329,258	1.89
CITY	32,041	31,413	1.96

TABLE 5:3

UNIVERSITIES' DEFICIT OR SURPLUS AS PERCENTAGE OF RECURRENT GRANT 1990 (Cont'd)

LEICESTER	43,995	43,130	1.97
BRADFORD	33,591	32,906	2.04
LOUGHBOROUGH	46,523	45,390	2.44
KENT	29,133	28,388	2.56
ST. ANDREWS	26,696	25,959	2.76
YORK	29,782	28,676	3.71
LONDON	696,408	668,880	3.95
BATH	33,410	32,077	3.99
ULSTER	50,209	48,099	4.2
BRUNEL	29,259	27,916	4.59
BIRMINGHAM	98,462	93,140	5.41
QUEENS BELFAST	62,086	57,980	6.61
CARDIFF	56,107	51,611	8.01
ASTON	32,682	29,948	8.37

Reductions in staffing have had a negative effect on research. For much of the nineteen eighties universities shed staff in large numbers, between 1981 and 1984 there were 2,000 voluntary retirements of staff over age 50, and less than 15% of staff were under the age of 35 at the time of the 1986 UGC report, with 60% being between 35 and 49.[18] The authors of the report did not expect the universities to be able to recruit more than about 700 new non-clinical staff each year, whereas there should, in their view, be 900 new appointments annually. *The Economist* commented: "The target for academic staff redundancies was 3,000. In fact 4,400 took the money and left.... Many of those who left were in the very departments, like engineering technology and computer sciences, which the government intended to protect. A lot of scientists and technologists could move easily to industry, some of them packeting large payments on Friday, and starting a new job on Monday at higher salaries. As a result, an extra 800 staff now have to be expensively recruited".[19]

The composition of university research staff changed radically during the nineteen eighties, with the rise of the contract worker, an ill-paid, insecure and poorly treated group who came to constitute a sort of coolie class. Thus in 1985-1986, "Taking academic appointments for that year as a whole,

---

[18] UGC, *A Strategy for Higher Education in the 1990's*, 1984.
[19] *The Economist*, 9 December, 1985.

only 5.8 per cent were tenured, with 74.7 per cent on fixed term contracts".[20] Researchers fully financed by universities declined 5% between 1976 and 1985, those financed externally increased by 71% (mainly via the Research Councils).

TABLE 5:4 COMPARATIVE UNIVERSITY SALARIES IN UNITS OF PURCHASING POWER

BELGIUM	XXXXXXXXXXXXXXXXXXXXXXXXXXXXXXXXXXX
GERMANY	XXXXXXXXXXXXXXXXXXXXXXXXXXXXXXXXXX
DENMARK	XXXXXXXXXXXXXXXXXXXXXXXXXXXXXXX
FRANCE	XXXXXXXXXXXXXXXXXXXXXXXXXXX
ITALY	XXXXXXXXXXXXXXXXXXXXXXXXXX
IRELAND	XXXXXXXXXXXXXXXXXXXXXX
BRITAIN	XXXXXXXXXXXXXXXXXXXXX
HOLLAND	XXXXXXXXXXXXXXXXXXX

Academic purchasing power

0   10,000   20,000   30,000

Difficulties lie ahead if competent research workers are to be found and then retained. A major problem is the ability to pay realistically. Table 5:4 gives a comparative estimate of university salaries in units of purchasing power throughout Europe showing Britain lagging behind all but Holland. With the Single European Act of 1992 and the impact of the single market, British academic competitiveness and reputation will undoubtedly suffer.[21]

Reductions in the number of postgraduates have also harmed research: "Restoration of postgraduate research studentships to a healthy level would be a very rapid and cost effective way of making good much of the erosion of the universities' research base".[22]

---

[20] AUT, *AUT Bulletin*, June, 1987.
[21] ACOST, *The Impact of the Completion of the Single European Market on UK Science and Technology*, 1991.
[22] UGC, *A Strategy for Higher Education in the 1990's*, 1984.

According to the UGC's 1984 advice, contained in the Government's 1984 Public Expenditure White Paper, there would be an average cut in recurrent grant of 0.5% p.a. in real terms up to 1986-7, and universities must expect resources to decline by 1.5% p.a. thereafter.[23] The report adds: "Since pay is the dominant component of university expenditure, accounting for about two-thirds of the total, each fall of 1% in the real income of the university system would mean a fall of at least 1% in the number of staff employed".[24] Implementing cuts would mean the closure of departments, possibly of entire institutions, and according to Sir Mark Richmond, at the time vice chancellor of the University of Manchester, writing in 1987, "There has been a 10 per cent cut in staff and a 20 per cent fall in the purchasing power of our recurrent grant while the number of students has risen marginally".[25]

Universities have, however, made vigorous efforts to increase their research income. This rose by £4,000 per head between 1986 and 1989 and some areas managed to double it.[26] Even in the arts, with no clear industrial application, income per capita rose from £1,580 to £2,330 during this period. Average staff research income now amounted to £16,500 per annum.[27] By the middle of the decade almost a quarter of total income now came from research grants, contracts and other services, representing an increase of 18%.[28]

However, most money from this source remained public in origin – 63.4% of it in 1983/84, with only 10.7% coming direct from industry. The state contributed especially towards defence (£9.4m), energy (£6.2m) and D.H.S.S. matters (£5.4m).[29]

Universities' initiative in the generation of research income has continued to strengthen. By the end of the decade UK universities' research competencies were being recognised by the European Economic Community, from which each university had received an average of £1 million. By that time too, it was being predicted that soon Government

---

[23] *Public Expenditure White Paper*, London, HMSO, Cmnd. 9189, 1984.
[24] UGC, *Ibid*, 1984.
[25] Sir Mark Richmond, *The Times*, May 1987.
[26] DES, *Science and Public Expenditure, A Report to the Secretary of State for Education and Science from ABRC*, 1987.
[27] ABRC, *The Support Given by the Research Councils for In-house and University Research*, 1983.
[28] DES, *Science and Public Expenditure, Ibid.*, 1987.
[29] DES, *Ibid.*, 1987.

would fund "less than half of universities' research expenditure".[30] At the University of Salford, "the value of research income secured per full-time member of academic staff reached an all-time high, of just under £11,000 in the academic year 1986/87, nearly five times the comparable figure in the year 1980/81, and two thirds of which was made from research council money....".[31] In some ways the pressure has relaxed recently. The UGC's successor, the UFC, said initially it would not conduct more subject reviews to close or merge departments; and the next round of research selectivity exercises will be in the mid nineteen-nineties, although pressure seems to be mounting to resurrect the former and the latter has been brought forward to 1992.

HAVE UNIVERSITIES CURRENTLY MET MORE OFFICIAL GENEROSITY?

Higher education was offered an extra 10% for the year 1990/91, roughly in line with inflation. Science won an extra £80 million for the same year, yielding a 27% rise in two years. Student tuition fees will rise to £1675 and student numbers expand by 50,000 over three years, but there will be no increase in funds to cover these extra students. Changes in the rating system and the law on charities in the 1990 budget also provided universities with more money and this would have amounted to £200 million over three years: it remains unclear how they will fare with the abolition of the poll tax. Capital grants will also rise by £30 million over three years. But no matter how this package is reviewed, it could not possibly be considered as generous, and does nothing to correct years of almost terminal decline. The 19% increase announced in 1992 to cover the period 1992/93 to 1994/95 does promise limited expansion, but much depends on the change in costs.[32]

RESEARCH FUNDING FROM INDUSTRY

Another source of research funds is of course industry. The official ideology is that industry should provide an alternative resource to the state for research funds, and that academics should show initiative in soliciting industry, modulating their research the better to satisfy its needs. Clearly

---

[30] J. O'Leary, "Britain Turns to Euro-Millions for 1992 Expansion", *THES*, 1989.
[31] Claire Williams, "Salford's Standards Restored to Pre-1981", *THES*, 1989.
[32] See p.182 below for details of the changes.

no sane policy maker would do other than wish such activities well and actively encourage them; considerable doubt remains, however, as to whether industry has much to offer research that is largely propelled by intellectual curiosity, and that traditionally symbolises the core of a university's mission.[33] British Petroleum's Venture Research International is an important contribution to these developments and has recently attracted financial support from Sony since becoming an independent company, with BP still providing substantial funding. The Squibb Corporation has shown extraordinary generosity to Oxford as has Upjohn to University College London. The big question remains though about future industrial injections, particularly during periodic economic recessions.

Between 1984/85 and 1987/88 university research income from industry did rise substantially by 62% (increasing to over £100m in 1989/90, a 20% increase over 1988/89), but over the same period research spending by industry itself on research and development increased by 38% from a much higher base. Of interest here too is the growth in overseas funding of industrial research and development in Britain, from £283 million in 1983 this rose to £742 million in 1986, a rise of 162%, but the multinational companies have chosen British industry to do their research and not British universities. Higher pay in the industrial sector, and hence the ability of industry to attract the best researchers, is part of the explanation. Table 5:5.1 shows the proportion of university research income coming from public corporations and from private industry. Table 5:5.2 gives details of the 1989/90 external research income that totalled £762m. Table 5.5.3 shows industry's expenditure on research. Finally, Table 5:6 gives the breakdown of the government's funding of Research and Development based on the 1989 Review.

---

[33] See the authors "Teachers and Traders: A Survey of Industry Attitudes to Universities", *Management Education and Development*, (forthcoming).

TABLE 5:5.1
UNIVERSITY RESEARCH INCOMING FROM INDUSTRY

£0 m	£20m	£40m	£60m	£80m

84/85	YYYYXXXXXXXXXXXXXXXXXXXXX	TOTAL £47.4
87/88	YYYYYYXXXXXXXXXXXXXXXXXXXXXXX	TOTAL £76.9

YY from public corporations   XX from private industry

Total increase £29.5m (62%)

TABLE 5:5.2[1]
UNIVERSITIES EXTERNAL RESEARCH INCOME

	£m
Research Councils	265
UK-based Charitable Trusts	156
UK Government Departments	106
UK Local Authorities	4
UK Public Corporations	9
UK Industry and Commerce	96
UK Health/Hospital Authorities	14
European Community Grants	38
Other Overseas	43
Other Sources	31
Total External Research Income	762

1. The top eighteen universities gained 75% of the external research income.

TABLE 5:5.3
INDUSTRY EXPENDITURE ON RESEARCH

0	£1000m	£2000m	£3000m	£4000m

1983	XXXXXXXXXXXXXXXXXXXXXXXXX	£2,622m
1986	XXXXXXXXXXXXXXXXXXXXXXXXXXXXXXXX	£3,621m

Increase £999m (38%)

TABLE 5:6
ANNUAL REVIEW OF GOVERNMENT FUNDED R & D

Expenditure on R & D by departments (in cash terms)

	Outturn		Estimate	Provision		£ million Plans
Department	1987/87	1988/89	1989/90	1990/91	1991/92	1992/93
Civil departments						
MAFF	113.8	115.0	114.0	120.8	119.1	121.8
DES	132.4	73.4	80.0	86.9	91.8	95.3
DEn	176.4	190.2	169.2	153.9	143.8	140.6
DoE	62.1	63.0	71.9	78.1	82.8	81.9
DH	47.3	50.3	56.6	65.7	67.9	70.9
HSC	5.1	6.3	6.0	8.2	10.3	9.4
Home Office	14.25	14.1	16.1	15.8	18.4	18.7
ODA	32.5	34.2	38.5	40.3	42.5	44.3
DSS		0.8	1.3	1.7	1.8	1.8
DTI	324.4	314.4	304.8	334.5	273.6	213.7
DTp	26.4	27.2	27.5	29.8	31.5	31.3
NI Depts	16.8	18.0	21.7	22.1	22.8	23.8
Scottish Depts	51.6	55.3	57.8	64.1	63.8	63.6
Welsh Office	1.9	1.9	2.4	2.7	3.1	2.3
DEmp	2.2	2.3	2.9	3.1	3.2	3.3
TA	23.9	45.3	47.4	51.1	52.5	53.9
Other departments	24.0	25.8	26.7	28.2	29.1	30.0
Total civil departments	1055.1	1037.2	1044.9	1107.0	1057.8	1006.6
Research Councils						
AFRC	49.4	55.0	65.9	62.3	61.5	62.4
ESRC	21.6	23.4	28.3	32.4	31.3	31.9
MRC	139.1	144.9	165.6	175.2	178.2	178.7
NERC	70.8	81.7	103.9	124.4	111.3	106.6
SERC	334.5	339.6	371.8	404.8	401.7	407.7
Unallocated					17.4	36.7
Total Research Councils	615.5	644.6	735.4	799.1	801.5	824.0
UFC	760.0	800.0	820.0	830.0	830.0	820.0
PCFC		60.4	61.1	57.0	50.9	50.9
Total civil R & D	2430.5	2542.2	2661.5	2793.1	2740.2	2701.5
Ministry of Defence						
–Research	370.3	360.7	400.2	403.4	419.5	427.5
–Development	1558.1	1574.6	1745.6	1848.0	1925.4	1961.8
–Staff and superannuation	56.1	56.1	56.0	63.6	66.2	67.4
Total defence	2014.5	1991.4	2201.7	2315.0	2411.1	2456.7
TOTAL	4445.0	4533.6	4863.1	5108.1	5151.3	5158.2
Indicative UK contribution to EC budget in respect of R & D (£m)	96.0	128.0	171.0	222.0	251.0	273.0
GRAND TOTAL	4541.0	4662.0	5034.0	5330.0	5402.0	5431.0

The report of the ABRC on industry and university research co-operation makes a number of interesting proposals:

(1) The government should create an industrial seed-corn fund to help basic research that will complement industrial and applied research.

(2) The Department of Trade and Industry (DTI) should help academics take 'exploitation leave' in small companies.

(3) The report stresses particularly the need for stronger academic-industrial liaison, it inveighs, as all such reports do, against "the way in which industry and the academic world have failed to come together in the U.K. compared, for example, with the US".

(4) The report suggests possibly 'more flexible' arrangements for new members of academic staff. They include:

(a) Industrial experience as a condition of appointment to a tenured post in industrially-oriented departments.

(b) More untenured short-term (5 year) appointments at higher salaries to make up for the lack of security and perhaps with a gratuity at the end of the term.

(5) The purchase of more teaching staff from industry, business and commerce.

(6) Permit academics to work part-time in business, perhaps even their own.

(7) More joint appointments, for example, integrated chairs on the Salford University model, whereby an individual has substantial professorial responsibilities in the university at the same time as exercising a senior managerial role in a firm or other corporate body. One of the main benefits envisaged is the generation of joint programmes of Research and Development.

(8) The appointment of industrialists to temporary top jobs in higher educational institutions, raising salaries to industry scales.

(9) £5m for projects 'contributing significantly' to the infrastructure for academic-industrial co-operation; closer collaboration between the DTI and the Science and Engineering Research Council (SERC); that the DTI and industry be first suppliers of money to assist new initiatives in academic-industrial

collaboration; the funding of 'enabling science' by DTI and not the research councils.[34]

Current industry-university liaison schemes include the Co-operative Awards in Science and Engineering; the Collaborative Training Awards; the Integrated Graduate Development Scheme; the Royal Society/SERC Industrial Fellowship Scheme; CASE studentships and the Link programme. Under the Teaching Company Scheme, graduates are supervised jointly by the firm and the institute, with a focus on the solution of problems in manufacturing.

Such ideas are most certainly to be welcomed and can do good, but without seriously addressing the central problem of salary size and rigidities they make limited sense, since the company-university staff mobility they call for would be frustrated. There is also the danger that a policy of fomenting industrial support simply becomes a substitute for a coherent higher education policy. For one thing, there is very little that industry could offer the arts; and, as our survey will show, industry has relatively short time horizons.[35] Certainly though the two spheres need educating about each other.[36]

PART THREE: CURRENT POLICY PROPOSALS : SELECTIVITY AND HIERARCHY

Currently a whole set of new research policies are prominently on the agenda: they are conceptually and administratively interconnected. They include 1) contracts, (enshrined in the 1988 *Education Act*); 2) the separation of teaching and research; 3) competitive bidding; 4) a three-tier university system, whether formal or informal; 5) teaching only universities; 6) the admission of the polytechnics into the university ranks; 7) a changed role for the Research Councils; 8) 1991 White Paper, *Higher Education : A New Framework*. And all such changes would take place in the context of an increasingly 'massified' higher education system.

The aim is to make British universities more research-efficient by creating an 'internal market' for funds, and more accountability: "At present, it

---

[34] ABRC, *The Support Given by the Research Councils for In-House and University Research*, 1983.
[35] See Chapter 9 below, p.280.
[36] British Technology Group (BTG) addresses this issue.

seems, a large sum of public money, arbitrarily set at about £800 million, or 40 per cent of the total grant, simply disappears into a black hole".[37] This particularly aggravates the government. It speaks of a feckless amateurism totally out of keeping with the ethos of the nineteen eighties and nineties.

It is not difficult to see what the 'hole' consists of: the generous research time that is factored into the task of every university lecturer, but is sometimes under-exploited or abused. That men and women, bored with marginal salaries, should use some of that time to generate external earnings should not arouse censure: though the case of those who choose to remain idle should concern and embolden the government to seek dynamic reform.

Current proposals, if implemented, will change universities. Theoretically they will make them sharper, more vigorous and less extravagant. Practice may conform to theory. On a more pessimistic interpretation they will create a level of turbulence and uncertainty which will drive able men and women, already disenchanted by pay and prospects, out the of system entirely. Our expectations of competition may be nullified if there is no reinvestment.[38]

(A) COMPETITION AND CONCENTRATION

The major development here is the split in the funding of teaching and research. Hitherto the block grant to the universities contained a substantial research component: this is factored into the conditions of each lecturer, so that perhaps half his time is research time. This has now gone, making academics much more accountable for their research time, very possibly forfeiting it for a much higher teaching load. Ministers apparently regard such an evolution as essential if a 'massified' system is to be developed, via the lowering of unit costs.

Under related proposals connected with the 1991 White Paper, *Higher Education: A New Framework*, universities and polytechnics would bid competitively for research funding in a sort of égalitarian melée. The extent of this has yet to be determined, but it could make life much less certain

---

[37] DES, *Science and Public Expenditure, Ibid.*, 1987.
[38] For a further recent account see "Sun, Sea, Sand... and San Diego", *The Independent on Sunday*, January, 1992.

for the universities, as research funding would cease to be assured. Certain of them would definitely end up as teaching only institutions in consequence, although the Secretary of State is already backtracking on the precise wording in the White Paper by arguing, now, that the new universities would retain their present applied research mission and not compete for funds from the existing UFC research pool. If this did happen, then on the basis of student numbers existing universities would lose half their present research funding.

A necessary concomitant of this would therefore be the stratification of universities, with research resources concentrated in the top ones. For the *Times Higher Education Supplement*: "Selectivity can only be produced by national planning – and planning, moreover, based on qualitative judgements, that are bound to be hotly contested".[39]

Professor R J P Williams, Professor of Inorganic Chemistry at the University of Oxford, identified the following dangers in the classification of universities as proposed:

"1. Ossification – try experimental nuclear physics in universities as run by Research Councils from 1950.
2. Loss of mobility – once in class Z always in class Z.
3. Loss of incentive in two thirds of the universities. Why bother to think new thoughts?
4. Fall off in calibre of research workers in two thirds of the universities. Why go to an institute which is labelled 'not to be funded properly'.
5. Lack of incentive for the young to join the system in Z universities (where they are doomed to start if they are *independent*).
6. A failure to teach how to do research using simple problems.
7. Heavy concentration of power in a few.
8. Disassociation of Arts and Sciences in universities".[40]

He argued that the checks and balances in university politics "generate a slow-moving, often frustrating, fairness".[41]

---

[39] "Mixed Motives: The Split Between Teaching and Research", THES, 1989.
[40] *The Times*, 27th August, 1989.
[41] *Loc cit.*

Croham also speaks the language of assessment, competition and targeting: "A claim to academic freedom cannot be translated into a right to be funded".[42] Yet funding decisions invariably have implications for academic freedom: they must establish priority areas, and without funding, academics cannot function whatever their legal "freedom". He stresses the importance of the block grant on the basis of negotiated academic plans, of performance indicators, adding that "selectivity may in future years underpin larger transfers of resources". He suggests that the UGC should give a triannual report to Parliament on university development.

(B) CONTRACTS

For some time it has been argued by the government that greater research efficiencies could be gleaned by placing universities in a formal contractual relationship with the state: they would thus be accountable.

A contract may, according to the Department of Education and Science (DES), embrace all of an institution's publicly supported activities – teaching and research – these could then be described in a single comprehensive contract; it might cover a three year period.[43] There could be subsidiary contracts covering more specific items such as the launch of new research and so on. Alternatively there could be several different contracts – (a) some for research, (b) some for courses, particularly those producing saleable 'results'. The DES suggest that contract (a) is the most facilitative and nearest to the current relationship. The report adds "some self-standing contracts – for the development of a new course or the launch of research in a priority area for example – might necessarily *define the provision contracted for in terms which left institutions little discretion*".[44] The report further says that the contracts will typically deal annually with the specification of provisions, the conditions under which they should be made, and procedure in the event of non-fulfilment. Clearly, in stipulating procedure in the event of non-fulfilment, the DES feels a need to provide personal punitive sanctions.

---

[42] *Review of the University Grants Committee*, Croham Report, London, HMSO, Cmnd. 811, 1987.
[43] Department of Education and Science, *Changes in the Structure and National Planning for Higher Education*, 1987.
[44] DES, *Ibid.*, 1987.

The report attaches great importance to performance data; central to the contracts will be much more intensive scrutiny of performance and delivery of services, with the associated accumulation and publication of data. When institutions fail to fulfil a contract it will be 'renegotiated' for a future year.

It is easy to see what the goals of the contract system are – to make research more 'relevant'; to make academics work harder and keep them agile; to avoid tenure and permanent commitments; to keep out mediocrity. But does it deliver them? Or does it, while perhaps delivering them more fully, create a new set of problems? Only experience will reveal what the government really means by 'contract', it could mean little, it could mean greatly heightened state supervision; everything depends on the implementation.[45]

Almost certainly, contracts will entail a separating out of teaching and research, with the consequent evolution of teaching-only universities. No longer will individuals be simply assumed to be doing research for part of their time, they will perhaps be paid for the teaching component and research will be something they can only do if they succeed in securing the funds; life under such a régime can well be imagined.

Note, too, the timescale of the contracts – three years – much too short for the purpose of much academic research planning; and consider too the costs of the bureaucracy.

There is also a fundamental fallacy with the 'contract' analogy, and its parallels with business. A university has only one customer, whereas a business has freedom to choose. Additionally, a 'contract' wrongly implies equality between partners and alternative customers. The long academic training necessary to teach and research in an area, plus the absence of alternative purchasers, unlike say construction engineers or junior hospital doctors and their contracts, makes the comparison risible. Thus the comparisons with other professions where contract plays a major role are phoney since:

(a) These pay far more, to compensate for the insecurity involved.
(b) There is a living market, not as with U.K. universities a moribund body which fitfully jerks into semi-consciousness.

---

[45] Professor J. Griffith justifiably painted a most gloomy picture of the future. Cf. "The Threat to Higher Education, *The Political Quarterly*, 1987, pp.50-62.

Therefore to imply that a contract system would make for a more adventurous, initiative-taking academic polity is questionable, they would be taking more risks than other professionals for more paltry rewards; in the real world outside Whitehall and Government White Papers, people have spouses and families: for them to work under the kind of system proposed would not be taking initiative. It would be folly.

Professor J A G Griffith has drawn eloquent attention to the potential menace of the new contract system. The contract, he says, will contain many controls, directions, conditions and earmarking not now imposed.[46] What must cause concern is the degree of detailed supervision the contracts seem to imply, indeed the report overtly states that contracting might leave institutions with little discretion over research. A contract has of necessity to be framed round achievements that are tangible and objects that are definable, and this is the great danger, for contracting demands supervision, possibly rather intense supervision, of results; all kinds of problems are associated with this, the bureaucracy and time filling paperwork, the rigid centralised control and consequent decline of innovativeness. All of this is a result of a central conflict in the government's philosophy, between its demand for accountability in the area of public funds, a *dirigiste* impulse, and its devolutionary belief in institutions running themselves rather than being the fiefdom of the nanny state: the government then as enabler rather than manager. Griffiths adds: "One man's value is another man's extravagance. And the National Audit Office, acting for the Comptroller and Auditor General (CAG), is not in the business of taking into account the value of knowledge for its own sake, of historical research which seems to have no bearing on contemporary problems, or of any cultural or aesthetic considerations. What have these to do with economy, efficiency and effectiveness?".[47]

Griffiths portrays the peripatetic nature of academic life under the new dispensation, the system of short-term and earmarked grants: "Many members of the academic staff will be expected to come and go and, under the redundancy provisions, this will be perfectly feasible". Thus we would create an entirely new caste of migratory academics – what will inevitably arise will be a project structure rather than a departmental structure for

---

[46] Professor J. Griffith, *Universities and the State: The Next Steps*, Council for Academic Freedom and Democracy, 1989.
[47] J. Griffith, *Ibid*.

research. It should be understood that the gains of a project structure – that is focus, urgency and measurability – may well not outweigh the losses of the departmental structure – difficulties of attracting staff because of insecurity, lack of a corporate image or spin-offs for students and an inability to create intellectual traditions. The idea of contracts is thus fallacious, since it threatens to undermine the continuities necessary to get together good research groups. Griffiths also refers to the "wholly remarkable penalty provisions in the Act".

The notion of penalty is indeed unprecedented. If adopted it would lead to risk aversion, and it is also a very real threat to academic freedom. People will only go in for 'safe', that is fashionable, areas – the pressures to do this are strong enough under the present arrangements, while we may anticipate a lack of challenge and stimulus to read widely. And a consequent stress on bulk publications rather than quality that will create an even greater proliferation of mediocre journals and militate against long term excellence.

What are the alternatives to a contract system? The need is to make institutions impose central mechanisms and then trust them to implement and monitor them and when they betray that trust, replace the vice-chancellor: punish the errant individual, not the institution. But the recent suggestions for state suzerainty at microscopic levels of detail is actually counterproductive: universities will become creatively bankrupt and the best staff will leave; they will produce a large amount of rather mindless hackwork.

Perhaps this is all a storm in a teacup, since contracts seem to be less emphasised, at the moment : "Contracts between the funding council and their client institutions, which were to have been the centre-piece of their new model régime, seem to have been all but forgotten. Instead there is enthusiasm for vouchers, bursaries paid direct to students, an entirely different and even antithetical idea".[48]

RESEARCH COUNCILS

Other recent proposals relate to reforming the Research Councils, perhaps by merging them, and creating a new one for the arts. Clearly 'competition'

---

[48] J. Griffith, *loc. cit.*, 1987.

would enlarge their role – they would be given the research funds for which universities compete.

Not surprisingly perhaps, there has been criticism of the operation of the Research Councils, some of it internal. The 1983 ABRC report was critical of the way the Research Councils spent their money: "We found evidence of a belief that councils were too inclined to support projects in 'safe' areas of well-known research activity and were prone to favour 'big' at the expense of 'small' science. It was also held that large, open ended international commitments, for example CERN, took too large a slice of council resources, to the detriment of funding for smaller projects in the U.K".[49] They pointed out that many good research projects were currently being turned down, solely for reasons of financial stringency. Each university, they suggest, should have a research committee. Nevertheless, the ABRC's 1987 paper, *A Strategy for the Science Base*, reinforced the predilection shown amongst the individual Research Councils for supporting large research projects, with a more recent emphasis upon interdisciplinary research centres combining applied and strategic work with industrial links.

Small grants have their place, in the view of the ABRC, and can be useful in innovatory areas where a larger investment might be unwarranted in the longer term. Directed programmes, encompassing coherent and comprehensive research programmes to stimulate research, are also important, although perhaps badly named, since programmes are 'built-up' rather than imposed from above. The Research Councils also put resources (currently £180 million) into so-called responsive research grants, initiated by individual researchers. International co-operation is another important dimension and here subscriptions and access to separate funding are crucial, particularly as the costs of complex apparatus continue to spiral upwards. In all these areas, the DES does not attempt to dictate research content, but rather seeks to ensure effective and efficient management of resources.

Nor have the Research Councils been without their external critics. Professor RJP Williams has commented: "For a long time now it is the Research Councils who have controlled the distribution of money... The

---

[49] Advisory Board for the Research Councils, *The Support Given by the Research Councils for In-House and University Research*, 1983.

only ones who can have failed in the distribution of the funds are therefore the Research Councils.... Why do they blame universities for failings in research, when most of what they do is controlled by the councils themselves?"[50] In the case of scientific research, one clear defect has been the decision to fund science selectively rather than the more profitable route of funding *scientists*.

Because of the ambiguity in the precise breakdown of the funding arrangements for research between the UFC and the Research Councils, the DES will be modifying the dual system of support in 1992/93, by transferring £150m of funds from the UFC to the Research Councils. Research sponsored by the Research Councils will thus become self-supporting and incorporate overheads. Funding of research in the humanities will remain with the UFC, with no transfer of funds to the other major sponsor, the British Academy, pending a decision on whether to create a single body for the funding of arts and social science research. This would envisage a merger of the British Academy's activities with the Economic and Social Research Council, at which stage some UFC funding may be switched. Present changes, however, mean that the Research Councils have more financial and managerial freedom over their affairs.

At present there is a hiccup in this transfer, since the ABRC require knowledge of precisely what the transferred funds are to cover, specifically the size of indirect costs as there is evidence of considerable undercharging by universities for research facilities. Indirect costs are estimated by the Sussex University based Science and Engineering Policy Studies Unit as £10-20,000 per research worker. Given these figures, ABRC believes that the Research Councils would not be able to fund the same volume of research as they currently do and therefore need a larger sum transferred. Because funding for research through the UFC and the Research Councils will rise next year, the precise figure transferred will be difficult to calculate in any case.

In the past, the universities have had a very chequered history in terms of their ability to recover fixed or overhead costs on non-dual support research projects. Recovery, as can be seen from Table 5:7 for the academic year 1988/89, varies from 59% at Salford, way out in the lead, to between 27% at Loughborough and 0% at Manchester Business School. This does not

---

[50] "Time to Grade the Research Councils", *The Times*, 27 August 1989.

augur well for efficiency in the distribution of research grants after the transfer of funds to the Research Councils.

TABLE 5:7
OVERHEADS RECOVERY BY UNIVERSITY RESEARCH DEPARTMENTS

		1988/89	*% RECOVERY*	*1986/87*		*1988/89*	*%RECOVERY*	*1986/87*
1.	Salford	59.3	(1. 31.4)	30.	Hull	13.2	(31.11.3)
2.	Loughborough	27.0	(3. 20.2)	31.	Leicester	12.7	(34.10.8)
3.	Aston	25.3	(27. 13.0)	32.	Heriot-Watt	12.2	(46. 4.2)
4.	Edinburgh	23.4	(45. 5.5)	33.	London	12.0	(38. 8.6)
5.	E. Anglia	22.3	(20. 14.2)	34.	Dundee	11.9	(49. 3.4)
6.	Birmingham	22.0	(22. 13.5)	35.	Essex	11.5	(35. 9.9)
7.	Southampton	20.7	(8. 17.5)	36.	Cambridge	11.0	(33. 11.1)
8.	Sheffield	20.6	(6. 17.5)	37.	Aberdeen	10.9	(28.12.2)
9.	Nottingham	19.8	(12. 16.7)	38.	Bangor	10.8	(23.13.5)
10.	Bath	19.6	(24. 13.4)	39.	Exeter	10.7	(29.11.7)
11.	Durham	19.3	(7. 17.5)	40.	Manchester	10.6	(36. 9.6)
12.	Warwick	18.8	(13. 16.4)	41.	London Business School	10.5	(2.28.3)
13.	Oxford	18.6	(11. 16.9)				
14.	Reading	18.1	(11. 16.1)	42.	Stirling	9.6	(40. 7.3)
15.	Brunel	17.7	(26. 13.1)	43.	Queen's	9.3	(47. 4.0)
16.	Bradford	17.6	(18. 15.7)	44.	St. Andrew's	9.1	(39. 8.5)
17.	Lancaster	16.9	(10. 17.0)	45.	UMIST	8.6	(37. 9.4)
18.	Bristol	16.8	(17. 15.8)	46.	Strathclyde	6.7	(42. 6.5)
19.	York	16.0	(5. 17.7)	47.	Ulster	6.3	(52. 1.6)
20.	City	15.9	(15. 16.1)	48.	Aberystwyth	3.1	(44. 6.2)
21.	Swansea	15.0	(9. 17.2)	49.	UWCM	3.1	(50. 3.0)
22.	Cardiff	14.7	(25. 13.2)	50.	Glasgow	2.0	(51. 2.6)
23.	Surrey	14.6	(4. 19.3)	51.	Lampeter	2.0	(48. 3.9)
24.	Sussex	14.4	(30. 11.6)	52.	Manchester Business School	0.0	(53. 0.0)
25.	Kent	13.6	(19. 14.3)				
26.	Leeds	13.6	(14. 16.3)				
27.	Liverpool	13.4	(41. 6.9)				
28.	Keele	13.3	(43. 6.3)				
29.	Newcastle	13.3	(32. 11.2)				

Future developments also include closer co-operation between Research Council Institutes and universities, with the former possibly located on campuses, and Interdisciplinary Research Centres to maximise the flow of bright graduates and potential researchers, something that failed to occur when the two were separate. This blends together the individual researcher model of research, following his own initiative, with the innovative and creative freedom of the university. The size of research grants have also increased, averaging £50,000 between 1987 and 1988 with large programme grants awarded by the SERC accounting for 44% of their funds in 1987/88 (up from 12% in 1985/86). Concentration figures for the Research Councils for 1988/89 are as follows:

ABRC	56.5%	of grant expenditure went to top 10 institutions
ESRC	42%	to top 10 and 64% to top 20 institutions.
MRC	61%	to top 10 institutions.
NERC	53%	to top 10 institutions.
SERC	50%	to top 12 institutions, 75% to top 26 institutions.
		In Astronomy and Planetary Science 50% went to three institutions and in Nuclear Physics, 50% to four.

SERC reported in 1990/91 that for the past three years eight of the top ten universities receiving funds had remained unchanged: Birmingham, Cambridge, Edinburgh, Glasgow, Manchester, Oxford, Imperial and University Colleges in London. Liverpool, Leeds, Sheffield and Southampton have been in the list in one or two of those years, confirming the emergence of a super-league for research in science and technology. The top four, in fact, took 27% of total SERC grants in 1990/91 (£30m each) and the rest of the group had £20m each.

Within SERC, planned science is crowding out undirected inquiry – strategic initiatives now account for some 30% of the grants pool, having been virtually zero in 1982/83. Physics, chemistry, biology and mathematics have all suffered as the grants spend has remained virtually constant. The falls were as follows, the latest figures being for 1986/87:

Physics	23.3%	down to 16.7%
Chemistry	29.7%	down to 20%
Biology	29%	down to 18%
Mathematics	6.5%	down to 4.7%

Because strategic work is included in support for core sciences, that support appears not to have fallen, but SERC expects strategic work to increase to 50% of the budget – any rise in grant will go to Interdisciplinary Research

Centres. Between 1978/79 and 1988/89 the basic/strategic balance has changed as indicated below, although basic will not be allowed to fall below 40%[51] :

	78/79	84/85	85/86	86/87	87/88	88/89
Domestic	45:55	35:65	33:67	31:69	30:70	32:68
Total	58:42	46:54	45:55	44:56	46:54	47:53

Grant applications are rising, more are being rated alpha projects, but fewer are receiving awards.[52]

From April 1991 the ABRC acquired quasi-executive power over the Research Councils, assuming a managerial and advisory role and having a full time chairman, Professor Sir David Phillips. Part of its new function is to iron out over-lapping research interests amongst the individual Research Councils and thus ensure interdisciplinary projects are not penalised.

PART FOUR: ASSESSMENT

The need to engage in research assessment exercises followed the more selective funding of universities post-1981. More selective funding of research in particular aimed to preserve the quality of research and the report on the 1989 Research Assessment Exercise prepared by the UFC makes the point. Research activities of "special strength and promise" were to be encouraged through a policy of redistribution of resources between individual universities and then departments within those universities. The UFC ostensibly would not transfer funds between broad subject categories or identify subjects for preferential treatment, but of course this is precisely the result of the assessment exercise.[53]

The first exercise, completed in 1985/6, had come in for strong criticism. Following the completion of a detailed questionnaire, requiring submissions on research income and expenditure, research planning,

---

[51] *Annual Review of Government Funded Research and Development*, London, HMSO, 1990, p.172.
[52] SERC, *A Strategy for Support of Core Science*, 1988.
[53] UFC, *Report on the 1989 Research Assessment Exercise*, 1989.

priorities and output, subject sub-committees of the UGC produced evaluative ratings, thus helping to provide the judgemental allocation of research funds through the Committee. The main points of conflict were: assessment criteria were uncertain; assessors remained anonymous; inter-disciplinary work did not fall easily within cost centres or university departments; larger departments received biased judgements as a consequence of the information sought; the rating categories were ambiguous; judgemental standards varied between subject committees; the ratings reflected completed rather than current and forthcoming research activity; and finally, there was no appeals procedure or possibility of consultation. Comparisons of research ratings might be more instructive if institutions throughout the world or in Europe were included in the exercise, since it might be that a UK institution is simply below average in an above average system.

The UGC's paper *The Next Research Selectivity Exercise*, did attempt to refine the criteria by which judgements on selectivity and performance were to be made in 1989. It dismissed an appeals mechanism as 'impractical': although no explanation was given (inadequate funding of the UGC/UFC maybe?). It admitted serious deficiency in the previous selectivity exercise; now the stress was to be on quality.[54] But how is quality to be judged? The committee considered that income from research grants and research contracts reflects research strength as perceived by industry, commerce and government departments (and research income of course, as an *input*, might not equate with quality research, an *output*). Yet, as our own survey of industry shows, what industry perceives as 'strength' is work with a tangible product dividend;[55] government departments similarly will be looking for clear and 'useful' results. The committee now wishes to know details of all members of staff, taking the laboriousness of central 'planning' to a new extreme.

In the event more weight was given to grant income from the Research Councils than from industrial and commercial sources in the 1989 exercise. Data inputs were weighted to take account of the size of departments and this countered a major criticism of the previous exercise. The assessments were essentially retrospective on the basis that past performance represented a good guide to the future.

---

[54] University Grants Committee, *The Next Research Selectivity Exercise*, 1988.
[55] See chapter 9, pp.279-81.

The 1989 assessments produced very few surprises and deal only with original research: teaching and unoriginal contract work are ignored. Two institutions emerge with almost universal excellence, namely Cambridge and Oxford, with Imperial College and University College London very close behind. Following these are the newer universities of Warwick and York and a solid core of older civic universities, all being rated through cost centres and then units of assessment on a five point scale. On the scale, 5 equates with international excellence in many areas and national excellence in all others, and 1 with little or no national excellence. Tables 5:8 and 5:9 give a league table based on percentage scores out of a possible maximum of 100 for cost centre and then unit of assessment. By way of comparison, A.H. Halsey's peer review for 1989 is shown in Table 5:10, where a first choice per subject receives a score of three points, a second choice two and a third one. The sum of these scores rates Oxford and Cambridge at the top followed by Manchester and Edinburgh, thus no great difference with the 1989 assessment. Individual subject breakdowns are also given in Table 5:11. Finally in Table 5:12 the 1986 research rankings are given so that positions in 1989 and 1986 can be compared (column six equates with the 1989 scores).

TABLE 5:8
1989 SELECTIVITY EXERCISE BY COST CENTRE % OF MAXIMUM POSSIBLE SCORE OF 100

CAMBRIDGE	93
OXFORD	91.42
IMPERIAL	91.25
UCL	85.83
WARWICK	81.53
LSE	80
BRISTOL	75
YORK	73.84
UMIST	73.84
MANCHESTER	72
ESSEX	68
LIVERPOOL	67.85
EDINBURGH	66.89
SOUTHAMPTON	66.66
SUSSEX	66.25
LANCASTER	65.5
DURHAM	65.3
QMC	64.28
SHEFFIELD	64.16

TABLE 5:9
1989 SELECTIVITY EXERCISE BY UNIT OF ASSESSMENT % OF MAXIMUM POSSIBLE SCORE OF 100

CAMBRIDGE	89.5
IMPERIAL	89
OXFORD	88.26
LSE	83.75
UCL	83.55
WARWICK	82.5
YORK	74.28
ESSEX	73.7
UMIST	73.3
BRISTOL	72
KING'S	69.71
MANCHESTER	78.1
SHEFFIELD	67
LIVERPOOL	66.94
SOUTHAMPTON	65.85
EDINBURGH	64.92
LANCASTER	64.8
EAST ANGLIA	63
QMC	62.4

TABLE 5:8
1989 SELECTIVITY EXERCISE BY COST CENTRE % OF MAXIMUM POSSIBLE SCORE OF 100 (Cont'd)

NOTTINGHAM	62.96
EAST ANGLIA	62.8
BIRMINGHAM	61.5
LEEDS	61.4
NEWCASTLE	61.3
KING'S	60.86
SURREY	60
BIRKBECK	60
EXETER	58.8
ST ANDREW'S	58.57
READING	57.89
GLASGOW	57.77
CARDIFF	57
BATH	56.8
ABERYSTWYTH	56
LEICESTER	55.78
SWANSEA	55.55
KENT	54.2
ABERDEEN	53.63
LOUGHBOROUGH	52.85
ASTON	51
BANGOR	50.76
RHB	50.76
HULL	50.5
DUNDEE	49
BRADFORD	48.7
STRATHCLYDE	47.2
WESTFIELD	46.66
HERIOT-WATT	46.66
QUEEN'S	46.15
ULSTER	45
STIRLING	44.28
BRUNEL	42.8
CITY	40
KEELE	40
LAMPETER	40
SALFORD	40
GOLDSMITH'S	35

TABLE 5:9
1989 SELECTIVITY EXERCISE BY UNIT OF ASSESSMENT % OF MAXIMUM POSSIBLE SCORE OF 100 (Cont'd)

BIRKBECK	62
NOTTINGHAM	62
BIRMINGHAM	61.7
DURHAM	61.6
ST ANDREW'S	61.48
READING	61.46
NEWCASTLE	61.3
SURREY	60
SUSSEX	60
BATH	59
EXETER	58.85
LEEDS	57
LEICESTER	56.96
GLASGOW	57.77
LOUGHBOROUGH	55.2
ABERDEEN	53.8
CARDIFF	53.5
RHB	53.33
HULL	53.3
SWANSEA	53.3
KENT	52.5
WESTFIELD	52.5
ABERYSTWYTH	51.85
ASTON	51
BRADFORD	50
BANGOR	49
STRATHCLYDE	48.83
DUNDEE	48.69
HERIOT-WATT	48.42
QUEEN'S	47.08
STIRLING	45.45
SALFORD	44.2
BRUNEL	43.8
CITY	42.5
ULSTER	41.81
LAMPETER	41.8
KEELE	40
GOLDSMITH'S	39.04

TABLE 5:10
INSTITUTIONAL AND SUBJECT RANKINGS 1989

Ranking	Institution	Sum Rate 1989
1.	Oxford	1,920
2.	Cambridge	1,902
3.	Manchester	678
4.	Edinburgh	592
5.	Imperial College, London	587
6.	London Medical (combined)	536
7.	Bristol	512
8.	UCL	481
9.	LSE	418
10.	Warwick	366
11.	Glasgow	268
12.	Leeds	260
13.	Nottingham	249
14.	Southampton	243
15.	Birmingham	218
16.	Sheffield	205
17.	Lancaster	173
18.	Newcastle	169
19.	Reading	159
20.	Kings College, London	157
21.	York	151

TABLE 5:11
SUBJECT GROUP BEST DEPARTMENTS 1989 – UNIVERSITY RESPONDENTS

Subjects	Institution	Ranking 1989	Sum Rate
Arts	Oxford	1	255
	Cambridge	2	220
	Bristol	3	47
	Edinburgh	4	42
	Manchester	5	37
	East Anglia/Warwick	6	34

TABLE 5:11
SUBJECT GROUP BEST DEPARTMENTS 1989 – UNIVERSITY RESPONDENTS (Cont'd)

Subjects	Institution	Ranking 1989	Sum Rate
Language/Literature and area studies	Cambridge	1	277
	Oxford	2	255
	UCL	3	76
	Edinburgh	4	68
	York	5	55
Architecture and other professional studies	Reading	1	13
	Sheffield	2	11
	Cambridge	3	10
	Bath/Cardiff	4	9
Social, administrative and business studies	Oxford	1	382
	LSE	2	372
	Cambridge	3	244
	Manchester	4	173
	Warwick	5	162
Science	Cambridge	1	821
	Oxford	2	698
	Imperial	3	306
	Edinburgh	4	241
	Manchester	5	154
Agriculture, forestry and veterinary studies	Glasgow/Reading	1	39
	Edinburgh	2	32
	Bristol	3	31
	Nottingham	4	26
Engineering and technology	Imperial College	1	253
	Cambridge	2	181
	Southampton	3	99
	Manchester	4	57
	Bristol	5	52
Medicine, dentistry and health studies	London (combined)	1	680
	Oxford	2	270
	Manchester	3	201
	Cambridge	4	133
	Edinburgh	5	130
Education	London	1	104
	Exeter	2	45
	Leeds	3	24
	Warwick	4	20
	Loughborough	5	19

TABLE 5:12
1986 UNIVERSITY RESEARCH RATINGS

UNIVERSITY (inc.main London Colleges)	No. of Cost Centres In Which Active	No. of Cost Centres Above Average	% Above Average (X)	No. of Cost Centres Below Average	% Below Average (Y)	X – Y	No.of Subject Areas Out-standing
1. LGBS	1	1	100	0	0	100	1
2. CAMBRIDGE	27	25	93	0	0	93	35
3. OXFORD	21	19	90	1	5	85	31
4. UCL	24	21	88	1	4	84	18
5. LSE	6	6	75	0	0	75	8
6. IMPERIAL	16	12	75	1	6	69	8
7. WARWICK	15	10	67	1	7	60	7
8. UMIST	16	11	69	2	13	56	4
9. BRISTOL	26	17	65	3	12	53	15
10. SUSSEX	16	10	63	2	13	50	3
11. YORK	12	6	50	1	8	42	6
12. MANCHESTER	28	16	57	6	21	36	11
13. ESSEX	10	5	50	2	20	30	6
14. QMC	15	6	40	2	13	27	2
15. GLASGOW	27	9	33	3	11	22	4
16. S/HAMPTON	27	10	37	5	19	18	7
17. BIRMINGHAM	25	8	32	4	16	16	4
18. KING'S	22	7	32	4	18	14	8
19. EDINBURGH	31	14	45	10	32	13	12
20. LEEDS	27	9	33	6	22	11	10
21. READING	19	5	26	3	16	10	4
22. UEA	14	4	29	3	21	8	3
23. BATH	19	4	21	3	16	5	2
24. NOTTINGHAM	26	9	35	8	31	4	5
25. DURHAM	16	4	25	4	25	0	4
26. KENT	14	5	36	5	36	0	3
27. LIVERPOOL	30	10	33	10	33	0	2
28. NEWCASTLE	29	8	28	8	28	0	4
29. SHEFFIELD	26	7	27	7	27	0	4
30. LAMPETER	3	0	0	0	0	0	0
31. UWCM	4	0	0	0	0	0	0
32. LANCASTER	18	5	28	5	28	0	3
33. ST ANDREW'S	13	3	23	4	31	-8	4
34. SURREY	18	5	28	7	39	-11	2
35. LEICESTER	19	5	26	7	37	-11	4
36. HERIOT-WATT	15	5	33	7	47	-14	1
37. EXETER	18	3	17	6	33	-16	1
38. L/BOROUGH	16	1	6	4	25	-19	1
39. STRATHCLYDE	26	5	19	10	38	-19	0
40. BIRKBECK	11	2	18	5	45	-27	0
41. RHBNC	15	3	20	7	47	-27	2

TABLE 5:12 (Cont.)
1986 UNIVERSITY RESEARCH RATINGS

UNIVERSITY (inc.main London Colleges)	No. of Cost Centres In Which Active	No. of Cost Centres Above Average	% Above Average (X)	No. of Cost Centres Below Average	% Below Average (Y)	X – Y	No.of Subject Areas Outstanding
42. CARDIFF	23	3	13	10	43	-30	2
43. ABERDEEN	23	3	13	10	43	-30	2
44. SWANSEA	19	4	21	10	53	-32	0
45. ASTON	15	4	27	9	60	-33	1
46. DUNDEE	22	4	18	12	55	-37	2
47. BRADFORD	18	3	17	11	61	-44	0
48. SALFORD	14	2	14	9	64	-50	0
49. STIRLING	14	1	7	8	57	-50	0
50. WESTFIELD	4	0	0	2	50	-50	2
51. ABERYSTWYTH	16	0	0	9	56	-56	0
52. HULL	21	1	5	13	62	-57	1
53. BRUNEL	15	1	7	10	67	-60	0
54. BANGOR	14	2	14	11	79	-65	0
55. KEELE	17	0	0	11	79	-78	0
56. CITY	15	1	7	13	87	-80	0
57. MBS	1	0	0	1	100	-100	0

Many have argued that the results reflect the Matthew Principle, of "to him who hath shall be given". The best universities already attract the best researchers and now the UFC will reinforce this by cutting off the weak, instead of giving them extra investment to establish and consolidate their strengths.

Several points need to be noted though in relation to the most recent exercise: (1) there has been an enormous improvement in the performance of almost all university departments since the 1986 exercise; (2) small departments do less well than large, because of the resource factor; (3) different modes of publication were not given an overt weighting and the speed of delivery of the assessments suggests cursory consideration of publications; (4) there now appears to be evidence of cheating in submissions. Units of assessment and the rating scale need to be well-defined before the next exercise is undertaken, and some guarantee of comparability between assessing panels established. For example, cost centres are more narrowly defined in the sciences than in the social sciences and this shows through in the results: 35 cost centres have a maximum score of 5 (international standing) in the sciences and 20 in the applied sciences, but only 4 in the social sciences and 1 in the arts. Weaknesses are also easily detectable, 25 in the sciences, 28 in the applied sciences, 2 in the social sciences and 2 in the arts. Problems with classification represent only part of the explanation for this state of affairs.

In late 1989 the UFC announced that the next round of assessment had been postponed until the mid-1990's, but it has now been brought forward to 1992/93 with the promise after consultation with the universities of more guidance on quality and fewer subject units, but peer review is to remain the major vehicle for assessment. This will encompass a move towards funding 'for' research rather than being based on research criteria, requiring, of course, more institutional accountability. All areas of research will be included – basic, strategic and applied, and the five point scale for ratings has been retained. Submissions will be scrutinised for accuracy.

THE 1991 WHITE PAPER

The 1991 White Paper, *Higher Education: A New Framework*, underpins the governments objective of "securing a high quality system of higher education... (whilst enabling) institutions to make yet more effective responses to the increasing demand for higher education".[56] It argues that national wealth will rise in the five years from 1992/1993 and that a fair share of this will go to higher education. However, the old clichés are rehearsed again to the effect that greater efficiency is required given the need for restraint on public expenditure: hence existing facilities need to be more intensively used through a system of flexible credits. The key to cost-effective expansion is thus greater competition for funds and students.

Research receives terse coverage in the White Paper, which accepts that universities undertake basic and strategic research, whilst the Polytechnics embrace applied and some strategic research.

Although both sectors bid for funds from the Research Councils, the universities receive the largest share of such funding. In 1989/90 the universities received £860m from the UFC; £260m from the Research Councils and £500m from other research grants and contracts, giving a grand total of £1,620m. Polytechnics in the previous year received £20m

---

[56] DES, *Higher Education: A New Framework*, London, HMSO, Cmnd. 1541, 1991, p.10.

from central (PCFC) funds; £10m from the Research Councils and £40m from other external sources, giving a grand total of £70m.

In the White Paper the government iterates its support for the dual system of support combined with selectivity, so that the universities are free to decide their own research priorities. It accepts that teaching and research are "linked together to allow a better overview of the financial position of individual institutions",[57] that the Research Councils should be responsible for meeting the full cost of research that they sponsor, and that commercial research should be self-financing. Funding of research on the basis of student numbers is to be phased out and, given an emphasis on applied and strategic research, research funds are to be selectively applied to preserve "the (unique) research mission of different institutions" whilst they remain essentially free market in what they choose to do.

The conflict between philosophy and practice comes towards the end of the White Paper. For it is argued that Polytechnics are no longer to be excluded from the dual system of support, which on the present basis of funding by student numbers would give them the lion's share of all such funds. Hence the Secretary of State was forced to recant almost immediately and make it clear that equal support was not his intention, rather a continuation of the present distribution, albeit more refined through a new and more thorough selectivity exercise. It thus becomes quite clear that the government has not thought out the implications of its new philosophy for jointly funding higher education and is in danger of disrupting an already fragile research base. On research alone it must accept that extra funding is required if the status quo is to change. The Bill that eventually emerges will need the closest scrutiny, not least on its provisions for research funding.

CONCLUSIONS – THE DEATH OF RESEARCH

British government policy in relation to theatre, the arts, museums and libraries has often been to award grants below the rate of inflation in the expectation that organisations will become more proactive and seal the gap with private funding.

But what if they do not? We are making all kinds of assumptions about the competence of these institutions to seek funding, to deliver more

---

[57] *Higher Education: A New Framework, Ibid.*, p.16.

commercial products, and about the culturally determined willingness of the private world to support them. A more imaginative approach would have been for the government to provide seed money to hire experts in the art of fundraising and such like. Ministers delude themselves if they think, as one minister has suggested, that the new rich they claim credit for will help fund universities, since such a proposition assumes they are prepared to and credits them with more disposable income than they actually possess, once the costs of English embourgeoisement – mortgages, private medicine, school fees and so on – are taken into account. And industry itself, as our survey has shown, is only really interested in near-market research (this is true of America as well) so that the basic research specialised in by universities will be neglected.[58]

There exists also a fallacious perception that universities can gain richly through contract research from industry. But given that so much of this work is invariably 'applied', it can represent the misdirection of scientific talent from what it does best in return for perhaps limited long-term gains. Moreover, comparisons with the U.S. are often phoney; those who make them usually believe that American academe is held aloft by substantial contract research with industry, but as we know this is not the case. The American system is actually propelled by fees, state grants and fundraising from alumni and business. Alumni fundraising works because: it is deeply rooted in culture and tradition; a favourable tax system; the elegance of U.S. campuses, compared with the brittle U.K. palaces of steel and concrete; a long-term policy of fostering student loyalty to the institution that begins in the freshman year. We should be sceptical about its immediate importability to Britain, since it is a practice which can only gain momentum over time.

Are there alternatives to a state that will consistently underfund, and therefore gradually debauch the system to mediocrity? Clearly yes in the case of applied research, but with basic research? The question that should be asked is not whether the very notion of state support is ideologically unsound, but whether it actually works. In the case of the car industry, for example, the process of state subsidy failed: government cannot run industry. But was the subsidised theatre, which can assume much of the credit for the excellence of British acting and the availability of great drama, equally a failure? Indeed, a policy of constant diminution of support

---

[58] See chapter 9 below, pp.278-9.

can of itself be extravagance, since the degradation of institutions into mediocrity raises the question of whether it is worth bothering to support them at all.

In twenty years time, if current trends continue, British universities will be for the most part the Dunciad of the North American and European league, many of them ossified schools, essentially teaching institutions like the polytechnics with which they are being merged. And the kind of people who work for them will be competent pedagogues with scant inclination or indeed competence to do research. *For academic excellence in research is a tradition and not a product.* If demolished it cannot simply be re-purchased. As the 1989 ABRC report stated: "Unless action is taken very soon there will be a critical shortage of suitably qualified and trained researchers in the 1990s", and the Board continues, "Too few children are opting for scientific subjects at school, applications for science and engineering places at universities are falling and the pool of excellent science graduates willing and able to go on to postgraduate work is declining. The career opportunities and high rewards now open to the most talented graduates in non-scientific occupations contrast strongly with the poor rewards open to scientists and engineers".[59]

Science Strategy for the 1990's, produced by the AUT, in response to Save British Science's analysis of the current state of British scientific research, gives a seven point summary of the major policies required to save British science. These are much wider than simply pumping in large sums of extra cash, and all of the points require urgent attention:

1. Schools: The teaching of school science is clearly suffering badly from a lack of qualified teachers. It will be essential to make careers in school science teaching more attractive to ensure success for science as a part of the core curriculum.

2. Higher education: Industry and research need a substantially larger production of trained people at all levels. We propose a long-term aim to increase the numbers by about 50%, with the largest increase occurring in the numbers of skilled technical workers.

---

[59] ABRC, *Science and Public Expenditure*, 1989.

3. The brain drain: Schemes like the Royal Society Fellowships and Professorships should be expanded to attract back some of the key scientists lost recently to the US. The numbers involved in the brain drain are not large, but the quality certainly is.

4. Europe: Given its economic and political position, the UK should be involved in European collaborative science projects to a degree that matches France and Germany.

5. Research and development: The United Kingdom should aim to raise its overall level of civil research and development towards that of Japan, Germany and France. Part of this development could be secured by progressively shifting the balance of civil and military research.

6. Industry: International comparative studies show the growth in industrial research and development still lagging well behind our competitors despite reduced corporation tax. Other fiscal measures are therefore required to stimulate essential growth.

7. Science-industry collaboration: Industry and private funds are already contributing as much, if not more, to higher education research as in other countries. SBS is strongly in favour of further growth in science-industry collaboration provided that government support for basic sciences ensures a proper balance between fundamental and applied work, and that collaboration is seen as a two-way process. Industries should consider appointing academic scientists to their boards, just as universities appoint industrialists to their governing bodies.[60]

EXODUS

What of the frequently alleged emigration of researchers? The Conservative Party, largely through the medium of Robert Jackson, has denied that it exists. In the 1989 issue of *Politics Today* for example, their research department states:

> "Apart from wild and unfounded accusations of 'cuts' in Government funding of higher education, the favourite ploy of the Government's critics is to accuse it of allowing a 'brain drain' to take place. They allege that academics from all areas are leaving Britain for jobs abroad because they do not receive either

---

[60] AUT, "Saving British Science", *AUT Bulletin*, September, 1989.

adequate remuneration or service to support their work. These charges are groundless".[61]

Others disagree and one example may suffice. According to a citation study by three emigrating economists:

> " ... five economists out of the complete British total ... are cited more than one hundred times in a year. Out of these five, only one now remains in Britain .... Adding together citations gives, for our group of emigrants, a total of 940 for the year. We have also calculated the citation total for the London School of Economics top eight economists. It comes to 530. By this crude measure of performance, the emigrants are nearly twice as good as the cream of Britain's top department... The entire faculty (50 strong) at LSE is cited a total of 1100 times in 1987. As far as (the authors) can judge, it is Europe's most highly cited economics department. Yet the emigrants alone come close to that total".

And they concluded: "The average (one) of our emigrants is typically worth more than an entire British economics department".[62] They cite some of the economists who have recently moved to the United States from British universities: W. Buiter (LSE > Yale); J. Campbell (Oxford > Princeton); A. Deaton (Bristol > Princeton); A. Dixit (Warwick > Princeton); D. Gale (LSE > Pittsburgh); O. Hart (LSE > MIT); T. Lancaster (Hull > Brown); A. Sen (Oxford > Harvard).

Clearly a significant exodus has important consequences for research policy; if the rising stars are to be constantly abducted, the consequence will be a climate of banality since a good researcher takes not only his mind and ideas, he also ceases to contribute to the sustenance of that quality culture by guiding generations of research students. And if mediocrity is the norm, would anything be worth preserving?

WHO PAYS?

Who, then, should pay for university research and education? Clearly the state ought always to have a major role if only because of the social and taxation return which graduates supply during their years of employment. Industrial and alumni sources must of course be eloquently solicited; another part of the answer may even lie, as we suggest elsewhere, in the

---

[61] "Higher Education", *Politics Today*, 16, 1989, p.287. The raw figures for the brain drain ignore the age, experience and level of the staff involved. From 1986-87 4,000 staff left British universities with no known destination. As the *Financial Times* noted (13 June 1989), "as the decades pass the correlation between economic success and educational attainment will become increasingly obvious. A university brain drain will become a real drain on the economy. The government should accept its responsibility to finance higher pay".

[62] A. Oswald et al., "The Cream Goes West", *The Guardian*, 13 June, 1989.

cash endowment of some universities. But if the state is unwilling to pay more in subsidy, and there is scant evidence that such reticence causes alarm among the populace, then the only alternative source of university funding is from the consumers of knowledge themselves, students and their employers.

The ideological right will certainly object to the grand strategy to deal with the problem of university funding advocated in this volume, which is an alternative to the Barr-Barnes proposal for specially appropriated National Insurance Contributions (NIC's).[63] Perhaps, then, the argument should be expressed in their own language. Our proposal is for a payment for a service which has greatly benefited the individual, not for a redistributive tax. As such it is fully in line with the Conservative credo, which is, we take it, to evolve from taxes differentiated only by income level towards a system where people pay for that which directly benefits them. Never in the life of the individual, unless they are seriously ill and for a long time, will they receive such a major transfer of equity from the state. It is fair that they should be made to pay more and it is just that they should do this through loans with repayment contingent upon income, but in such a way as not to destroy a major raison d'etre of that ethos and system, which is access and mobility via an intellectual meritocracy.

But is this fair, bearing in mind that students and their employers would then actually be subsidising university research, as well as their own tuition? The answer is clearly, yes, because there is limited utility in giving to students a moribund body of knowledge, and to industry personnel whose information is dated. The notion of 'good' university teaching must rightly imply lucidity of presentation. But it must also draw from a living intellectual body. There is no pedagogic excellence in recycling dead knowledge however good the exposition.

POSTSCRIPT – HOW IS UNIVERSITY RESEARCH FUNDED?

How does the process of distributing research monies now currently work? The £1.6 billion allocated through the Research Councils and UFC actually

---

[63] N. Barr and J. Barnes, *Strategies For Higher Education: The Alternative White Paper*, Aberdeen University Press, 1988 and N. Barr, "Student Loans: The Next Step", in *The Management and Funding of Universities*, Edited by S. Sexton, Institute of Economic Affairs, 1989.

results from the Public Expenditure Survey, with inputs from the UFC and the Advisory Board for the Research Councils (ABRC), and this produces the government's block grant for the universities and the science budget.[64] The UFC then allocates funds for research and teaching according to the following methodology: (a) what level of resources should be devoted to subjects on a national basis and (b) how these totals should be divided into a teaching and research component. This teaching allocation goes to individual universities on the basis of funded student places. Research allocations depend on more complex criteria, half depending on student numbers in each university cost centre, a proxy for staff numbers, the other half allocated on the basis of: (a) the department's rating in the UGC's research selectivity exercise; (b) the department's income from the Research Councils and charities and (c) the department's other external research income. After special items like London weighting are taken into account, expected fee income from home and EEC students is subtracted from the total figure and the difference represents the UFC grant to the university.

Universities determine the precise split between teaching and research from their block grant until 1992/93, when virement becomes impossible. But from January 1989 judgemental criteria became crucial in the UFC's allocation of research funds and this process is bound to be extended and refined as assessment becomes the norm. Inevitably research monies will be applied more selectively and in greater concentration, but this does not, of course, produce an evolutionary process through which weaker departments will rise as they improve and currently stronger ones, if they lose momentum, fall. To facilitate selectivity the UFC now identifies the research funding in each university's block grant. Nevertheless, universities will retain the ability to determine what research avenues to explore, except that greater accountability and more effective allocation and management of resources will become standard practice.

As a result of the implementation of the selectivity exercise, the distribution of the UFC grant in favour of research has changed. The UFC grant at present is as follows: Teaching 63%, Research 33% and Special Factors 4.0% (mainly London weighting). The 33% presently divides up as:

---

[64] ABRC advice was given publicly until the 1991 round, but thereafter is to be private, including the earmarking of funds for particular projects and the correction of structural problems arising out of changed research priorities.

(1) 5.4% depends on research grant income from Research Councils and charities (DR).

(2) 0.7% depends on contract income (CR).

(3) 12.0% depends on student and staff numbers (SR).

(4) 14.9% depends on research selectivity reviews (JR).

Some virement between these categories of course takes place in individual universities, however by 1994/95 the balance between (3) and (4) will change to 9.75% and 19.25% respectively (1990/91 13.5% and 14.46% respectively). As we have already noted, from 1992/93 a tranche of UFC research grant income will be transferred to the Research Councils, some £150 million. The control of funds from the centre will therefore reiterate the research position of a department, although the UFC does acknowledge the close relationship between research and teaching in its 22/89 statement on research policy.[65]

Considering the comparative position of universities between 1985/86 and 1990/91, and dividing them into three divisions based on research ratings, it is possible to identify the winners and losers in grant terms. The top 13 gained 8% of exchequer grant (or £51m), the second 18 lost 4.5% (or £20m) and the bottom 15 lost 13% (or £31m).[66] In the first group, London gained 16%, Oxbridge 9% and the others 0.25% with two losing 11%. All those institutions in the second and third group lost their share of income bar one in each group. Clearly therefore historical developments and the shift in emphasis to judgemental criteria, mean de facto division of universities into X, Y and Z categories is only a matter of time and the inclusion of the new universities (ex polytechnics) in the pool, can only speed up the process.

SCIENCE

The science budget is determined by the Secretary of State in response to the ABRC's advice and includes some earmarking of funds for particular projects and the correction of structural problems as research priorities

---

[65] UFC, Circular Letter, 22/89 (statement on research policy).
[66] Top 13 equates with 65% of maximum possible research score;
Middle 18 equates with 55-64% of maximum possible research score;
Bottom 15 equates with 40-54% of maximum possible research score.

change. The division of the 1989 budget of £825.6 million is indicated in Table 5:13 together with planning figures for the years 1990/91 to 1991/92.

TABLE 5:13
SCIENCE BUDGET: RECOMMENDED ALLOCATIONS FOR 1989-90 AND PLANNING FIGURES FOR 1990-91 AND 1991-92.

	£m 1989-90	%	£m 1990-91	£m 1991-92
AFRC	76.3	9	78.2	81.7
ESRC	32.0	4	32.4	31.6
MRC	176.3	22	181.4	184.5
NERC	123.4	14	106.2	103.3
SERC	404.8	50	410.2	407.0
Royal Society	11.64	1	12.29	12.73
Fellowship of Engineering	0.97		1.04	1.11
Science Policy Studies	0.11		0.12	0.12
CEST	0.08		0.08	0.08
Flexibility Margin			15.7	33.6
TOTAL	825.6	100	837.6	855.8

TABLE 5:14
DES SCIENCE PROVISION 1991/92 TO 1994/95

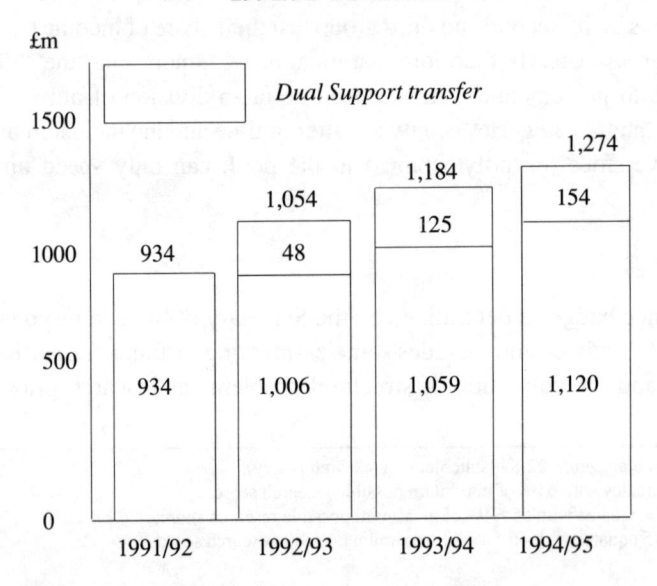

£m	1991/92	1992/93	1993/94	1994/95
Total	934	1,054	1,184	1,274
Dual Support transfer	—	48	125	154
Base	934	1,006	1,059	1,120

The planning figures given in Table 5:14 indicate a 19% increase for science over the next three years, although pay awards and inflation will obviously take their toll. The budget rises from £934m in 1991/92 to £1,006m in 1992/93, £1,059 in 1993/94 and then £1,120 in 1994/95. When monies transferred from the UFC are included, the relevant figures become £934m; £1,054; £1,184m and £1,274m respectively. The precise allocation of the money will depend on ABRC advice, but at least some new initiatives in science should prove possible.

The Research Councils and universities obviously co-operated in the system of dual support for research, with the universities providing basic funding to enable all academic staff to pursue research and 'well-founded' laboratories, or an infra-structure, to enable work to be undertaken that is supported by the Research Councils. However dual support in 1992/93 is substantially modified, in the sense that Research Councils assume responsibility for overheads connected with research sponsored by them.[67] The Research Councils have their own Institutes, Units and Centres, but support university research through grants, post-graduate studentships, fellowships, the provision of access to central 'domestic' facilities and by subscriptions to international bodies. Research Council support for universities amounted to £825.6 million in 1989/90 representing an increase of 82% in real terms since 1979/80. Funding from other sources, government departments, industry and commerce, reached £350 million in 1987/88, a threefold increase since 1979/80.

---

[67] See above p.162.

CHAPTER SIX

DECONSTRUCTING THE IVORY TOWER: INTERNATIONAL COMPARISONS OF RESEARCH FUNDING

"Most future historians who judge Margaret Thatcher will, in the nature of things, be in universities – which are my major association with Britain. Those historians will tell how British university scholarship and research, once in my lifetime pre-eminent in the world, were scrimped, bashed and diminished in her years as Prime Minister. Perhaps in pursuit of more comprehensive truth they will mention other matters, but the above they will surely say".
John Kenneth Galbraith,
The Economist, 29 April, 1989.

"I beg to differ with Professor Galbraith. I am confident that future historians – and indeed many commentators writing on the subject today – will praise the revolution taking place in Britain's education system under Prime Minister Thatcher. The revolution is under way at all levels of the system. It is part of a necessary process, given the changing needs of the new Britain. The revolution will invigorate scholarship and research in Britain's universities. It will help them realize their full potential and regain the eminent position of the past mentioned by Professor Galbraith".
Ambassador Charles Price,
The Economist, 29 April, 1989.

INTRODUCTION: LESSONS FROM OVERSEAS?[1]

International comparisons are notoriously misleading: Britain has fewer universities in relation to its size for instance, and what is here called a polytechnic is elsewhere called a university. But, *prima facie*, the United Kingdom academic would appear to be doing relatively well compared with his continental and Japanese peers in terms of abundance of research time. Research expenditure in other countries tends to be between 3-7% of university expenditure; in the United States and the United Kingdom it is much higher.

But one is not comparing like with like. Statistics are obtained in different ways and can in fact be measuring different things. In Japan and the United States of America there is a major private component to the university system. In Europe there is a state system with elements of a Roman Catholic system, and unlike the United Kingdom's it is not élitist but massified, with students actually going to university much later. Most institutions of higher learning are designated 'university', and it is perceived as the right of anyone within a generously defined ability range to go there; selection is actually done during the course itself. It is an égalitarian system in Europe and universities are often formally equal, however there must be doubts about a system with such a high drop out rate, unlike the United Kingdom where this is negligible.

Research, however, is often siphoned off into specifically focused institutions: "A typical arrangement is independent research institutes which may (or may not) be located on university or college campuses, but are not integrated with teaching departments and which are staffed by a separate corps of researchers who only rarely and incidentally teach students".[2]

Whilst international comparisons of research and development as a proportion of GDP are tricky, Table 6:1 shows that Britain has not increased its spending on these areas, unlike six of its major competitors. This will inevitably have serious consequences for Britain's economic

---

[1] Evidence presented here arises from the Organisation for Economic Co-operation and Development's 1989 studies, *Changing Patterns of Finance in Higher Education*, that included: United States of America, Japan, United Kingdom, France, Germany, Denmark, Netherlands, Portugal, Spain, Greece, Finland and Norway. Cf.G. Williams, *Financing Higher Education*, OECD, 1990.
[2] G. Williams, *Universities Under Stringency*, OECD, Paris, 1989.

performance in the future, for she lags behind in fifth place (sixth if military research is excluded, for Italy then moves ahead of her).

TABLE 6:1
GENERAL EXPENDITURE ON R AND D AS PERCENTAGE OF GDP 1981 – 1988

ITALY	XXXXXXXXXXXXXX	1981
	XXXXXXXXXXXXXXXX	1988 (1.3)
FRANCE	XXXXXXXXXXXXXXXXXXXXXXX	1981
	XXXXXXXXXXXXXXXXXXXXXXXXXXXXX	1988 (2.3)
WEST GERMANY	XXXXXXXXXXXXXXXXXXXXXXXXXX	1981
	XXXXXXXXXXXXXXXXXXXXXXXXXXXXXX	1988 (2.8)
JAPAN	XXXXXXXXXXXXXXXXXXXXXXXXXXX	1981
	XXXXXXXXXXXXXXXXXXXXXXXXXXXXX	1988 (2.7)
SWEDEN	XXXXXXXXXXXXXXXXXX	1981
	XXXXXXXXXXXXXXXXXXXXXXXXXXXXXX	1986 (2.7)
USA	XXXXXXXXXXXXXXXXXXXXXXXX	1981
	XXXXXXXXXXXXXXXXXXXXXXXXXXXXXX	1988 (2.9)
UK	XXXXXXXXXXXXXXXXXXXXXXXX	1981
	XXXXXXXXXXXXXXXXXXXXXXXX	1988 (2.3)
	0 0.5% 1% 1.5% 2% 2.5% 3%	

SOURCE: OECD

In terms of expenditure by member governments of the European Community in billions of pounds sterling, in 1988, France spent £6.3; Germany £5.5; Britain £4.5; Italy £3.6; Netherlands £1.1; Belgium £0.4 and the others £1.5. The EC itself spent a further £1 billion on the production, distribution and rational utilisation of energy.

Table 6:2 looks at government funding of research and development by socio-economic objectives in 1988. Again, Britain is shown to be lagging behind, particularly in industrial development and the advancement of knowledge. As expected, only in the area of defence is Britain comparing favourably, but the benefits for industrial development from this expenditure are extremely marginal.

TABLE 6:2 GOVERNMENT FUNDING OF R AND D BY SOCIO-ECONOMIC OBJECTIVE.

	Agriculture, forestry and fishing % GDP	Industrial development	Energy	Health	Advancement of knowledge	Civil space	Other	Defence	Total
Italy	0.02	0.12	0.07	0.04	0.33	0.07	0.07	0.08	0.81
France	0.06	0.18	0.05	0.04	0.38	0.01	0.07	0.52	1.38
FRG	0.02	0.15	0.07	0.03	0.48	0.06	0.11	0.13	1.05
Japan	0.02	0.02	0.11	0.01	0.24	0.03	0.01	0.02	0.47
USA	0.02	0	0.04	0.15	0.04	0.08	0.05	0.83	1.23
UK	0.04	0.09	0.04	0.05	0.23	0 03	0.06	0.43	0.98

SOURCE: OECD.

Similarly, Table 6:3 demonstrates Britain's failure to keep pace with its European partners in government funded civil research and development, particularly in : exploration and exploitation of space; production, distribution and national utilisation of energy, and industrial production and technology. Again the implications that follow are extremely serious.

TABLE 6:3 GOVERNMENT AND EC FUNDED CIVIL RESEARCH AND DEVELOPMENT.

	Exploration & exploitation £million except EC ECU million	Production distribution & rational utilisation of energy	Non-oriented research	Industrial production & technology	Other	Research financed from general university funds
FRG	303	386	793	768	857	1707
France	437	248	985	803	742	736
Italy	328	316	307	551	601	1151
UK	146	171	216	395	765	860
Other	68	40	184	278	464	392
EC (mecu)	25	412	24	266	246	0

SOURCE: *Annual Review of Government Funded Research and Development*, 1990.

The funding of research in specific OECD countries and in particular the role of universities, is examined in the rest of this chapter.

GERMAN EXPERIENCE

In Germany research funds come from the government and are co-ordinated by the Federal Ministry for Research and Technology, though there is some private funding. Government grants are supplemented by the German Society for the Advancement of Scientific Research. But institutions are given little sovereignty over their budgets. There is no long term planning strategy and budgets are liable to be cut if there are economic difficulties (there was a large cut in 1982 for example). Third party finance of research is important: from international organisations, foundations, industry and trade associations. The Länder promote research, but most pressure comes from industry now. Recurrent expenditure in real terms on teaching and research has fallen 50% between 1970 and 1985. Research laboratories and industrial sponsorship benefits university research, and much more specialisation in research by institutions is expected to follow in the future.

Again then, we see the government as the mainstay of research, with autocratic control and a considerable fall in research expenditure.

FINNISH EXPERIENCE

Teaching and research are closely linked together here. External funding of higher education is increasing at all levels (8% increase in industrial funding), but there are also plans to raise the level of state funding of research down to 1991 by 15%: all research is subject to assessment. The Academy of Finland and the Technological Centre both fund research as well as various Ministries and enterprises. The Academy maintains a fine balance between pure and applied research funding, including ethics of science and technological discoveries as well as ecology and the environment.

By 1991 all institutions are to have the same level of resources at their disposal to ensure equality of opportunity and make assessment more penetrating. Co-operation, the sharing of equipment and, therefore, cost effective research, is to be encouraged. Research priorities will be bio-technology, molecular biology, cancer research and information technology. A University Holding Company has been created for development projects and income divides between department, university and the company.

DANISH EXPERIENCE

The Danes aim to integrate their universities' research effort much more with trade, industry and international agencies. They have embarked upon this course to ensure that the universities face up to the needs of the contemporary Danish economy. The central allocation of budgets and research funding is linked to student admissions which are also controlled by the government, and the funding of research now emphasises new areas: bio-technology, the environment and internationally orientated projects, which have a familiar ring to them. The private sector is offering sponsorship to the universities and a good example of this is the Technical University of Denmark: industry is expected to make an even greater contribution in the future.

In Denmark then there is the same pragmatic belief as in the UK, that universities should service industry, and as in the UK a strong linkage between research funding and student admissions, with research funding largely from the state.

DUTCH EXPERIENCE

Although the funding of teaching and research are linked together in the Netherlands, they are now to be separated and subjected to performance indicators to ration declining funds. The Minister of Education is responsible for the 10% of funds withheld for capital expenditure, computing and innovative projects. The division of resources is as follows: Teaching 69%, Research 23%, and Administration 8%: the research grant is one third of the teaching grant, and the scale of research is set at 1500 academic posts, or 10% of the universities overall workload.

Sixty five per cent of research funding is from the Ministry of Education and a further 15% is government sponsored via the Netherlands Organisation for Scientific Research, and 20% of research is contracted by industry.

From 1982, research funding has been linked to quality criteria and no longer to student numbers, with ex-post assessment of establishments. Criteria used in this assessment of research include: quality, relevance, accountability and peer group review, and the effect has been to produce better programmes with no identifiable loss of accountability. Starting from 1987, any programme guaranteed by a university is to be assessed once every 5 years, and all programmes in the same discipline are assessed in the same year for comparative reasons. From 1990 onwards there will be more direct guidance on research priorities as well as a system of incentive grants to ensure innovation and differentiation of projects.

NORWEGIAN EXPERIENCE

Research in Norway is supported by the Research Councils, public agencies and private corporations. Research foundations are attached to universities, and external finance generally covers a large proportion of total expenditure. These foundations are not thought to exert undue policy influence, but efforts are now being made to strengthen support from the central budget to guarantee a larger measure of independence, and institutions will be given more discretion and autonomy in the allocation of their central government grants.

Research Councils constitute an important allocative mechanism between institutions and attempt to remove institutional distortions. Oil related research generates the greatest outside support, some 5% of the total higher education budget, and since the 1980's some ministry funds have been channelled through the Research Councils. There is a recognition of the need to link together researcher and users more closely.

In theory 50% of an academic's time should be devoted to research, but in practice lack of resources prevents this from happening. Twenty per cent of total Norwegian research expenditure goes to universities, and this covers 80% of fundamental research, while of this 20%, 75% is from the central budget, 13% from the Research Councils, 3% from public agencies, 5% from private enterprise and 4% from research foundations. In recent years, in fact, foundations have been funding as much as 25% of Norwegian research and development. Science Parks are also of growing importance and in the 1990's the emergence of an Industrial University, based on large Nordic companies, is a distinct possibility.

In Norway the role of the Research Councils are therefore key and all research monies are arbitered through them, earnings from private enterprise are low and the system is in fact very similar to that in the UK – externally funded with some Research Council input. As in the UK there is a concentration on fundamental research.

In relation to Finland, as well as other Scandinavian countries, one should stress their small size, which may argue for a different type of research régime to that which pertains in the UK. But in Finland state research funding is to increase, as is assessment; there is an égalitarianism as between institutions, and considerable co-operation.

In the Netherlands too there is greater emphasis now upon assessment. The proportion of resources going into research seems somewhat less generous than in the UK – one third in proportional terms, central direction is strong, the government is the main sponsor of research and much bigger than any other agency. Industrial support is significant, but not dominant. The separation of research income from student numbers surely portends imminent developments in the UK and also Australia?

GREEK EXPERIENCE

The system of funding is tightly controlled by the state and there is concentration on teaching activities at the expense of research. With outside funding of research, there is often a staffing problem when it comes to executing the project. Since 1982 it has been possible to set up public or private enterprises to exploit a university's resources, but so far there is little use of this facility.

SPANISH EXPERIENCE

From 1986 there has been a National Plan for Scientific Research and Technological Development in Spain to reproduce the scientific tradition that flourished in the 900 years before the eleventh century, but the financing mechanism is yet to be decided. However, the intention is to raise expenditure from 0.35 to 0.85% of GNP. Under the plan for scientific research twenty programmes are under way with a budget of $5,000m (£2.800m) in four target areas: agriculture and food; technology and communication; quality of life; and a special programme including (for example) high energy physics. Two bodies are the focus of attention here: the Advisory Commission for Scientific Research and the Higher Council for Scientific Research. In 1989 the Offices of Transfer of Research Results completed 3,000 deals between universities and business worth some £46.5m.[3]

Research is funded through subsidies from state departments, though links with business are increasing. Scientific and technological research are subject to targets and objectives – more public resources are being invested here. Autonomous Committees within each region have assumed responsibility for funding research at the local university and this is of growing importance to the total national effort. There is a tendency to promote joint ventures and consultancy in research, but this gives rise to the problem of integrating research into other mainstream activities. Certainly more input from industry is expected in the future.

---

[3] The OTRR markets university research to business.

While in Greece the focus is very largely teaching rather than research, with strong state control, in Spain we see state financing of research with growing investment in it. The role played by business is increasing, and there are now familiar moves to more assessment. However, there is in Spain a great deal of institutional independence – at variance with moves in this country.

UNITED STATES EXPERIENCE

We must distinguish in the US between private and state universities. Tuition fees in the private system are high – $50,000 (£28,000) at Harvard for a four year degree including living expenses, and some of this money is siphoned into academic research. Alumni fund-raising is another source of research income: an Ivy League business school such as Columbia, could and would annually raise sums of between $200 (£112) and $50,000 (£28,000), from each of some 4,000 donors.

The very size of the US system makes comparisons with the UK misleading. Forty per cent of Americans go to college or university compared with only 14% in the UK at present. One should not expect so much of researchers in such a massified system: "the US statement to the Organisation for Economic Co-operation and Development (OECD) in 1985, claimed that only 20% of staff were active researchers, only 10% published regularly, and of their work, only a small proportion was significant".[4] The system "has clear strategic goals, strongly assented to by the States' political class(es) but its institutions are self-planned and flexibly managed".[5]

In the 1970's the federal government provided increased support for research; the shift to greater competitiveness in higher education has led to increases in national funding despite the deficit in the budget, and prestige colleges in the state system are given extra research funding by the state. In general terms, research funding fell in the 1970's and picked up in the 1980's. Corporate financing of research is growing, but following changes in the tax law in 1986 this may become a less important feature in the future. The government remains a big purchaser of research and

---

[4] "Mixed Motives: The Split Between Teaching and Research", *THES*, 1989.
[5] "California Dreaming", *THES*, 1989.

President Reagan decided to double science funding over 5 years, though much of this kind of spending goes to military research.[6]

High salaries help enormously to attract the good people, nationally and internationally, so that a twenty-eight year old economist starting teaching would be paid $40,000 for nine months work: then there would be added summer earnings. The UK equivalent would be on £12,000. The earning curve rises more steeply: at 37 the American would be on $55,000 plus (£30,900 plus) compared with £20,000 for an Englishman.[7]

In 1981 the National Science Board suggested that higher education institutions produced 9% of America's Research and Development (R & D). Of the academic R & D budget, 3.5 – 6% came from industry, and of the 200 élite research universities/institutes, 25 had more than 10% of their research budgets subscribed by industry.[8] But a common misapprehension is that US firms order a large amount of contract work from universities, and that such work is a major source of university revenue: this is not the case, and the figures that emerge here are comparable to that in the UK, suggesting that, everywhere, business is not interested in subsidising basic research, and government would be wrong to predicate strategy on the assumption that it is.

However, of considerable importance to American universities is the practice of their staff conducting consultancy for firms, and according to the report one study of circa 500 business-university collaborations discovered that three quarters arose as the result of previous consultancy.[9] Thus industry in America does not so much fund the university as an entity, but rather the individual academic who gives of his private time to the firm, and this is partly because of a cultural conditioning that encourages academics to interact with business; but also, the cultural milieu gives industrialists a predisposition to seek academic help, partly because they are themselves the product of an academic training.

Where such university-industry links are pronounced, according to the report, regions are economically successful. It cites the new companies along Route 128 to Boston, founded by Massachusetts Institute of

---

[6] *The Sunday Times*, 2 August, 1989.
[7] *The Guardian*, 2 June, 1989.
[8] Advisory Board for the Research Councils, *Support Given by the Research Councils for In-House and University Research*, 1983.
[9] Centre for Science and Technology Policy, New York University, 1989.

Technology (MIT) graduates and ex-faculty, and the electronics industry derived from Stanford and similarly evolved by graduates and ex-faculty.[10] In addition, according to the report, large companies – often in pharmaceuticals – have given long term commitments to university research: Hoechst apparently donating sixty-five million dollars for research at Massachusetts General Hospital.

The report also describes the attempts of the National Science Foundation (NSF) to forge associations between universities and industry. Thus, the Industry-University Co-operative Research Programme helps university-industry projects, by covering the university's costs and half of the company's (90% in the case of small businesses). Six Co-operative Research Centres were operating at the time of the report. The NSF also gives seed money to interdisciplinary research centres. Another programme screened by the NSF is Small Business Innovation Research. Projects are given up to $100,000 for feasibility studies and up to $1 million for a main contract, though private capital is expected to finance the commercial exploitation phase: private additional money provides a multiplier effect of eight. "The companies concerned have known a 125% increase in employment since 1977".[11] Various laws to encourage discovery, such as the Small Business Act or the Economic Recovery Tax Act of 1981, have also been introduced in the United States.[12]

AUSTRALIAN EXPERIENCE

In Australia the government is preparing to emphasis 'quality' much more in university teaching, partly because the degree completion rate is under 60% – an invidious comparison with the UK.[13]

More controversially, the government proposes to end an academic's right to resources, with a movement to the Canadian model of separate funding for teaching and research: according to the chairman of the Australian University Research Council (AURC), "The shape of Australian basic research firstly tells you more about the performance of university students for courses than it does about Australia's national needs".[14] He claims that

---

[10] Advisory Board for the Research Councils, *Ibid.*, 1983.
[11] Advisory Board for the Research Councils, *Ibid*, 1983.
[12] Small Business Innovation Development Act, 1982, Public Law 97/219.
[13] Geoffrey Maston, "Researching the Last Chord", *The Times Higher Educational Supplement*, 1989.
[14] Advisory Board for the Research Councils, *Ibid.*, 1983, pp.65-67.

only 50% of academics are active researchers, (in engineering, 25% had published nothing in refereed journals for five years). US academics can probably be similarly categorised.

The high drop out rate in Australia mirrors the continent of Europe, and actually leads to an urgent emphasis on the quality of teaching. The limiting of research may even be viewed as eminently sensible in a move to a massified system, and the separation of teaching and research reflects European developments, with an ending of the automatic connection of resource endowment to student numbers.

FRENCH EXPERIENCE

Research income and expenditure are expected to be in balance and the State supervises the budgets of institutions through the Minister for Research and Higher Education. The financing of teaching and research is separate (note the exclusive research organisation Nationale des Recherches Scientifiques that conducts basic research in nearly all scientific disciplines).[15] Research budgets fell 5-7% between 1977 and 1980, but then there was a 116% increase down to 1988. Since 1977 there has been much less use of established formulae for determining research grants. Evaluation of university programmes is now quite common and since 1983 there has been a system of four yearly contracts between the Ministry of Education and the universities, while local authorities share some of the research costs, but only where the research is of direct benefit to regional development. In future the National Scientific Research Council will give its grants direct to the researchers rather than the university institution. University firms were also permitted to be established after an amendment to the relevant law in 1985. Viable scientific projects and profit potential are two important criteria for the acceptance of proposals.

Research contracts are 7% of total university funding and employ a further 9% of the universities' own resources. Public and private enterprise are now of growing importance in the finance of research. Universities recruit staff for research projects on three year contracts (all other university staff are recruited by the state). Some contracts have been underpriced though. The finance law of 1987 allows firms to deduct sums from taxation on

---

[15] See below Chapter 7, pp.221-2.

profits up to 2% of their turnover, as gifts to higher education (amended to 3% since 1988). In 1991/92 200 chairs of research are to be filled having been identified by an international advisory body: these have ten year renewable contracts and involve little or no teaching.

Can any regular pattern be deduced in these case histories? Are there lessons for Britain? France exhibits both strong state control and the separate financing of teaching and research, note also the movement in France towards the evaluation of programmes and to contracts. But the nineteen eighties produced a big increase in research expenditure, unlike Britain, though staff are often on contracts as is increasingly the way here, and the involvement of private enterprise has increased. But firms are given generous tax concessions, yet are also made to give – examples here perhaps, for the UK – thus they are taxed to compensate the state for training (tax d'apprentiseage), and this money goes to public research institutions if they have provided the training.

JAPANESE EXPERIENCE

According to the ABRC report "only a modest proportion of Japan's universities enjoy a reputation for high grade research which is relevant to industrial innovation".[16] It stresses the value of networking, that is, the strong links between graduates of the same class and how this boosts the connections between industry and academe, and it also points out the position of Japanese professors as employees of the Ministry of Education: as such, national research programmes are more easily fostered (the Report cites the Fifth Generation Computer Project) and academics, who play a major role in these programmes, develop links with business. Also researchers from industry stay in university departments for periods of more than one year, hence linking the research of two very disparate kinds of organisation.

Public institutions, concentrating on natural sciences, engineering and education, emphasise post-graduate training and research. The Ministry distributes 3% of its funding for research, but this excludes direct expenditure by research institutes, supported by the Ministry of Education, Science and Culture and other government departments. Grants for research cover 1-3 years and are directed by the Ministry: of 51,000

---

[16] ABRC, *The Support Given by Research Councils for In-House and University Research, Ibid.*, 1983.

applications for grants in 1986, 14,000 were given and 72% of them were in the public sector. Seven per cent of total government expenditure on higher education goes to research institutes. Government codes of auditing tend to inhibit innovative research, however, which is too dependent upon national funds.

Under changes in accounting codes it is now much easier for outside bodies to fund research, and since 1980 large increases in funding have come from business and industry. So-called Attached Foundations have been established post-1982, with funding from private corporations, but the problem here is that only prestigious colleges and applied research have benefited.

Per faculty expenditure in national institutions on research has been static over the past five years and this has had a negative impact. However, Grants in Aid for Scientific Research increased and some compensation was thus afforded: between 1980-1985 expenditure here rose 18%. Between these dates average research expenditure rose 16% in higher education as a whole, 36% in research institutes and 41% in private corporations, and yet the share of higher education in total research expenditure fell from 24% in 1981, to 20% in 1986. Nevertheless, it is recognised that research expenditure is the key to international competitiveness.

In Japan therefore we see a high degree of state control and national planning, with substantial interchange between university and industry. The private system – 73% of universities are privately funded – is generally viewed as intellectually shallow, with its lecturers moonlighting.

The main distinction of the Japanese system is the concentration of research in specialised institutions, and we may compare this with moves in the UK to concentrate research, perhaps with the foundation of graduate research schools. There is strong ministerial direction, again presaging events in the UK, but unlike here there was significant growth in research funding from the state in the eighties, as well as growth in industry's own research as Japan moved to industrial maturity. Traditionally, Japan has stressed development not research: this is having to change, since intelligence gathering abroad is no substitute for a proper programme of domestic research.

The role of private money is certainly useful, in that it reduces considerably the total amount that must be allocated to teaching/research. Research policy concentrates on science and technology – the 'useful' areas – and amounts spent on research are now similar to those in Europe, but such a 'massified' system is not directly comparable with the UK. Nor does government subsidise the research of industry itself: Japanese firms fund 98% of their research development, Americans and Europeans 80%, the UK 66%.

CHAPTER SEVEN

ATHENA DISROBED: INTERNATIONAL COMPARISONS OF THE FUNDING OF UNIVERSITIES AND STUDENTS.

"Seafaring men, for example, range from one end of the earth to the other; but the multiplicity of external objects, which are encountered, forms not a symmetrical and consistent picture upon their imagination; they see the tapestry of human life, as it were on the wrong side, and it tells no story. Everything stands by itself, and comes and goes in its turn, like the shifting scenes of a show, which leave the spectator where he was. For in fact he has no standard of judgement at all, and no landmarks to guide him to a conclusion. Such is mere acquisition, and, I repeat, no one would dream of calling it philosophy".
J.H. Newman,
The Idea of a University, New York, 1959.

"That only is true enlargement of mind, which is the power of viewing many things at once as one whole, of referring them severally to their true place in the universal system, of understanding their respective values, and determining their mutual dependence".
J.H. Newman,
The Idea of a University, New York, 1959.

"I protest to you, Gentlemen, that if I had to choose between a so called University, which dispensed with residence and tutorial superintendence, and gave its degrees to any person who passed an examination in a wide range of subjects, and a University which had no professors or examinations at all, but merely brought a number of young men together for three or four years, and then sent them away as the University of Oxford is said to have done some sixty years since, if I were asked which of these methods was the better discipline of the intellect, – mind, I must determine which of the two courses was the more successful in training, moulding, enlarging the mind, which sent out men the more fitted for their secular duties, which produced better public men, men of the world, men whose

names would descend to posterity, I have no hesitation in giving the preference to that University which did nothing, over that which exacted of its members an acquaintance with every science under the sun''.
J.H. Newman,
The Idea of a University, New York, 1959.

INTRODUCTION

We have noted in chapter six that international comparisons are misleading, with information uneven and comparative costs difficult to work out; the very name 'university' applies to so many different institutions as to render it descriptively almost valueless. With this important caveat in mind, comparisons should be attempted. These will tell us what we should seek to emulate. They will also remind us of what we do well.

What kind of pattern then emerges? The culture, organisation and financing of overseas universities is radically different from our own, but in the nineteen eighties the same politically-inspired trends and themes have coloured their systems as they have coloured ours. So within a pattern of divergence, similarities leap forth.

First the differences, for they are numerous and fundamental. Their systems are 'massified', with all of the implications that flow from this. A considerably higher percentage of the relevant age group actually goes to university, and there are many more universities. Table 7:1 gives comparative figures for a large number of European countries in 1989, many more than are surveyed here, but some idea of diversity is shown under headings of: Students, Students as a Proportion of Total Population, Education Expenditure in local currency, Proportion at Third Level (that is higher education) and the Number of Universities. But by no means are they more pleasant places for students: there is a lack of individual attention in their education and they are likely to find themselves passive recipients in a lecture theatre for five hundred rather than intellectually challenged in a tutorial group: and the campus might even resemble an educational factory.

TABLE 7:1 HIGHER EDUCATION IN EUROPE 1989

		No. of University Students	No. of students per 100,000 population	Education Expenditure[1]	% 3rd level	No. of universities
1.	Albania	22,403	719	-	-	1
2.	Austria	168,182	2398	85,814,800	18.8	18
3.	Belgium	103,505	2546	277,235,300	17.3	18
4.	Bulgaria	113,816	1381	1,911,982	12.1	23
5.	Czechoslovakia	169,723	1088	29,466,873	14.4	23
6.	Denmark	91,450	2271	476,960,000	20.7	19
7.	Finland	95,919	2733	20,607,936	18.5	19
8.	France	980,337	2358	258,880,000	12.3	72
9.	East Germany	153,178	2608	-	22.4	17
10.	West Germany	1,336,395	2546	83,691,000	20.8	61
11.	Greece	111,446	1709	100,293,521	22.3	16
12.	Hungary	61,603	923	59,469,000	17.2	26
13.	Iceland	4,949	2040	4,196,000	-	1
14.	Italy	1,132,386	1989	25,112,000,000	10.1	54
15.	Luxembourg	843	232	13,114,700	2.5	1
16.	Malta	1,449	377	17,899	7.7	1
17.	Norway	41,658	2124	34,584,000	14.5	14
18.	Poland	354,492	1205	-	18.1	25
19.	Portugal	81,293	1112	181,841,000	13.7	16
20.	Rumania	159,798	694	17,940,900	-	11
21.	Soviet Union	5,088,400	1814	40,060,100	12.6	69
22.	Spain	903,166	2626	1,010,445	14	36
23.	Sweden	219,757	2635	69,825,200	12.9	34
24.	Switzerland	76,664	1789	11,696,300	18.1	9
25.	Turkey	380,844	1003	795,892,000	25.3	28
26.	United Kingdom	352,419	1806	16,678,000	21.4	46
27.	Yugoslavia	293,070	1509	953,793,000	16	20

1. In local currency

Admissions policy will be more open than in the UK, it may be politicised and entirely open to all secondary school graduates, with universities a much bigger public issue; selection will take place in successive examinations after entry. Such universities will have a much higher drop-out rate than is the case here. And the degree structure will be more flexible. There will be many mature students. Degrees will often commence at a later age and last longer, some doing the degree in stages via accumulated credits and mixing it with work experience, while many students will come from the immediate locality. The syllabus they study will be much broader, with a range of consumer choice.

And students will be charged tuition fees, or it is planned that they will be paying them soon. Loans will be almost universal, consequently the state will spend a lower per capita amount on students in both support and tuition, enabling it to educate many more. In these countries there is generally a greater willingness among the middle class to pay for the university experience. Academics themselves will enjoy higher status and generally better pay. Their tenure, if they have been awarded it, will not be under state threat of abolition. Some of the best of them will actually work in specialised research-only institutions. But within this broad canvas there are many aspects specific to the indigenous systems. Some countries, for example, have extensive private institutions.

The consequences for society of generous higher education arrangements include a more intellectually trained and oriented business management, and while each nation exhibits its own form of social delinquency, we might also suggest that the consequence of a better educated population is a less immature and slovenly public culture, where values are informed by learning. For market forces do not operate in a vacuum. They articulate the preferences and values of the culture in which they are liberated, they celebrate its richness, or they express its banality. The wealthy young man may choose to motor in a red Ferrari, or enjoy the fine arts. The choice is neither morally nor aesthetically neutral.

In spite of monumental national divergences, the political demands on universities during the last decade have been similar. There is the same demand for 'relevance' and moves to central 'planning', with a sclerosis in academic opportunities and reductions in public funding as legislators begin to demand value for money and perceive higher education as a bottomless pit. Universities are encouraged to seek business links, to serve the needs of industry more effectively and raise money from it; in this aspiration they are assisted overseas by much more creative tax systems. Student support is increasingly targeted. The formal evaluation of teaching and research is becoming universal with a rise in contract funding. Generally, the pressure is for universities to become more market oriented with a stronger vocational input.

HIGHER EDUCATION IN THE UNITED STATES OF AMERICA

The United States of America has the most diverse system of higher education in the world, with 3,300 accredited institutions and funding based on a spectrum from total state funding to total private funding. But while the USA may seem prima facie an example of how to use private sources, the example is misleading, and even for the private system too, there is a large element of hidden subsidy from the state (via tax right-offs and the like).

The state plays of course a substantial role in the state university; there is state support of students, though it is much less than in the UK, students even have to pay tuition fees at state universities and support is targeted (for example the Pell grants with their focus on poverty). Students and their families therefore assume much more of the university's costs, liberating resources for other demands like libraries, salaries, expansion and so on. As many as 53.6% of students do some form of work to support themselves at university.

In the United States it was the nineteen-seventies, not the eighties, that the universities found to be their most vexatious decade. Budgets were hit hard in the 1970's as costs rose; inflation, rising administrative costs, and the price of compensating for poor pre-university education all explain this imbalance in accounts. However in the 1980's, as a result of three reports (the 1983 National Commission on Excellence in Education, established by President Reagan, the 1984 report Involvement in Learning, commissioned by the Department of Education and The Undergraduate Experience, commissioned in 1986 by the Carnegie Commission) Congress raised the level of funding whilst disregarding the budget deficit. The individual states had also increased their support for higher education, with sometimes up to 50% of their budget going to education, until the recession in the late eighties and early nineties led to retrenchment. Unlike in Britain, the Reaganite eighties proved to be a decade of optimism for universities.

UNIVERSITY REVENUE SOURCES, PRIVATE AND PUBLIC

Compared with the U.K., U.S. universities enjoy far more variegated forms of finance. Besides Federal and State support, they derive their revenue from student tuition fees, private philanthropy, the sale of services, and endowments, while there are also substantial indirect contributions through the system of tax breaks enjoyed by benefactors. Revenue in fact rose from $21.5 billion in 1969 to $92.4 billion in 1985, and whilst revenue kept pace with expenditure in the 1970's, in the 1980's a surplus emerged and was invested by extending endowments. In point of fact the federal government only provides 12% of total resources in the public sector and this has fallen over the decade 1975 to 1985. Tuition yielded 14.9% in 1985 (up from 13% in 1975) and the contribution from the state and local government, after rising, fell back to less than 4% each, whilst the share of gifts and grant contracts rose from 2.3% to 3.0% over the same period.

There are essentially two models of higher educational institution, the one state or public and the other private. Only the U.S. and Japan have large private sectors. Public institutions are chartered by the state and governed by a board of trustees with a president or chancellor as the administrative head and accountable to the board. Revenue comes principally from the state and the amount depends on full-time equivalent enrolments, although prestigious universities or those distinguished by research are allocated additional funds, an allocation not without political overtones. Thus tuition fees are an additional source of finance and their level reflects the environment in which the university operates. Hence the presence of private universities charging high fees will act to lever up fees at public universities: witness the position in the New England States – in 1987 fees at public Vermont University were $3198 compared to $1346 at public Berkeley California, and as little as $100 at some 100 community colleges in California. Between 1980 and 1988 costs rose 26% in real terms from $14,400 to $25,000 on average at public colleges, $26,600 to $50,000 at private colleges. Table 7:2 shows tuition fees at state universities, where the average is $1,972.

Donations from corporations and individuals may be tax deductible and therefore represent an indirect public subsidy, and the universities themselves pay no tax on activities which if executed in the commercial world would attract taxation.

Private universities derive their revenue from tuition and other fees, although if a tuition fee equalisation scheme operates to keep tuition fees level at all institutions in a state, as in North Carolina, then private universities receive a subsidy from the state government. Gifts and endowments are particularly important in the private sector and the tax advantages are utilised to the full.

INCREASE IN STATE AND PRIVATE SUPPORT

Federal funds for the support of students have increased over the period 1970-1985 but those available for capital construction projects have been severely curtailed, despite the fact that many facilities are now in need of replacement. After declining in the 1970's, Federal support for research has increased in the 1980's, but inflation and high rates of interest remain a problem for higher education in a period of stringency. But while state support for higher education increased in the 1980's the major growth area has been in private donations, expanding from $2.1 billion in 1980/81 to $3.1 billion in 1984/85, while the universities themselves have been earning more from the sale of services. Changes in the tax laws in 1986 however have curtailed the scope for tax breaks, but the full impact of this is not yet apparent. The recession is causing some cut backs to be made in recent years.

ORIGINS AND GROWTH OF FEDERAL STUDENT SUPPORT

Loans rather than UK-style grants remain the chief feature of student support in the U.S.A. Existing schemes were incorporated in the 1965 *Higher Education Act* and two new support programmes emerged: Educational Opportunity Grants and Guaranteed Student Loans. The former, a campus based scheme, offers annual grants of up to $800 (now $4000) to financially needy students, the latter utilises Federal funds to pay an interest subsidy to private banks and to guarantee loans against default, death or disability.[1] The current rate of interest is 8%.

---

[1] The subsidy has three components (a) payment of interest when a student enrolls and extending over the deferment period; (b) a special allowance or the difference between the borrowers preferential rate and the lenders highest rate of interest and (c) re-insurance to cover claims due to default, death or disability.

Other sources of revenue in the USA include the following:

(a) Grants from the Federal government.
(b) Sponsored research contracts awarded on a competitive basis by the Federal government, state or local government agencies.
(c) Local government agencies.
(d) Gifts from private corporations, foundations and alumni fundraising.
(e) Revenue from the sale of patents, inventions and campus activities.
(f) Revenue from endowments.

TABLE 7:2
TUITION AT STATE UNIVERSITIES – TUITION PLUS FEES 1989-90*

State	Tuition
Arizona	$1,362
California	$1,673
Colorado	$2,060
Connecticut	$2,631
Florida	$1,195
Illinois	$2,919
Massachusetts	$2,629
Michigan	$3,395
New Jersey	$3,170
New York	$1,490
Ohio	$2,190
Oregon	$1,782
Pennsylvania	$3,754
Texas	$969
Washington	$1,827
Wisconsin	$2,003
National average	$1,972

* The national average for tuition at public universities is almost $2,000 a year (£1,120).

Source: *The New York Times*, 3, March 1991.

Since 1980 the Educational Opportunity Grants have been known as Pell Grants (after the Rhode Island Senator) and these approximate to a voucher and can be used at either public or private institutions. Eligibility depends on family income and student assets and the cost of the course undertaken, up to a limit of 60% of the cost. Pell awards themselves are also subject to a maximum rate (a percentage limit at public university and a dollar limit at private university). These awards amounted to $122m in 1973/74 covering 176,000 students and rose to $2.2 billion in 1980/81 covering 2.9m students, 75% of the total going to students whose families were below the poverty line. The variety of funds available to students is indicated in Table 7:3.

TABLE 7:3 US STUDENT AID PACKAGES

1. Pell grants for undergraduates only, maximum award $2,300 a year, given to students in need. This depends on family income, assets, size. Approximately 82 per cent of this money goes to students whose families have adjusted incomes of $15,000 or less and more than 46 per cent to students with family incomes of $6,000 or less.

2. Supplemental Education Opportunity Grants (SEOG) for undergraduates maximum award $4,000, can supplement Pell grants, and the amount given depends partly on funds available at each college.

3. College work-study programmes for undergraduates and graduates given jobs on and off campus in areas that are related to their studies. Amount earned cannot exceed need.

4. Perkins loans (formerly the National Direct Student Loan Program) for graduates and undergraduates with exceptional need. Interest rate 5 per cent. Students in the first two years of study can borrow $4,500. This goes up to $9,000 in the last two years at undergraduate school and up to $18,000 at graduate school.

5. Stafford loans, new name for Guaranteed Student Loan Program, for graduates and undergraduates. Interest rate 8 per cent rising to 10 per cent. Government pays interest while students are at college and, to a lesser extent, after graduation. Undergraduates may borrow up to $2,625 for their first two years of undergraduate study, $4,000 for each subsequent year and $7,500 for graduate study. Total limits are $17,250 for undergraduates and $54,750 for graduates.

6. Plus and Supplemental Loans for Students Programme. Plus is for parents to borrow for their children and SLS is for student borrowers. Interest rates vary and borrowing can range from $14,000 a year to $20,000.

LEVEL OF TOTAL SUPPORT, MID-EIGHTIES

Federal aid for students in total slowed in the 1980's, and in 1984/85 amounted to $6.2 billion with state aid at $1.2 billion and private aid $3.2 billion for an enrolment of 9 million students (from 5 million in 1965).[2] Aid therefore totalled $13.4 billion in 1984/85 for an enrolment of 12.5 million, or $21,000 per student. In 1991 the student aid bill amounted to $19 billion giving an average loan of $4,000 (£2250); the highest was in medicine at $50,000 (£28,000).

The means test for Guaranteed Student Loans was lifted and the value of loans rose from $2.4 billion in 1978 to $7.2 billion in 1984. However to prevent abuse, a means test was added again in 1981 and set a cut-off point where family income exceeded $30,000. In 1986 Congress re-authorised the student aid programme down to 1991, but concern has been expressed over the level of defaults on loans which reached $2 billion in 1990/91, equivalent to 50% of the cost of annual subsidies (see Table 7:4).[3] Student aid rose 10% in 1991 – Perkins, Supplementary Opportunity Grants and Pell Grants – but by 1995 £1.7 billion is to be cut from the student loan programme to reduce the default deficit, some colleges will be excluded from the programme and loan cheques will be delayed by 30 days. Plans also exist to decentralise student support by making it the responsibility of the individual States, and by targeting grants on families with income below $10,000 whilst removing eligibility from those students with low entrance marks. The latter could well save one million grants. Parents are to be encouraged to save for higher education through US Savings Bonds, whereby income falling below $75,000 entitles holders to income, tax free. Finally, institutions will undoubtedly do more fund-raising for themselves: in 1969/70 23.5% of income came from fund-raising and 28.9% in 1984/85.

---

[2] Federal grants have fallen from 41% of the education bill to 29% and federal governments impose more severe means tests.

[3] In 1988/89 the average loan amounted to $2,555 per annum and in the same year the average debt on graduation was $7,000.

TABLE 7:4 ANNUAL STUDENT LOAN DEFAULT COSTS

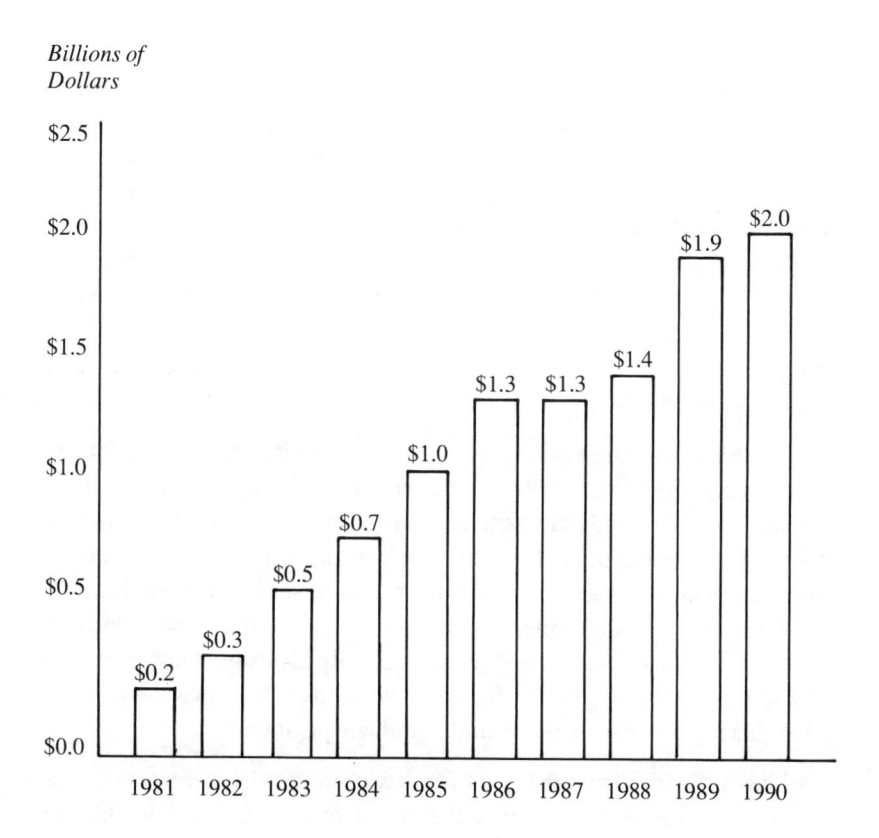

Billions of Dollars

1981	$0.2
1982	$0.3
1983	$0.5
1984	$0.7
1985	$1.0
1986	$1.3
1987	$1.3
1988	$1.4
1989	$1.9
1990	$2.0

HIGHER EDUCATION IN JAPAN

Japanese higher education is constructed thus: (a) four year colleges and universities; (b) two year junior colleges; (c) fourth and fifth grade technical colleges and (d) post-secondary courses at special training schools. The four year colleges are called *DIAGAKU* and there were 500 in 1987 offering courses to 1.9 million students, of which 54,000 were postgraduates. Technical Colleges, or *KOTO SENMON GAKKO*, specialise in technical and engineering subjects requiring five years of study and cater for only 1% of the total higher education enrolment. Higher education in its totality takes 48% of the relevant age cohort: gaining admission is difficult, but graduation is easy.

Higher education is divided between public and private institutions. Institutions of higher education fall into one of three categories: (a) national; (b) municipal or (c) private. There are 95 national universities and colleges representing 25% of total enrolments and these include the most prestigious institutions, some dating back to the Meiji. Staff are employed by the Ministry of Education, Science and Culture, although academic staff in reality are appointed by the relevant faculty. Finance is unambiguously under the control of the Ministry. Municipal or local public institutions are established and financed by the cities and prefectures and in 1986 there were 37 four-year and 53 two-year institutions. In the same year, private universities were the largest single sector, these cater for 75% of students in Japanese higher education. In 1991/92 six more private universities have been sanctioned bringing the total to over 800.

The existence of a large private system is a particularly noticeable feature of Japan and the U.S., distinguishing them from Europe and particularly Britain. It enables the Japanese to educate far more, but creates tensions of its own. The national or public institutions specialise in the natural sciences, engineering and education, whereas the private institutions concentrate on the humanities, social sciences and home economics, the relatively speaking low cost areas. There is also a disparity in postgraduate provision with the national institutions educating two thirds and the private only one third, exactly the reverse of the undergraduate position.

Looking at finance from the point of view of the public institutions, 63% of total revenue derives from government and 29% from the sale of services, including student fees. Private institutions rely on tuition charges and currently receive a subsidy equivalent to 10% of their revenue from the government, down from a peak of 24% in 1979, so they are best described as semi-private.

The most expensive courses are those in medicine and dentistry, with the social sciences being the cheapest. Expenditure per student averages 30% more in the national institutions in comparison to the private, reflecting the bias in favour of the social sciences at the latter.

CUTS

Expenditure per student had risen by 220% between 1970 and 1985. Latterly expenditure was curtailed and the budget cut in real terms, so that by 1985 only 0.45% of GNP went to higher education. The contribution of households however has soared from 0.265% of GNP in 1970 to 0.439% of GNP in 1985. But with the increasing level of financial stringency the value of the government contribution fell in real terms in the 1980's and represented only 15% of total revenue in 1985.

During the recent period of restraint, the private sector fared much better than the public – real expenditure rose 2.2 times – thereby accentuating the disparity between the two sectors. Globally the cut-back represented a serious threat to research and graduate education, although some amelioration came through increased tuition fees that expanded from 0.26% of GNP in 1976 to 0.43% in 1985.

REFORM

The crisis in Japanese higher education led in 1984 to the establishment of the National Council for Education Reform and this body called for a significant change in the nature and extent of government funding. The government in its turn charged the universities with the inefficient use of funds already granted and wished to curtail the level of its support (as governments were doing everywhere). Clearly a major problem existed and this was due mainly to the method of funding adopted, based as it was on 'standard unit pricing per student' at national institutions – a quantitative and not a qualitative criterion for support. Budgets tend to be inflexible and resources allocated according to the size of the faculty, thereby killing innovative research, lessening the ability of the institutions to respond quickly to changing economic and social needs.

PUBLIC AND PRIVATE

Given the generally inferior quality of Japanese higher education, great pressure built up on the best universities where the demand for places outstripped the supply, since there was no encouragement for them to increase the number of places available. Hence the shortage of places led to the rapid development of the private sector, which as early as 1969 accounted for 65% of total enrolments: in these institutions, tuition fees were the major source of income and consequently they were quite high.

Since 1971, the government has attempted to deal with the disparity between the public and private sectors on two fronts. Firstly, by paying a subsidy to private universities, and secondly by raising tuition fees at public institutions. Fees have been raised significantly, in fact, and between 1970 and 1987 rose from some 2% of GNP to 10%.

STUDENT SUPPORT

In the peak years of expenditure, the average Japanese family devotes 34% of its income to the education of student siblings, an extraordinary figure to spend on education, representing an ethos and dedication that would astonish the British. In total, only 21% of full-time students received financial assistance through loans according to the 1984 Students' Living Survey, and many of these attended national institutions reflecting the lower incomes of the students' parents. These loans are by no means generous however, for in 1984 they covered only one third of the cost for those living away from home and attending national or public institutions. Ninety per cent of students obtain income from some form of part-time employment.

The institutions recommend students for loans, and the Japan Student Foundation is then unlikely to reject them provided the loans have not been oversubscribed. Category one, or interest free loans, are awarded on the basis of academic criteria and family income, but those rejected are eligible for category two loans at interest. Academic achievement is monitored during the duration of the loan, fines may be imposed and this acts as an incentive, and repayment commences six months after graduation with a maximum repayment period of twenty years. Minimum repayments apply and the length of repayment averages eleven years. In 1986 defaults amounted to 13% of total repayments and this is kept within bounds by a strict procedure for recovery. Exemption from repayment applies to those entering the teaching profession or certain areas of government service, but does not operate until a few years of service have been gained, presumably to prevent any abuse of this escape route from repayment.

However, given their small global size, there remains great competition for research awards, with the research institutions and private corporations together investing 500% more in research than all the institutions of higher education added together. Since the 1970's the government has made loans available for postgraduate research, but these singularly failed to meet the demand for them. In the future, in order to maintain international competitiveness, the government has conceded that the amount of resources devoted to research in Japan will have to increase.

HIGHER EDUCATION IN GERMANY

Germany also reveals the customary European litany of cuts, selectivity, increasing industrial contributions and blockage on appointments. However, although countries are adopting similar strategies, comparisons are misleading since they start from different base points: Germany has a 28% participation rate as against 14% in the UK. Like nearly all the rest of Europe, Germany operates a loan system. Its university education is technical in its concentration and, as with other European countries, begins later and lasts longer – many graduate at age 27.

But the theme – heady expansion, followed by fretful stasis – is familiar in Britain and throughout Europe. Public expenditure on higher education fell 8% in real terms between 1975 and 1986. Generous financing in the 1970's produced an air of complacency in higher education, but to provide greater motivation and ensure higher completion rates more selective funding is envisaged in the future. Nevertheless expenditure is set to rise by 20% in 1991, but linked to performance criteria that will be rigidly upheld.

FUNDING

As throughout Europe funding is primarily provided from government sources, although there is growing private sector support for research and some contribution from this quarter for the support of junior academics. Recurrent expenditure is covered by the Länder and covers staff salaries, materials, operating charges, teaching, research and maintenance for a variety of institutions: 51 universities, 7 comprehensive universities, 13 colleges of education, 25 colleges of art and 74 polytechnics (no identity crisis here). Since 1969 the Federal Government has assumed responsibility for 50% of capital expenditure and the purchase of large items of scientific equipment.

The Federal Government, in conjunction with the Länder, funds research through the German Society for the Advancement of Scientific Research, and funds students through the Federal Education Assistance Act, effectively covering two thirds of the cost of the programme. In addition, doctoral scholarships are provided as well as scholarships for international exchange programmes involving students and researchers. Those institutions funded out of Länder budgets have no sovereignty over their affairs. Academic posts were planned to expand in 1986 and 1987, given the decline of 6% during the previous ten years. The staff/student ratio had risen from 29:1 in 1975 to 34:1 in 1985.

In the nineteen eighties state priorities began to influence universities, dictating what was cut and what increased, a familiar pattern. The budgetary allocations for teaching and research were liable to be cut at short notice, because unlike that for staff there are no clearly defined long term plans. In 1982, for example, there occurred a large cut in teaching and research expenditure. These two categories account for 16% of total expenditure and were to increase in 1986 by 4.7%, little compensation for the fact that expenditure per student had halved since 1970. From 1985 onwards, a differential approach to funding the universities reflecting national priorities for science and technology resulted in technical universities experiencing a 23% rise in real resources, whilst polytechnics gained a modest 12% in real terms and the others suffered a 1% loss. Capital expenditure and expenditure on large scale scientific equipment boomed in the 1970's, but assumed a fairly settled pattern in the 1980's at half the earlier level – about DM2,000 million (£700m).

Research funding is more variegated in Germany than the U.K. Besides the Federal Government, contributors include: government institutions,[4] Federal ministries for education, Länder ministries,[5] international organisations, foundations, industry and trade associations, all giving to the total research budget. Industry sources produced the largest increase in research funding, with the total budget from all sources increasing 100% between 1975 and 1985, or 38% in real terms. In the case of the 27 medical establishments attached to universities, the income derived from the sale of services increased enormously, covering 53% of total expenditure in 1978 but reaching 70% by 1986.

STUDENT SUPPORT

There is substantial participation in German higher education. The number of students registering in 1983/84 recorded a fall for the first time and a slow decline in enrolments has continued since: the fall in 1984 was 5.1%

---

[4] Including: German Society for Advancement of Scientific Research; Alexander von Humboldt Foundation; German Academic Exchange Service.
[5] These are funds outside the regular budgetary allocations.

and in 1985 6.6%, down 10% on the peak enrolment of 1983. Nevertheless, 28% of the relevant age cohort entered higher education, with increases in student numbers registered at the polytechnics. There are limitations imposed on student recruitment in certain subjects. On average a course takes six years to complete, so that the average graduate would be 27, but the recent slow-down in the number of examination passes indicates that completion rates are deteriorating and this is giving cause for concern.

In this state sponsored system there are no tuition fees so that financial aid consists of a cost of living subsidy under the Federal Education Assistance Act, passed in 1971 and amended a number of times since. The aim of the system is to create equal opportunity for all, and this replaces the previous reliance upon demonstratable above average ability *as a prior condition for aid*.

Scholarships played a dominant part in German student support, a feature unique in Europe apart from the U.K. After 1974, as a result of budgetary constraints, part of the support came as a loan, except in the case of those studying abroad who continued to receive a grant. Loans were interest free and repayment commenced five years after graduation, with twenty years to repay via fixed monthly instalments: these repayments could be waived in exceptional circumstances. The state provides support if there is evidence that the student and/or his parents are unable to do so. However, the number receiving aid has fallen since 1981, down from 45.3% to 30% of the student population. The Federal Government makes a contribution to the support of doctoral students too by channelling scholarships through a number of foundations. Of particular interest in Germany is the clear trend for more young people to undertake some kind of vocational training before proceeding to university, but under present arrangements this also has the adverse effect of raising the average age of graduation.

In 1990 a large part of the loan reverted to grant, and the parental threshold, below which students are entitled to assistance, rose from DM4,800 to DM6,200 monthly (£1,670 to £2,160 monthly) – higher for those living at home. Monthly loans to students therefore amount to DM890 with 50% repayable where appropriate, giving rise to a 30% rise in those qualified for a grant (428,000 in total).

Funding arrangements presently favour engineering subjects mainly for economic and labour market reasons, but this seems to have little impact on demand (down nearly 10% in this subject between 1982/83 and 1986/87). Two billion DM are currently being expended to deal with the chronic problem of overcrowding, but reunification of the two Germanies will now place additional strains on the whole financial régime for higher education.

The major criticisms of the universities can be summarised as follows; again the refrain is familiar:

- overloaded curicula and slow adaptation of content and organisation to developments in research;
- excessively long, subject-related study periods and an advanced age of entry into professions with detrimental consequences for the development of personal, professional and family lives;
- too little flexibility of courses in adjusting to labour-market requirements;
- lack of opportunities for junior researchers with regard to post-graduate studies, research work and funding;
- limited research opportunities.[6]

RESEARCH

Research has benefited, however, from links with research laboratories and industry – for example, the volume of research undertaken through the German Society for the Advancement of Scientific Research has steadily increased, and similar advances have been achieved by the Max-Planck-Gesellschaft and Fraunhofer-Gesellschaft Institutes. The unity of teaching and research has been maintained and is recognised as a reinforcement of both. There appears however to be a blockage in appointments, owing to the expanded recruitment of young, and in some cases poorly qualified, candidates in the expansionary 1970's: expenditure on both teaching and research per student has in fact fallen by 50% since 1970. Financial pressure will undoubtedly lead to further rationalisation here and strengthen ties between science and industry, thereby ensuring an exchange of bright ideas and bright people. Thus German research is noteworthy for the substantial collaboration between universities and industry it involves: in this aspect its evolution is ahead of the British.

---

[6] OECD, *Changing Patterns of Finance in Higher Education: Country Report Germany*, 1989, p.32.

WHAT OF THE FUTURE?

Whilst no new funds for higher education are likely to be forthcoming, investment in new plant is seen to be essential with 2 billion DM allocated to relieving overcrowding. This and other pressures raise the possibility of the introduction of fees, which the President of the German Society for the Advancement of Research described as necessary to "strengthen the students' self-responsibility and the achievement orientation of institutions and their staff."

HIGHER EDUCATION IN FRANCE:

AN OVERVIEW

France reveals some similarities to the UK. The same trends are in evidence – towards vocational education, higher fees and evaluation, with contract funding. Whereas the overall structure of French higher education is not worth replicating, some of its details are of value. It exhibits much more variety than is the case in the UK: the system is more flexible with less rigid distinctions between institutions. We might also note the customary use of loans and students fees, the importance of family support and the fact that grants are much lower and more targeted. Useful too are the tax incentives for industry to give to higher education: the apprenticeship tax and gift tax breaks. Noteworthy also is the 27% increase in expenditure on higher education between the years 1975 and 1988, and the 13.3% academic employment increase, compared to the constant attrition in the UK (though there have recently been economies in France). Spending will rise by some 10-12% in 1991/92 reflecting the priority awarded to higher education by the Mitterrand government (5.6% education, 5.8% research) and a five year expansion programme costing some £1,500m is also envisaged.

The French system of higher education is very much conditioned by its historical origins with much that is specific to France. Following the baccalauréate, students have a choice of higher education courses, essentially differentiated by duration. Short courses lasting two years may be followed at University Institutions of Technology (IUT), technical lycées (STS) or institutes offering social or para-medical qualifications. Long courses, covering upwards of three years, are followed at univérsities and Grands Écoles. In total three cycles can be distinguished for university courses:

First Cycle: diplôme d'études univérsitaires générales (DEUG), awarded after two years and usually followed by:

Second Cycle: licence, awarded three years after baccalauréate; masters, awarded four years after baccalauréate.

Third Cycle: selective entry for those having a diploma or award at second cycle: diplôma d'études supérieures spécialisées (DESS), a one year sandwich course; diplôma d'études approfondies (DEA), a one year preparation for doctoral studies.

The Grands Écoles recruit by competitive examination two years post baccalauréate, and the preparatory classes are conducted at lycées where admission depends upon selective attainment (Les classes préparatoires aux grandes écoles (CPGE)).

Virtually every student obtaining the baccalauréate enters a course of higher education, a permissiveness of entry that would shock the British, and numbers have increased from 205,000 in 1975 to 278,000 in 1987. The distribution of students between the various types of institution in the academic year 1985/86 were as follows:

TYPE	%
IUT	8.9
STS	18.6
Social/paramedicals	4.6
Universities	47.1
CPGE	9.8
Others	11.0
	89.0

Approximately half the baccalauréates eventually go on to long courses, but the number entering short technical courses has been increasing (STS 18.6% in 1985 against 10.2% in 1975 with IUT roughly constant).

The distinction between institutions is not rigid and some movement between categories does occur: this adds flexibility, but creates complexity and financial consequences. Another distinguishing feature of the French system is the existence of a private sector. In total there are 17,782 students attending private, mostly catholic, universities, equivalent to 1.8% of the total student population. Under the *Université 2000*, seven new universities are planned, 5 new engineering schools and 160 new institutes of technology attached to existing universities.

FUNDING

Accounts for education are part of national accounts and cover a wide area of post-secondary education. The last definitive version is for 1983 and separates teaching and research expenditure: as a percentage of GDP, France spends 0.7% on higher education and this figure varied little between 1975 and 1983. The state's share fell slightly, from 91% in 1975 to 88% in 1983, the private household and business share rose from 4.5% to 5.17% between the same dates, and the local authority share was below 2% until 1983, when laws covering decentralisation made the regions responsible for the finance and operation of lycées and regional post-secondary education more generally. From 1975 to 1988 the budget for higher education increased by 27% in 1975 prices (a level that would shame the British who were enthusiastically hacking at finances during the same period), virtually the same increase as for the number of students at 28%. In 1988 credits per student were F8,219 (£913), much the same as the 1975 level, F8,296 (£866).

Those credits for maintenance and investment, excluding research, fell from 23.3% of the budget in 1975 to 17% in 1988. The credits for research fell 5.7% between 1977 and 1980, but from 1980 to 1988 experienced a massive increase of 116%. Overall, higher education benefited from a number of government inspired initiatives, including: the machine-tool national plan which provided modern equipment for higher education; funding for energy conservation; the national plan for electronics; the plan for information sciences; other funds for industrialisation, modernisation and the development of Lorraine.

Vocationalism has been the hallmark of recent developments in French higher education, as it has been here, with short professional courses particularly in demand. Between 1980 and 1986 the student population rose by 12%, but the following increases in particular areas took place: university institutes of technology (IUT) 15%; engineers 39%; Masters in Science and Technology 55%; Masters in Management Science 100%; Management Information 51% and Higher Diplomas 44%.

In other areas, the methods of finance have been rationalised. Since 1978, for example, much less use has been made of an automatic formula for research grants and increased evaluation of programmes has occurred. After 1983 four yearly contracts became the norm between the ministry and institutions. All of this presages developments in Britain. Allocations for buildings under maintenance grants are proportional to size in square metres, the allocation for teaching activity is linked to the number of hours of teaching and includes the cost of maintaining equipment, and some maintenance grants are linked to supplementary or overtime hours. However, on the negative side, such arrangements for allocations have been found to encourage universities to pursue excessive diversity in the provision of courses. New legislation and rules have placed severe restraints on the recruitment of personnel in an attempt to reduce costs, but this has come at a time when student enrolments are increasing and universities are being opened up to a wider public with a participation rate of 48% envisaged, an astonishing figure and one that could only make our 'educationists' gawp. Nevertheless, the drop-out rate remains excessively high at 50% and little has been done to reduce this (20% is accounted for by financial pressures on students).

SUPPORT FOR STUDENTS

Student aid programmes have a long history with measures in 1877, 1880 and 1886. For non-aided students, a system of advantageous loans was organised by the state between the wars. Indirect aid followed, and in 1936 low cost student restaurants (a malodorous memory to those of us who have used them) and lodgings became available. Grants are the oldest and the most numerous form of aid and are based on social considerations, whilst others are based on university criteria. Grants are supplemented by loans.

Grants are given in addition to family support, since parents are legally obliged to feed and support their children until the end of their studies. To qualify a student must be French, or if foreign satisfy general conditions, and be less than 26 years old at the start of the period of study. In 1986/87

15.8% of students obtained the minimum grant and 44.5% of students obtained the maximum grant.

There appears to be a growing consensus in France that direct aid to students needs to be revalued and the number of beneficiaries increased. The policy operating at first and third cycle levels remains very much the same, but at second cycle level new proposals aim to emphasise educational criteria (whilst not altogether abandoning social criteria), with the intention of enquiring into the probability of successfully completing courses of study at the first level.

From the 1991/92 academic year student loans are available for the first time to those in the second year of study and beyond for a maximum of three years. Annual loans are worth £1,300 and must be paid off within six years of graduation, being underwritten by the state and insurance companies/universities on an equal basis. These loans are intended to help the least well-off families and it is hoped that employers might be tempted to write them off when employment is taken up. Grants will rise at the same time by 21% to £650 (student unions demanded £3,000 p.a.) but still only 20% of the student population will receive one. The authorities hope that the combination of grants and then loans will help to reduce the high drop out rate – currently a staggering 50% of all those entering higher education, making Britain by far a cheaper and more efficient educator at degree level.

Given the fall in total resources available to the state, and the growing demands from higher education in particular, the search for alternative sources of finance has assumed paramount importance. Local authorities – commune, department and region – have been more involved with university institutions over the last fifteen years or so. In some cases help came in the form of specific grants to establish new institutions. Indeed the report of the Dèlègation à l'Amènagement du Territoire et à L'Action Règionale stated that higher education was a fundamental component of regional policy. French planning policy for the period 1989-1993 has two main themes: higher education and transport infrastructure, and each region has its own plans for a technopolis.

French universities mirror the international trend towards increased commercialism. Since legal difficulties have been resolved, universities are able to create their own firms, and in 1985, of 40 applications to do so, 25 were accepted. Research contracts with public and private enterprise have increased, and represent 7% of university income and around 16% of their own resources.

Another income source is a forced levy from industry itself. The apprenticeship tax, levied on the salaries and the expenses of personnel at a rate of 0.5%, may be donated to either the public treasury, Chambers of Commerce and Industry or to teaching institutions. In 1986, the universities collected 206 million francs (£23m) from the apprenticeship tax, equivalent to 3% of their total receipts or 7% of their own resources. The areas which benefit are quite restricted and include IUTs, the engineering schools and some diplomas with a professional bias. In addition, the 1987 Finance Law allows firms to make deductions from the tax on profits up to a maximum of 2% (now 3%) of their turnover, payable as gifts to higher education institutions.

Greater autonomy for individual higher education establishments will undoubtedly lead to more market orientated fund-raising efforts in the future.

HIGHER EDUCATION IN NETHERLANDS

The Netherlands represents in some of its features an alternative paradigm to the UK. Students are more mature and there are longer periods of study but also the common European problem, thankfully still absent in the UK, of low completion rates. Otherwise there are many parallels between the two systems – the huge size of state support and its monopoly on higher education, the overly formulaic funding, the mixture of loans and grants, the drive to research accountability and relevance. The increasing possibility in the Netherlands of full-cost tuition fees is not however present in the UK.

The *Universities Administration (Reform) Act* of 1970 guaranteed democratically run institutions, where resources were related to student enrolment with teaching and research indissolubly united. Expenditure rose throughout the decade from 14.5% to 23% of the total education budget, representing an increase in the proportion of GNP devoted to higher education from 0.8% to 1.9%. Planning of the system remained rudimentary in the 1970's, there were few incentives for innovation and resources were not meaningfully linked to objectives. Again there were economic pressures coming to bear which meant resources had to be cut back and there was little in the way of private finance to offer amelioration from the enforced retrenchment.

This pattern – growth without accountability followed by disillusion and cuts – was repeated throughout Europe. A discussion paper, *Main Features of a Future Higher Education System*, that considered higher education down to the mid-1990's, envisaged a separate funding mechanism for teaching and research; administrative changes to make decision-making more market oriented; a voucher system establishing consumer sovereignty; performance indicators to determine the size of budgets; and government as the co-ordinator, catalyst and creator of opportunities within the university sector. Many of these have a thoroughly British or more generally market oriented ring about them, but the last group seem to accord government unwarranted foresight and innovative flair, not borne out by history. At the present time, however, budgets are being applied more selectively and less formulaically and mixed funding receives positive encouragement, with resources and performance closely linked together. Macroeconomic inefficiency has been identified in the form of the overlapping supply of courses making some rationalisation necessary. As with Denmark, questions have been raised about the low completion rates for undergraduate degrees, and the authorities are attempting to find a solution to this problem in particular.

FUNDING

As in the UK, universities are almost entirely dependent on the state with its concomitant of political interference. The state meets 80-95% of the cost of higher education and this global grant is fixed annually in the Finance Act. Teaching and research contracts together with patent revenue make up the roughly 10% outstanding, but any tuition fees are deducted from the government grant. There are two tiers of funding: a 'normal' funding formula and secondly 'special features funding', accounting together for 90% of funding.

The Ministry of Education and Science provides 65% of research funding and this goes direct to the universities. Secondary sources include the Netherlands Organisation for Scientific Research (15% and funded by the Ministry) and contracted research from industry (20%). Since 1982 the funding of research and teaching has been separated and the allocation for the former depends upon the fulfilment of quality criteria and not simply student numbers. Ex post assessments of research have become the norm and it is upon these that the continuous funding of research projects depend.

As usual in the eighties, objective quality assessment criteria began to be imposed, with the customary obeisance to 'relevance'. Research funding over the period 1982-86 fell under the terms of the memorandum, *Conditional Funding*, where quality, relevance, accountability and external assessment were important judgemental criteria. The end result has been the formulation of better programmes of research with no noticeable loss of autonomy and the full utilisation of funds to ensure no subsequent reallocation. On the negative side there may be a tendency to plan research too rigidly as a consequence of this procedure and the 'publish or be damned' mentality engendered might very well damage the quality of research.

STUDENT SUPPORT

In the wake of public debate, the 1986 *Financial Aid to Students Act* covers provision for the 18-30 age group in full-time education. Under the Act, every Dutch or EEC national student is eligible for a grant, child benefit and tax allowances having been abolished. The grant covers a six year period of study at a university or six years at a higher vocational college plus the 10% transferring thereafter to a university, giving them the possibility of twelve years grant: in the near future the second grant is likely to be restricted to a maximum of two years.

The monthly budget for students resident at home is estimated at 620 gilders (£206) and for those living away 920 gilders (£306). The basic grant covers part of the budget and then there are allowances, supplementary loans (at interest) and a supplementary grant. The supplementary loan and grant are both dependent on the level of parental income and in 1987, 55% of students received the basic grant alone, the rest a combination of the three. Repayment of the loan commences within two years of graduation and can be spread over a period of ten years for interest free loans, or fifteen years for those bearing a rate of interest, where the rate is 2.5% below the market rate. All of Europe uses a grant/loan mix: Britain alone preserved for a long time the chastity of an exclusive grant system. From 1990 however, in the Netherlands the grant was reduced by £200 in exchange for free unlimited travel on public transport in an attempt to reduce the education deficit by some £200m. Grants are no longer index linked and are paid for five rather than six years with repayment commencing from the inception of the loan rather than graduation. Fees are to rise by £30 per annum for the next five years and government loans attract a rate of interest still subsidised but 0.5% higher than it was.

Unlike Britain the liberal welfare-minded Dutch nevertheless exact tuition fees from their students. Tuition fees were fixed by the 1984 *Memorandum Towards a New Policy of Educational Fees*. From 1988/89, with fees statutorily determined, they are set at 1750 gilders (£580) and accommodated within the total package of financial support for students.

In the future, the block grant may very well be split into two parts, one part covering the original government grant, and the second operating as a type of mission budget. Government would thus be able to influence the shape and development of each institution taking into account the changing needs of society and the economy. A substantial consultation procedure is envisaged every 5-6 years between government and the institutions, with the reapplication of the mission budget dependent on satisfactory past performance.

Certainly institutions can expect much closer monitoring of effectiveness, and this must be seen as a positive development, since it ensures that an institution never loses sight of its objectives and operates at maximum efficiency. A system of vouchers offering an entitlement to use public funds might yet be a better alternative to ensure high standards and maximum flexibility. The government for its part wishes to encourage differentiated products; variable course lengths; part-time study; modular degrees across disciplines and institutions; a diversified approach to teaching and greater weight attached to post-graduate education. Vouchers can help to achieve this.

Despite the emphasis placed upon these alternatives, grants for all plus loans at a commercial but guaranteed rate of interest, are not ruled out. Variable but full-cost tuition fees are a further possible option, a notion unthinkable in the U.K., and to increase the availability of independent resources, universities could be given the power to borrow on the capital markets. At the very least the government wishes to break the collusive oligopoly that is Dutch higher education, allowing market forces to operate whilst retaining some degree of control, particularly over standards. The funding of core research would remain as an almost exclusive governmental responsibility.

HIGHER EDUCATION IN DENMARK

The Danish system exhibits conflicts and confusions that too closely approximate to those in the UK. The state similarly has financial and numerical control of the system, with the usual outcome, a rationing of places: society is faced with the incubus of free education and the consequences of lugubrious central 'planning'. Now universities are to sell services to business and encourage private sector involvement: there will be a new commercial focus: relevance and utility are the new commandments, and the state is even thinking of introducing tuition fees because of the financial drain represented by universities. The pattern of student participation is however radically different from that which pertains in the United Kingdom, with courses extending over ten years, employment while studying, and graduation up to the age of thirty. Certainly this represents a waste of manpower, with able people in mundane jobs 'working their way' through college. This is not an economic use of human resources and we would not wish to see the migration of such a system here.

Many students take ten years to complete their studies, so that the average age at graduation can vary between 25 and as high as 30. There are no tuition fees, but annual admissions are strictly controlled and nearly all study is on a full-time basis.

FUNDING

Danish higher education is state financed and, obtrusively, state controlled. At the present time the state provides most of the financial resources for higher education. Through legal and ministerial edict, admission requirements, validation of study programmes and the formal conditions for the granting of degrees are all centrally controlled. The number of students admitted in any one year is also subject to strict control. Through the Directorate, student intake has been adjusted to manpower needs to improve the efficiency of the economic system, although elsewhere in Europe this came to be recognised as a chimera. Through the 1976 Act on the *Regulation of Admissions*, the Minister of Education can determine the maximum intake, set that year at 20,000 per annum, or 27% of the age cohort.

Admission depends on the availability of resources and resources are made available on the basis of student numbers and courses followed. Students are also recruited from non-traditional backgrounds in larger numbers than in the OECD countries – both mature and part-time. The Danish government in these instances is actively considering the introduction of tuition fees to reduce the financial burden on the public purse, and the universities ordinarily are encouraged to sell services to business and industry to raise revenue.

STUDENT SUPPORT

As there are no tuition or registration fees, student support is entirely independent of university finance. Grants were originally the only method of student support and these covered maintenance, books and food and were awarded so as to ensure equality of opportunity. However in 1964, a state guaranteed bank loan scheme commenced a quarter of a century before a British Tory Government toyed with the idea against much simulated uproar.

Repayment of all loans must commence one year after graduation, is by instalments, and must be fully repaid after a maximum of 15 years, with some exceptions. That a connection exists between taking paid employment and the duration of degree courses is entirely evident and clearly conditions the amount of financial support required. During studies, income from paid employment remains a substantial contributory factor towards total student income, particularly for mature students.[7]

Revision of the state support scheme was expected in 1988, with the abolition of state guaranteed loans, leaving only grants and state loans available for those aged 19 years and over with assets of less than 100,000 DKK (£10,000) or annual income below 34,000 DKK (£3,400) *excluding the grant.*

---

[7] A study of Copenhagen University, for example, found that between 1980 and 1986, those students who were under 23 spent less time in paid employment. Examining student income in 1989, Statistical News found that those aged 20-24 commanded 45% and those aged 25-29, 55% of their respective peers income: these figures show part of the opportunity costs that accompany study in Denmark.

THE THREAT TO AUTONOMY

University autonomy is clearly under threat in Denmark as it is in the UK, and to a lesser extent throughout Europe though not the U.S. The Ministry of Education is charged with a lack of professional expertise and indeed legitimacy to act as the administrative authority. Once again, the state now demands much more than qualified students from the universities in return for streamlined funding: value for society, technology, exports, health, environmental improvements and so on. It should be noted however that the financially most rewarding areas of activity may not coincide with the core research areas, thereby starving them of the most dynamic staff and resources. User-payments look attractive to politicians nevertheless, but the need to maintain the concept of free education and free admission may require a two tier and potentially divisive system of higher education in the future, with free universities and those charging fees.

HIGHER EDUCATION IN NORWAY

Total expenditure on higher education in Norway in 1987 amounted to NoK 6,000 million (£517m) with less than 3% attributable to the private sector. The state thus, as in the case of Britain, plays a predominant role in financing higher education, meeting some 90% of the bill, mainly through the Ministry of Culture and Scientific Affairs, but with a minor contribution from both the Ministry of Agriculture and Ministry of Defence. External finance covers the remaining 10%, channelled mainly through the Research Councils, but including research grants from private enterprise and other public agencies. Attached research foundations made a significant contribution to the finances of the universities, some NoK 600 million (£57m) in 1987, in return for research expertise. Total research income amounted to NoK 2,200 million (£210m) in 1987, of which 25% was externally financed.

Expenditure on the university sector increased in real terms between 1975 and 1987, as against the corrosive trends in this country. External financing however doubled over the same period from 5% to 10% of the budget, mirroring developments here, and some 5% of the total budget was allocated to private sector institutions (amounting to NoK 115 million (£11m)). Higher education student numbers rose by almost 50% from 1975 to 1987, in radical contrast to the more static UK, increasing from 67,000 to 92,000, and the number studying abroad rose from 4,000 to 7,000 over the same period.

Of a total student population of 96,000, some 45,000 attend university and 10% of the this total are enrolled in the private sector, which is much greater than here and where numbers are larger than the full-time equivalents suggest, because many are part-time: these private institutions offer courses extending over two or three years. Sixty per cent of the higher education budget is absorbed by the university sector and the state funds 90% of the university research budget: as here, it has a near monopoly of financial support. Whilst external funding has been encouraged, the general view is taken that it should not rise to such a level that it might encroach on higher education policy as it is envisaged by the state. Partly to ensure that this criterion is met, the government intends to strengthen the support research receives from central government: research contracts that used to be contracted through individual ministries, are now centralised and channelled through the Research Councils. And yet the state recognises that irrespective of its central planning function, individual universities must receive a greater degree of autonomy in the allocation of resources and in the determination of educational priorities, in direct contradiction to the official thrust in the U.K.

Student support includes three distinct strands and compares favourably with that in Denmark and Finland. Students are offered a combination of grants, subsidised loans and student welfare benefits. Loans and grants are both means-tested against student rather than parental income, and consequently a large number qualify for support. In 1987, NoK 3,350 million (£319m) was distributed in student grants, NoK 1,400 million (£133m) in loan subsidies and welfare grants, the two together being almost equal to expenditure on the universities themselves. However, the rise in interest rates has effectively reduced the real value of the loans available and many students have been forced to seek paid employment to continue their studies.

Of particular interest in Norway is the fact that an egalitarian student mix has been achieved much more successfully than in many OECD countries, and this will be a reference point for any reforms in the future.

FUNDING

Grants from the Ministry of Culture and Scientific Affairs cover the bulk of expenditure on public institutions and cover 90% of the student population. These grants are in line with the overall government development plan, but are also determined in conjunction with plans received from the individual institutions. Once the institutions receive their budget they are free to determine its allocation through a process of virement. Provision for new courses and changes in student numbers must be agreed with the Ministry beforehand.

Three quarters of the budget for fundamental research is covered by the universities' allocations from the Ministry, the remaining 25% being split as follows: 13% from the Research Councils; 3% from public agencies; 5% from private enterprise and the remaining 4% from research foundations. Research contracts that are externally financed are rare and these relate mainly to adult education programmes.

In recent years research foundations have been established to utilise research from the universities and these are often organised regionally with a view to encouraging the growth and regeneration of the regional economy. Their work is mainly applied and developmental and they absorb funds equivalent to a quarter of the universities' research and development budget. Foundations are also beginning to spawn science parks.

Private universities cater for 10% of the student population, measured in full time equivalents, but given that many attend part-time they represent a larger numerical share of the total student body. The private sector has responded quickly to changes in demand for courses and introduced new and innovative schemes of study, but their research function is very much underdeveloped mainly because many of their staff are themselves part-time.

STUDENT SUPPORT

Most students are entitled to a loan and a smaller number to grants. In 1987 the bill for student support amounted to NoK 5,000 million (£476m), almost equal to the budget for university education. Of the total, some NoK 2,400 million (£230m) covered grants and interest rate subsidies.

Loans are available free of interest for the first four years and must be repaid over a maximum of twenty years, with some flexibility over repayment, including writing off the loan under certain circumstances. Applications for loans and the amount borrowed have both declined and more students have taken paid employment to meet their commitments. Loan repayments are reduced for those graduates taking employment in northern Norway as part of a regional development programme.

Finally the establishment of an Industrial University is a distinct possibility, based on the resources of the larger Nordic companies and this would boost competition with other universities in the engineering and business areas in particular.

Norway, like Britain, sees the evaluation of institutions as a guarantee of efficiency in the expenditure of public money and several schemes have been put forward. In the event, internal self-evaluation has been found to be the most constructive modus operandi because it facilitates institutional change.

HIGHER EDUCATION IN FINLAND

In Finland we see again a resemblance to the UK – the growth of the concept of a 'market' in higher education, the mix of loans and grants, the allocation of research priorities, the central planning, the increase in monitoring. However, there is much less support for students and – possibly connected with this – a much higher rate of non-completion; students do part-time work in order to finance degrees, and consequently spend much longer on them – not necessarily an economically desirable arrangement. Note however that central funding is projected to increase 15% between 1986 and 1991 – an impossibility in Britain if present thinking persists. If the 1970's were characterised by State planning and the 1980's by self-regulation, the 1990's saw the emergence of the evaluative state.

University education in Finland is well provided for and geographically dispersed, with demand for graduates an important element in planning arrangements. The majority of the necessary funding comes from the state and there are no charges for tuition, an unusual feature, and one shared with Greece and the U.K. Institutions of higher education have extensive autonomy and the teaching and research functions are viewed as very closely linked together. The idea of satellite teaching in the immediate region of a university is seen as important.

The major developments in funding arrangements encompass the assumption by the state of responsibility for core funding in place of the private sector, whilst more recently, additional funding has been raised through market orientated developments in conjunction with the private sector. External funding has been increasing and state funding is now determined not by the number of students enrolling, but by the number graduating. This might encourage a reduction in academic graduation standards. Future developments include greater equality in the provision of resources between disciplines, and distribution based upon performance indicators, although these have yet to be specified.

Students pay their own fraternity and health care fees, but for maintenance and subsistence have guaranteed loans, study grants and subsidised housing and meals. However, the total package has failed to maintain its real value, so that students find it necessary to take temporary jobs consequently lengthening the period of study.

FUNDING

There are twenty universities in Finland, 10 are multi-disciplinary, whilst the rest concentrate on a single subject: veterinary science (1); technology (3); economics (3); industrial arts (1); music (1) and theatre (1). Finance is mainly provided by the state and the teaching and research functions are not dealt with separately. Since the 1960's medium term planning has been used involving a rolling five year time horizon updated every couple of years, but subject to further revision as necessary.

Resource allocation depends upon student places and covers teaching, research, staffing and administration. In 1986 a new *Higher Education Development Act* superseded the earlier one giving universities extra resources to match rising costs. In addition, expenditure on staff and research was to increase by 15% in real terms between 1986 and 1991 (insidious comparisons with the UK for the same period may be drawn here). The government's new planning strategy encompassed the following areas:

(1) Management by objectives, but with more autonomy for institutions and clear specification of teaching duties;

(2) Greater emphasis on research, but coupled with co-operation between institutions to achieve economies of scale;

(3) Periodic evaluation of teaching and research activities;

(4) Publication of reports on activities and performance;

(5) Resource allocation that reflects the results of selectivity exercises;

(6) Faster completion of degrees; and

(7) Improved research training programmes including that for PhD.

External funding grew rapidly until fairly recently, reaching 15% of total funding in 1987. In total, funding increased tenfold over the period 1975-87. The average cost of a degree is $60,000 (£37,500), ranging from $120,000 (£75,000) for medicine or veterinary science to $20,000 (£12,500) for law. From 1966 to 1987 student intake rose from 10,000 to 13,300 and the total number of students from 45,000 to 80,000.

Basic research funding comes through the Academy of Finland which is geared up to developing a longer term research and science policy (comparisons here with U.K. Research Councils and similar bodies elsewhere). It plays a central role in the evaluation of research results through selectivity exercises, organising co-operative research projects, and places considerable emphasis on post-graduate training. The Technology Development Centre, established in 1983, promotes the planning and finance of technological research. In general terms, research in Finland has been funded from external sources, but more recently the state has taken a more proactive role, giving extra resources, but also new direction and focus encouraging the sharing of equipment. A University Holding Company encourages joint industry/university development projects and allocates the funds generated between company, university and departments.

STUDENT SUPPORT

The over-riding aim of the programme of student support is to ensure equal opportunity for all potential participants in higher education. Earlier plans for funding students involved the creation of a system of state loans but as the volume of funding involved proved to be too great, commercial bank involvement became necessary. Fees are negligible.

The system of support includes the now customary mix of:

(1) State grants;

(2) Guaranteed loans with a subsidised rate of interest and

(3) Other benefits which aim to reduce living expenses.

Academic progress, the income of students, their partners and parents, are all factors that influence the level of support, and continued support depends upon steady progress being made towards graduating.

Loans are obtained from commercial banks and repayment commences after graduation, encouraging slow completion rates – anything between 7 and 10 years and part-time rather than full-time study. For the duration of the course and the first eighteen months after graduation the rate of interest is subsidised by the state (3.25% in 1987) but thereafter variable commercial rates apply (actually 6.45% in 1987). The repayment of the loan must start two years after graduation with a maximum repayment period of ten years: unemployment, military service or maternity leave allow the term of the loan to be adjusted. The grant, on the other hand, is non-repayable and provides for a housing allowance in the case of students living away from home. There was a doubling of student numbers between 1966 and 1986, and the distribution moved in favour of engineering and medicine.

Following the 1988 budget it is evident that higher education will assume a higher priority in state planning, with research and its application in industry being crucial to economic health and stability in the future. Greater financial support is to be provided for adult students resuming study and this is a trend observable in other OECD countries, particularly Britain. Students are also to be encouraged to spend six months at a foreign university.

Unlike the continued financial reductions in the U.K., which set the U.K. apart from every other country, financial resources will rise by about 15% per annum down to the early nineties with any increase in costs being fully compensated for. The research priorities identified have a familiar ring to them and include: bio-technology, molecular biology, cancer research and information technology. Greater external (private) financing is also expected, particularly for technology centres and business enterprises where the benefits to collaborators are obvious.

HIGHER EDUCATION IN SPAIN

Although the growth in student numbers and in the number of institutions peaked in 1978, there were renewed pressures for growth despite the apparently unfavourable demographic position such that since 1982 numbers have risen by 30% (75% completing secondary education go on to university).[8] Following the 1983 *University Reform Law*, a process of internal reform of the degree structure has been initiated, partly in response to the reform of secondary education that raised the school leaving age to 16. The costs of higher education are largely met by the state with some contribution from fees that are met by the students, a usual practice throughout Europe apart from the U.K., Greece and Finland. These registration fees vary between universities, but on average the ratio between state support and fee income is in the order of 80:20, with the latter on a rising plane since 1979. Living expenses are met by the student and/or his family and the limited system of student support available takes into account academic and financial criteria in its distribution. With a period of further expansion envisaged, the present system is recognised as inadequate and in need of radical reform with the emphasis on accountability and the assessment of teaching and research on a regular basis.

Universities now have a greater degree of freedom than they were afforded under the Franco regime with consultancy and the sale of academic services actively encouraged. Post-graduate programmes are in the process of being introduced, but no method of financing them has been settled. Certainly contributions by students at all levels will increase and the pursuit of outside funding has become a major preoccupation, reflecting developments elsewhere in Europe. Since 1989 performance related pay has been introduced for academics with a National Commission evaluating candidates. Teaching is assessed every five years and research every seven years.

FUNDING

Private universities play a negligible role in Spanish higher education and are financed through registration fees and a system of private subsidies, but seven new ones are planned and the sector is set to expand further with the emphasis on law, economics and engineering. There are currently 32 state universities and 4 private ones offering three cycles: diploma (3 years), licenciatura (degree 2 years); doctorate. Public universities are state financed, although students do pay a small registration fee: the public subsidy accounts for 80% of costs, but this varies between institutions. Research is funded out of subsidies associated with individual departments

---

[8] Furthermore entry standards are rising in order to restrict the numbers entering university.

of state, but links with business and industry through sponsored research are expanding. Nevertheless, the contribution from fees has also been increased in the last two years, and these now cover 20% of costs.

Spain did not escape from the great debates on the future of university education that occurred in most European countries during the 1970's, and the issues raised have a familiar ring to them. As late as 1986, a report published by the University Council argued that fees should reflect the real costs of higher education, but a report published the following year took the diametrically opposite view, so that the financing mechanism remains unchanged. Indeed the sensitivity shown by all parties on the issue of funding makes it extremely difficult for Ministers to plan for any increase in the level of private funding, perceived by them to be in the best interests of a vibrant and expanding system.

Between 1982 and 1986 spending on universities doubled to 85,755m pesetas (£483m) and further growth in expenditure is expected down to 1994. Absolute expenditure per student relative to other OECD countries remains at a low level in Spain, but the average rate has increased between 1975 and 1985, from 33,268 pesetas (£190) to 39,273 pesetas (£224). To counter the neglect of research, the proportion of GNP spent on research is to rise from 0.35% to 0.88% with a doubling of scientists and tripling of trainee researchers.

STUDENT SUPPORT

Student support encompasses the following:

(1) A state financed scholarship and aid system that has not been disturbed by the activities of autonomous communities;

(2) A system of grants;

(3) Scholarships subject to academic and economic assessment of the students' status, with economic criteria assuming greater importance;

(4) Family income determines the level of support so that a student is not financially independent;

(5) Residences and food are subsidised to a limited extent; and

(6) Low income means the suspension of the registration fee and some help with living expenses, study materials and transport if living away from home.

Scholarship and student aid expenditure rose from 1.749 million pesetas (£10 million) in 1976/77 to 8.922 million pesetas (£51 million) in 1985/86.

HIGHER EDUCATION IN GREECE

The Greek system is certainly demoralised and there is nothing that we can borrow from it. It has a similar set of features to the U.K., but much exaggerated. There is low political value placed on higher education; lack of private input; an absence of forward planning and budgetary rigidity; heavy student subsidy and total state support for universities, with the similar result that few are permitted to go to university because of the immense per capita cost. As in the UK, the less well off are paying for the education of the better off. The example of Thrace, where 82.6% of academic vacancies are unfilled, illustrates the dangers of excessive state control. Greek universities are non-market orientated and prone to political subjugation; as in the U.K. cuts are being implemented while government demands that institutions take on more students.

Higher education in Greece is located mainly in the public sector and this grew at about 3% per annum between 1974 and 1988, although this growth rate compares unfavourably with the nearly 18% rate in the technical, non-university sector. Admission to university depends on the operation of a *numerus clausus*, and expansion reflects the government's response to rising demand pressures with the reform of entrance examinations also promised to limit numbers. Although numbers have increased, expenditure per student has fallen, as resources have not increased at a sufficient rate. Fees were abolished in 1965 and under the 1975 Constitution admission became free and private university institutions were banned. Along with free tuition, students were provided with text books and medical care. Additionally, those from low income families received special grants for meals and accommodation and there are interest free loans and scholarships available provided academic criteria are met.

FUNDING

Capital expenditure and recurrent expenditure are met by the state and combined grew at 12.4% per annum between 1974 and 1988, rising to 15% per annum between 1981 and 1988 (a familiar rhythm). Nevertheless, the rate of growth in expenditure on other sectors of higher education outpaced that on universities. Expenditure per student fell significantly during the period 1986-88, suggesting that the government placed less importance on the role of the universities in supplying skilled manpower.

There are two guiding principles that lie behind university education: these are that all Greeks have a right to free education and that only state universities may operate, with the private sector limited to higher education outside the university sector. In Greece growing pressure on government resources has led to debate of both principles: on the first with a view to introducing student contributions subject to a means test, and on the second, with plans to revive private universities. More optimistic commentators have proposed the injection of more state funds, and others argue that existing facilities should be used to generate greater revenue, with the second option favoured by the Minister of Education.

Public accounting procedures mean that at the present time government control over the universities is exceedingly tight, a situation that does not square with the supposedly self-governing status of universities set out in the Constitution. With predictable regularity the government only agrees part of the budget requested by the universities, on the grounds that they always exaggerate their needs. Currently there are a set of proposals under discussion that would base funding on staff/student ratios and faculty type, so that greater certainty of funding would be possible together with some measure of long term planning. Some kind of change is inevitable given the pressure on existing budgets as a result of extant arrangements.

Absurdly, 35-40% of the student population in Greece studies abroad because of the shortage of higher education places. This represents a drain on the exchequer of some $225m (£126m) per annum in foreign exchange, at a rate of $5,000 (£2,800) for each of the 45,000 students involved. Viewed another way, this level of expenditure amounts to 50% of the cost of higher education in Greece, although it should be remembered that most of these costs are borne by the students' family and not the state. But it is a silly price to pay for dogma and parsimony.

STUDENT SUPPORT

Tuition in Greek universities is free and aid is available in the form of: meals, accommodation, books, scholarships, loans and medical care. In addition, parents are able to deduct expenditure on students' education from income tax. State aid as a percentage of total expenditure on higher education amounted to 12.3% in 1987, up from 11.2% in 1984.

But even Greece started loans earlier than the British. From the academic year 1983/84 interest-free loans have been available and these are means tested and subject to satisfactory performance during the period of study. The annual loans are available for a period of time that matches the minimum duration of a degree course, and their size depends upon the nature of the degree taken: 54,000 dras (£206) for all except dentistry students who receive 72,000 dras (£274). Repayment must commence within two years of graduation or one year after completion of military service, by monthly instalments. If a student interrupts his studies, repayment of the loan must occur after six months. If a student fails to graduate within one and a half times the minimum duration of the course, the loan becomes repayable immediately: this provides a useful imperative to finish the course on time. For those graded excellent upon graduation, the loan is cancelled, offering an enormous incentive to the enterprising. Scholarships are also available subject to status, financial means and academic ability. These are renewable, with continuation dependent upon academic merit.

The financial arrangements for higher education that currently prevail in Greece result in an entirely arbitrary limitation on access to higher education, as they do here. They were set at their present level by the Council of Higher Education in 1985, as if they somehow met desired economic and social criteria, which they most certainly do not. Thus deadening rigidities affect the Greek system far more than our own.

MORE RECENT DEVELOPMENTS

Recruitment of academic staff is subject to Ministry approval and there exists little scope for exercising any degree of flexibility, a problem rendered more acute when students may be transferred from one institution to another, or indeed from a foreign institution to a Greek one, ''according to specified criteria'', not actually discussed in the relevant OECD report. There exists, in fact, no national educational development policy and the exercise of political expediency makes a mockery of any attempt at forward planning of even the most limited kind. Budgetary allocations are too rigidly applied, based on the previous years realised expenditure and an additional sum calculated by civil servants *according to their perception of educational need.* Consequently resources are mainly concentrated in the area of teaching to the exclusion of research and innovative activities of any kind. If, on the other hand, additional funds for research are obtained from sources outside the government, the inability of the institution to recruit additional staff makes successful completion of the research project or programme problematic. Institutional autonomy is thus all but absent and "discourages the institute of higher education from innovating, doing research, diversifying the subjects taught, enriching teaching, inviting outside scholars and in general doing anything that will contribute to ameliorating the quality of the education offered but which, on the other hand, could be considered as an unnecessary luxury by those responsible for allocating public resources".[9]

In theory equity should be the basis of a free system, but in Greece there is no equity in the admissions system, so that the rich are always over-represented, as indeed they are elsewhere in Europe. Hence support for the needy becomes essential if their studies are to be completed. As things stand though, in the absence of a vigorously progressive tax system, the relatively poor end up paying for the free education of the rich. Government 'policy' or rather rhetoric on higher education, includes the customary provision of more places, particularly in technical education, but this will undoubtedly put a strain on already limited resources since new funding is not on the agenda. Standards of education are perceived to have fallen as a result of attempts to recruit more students.

Despite expansionist intentions and concern over the leakage of students to foreign institutions, the government has severely limited expenditure on higher education. In 1978 higher education consumed 12% of the total public budget, but in 1986 that figure had fallen to 8.5%. The government in actual fact plans to reduce the level of admissions and simultaneously wants individual institutions to make more effective use of their resources. A return to fees and the revival of private universities is not inconceivable, although both would require a change in the Constitution. Greece's membership of the EEC will probably accelerate the return of private universities as domestic policies are realigned in the wake of competitive forces operating amongst member states. Pressure is mounting to save families the cost of sending students abroad to study and the government itself badly needs to save the foreign exchange it looses.

---

[9] OECD, *Changing Patterns of Finance in Higher Education: Country Report Greece*, 1988, p.23.

Student unrest has accompanied the publication of plans in 1991 to abolish free education, food and books, with the introduction of tuition fees and a time limit on the duration of degrees: this would be course length plus 50% if these proposals are enacted. Academic criteria would be applied to future grant eligibility with brighter students paying less for their degrees: a system of scholarships and grants in fact, based on strict assessment. These are radical reforms and it remains to be seen whether Greece's fragile Parliament can push them through.

Universities themselves have had the ability to establish special enterprises, either public or private, to exploit their special skills and resources since 1982, but as yet limited use has been made of this possibility. Education specialists, however, foresee increased use of these enterprises in the near future. The Council for Higher Education has re-established a dialogue between the various institutions of higher education and the government, so that a change in the funding and management of the institutions reappears on the agenda – the adoption recently of resource allocation indicators, albeit unsuccessfully, represents an important step towards greater freedom.

The nineteen eighties inflicted the same trends towards reduction in the level of research funding as in the United Kingdom, though we must again caution against comparisons since the systems start from different points. In general, the decade saw a move to increased state direction of research and increased applied research, with private and industrial sources solicited much more extensively for funds. Another movement is towards competitive tendering for research as in Denmark, the Netherlands and now Britain.

CONCLUSIONS

The European present could anticipate our future: vast classes, high drop-out rates, home domiciled students and local universities, long and very general courses sustained by peripatetic, low status employment. The Oxbridge model of intimate teaching groups could become anachronistic – except in Oxbridge. Research would no longer define any university institution, but rather would become the distinctive badge of the elite.

These authors believe such a course is inevitable unless we take the kind of action recommended in this book: we do want universities expanded, but not 'massified' on the European model.

Mass higher education is anyway a meaningless goal without improvement in secondary standards and a change in cultural and parental attitudes towards education. But do we want massification anyway? Is it merely an expensive form of remedialism? Is not the need really to focus on 16-19 training and education, and will expansion of the universities be carried largely by the (economic) arts disciplines, and, therefore, contribute little to the furtherance of national competitive advantage?

Our future could well be mirrored in Europe unless we take action now to change course. If we do not, most universities will become a kind of pedagogic granary: knowledge will be stored but not added to, and the solemn, anonymous task of milling will roll ever onward to the murmurs of the stream.

SUMMARY STATISTICS OF INTERNATIONAL COMPARISONS

Notes: * In each table indicates that figures are confirmed with the authors of the individual OECD Reports.

Exchange rates are the daily average of the year in question.

TABLE 7:5.1 PERCENTAGE OF GNP DEVOTED TO HIGHER EDUCATION

	Institutional aid			Student aid		
	Year	Early 1970s	Mid 1980s	Year	Form of aid	% of GNP
Australia	1975-88	1.36	0.99	1988	grant	0.13
Finland*	1970-88	0.60	0.71	1987	loan/grant	0.19
France*	1975-84	0.68	0.67	1984	loan/grant indirect aid	0.08
Germany*	1970-86	1.02	1.18	1986	loan	0.12
Greece	1974-88	0.54	0.83	1987	indirect/loans	0.10
Japan	1970-85	0.66	0.88	1985	loan	0.03
Netherlands*	1970-84	1.87	1.97	1984	loan/grant	0.20

TABLE 7:5.1 PERCENTAGE OF GNP DEVOTED TO HIGHER EDUCATION (Cont'd)

	Institutional aid			Student aid		
	Year	Early 1970s	Mid 1980s	Year	Form of aid	% of GNP
Norway*	1975-87	1.08	1.04	1987	loan/grant	0.50
Spain	1972-86	0.22	0.51	1987	grant	0.05
United Kingdom*	1984		0.80	1983	grant	0.30
United States*	1970-85	2.10	2.33	1986	loan/grant	0.17

Notes:

Australia	:	Total Commonwealth government grants to higher education as percentage of GDP.
Finland*	:	Total expenditure on higher education as a percentage of GNP.
France	:	Total expenditure on higher education as a percentage of GDP (excluding funds for research).
Germany*	:	Total expenditure on higher education as percentage of GNP.
Greece	:	Total expenditure on higher education as percentage of GDP.
Japan	:	Public and private expenditure on higher education as percentage of GNP.
Spain	:	Total expenditure on higher education as percentage of GNP.
Norway*	:	Total higher education expenditure as percentage of GNP. The grant/loan figure includes all new loans.
Netherlands	:	Total expenditure on higher education as percentage of GNP.
United Kingdom*	:	Public current expenditure on higher education as percentage of GNP; institutions as percentage of GNP.
United States	:	Total expenditure on higher education as percentage of GNP (includes purchases of land, buildings and equipment).

TABLE 7:5.2 ANNUAL RATE OF GROWTH OF CURRENT EXPENDITURE ON HIGHER EDUCATION INSTITUTIONS.
(at constant prices)

Australia*			
Commonwealth government grants only		1975-80	1.9
		1980-88	1.2
Denmark		1973-80	2.39
		1980-85	-1.20
France*			
Total recurrent public expenditure		1975-80	2.64
		1980-83	5.40
Germany		1970-80	2.63
		1980-86	1.53
Greece			
All higher education		1974-80	7.18
		1980-88	5.30
Universities		1974-80	5.84
		1980-85	4.39
Japan			
Public institutions		1970-80	13.83
		1980-87	2.64
Private institutions		1971-80	19.84
		1980-85	7.39
Netherlands			
All higher education		1975-80	2.29
		1980-85	-3.63
Spain			
Universities, including capital		1975-80	10.91
expenditure		1980-85	6.18
United Kingdom			
Universities		1970-80	1.30
		1980-86	1.89
Polytechnics (England only)		1982-86	0.51
University general grants		1970-80	1.28
+ subsidised fees only		1980-86	-1.46
United States			
Public institutions		1970-80	3.57
		1981-85	2.57
Private institutions		1970-80	2.20
		1981-85	3.92

TABLE 7:5.3 AVERAGE CURRENT INSTITUTIONAL EXPENDITURE PER STUDENT

		National currency	Exchange rate $	$ (current)	Constant prices in National Currency
Australia					
All institutions	1975				10 170
	1980				10 161
	1987	8 754	1.43	1 126	8 754
Denmark					
Universities	1973				40 950
	1980				46 660
	1985	37 030	10.59	3 495	37 030
All institutions	1973				52 235
	1980				53 177
	1985	40 068	10.59	3 784	40 068
France*					
All institutions	1975				6 528
	1980				6 617
	1988	17 513	5.96	2 915	6 227
Germany*					
All institutions	1985	11 700	2.94	3 976	
Greece					
All institutions	1974	22 402	30.00	747	58 400
	1980	70 800	42.64	1 660	70 800
	1988	285 849	141.64	2 018	67 000
Universities	1974	22 939	30.00	765	59 800
	1980	79 600	42.64	1 876	79 600
	1988	343 019	141.64	2 422	80 400
	1974	18 720	30.00	624	48 800
Other	1980	46 000	42.64	1 079	46 000
	1988	182 175	141.64	1 286	42 700
Japan					
National institutions	1971	468 000	348.94	1 341	468 000
	1980	1 215 000	226.70	5 360	545 000
	1985	1 424 000	238.62	5 968	558 000
Private institutions	1971	165 000	348.94	473	165 000
	1980	704 000	226.70	3 105	316 000
	1985	1 062 000	238.62	4 451	416 000

TABLE 7:5.3 AVERAGE CURRENT INSTITUTIONAL EXPENDITURE PER STUDENT (Cont'd)

		National currency	Exchange rate $	$ (current)	Constant prices in National Currency
Netherlands					
All institutions	1975	15 400	2.53	6 087	21 000
	1980	18 800	1.98	9 457	18 800
	1985	18 000	3.32	5 608	16 800
Universities	1985	23 665	3.32	7 126	
Other institutions	1985	8 262	3.32	2 488	
Norway					
Universities	1975	32 857	5.22	6 291	
	1981	48 922	5.73	8 535	
	1987	67 556	6.74	10 028	
Non-university	1981	26 733	5.73	4 664	
	1987	43 137	6.74	6 403	
Portugal					
Laboratory subjects	1987	371 200	140.79	2 637	
Other subjects	1987	129 500	140.79	920	
Spain					
All institutions	1975	33 268	57 40	580	33 268
	1981	99 525	92.26	1 079	38 816
	1985	154 070	170.06	906	39 273
United Kingdom					
Universities (all recurrent income)	1970-71	1 333	0.41	3 259	5 787
	1980-81	5 010	0.50	10 060	5 010
	1986-87	7 926	0.61	12 950	5 58
Universities (grants + fees)	1970-71	1 033	0.41	2 526	4 485
	1980-81	3 998	0.50	8 028	3 998
	1986-87	3 555	0.61	8 897	3 836
Polytechnics (all recurrent income)	1982-83	3 429	0.66	5 196	3 041
	1986-87	3 770	0.61	6 160	2 655
Polytechnics (grants + fees)	1982-83	3 330	0.66	5 045	2 608
	1986-87	3 555	0.61	5 808	2 352

TABLE 7:5.3 AVERAGE CURRENT INSTITUTIONAL EXPENDITURE PER STUDENT (Cont'd)

		National currency	Exchange rate $	$ (current)	Constant prices in National Currency
United States					
All institutions	*1969-70	2 452	1.00	3 349	7 536
	1980-81	7 263	1.00	7 263	7 263
	1984-85	10 049	1.00	10 049	8 065
	*1986	11 049	1.00	11 049	
Public institutions	1969-70	2 908	1.00	2 908	6 536
	1980-81	6 365	1.00	6 365	6 365
	1984-85	8 724	1.00	8 724	7 001
Private institutions	1969-70	4 510	1.00	4 510	10 135
	1980-81	10 003	1.00	10 003	10 003
	1984-85	13 955	1.00	13 955	11 200

Notes

Australia	: Commonwealth grants to institutions (1987 prices).
Denmark	: Ministry of Education appropriations (1985 prices).
France*	: Budget of Ministry responsible for Higher Education (1974 prices) excludes expenditures specifically for research.
Germany*	: All institutional expenditure except hospitals attached to universities.
Greece	: Ministry of Education budget (1980 prices).
Japan	: All institutional expenditure (1971 prices).
Netherlands	: All recurrent expenditure (1980 prices). If research is excluded, the university figure for 1985 is about Gld 12,000 or $3,000.
Norway	: Net current expenditure in public institutions.
Portugal	: Institutional expenditure.
Spain	: Institutional budgets (1975 prices).
United Kingdom	: Institutional expenditures (1980-81 prices). If research is excluded, the universities' grants-plus-fees figure for 1986-87 falls to about $6,600. Polytechnics figures are for England only.
United States	: Current fund expenditures – all sources of income (1980-81 prices).

TABLE 7:5.4 PERCENTAGE SOURCES OF INCOME OF HIGHER EDUCATION INSTITUTIONS

		General public funds	Fees	Other income
Australia*	1987	87.96	2.11	9.93
Finland				
Public institutions	1987	85.00	n.a.	15.00
France*	1975	93.00	2.90	4.20
All institutions	1984	89.50	4.70	5.80
Germany*				
All higher education	1986	68.50	0.00	31.50
Japan				
Private 4-year institutions	1971	9.00	75.80	15.10
	1985	15.00	65.80	19.10
Public institutions	1970	83.10	2.00	14.90
	1987	63.10	8.80	28.00
All institutions	1971	53.06	31.69	15.20
	1985	41.99	35.78	22.20
Netherlands*	1985	80.00	12.00	8.00
All institutions	1975	95.00	n.a.	5.00
Norway				
Public institutions	1987	90.00		10.00
Spain				
Universities	mid-1980s	80.00	20.00	n.a.
United Kingdom	1970-71	71.20	6.30	22.40
Universities	1986-87	55.00	13.70	31.30
Polytechnics (England Only)	1986-87	72.40	16.20	11.40
United States				
Private institutions	1969-70	20.70	38.60	40.60
	1984-85	59.30	14.50	42.90
Public institutions	1969-70	61.10	15.10	23.70
	1984-85	59.30	14.50	26.30
All institutions	1969-70	46.50	20.50	29.90
	*1986	44.80	22.40	32.80

TABLE 7:5.4 PERCENTAGE SOURCES OF INCOME OF HIGHER EDUCATION INSTITUTIONS (Cont'd)

Notes

Finland	:	Figures for fees not available but very small.
France*	:	Expenditure of National Ministry of Education.
Japan	:	73 per cent of other income is revenue of hospitals attached to universities.
Norway	:	Figures for fees not available but very small.
United Kingdom	:	Almost all the fees of undergraduate students are paid out of public funds. This amounts to about half the fee income of universities and probably a greater proportion of the fee income of polytechnics.
United States	:	Figures include all government expenditure at all levels. Loans and grants to students amounted to about 80 per cent of fees in 1969-70 and 95 per cent in 1984-85.

TABLE 7:5.5 PERCENTAGE OF INCOME FROM INDUSTRY AND COMMERCE AND FROM MEDICAL SERVICES (OTHER THAN TUITION FEES)

		Industry and commerce	Medical services
Denmark			
Technical University of Denmark	1985	2.55	n.a.
Finland			
All institutions	1987	3.90	n.a.
France*			
All institutions	1984	5.80	n.a.
Germany			
All institutions	1986	6.50	25.00
Japan			
National (public) institutions	1985	3.40	18.40
Netherlands*			
All institutions	1987	2.00	0.00
United Kingdom*			
Universities	1986-87	2.70	1.85
Polytechnics (England only)	1986-87	0.90	0.00
United States			
All institutions	1984-85	7.60	8.10
Private	1984-85	11.40	9.90
Public	1984-85	5.50	7.10

TABLE 7:5.5 PERCENTAGE OF INCOME FROM INDUSTRY AND COMMERCE AND FROM MEDICAL SERVICES (OTHER THAN TUITION FEES) (Cont'd)

Notes

n.a.	:	Not available but probably very small.
Denmark	:	Sale of services in one university only.
Finland	:	Enterprises, foundations and international sources.
France*	:	Income from enterprises.
Germany	:	Includes contract research from public funds.
Japan	:	Corporative research grants and contracts.
Netherlands*	:	"Third flows of funds".
Norway*	:	External income except Research Council grants.
United Kingdom*	:	Universities, research grant income only (about another 1.9 per cent can be accounted for by short-course income, most of which comes from non-government sources.
Polytechnics	:	Non-public sector income.
United States	:	Private gifts, grants and contracts and sales of educational services.

TABLE 7:5.6 STUDENT FINANCIAL AID

		Form of Aid[1]	Maximum per student (national currency)	In $	Average per student (national currency)[2]	In $	% Receiving aid
Australia	1987	Grant		0	825	578	43
Denmark	1986-87	Grant +Loan					
Students under 22			39 300	5 266			
Students 22+			43 800	5 869			
Finland	1987	Loan Grant	18 274	4 157	7 832	1 782	Most
France	1988	Grant and			1 190	200	
	1986-87	indirect	12 996	2 009			18
Germany	1986	Loan			1 321	608	
Greece	1987	Indirect Grant			28 215	209	
Japan	1986						
Graduate students		Loan	80 000	475	28 418	169	34
Undergraduates		Loan	45 000	267	5 075	30	10

TABLE 7:5.6 STUDENT FINANCIAL AID (Cont'd)

		Form of Aid[1]	Maximum per student (national currency)	In $	Average per student (national currency)[2]	In $	% Receiving aid
Netherlands*	1988	Grant	9 700	4 856	8 000		95
		Loan	3 500		1499	412	45
Norway	1987	Loan			33 500	4 970	Most
		Loan subsidy			8 500	1 261	Most
		Grant			6 250	928	Most
Portugal	1987	Indirect and grant			7 993	57	8
Spain	1986	Grant			16 134	115	
United Kingdom	1984-85	Grant			1 123	1 467	
	1988-89	Grant	2 050	3 648			82
United States	1984-85	Loan and Grant			2 142	2 142	30-50
	1986	Grant			742	742	

Notes:

1. Most countries also have some form of indirect financial aid for students. This is usually available to the majority of students. It is included in this column only when it constitutes a significant part of the total financial support. Indirect aid is excluded from the rest of the table.
2. Averaged over all students whether or not they received any aid.

Netherlands*	:	Excludes fee component of grant. All students receive the basic grant; otherwise eligibility is severely limited by family income. 55 per cent of students receive only the basic grant.
Norway	:	Loan + grant figure includes interest rate subsidy. Loan figure is amount of value of loans made each year.
United Kingdom	:	The maximum figure for students living in London is £2,425. Last column refers to full-time undergraduate students. All students receiving grants have fees paid as well.
United States*	:	Estimates of percentage of students receiving support based on figures given by Bruce Johnston (1987) in "Sharing the Costs of Higher Education". 1984-8 figures refer to gross loans plus grants available. 1986 figures refer to grants only.

CHAPTER EIGHT

THE COURTIERS OF LILLIPUT: A SURVEY OF VICE CHANCELLORS AND PRINCIPALS

"It is unrealistic to expect anything more than marginal funding from business, which is, after all, only one of the users of the higher education system".
Confederation of British Industry,
Quoted in Eamon Butler, *A Degree of Privacy*, 1987.

INTRODUCTION

Our survey of colleges and universities was, in some ways, a failed enterprise. We wrote to all the universities, and to the Oxbridge colleges. Understandably many of the colleges replied saying they felt the questions were not applicable on a collegiate basis. Unlike the managing directors, however, who we also surveyed, the vice chancellors claimed they simply did not have time to answer our questions. Because of the disinterest of vice-chancellors we cannot represent the universities' position as accurately and elaborately as the industrialists'.[1]

There were a few respondents – a large civic university; a collegiate university; a major London college; a small technological university; and three Oxbridge colleges (a mainstream one; a wealthy one; a postgraduate one). Their replies, though illuminating, carry an import caveat against generalising them throughout the university system. Nevertheless the value of this survey is that, though tiny, each respondent represented a major category of university archetype, all being afforded anonymity in the interest of the fullest possible reply.

What emerged from the replies was not in any way stereotypical and the respondents were open to innovation and to the challenging of traditional models, but it was clear that the less generously endowed institutions had a hard time over the past ten years.

PART ONE: FINANCING THE SYSTEM

The first major theme of our survey was the whole question of university funding. What was the nature of the crisis; were there alternatives to the state; how zealously had they solicited those alternatives?

IMPACT OF THE 1981 CUTS

First we needed to diagnose the scale of their crisis. To the question "What has the impact of the 1981 cuts in university funding been on your institution?", one major London college reported a drop of nearly 10% in UGC income in the first half of the eighties as a proportion of total income: it was now only slightly over half of annual income: overseas student numbers had nearly doubled in the eighties, during which period monies

---

[1] See chapter 9.

from research grants and contracts as a proportion of total income had increased by 5%. "Considerable effort has been expended on attracting industry to sponsor academic posts at the college and to economise on expenditure". A small technological university simply described the impact of the cuts as "severe". An Oxbridge college pointed out that despite its endowment income, more than half of its fellows held university academic posts, but the impact of the cuts had been indirect – for example a university readership held at the college had to be left vacant by the university for six years.

One of the country's largest civic universities described the impact of the 1981 cuts as serious – in particular, reductions in medical and dental training and patient provision; Italian discontinued as a single honours degree; few additional recruitments to permanent posts; great difficulties in getting good staff in marketable areas, for example computer science; more emphasis on overseas students, research, research grants and so on. The collegiate university described the impact thus: "Has speeded the university's rationalization programme, at the expense of worthwhile areas of creativity. Hard to retain quality while reorganizing and contracting simultaneously". However, an eminent Oxbridge college found the impact "not great", they now had to pay the whole cost of two tutors out of 23, though another said that the college had suffered a decrease in tutorial posts as a result of a Register of Suspended Posts. The impact of the cuts therefore varied according to the institution's existing capital and its ability, most broadly defined, to act as a cushion. For the less famous and endowed the cuts engendered real severity. For the top echélons however the problems were sustainable.

"How serious do you regard the shrinkage in the UK science base?"

"Extremely serious. We have to recognise that, if we are to keep our place, level funding will not be enough in this area. Other countries are increasing their civil science research expenditure in real terms". The other respondents perceived it as "very grave", "serious" and so on.[2]

---

[2] Such a view is confirmed by the House of Lords Select Committee on Science and Technology, *Civil Research and Development*, Volume One Report, London, HMSO, Cmnd. HL20-1, 1986, p.13 and pp.55-6. Cf. for a typical reply on this point the evidence of Professor E. Ash, Imperial College, London. *Ibid.*, Volume Three, London, HMSO, Cmnd. HL20-III, 1986, p.7.

Interestingly enough it was the industrialists who were more eloquent in criticizing the contraction of the science base: the academic denunciations were more ritualistic.

Then: "Have the cuts in funding affected your ability to give quality teaching to undergraduates and postgraduates?" Yes, said the London college – partly because of the time lecturers now had to spend raising external finance. One of the Oxbridge colleges had only been marginally affected by the cuts; the other wealthy one not at all; for the small technological university cuts had not initially been hurtful "but post-1984 it is now evident that they had been".

HOW MUCH MORE STATE SUPPORT?

We pondered the scale of resourcing necessary for all this to be remedied, asking how much greater should state support of your university be in order to achieve, in your view, a wholly satisfactory level? The major London College said: "An increase of 5% would ease the most pressing difficulties but for equipment to be brought up to modern standards and for buildings to be properly maintained and adapted an increase nearer 10% would be necessary". Another small technological university commented tersely "with the present range of activities 20%". Said the major civic university:

> "Regrettably we consider this question to be unanswerable. There are some who would argue that the level of funding we receive now from the Government is satisfactory, as presumably the Government does. At the other extreme to reimburse marketable staff at realistic rates, invest in new plant and equipment, and maintain the Library and estate in proper order would require an increase in grant of between 5 and 10 per cent".

This question seems to have elicited an interesting consensus. A 10% increase in funding would achieve most of the universities' aspirations: such an increase could in fact be the consequence of the graduate tax advocated elsewhere in this book, and if ways could be found of returning this amount to the university system its morale, efficiency and sanity would improve enormously.[3] This does not seem like an unattainable objective, and the reward would be a university system that looked brightly to the future and did not mourn for a (highly sanitised) past.

---

[3] See chapter 10 below, p.318.

Another university argued: "Level-funding since 1981 would have been fine. A 10% increase in UGC grant would solve most of the present pressing problems". Remarked the rich Oxbridge college:

> "I am afraid I do not think this is a very good question. A wholly satisfactory level would be interpreted in different ways by different people. I myself should not mean by it that we saw each university resuming and then sustaining its pre-cuts pattern of activities".

ENDOWMENT INCOME

Perhaps institutions themselves could mitigate the effects of state parsimony? On the question of the extent and sources of endowment income, the major London college said that it had increased from 0.4% to 1.21% in the years under review, sources being charitable trusts and industrial support. One Oxbridge college cited "Fee income, conference income, fellowship and scholarship endowment by industrial concerns".

An Oxbridge college pointed out that the sources of endowment income were largely the original endowments of the college; endowment income represented a little over 85% of the total income, excluding short-term research grants. The major civic university said that in 1980/81 income from endowments amounted to £800,000 or 1.4% of the university's gross income. Another university simply dismissed pre-81 endowments as "negligible" and an Oxbridge college described sources of endowment income as agricultural land and stocks and shares: such sources produced an annual income of £625,000 with fees producing another half million. Of non-endowment income, the major London college had seen its block grant doubled between 1975 and 1986; but research monies from government departments had increased by more than six times and Research Council money by four times. The category "Charities, Industry, Overseas" had increased its yield five-fold. The Oxbridge college emphasised the research grants it received, especially from the ESRC, foundations, government departments and a trust fund providing an annual income.

Another university listed its income thus: "grants (UGC) 50%; grants and contracts 24%; fees 12%; services rendered 6%; other 8%". An Oxbridge college wrote: "for the year ending 31 July 1987 net endowment income was £1,163,000 and from fees, dues and charges was £1,028,000; income from grants and donations was £12,000: none of this came from government, Research Councils or industry".

Outside Oxbridge therefore, current endowment income is paltry. Eminent institutions enjoy great success in getting money out of the government in other ways – via the Research Councils, government departments and so on. They also increased their industrial earnings significantly, but the base point here was very small.[4]

FUNDRAISING EFFORTS

Perhaps industry might help. So then we asked: "How extensive and formalised are your efforts to get industrial/commercial funding?" The major London college answered:

> "The effort expended is considerable, but industry and commerce retain the belief that state support of higher education is met in great part from their payment of corporation tax. The tax régime in the UK does not encourage the business world to be generous to universities. It will take some time for entrenched attitudes to change".

The small technological university said "such efforts extended throughout the organization". Commented the big civic university:

> "There has been a considerable push on the part of academic departments individually to attract greater funding in this area. The university has not so far found it necessary to centralise this part of its operations, and indeed feels that such a move would be counterproductive.
>
> In conclusion, our efforts in this direction are extensive though they are not formalised".

And the collegiate university replied that each major college had industrial liaison staff who worked collaboratively. Added the rich Oxbridge college "We are only beginning to crank this up. Our efforts are at the moment vigorous but elementary", and "our appeals within the 10 year period of my headship have been made largely though by no means entirely to Foundations here and abroad".

All then made energetic protestations of their vigour in this direction, anxious to make up for past neglect and wishing to distance themselves from the arm of the government. Again – a recurrent theme in their replies

---

[4] For the proportion of endowment income, see Table 2:7, chapter 2, p.60. In the academic year 1989/90, the last for which full data is available, the top eighteen universities out of fifty one, gained 75% of external research income that amounted to £762m.

– there are serious doubts about the willingness of industry to assume much more of the burden of higher education; quite rightly they recognise that there does not necessarily exist a specific 'industrial opinion' and that often industrialists merely reflect the views of the larger culture – especially in seeing education as the prerogative of the state.[5]

TAX INCENTIVES

As to the question, "Would you favour greater industrial support if continuity of such support could be ensured by appropriate tax breaks/incentives?" The major London college replied: "Yes. Such would certainly help in (i) improving liaison with industry and (ii) expanding the more applied research in for example engineering". The small technological university agreed. One of the Oxbridge colleges answered: "I do not think that this university or this college would be in danger of an improper degree of influence on the part of those providing such support". Said a major civic university:

> "Tax breaks/incentives is just another method of Government funding. It is doubtful if these would produce any more income than simply giving the equivalent sum direct in the first place. Industry usually wishes to contribute only if there is some benefit (gain) likely to accrue to them".

The other university replied simply "yes", as did the (rich) Oxbridge college.

Again then, greater confidence that Oxbridge would be able to maintain its own. Others felt they could not really protect uncommercial subjects.[6]

ALUMNI SUPPORT

In addition to commerce, former college/university members might be led to contribute. Thus we asked: "Do you see alumni as a potential source of

---

[5] This view is confirmed by the evidence given to the House of Lords Select Committee on Science and Technology by the CVCP, *Ibid.*, Volume Three, p.83. On the other hand, industry is ignorant about the potential of the universities, "some industrial firms are not aware of the potential for collaboration; others, especially hi-tech companies, find present university facilities, hit by the cuts in equipment grant, inadequate", *Ibid.*, Volume One, p.31.

[6] Again the House of Lords found many respondents to its Select Committee on Science and Technology favoured tax breaks of greater or lesser generosity, *Ibid.*, Volume Three, pp.16,18,83,156 and 216. Save British Science submitted evidence from the CBI that undermined the whole notion of industry support, "current policy and successive reductions in funding have seriously undermined morale and effectiveness in higher education..... there is no prospect of industry collectively intervening to shoulder a large part of the cost burden (of research) in higher education", *Ibid.*, Volume Three, p.233.

significant support: do you plan to solicit them and open an alumni funding office?"

"Our college is not planning to call on its alumni (except in the case of small 'memorial funds'). Oxford University has recently established an office of the type mentioned and will be seeking the support of alumni". (Oxbridge college).

"Alumni are a source of support, but we do not see them as providing a major input to the university in financial terms. However, we do plan to make approaches to our alumni for particular projects". (Civic University).

"Yes". (Rich Oxbridge college).

"Yes. In terms of private giving on the American scale it is doubtful that alumni working in the U.K. could provide major support in the short term, but their influence in the industrial and commercial sectors can be considerable. The college has opened what can be regarded as an 'alumni funding office'". (London college).

"Already happens, but not a major source of income. Far greater revenues would need to be put into Alumni relations to increase income". (Collegiate University).

"Yes. The University, but also colleges such as this one, now have a substantial funding office". (Oxbridge college).

"Yes but the timescale is long, most probably 50 years". (City technological).

While some alumni solicitation was therefore promised by everyone, there does not seem from the evidence of these replies to have been any great enthusiasm for it and this is a pity. Evidently too much of an assumption that alumni are parsimonious exists, and this would appear to assume the nature of a self-fulfilling prophecy. There is not enough vigour or technique or optimism in their pursuit.

PART TWO: INDEPENDENCE

Our second major theme was independence, and more generally the influence, positive and negative, of more forcible applications of market dynamics to the universities. We explored the question of whether, if the government could no longer be depended upon to support universities, independence might be a possible alternative.

To the question "What is your reaction to the continual decline in government support, and can universities be independent of government support", the major London college replied: "Universities cannot be independent of government support if tuition fees do not meet the full cost of teaching, nor can sufficient funds be attracted from industry or commerce to meet the costs of 'pure' strategic research, especially in 'big' science, where some projects require international collaboration in order to achieve objectives". Another university simply said "No, even Buckingham is not". One of the Oxbridge colleges said "I would not judge that a University such as this which supports major research in the natural sciences could become independent of government support, if it is remembered that the Research Councils receive their support from the government. Our college is able to draw on alternative sources of support". The major civic university replied:

> "We regret the philosophy that has led to a reduction in university funding as we do not believe it to be based on an accurate analysis of universities' financial positions. A second reaction is a determination that this University will maintain its commitment to teaching and research despite the reduction in funding. We know that one university – Buckingham – is independent of direct Government funding and have no doubt that the economy would support one or two small liberal-arts-based institutions. We do not, however, believe that industry and commerce would be prepared to provide funding for a major civic university. Thus the answer to your second question is that universities as a whole cannot be independent of government support".

Another university thought that universities could not be independent of government support in the modern industrial state: "Universities need to be more independent of short term government decisions". An Oxbridge college answered:

> "I must here make it clear that I speak as an individual and not for my College. I think that the modes in which we handle University finance increase the difficulties of dealing with any decline in Government funding to the system as a whole. I believe decline is in principle manageable if consequentially liberating steps are taken (for example to turn educational support over to a fee-led basis, to create a competitive fee structure and to abandon national salary scales). I do not think that a university can be independent of Government support in this country however, since the Government is always likely to be a substantial consumer of some of our services. This is so in the U.S., for example. That the universities could be more independent I have no doubt".

There was universal agreement that a total independence, in the sense of no government support for the research mission of universities, would be impossible and absurd, and the need really was to find mechanisms to distance government interference while retaining support. Nowhere in the world were universities and their research not in receipt of considerable funds from the state: and this was particularly so in the U.S.A. Industry would never meet the costs of pure research or of the support of a major university, and independence would only be an option for the small liberal arts college on the U.S. or Japanese model, but not for institutions with major science and engineering components. Our original question was perhaps a little naïve, and the universities' answer was based not on ideological animus against the concept of privatisation, but rather a simple disbelief in the willingness of British industry in particular to carry the burden.

A MIXED ECONOMY

"Is a mixed economy of state and private universities possible in the U.K. as in the U.S. and Japan?"

> "A mixed economy of state and private university already exists to a small extent in the U.K. Given proper tax incentives for private funding of university services and for private fee payments and student support then there is a possibility that a greater mix could exist in the universities. At present though the reluctance of industry and private benefactors to donate meaningful sums to universities (as they used to do before 1939) is the limiting factor". (Civic University).
>
> "Why not for example University of Buckingham". (Oxbridge college).
>
> "Yes – depending on tax and other financial arrangements". (Collegiate University).
>
> "Only if a great change takes place in public attitudes and perception in Britain". (Oxbridge college)
>
> "All things are possible but the setting-up costs have to be recognised and met from extended external funding". (City Technological)
>
> "The existence of the University of Buckingham proves that it is possible, but for purely 'private' institutions to increase in number and flourish will require considerable sociological changes, as well as those in monetary and employment policies and traditions. Much depends on the definition of a 'university' in terms of its nature and scope in teaching as research". (London college)

Again replies were subtle and qualified. A mixed economy might be possible, but this was predicated on a cultural change, that of willingness on the part of industry to support universities. Social and attitudinal maturity were seen therefore as prerequisite, something that it is beyond the power of government to ordain.

Then we asked, "How do you react to proposals made by Professor Kedourie of the London School of Economics that universities should be privatised with endowments equal to a significant number of years' recurrent grant? Is there any support for this proposal amongst your staff?"[7] The head of the rich Oxbridge college said: "I like Professor Kedourie's proposal and suggested something similar to Sir Keith Joseph, but without getting anywhere. I very much doubt if there is any support for the proposal among my colleagues".

Others were also interested:

> "If this was accompanied by a general property endowment on a comparable basis between institutions we would consider (it) seriously". (Technological university)

And:

> "Interesting idea, with benefit of freeing universities from enormous political interference. Would depend on student support". (Collegiate university)

The major civic university was sceptical of the interest of government: "We cannot conceive that the government would be prepared to provide the capital sum required to initiate the outcome". The degree of interest in this idea – which we would like to see one day realised – was very surprising, and doubt related largely to the willingness of government to entertain such a radical proposition.[8]

We asked:

> "Would privatisation give universities greater freedom? Would it lead, in your view, to universities becoming extensions of the R and D departments of large companies? Do you perceive any merit in the idea?"

There was not a uniform hostility to 'privatisation' but a recognition that it could not apply across the system and was in practice difficult to implement. Universities were principally concerned with autonomy, and feared that privatisation would mean merely swapping one unequal and dictatorial relationship – with government – for another: with industry.[9] 'Private' universities, it was generally feared, would do less basic research.

IS THE MARKET A THREAT TO STANDARDS?

Clearly the pursuit of greater independence, even when not taken to the extreme of severance from the state system, has implications for the nature

---

[7] E. Kedourie, *Diamonds Into Glass: The Government and the Universities*, The Centre for Policy Studies, 1987.
[8] N.F.B. Allington and N.J. O'Shaughnessy, *Learning Independence*, Adam Smith Institute, London, 1987.
[9] This view is borne out by experience related to the House of Lords Select Committee on Science and Technology, *Ibid.*, Volume Three, pp.142, 261 and 266.

and quality of what is taught and researched in universities. We asked whether more market driven universities would threaten standards. They thought:

> "Yes, but other factors can equally threaten standards". (Technological)
>
> "This would appear to be inevitable in that increasing dependence on particular sources of income could lead to a 'more means worse' situation. The qualifications for undergraduate entry could become increasingly marginal; the scope of research could become narrower, with more emphasis on short term gains at the expense of objectivity". (London college)
>
> "American and other experience suggests that it does not go where the institutions commanding greatest prestige are concerned. I would be less confident about the effect of the market forces on institutions regarded as somewhat less eligible". (Oxbridge college)
>
> "I very much doubt it". (Rich Oxbridge college)
>
> "Standards are set internationally – universities who wish to compete internationally would need to meet these standards". (Collegiate University)
>
> "Quite possibly a threat to standards of the kind a fully independent university would wish to maintain". (Oxbridge college)
>
> "All universities are to some extent market driven, but if by this question is implied the contracting of universities to produce so many graduates in particular disciplines then some universities might be tempted to reduce assessment and entrance levels in order to comply with the terms of the contract. We cannot envisage other circumstances in which a lowering of academic standards would be likely". (Large Civic)

Replies here were somewhat ambivalent, and many qualifications were made, but a general fear existed that indeed they might threaten standards.

PROTECTING THE WEAK

Then we asked: if industrial funding and endowments became the major or exclusive source of income, how or to what extent would you protect the less commercially attractive subjects? The major London College said:

> "The reduction in government support already makes it difficult to fund 'pure' research in the physical sciences and mathematics. Industrial funding is normally devoted to specific research objectives, and cannot be diverted to 'blue sky' ventures. Endowment income is too marginal to be relied upon to offer protection to subjects which are commercially unattractive".

The small technological university added "we scarcely have any", and one Oxbridge college said "this is not a problem which would be likely to apply to a college such as this which enjoyed a substantial general endowment, applicable to any of the purposes stated in its charter''. Added the major civic university:

> "I regret this question too is almost unanswerable and is, for the moment, hypothetical. If a university's income derives from industrial funding, only by the charging of realistic zero-based overheads could one hope to side-track sufficient monies to enable financial support for less commercially attractive subjects to be retained. It is to be hoped that industry and commerce, charities and Research Councils, will be prepared to pay overheads at a proper level as we perceive them.
>
> Endowment income is of course a quite different matter, as endowments tend to be provided for quite specific projects. Quite unbalanced institutions may result from specific endowments which tend towards particular objectives (commonly medicine or theology, say) with less popular subjects such as history or sociology quite neglected. One would need to develop a formulaic approach which ensured the most equal distribution possible''.

Another university thought that it was unlikely that commercial funding would become the major resource, but that prestigious humanities departments should be attractive for sponsorship and so on. Commented the (rich) Oxbridge college:

> "There has been no difficulty in protecting these subjects through endowments. So far as industrial funding is concerned we should have to seek the psychological and cultural change which would allow British industry, for example, to record the maintenance of a major library as an activity as prestigious as pouring money into the bottomless well of Covent Garden''.

RESTRAINT ON FREEDOM?

We also asked, "Would greater reliance on industrial support restrain research freedom and make for a short-term approach to research?" Several institutions – those with a clear technological bent – thought definitely yes.[10] So did the collegiate university, given the "widespread industrial view that basic research should be government funded". Others were more qualified. The major civic university stressed the likely shift towards commercial exploitability away from the 'broad academic base'. The Oxbridge colleges were less sceptical, one citing the complete freedom which a current commercially financed project allowed them, another that "some sponsors give great scope for disinterested research".

Again there appears to be a class divide. Commercial support for Oxbridge

---

[10] The short-termism of industry was echoed by D.A. Walker, Executive Director, Bank of England to the Glasgow Finance and Investment Seminar, October, 1985.

apparently gives the institution more freedom than in the case of the less urbane and more technological universities. Presumably firms think more in terms of a commercial purchase from the latter; they perceive the former more as prestigious giving to an élite institute.

Clearly the pursuit of greater independence even when not taken to the extreme of severance from the state system, has implications for the nature and quality of what is taught and researched.

In our original communication with the masters and vice-chancellors we suggested that, after these first fourteen questions, they need not answer the rest. At this point several institutions, including the major civic university, dropped out, and hence our survey became even less 'representative' than it was before, and its counsels should therefore be treated in a more qualified way.

PART THREE: ADMINISTRATION

The third major theme of our survey was the efficiency and effectiveness of university government, a subject we approached with some scepticism.

STAFF CONDITIONS

On the question of paying academic salaries "according to outside market forces in each subject", the institutions were in the main strongly opposed, only the wealthy Oxbridge College was in favour. Such a course would be "divisive", apart of course from medics since there "needs to be compatibility with the health service" (why only in medicine?), whilst "the concept cannot apply in some subject areas".

This is perhaps a pity. In so many other ways, our respondents were forward looking – their keenness for links with industry, staff training and assessment and so on; their lack of any rhetorical dogma on the issue of tenure – quite the opposite to what many would imagine to be the attitudes of university vice-chancellors. But rigid salary structures perpetuate the mediocrity of 'vocational' areas, and stunt the future of universities which happen to be located in high cost parts of the country. Of course in the scale of moral, intellectual and aesthetic worth, no one weighs an accountant near a professor of poetry, but whoever said that market forces, which reward a pop musician with many times the earnings of a prime minister, ever represented any criterion of ethical merit? For a market-place yields a judgement of price, not value.

However, there was universal and strong assent to the proposal that universities should provide training for academic staff.[11] There was also firm support for interchange of staff with industry, with respondents pointing out that it was already taking place; transferable pensions would help, according to one. Another pointed out that "we have a scheme for Visiting Professors which allows us to appoint industrialists who make a valuable contribution to the College. There are currently 50 Visiting Professors". The non-Oxbridge institutions had plans for staff assessment. No one regarded the pressure as unwelcome, and three of the four also had plans for student assessment of faculty.[12]

UNIVERSITY GOVERNMENT

Staff conditions however are intimately related to the quality of the management systems adopted and evolved by the universities over the years. The received orthodoxy has been that they are ineffectual.[13]

What were the major deficiencies in the system of university government in their institution? "The large size of the 'statutory' committees, representative of a broad spectrum of interests, can inhibit rapid reaction to changing circumstances" (London college). "Division of responsibility between senate and council" (Small technological). "Over-respect for entrenched interests and caution" (Rich Oxbridge college). A feeling here then that the administrative structure is overly deferential to the myriad interest groups, that the gaining of consensus and co-ordination in a fragmented policy is a slow process.

Should the Vice-Chancellor be regarded as a managing director and therefore, if you agree, to what extent is it necessary for them to be academics? "The nature of university decision-making processes, involving built-in checks and balances, differentiate the role from that of an industrial Managing Director. The academic ambitions and traditions of a university are such as to make it difficult to envisage a head who had

---

[11] This is now being undertaken of course, see above chapter 4, p.114.
[12] Since this survey, of course, assessment has been accepted as part of a pay agreement.
[13] J. Fielden and G. Lockwood, *Planning and Management in Universities*, Chatto and Windus, London, 1973; L. Wagner, (editor), *Agenda for Change in Higher Education*, Leverhulme Programme for Study into the Future of Higher Education, 1982.

not established an academic reputation" (London college).[14] This argument was broadly agreed with, the master of the wealthy Oxford college summarizing the role thus: "I am sure a Vice-Chancellor should wherever possible be an academic but that he should try to act as a managing director". So there was little support for our wish to cast the net wider, and there exists an entrenched belief that only academics can run universities.

What improvements could most usefully be made in the administration of universities?

> "Fewer arms-length Treasury controls via the UGC; fewer or smaller committees; provision for greater investment in first rate, modern equipment especially computing equipment; flexibility of pay scales to attract experts in areas of skills shortages".

> "Less external interference and direction by special initiatives".

> "Clearly, greater independence from the government is an important facet: it thus behoves us to dream up a system of university finance that can best guarantee that".

Respondents were also against the UFC's new statutory powers of control – it would damage diversity and limit freedom while "past experience in this and other countries requires us to beware of aspects of government forecasting and manpower planning".

Do you regard small departments as undesirable and, if so, why?

> "In general, yes, because of the high 'overhead' costs associated with them, for example, space usage, support staff, communication problems".

> "Not per se, most babies are small and develop with time. Oxford is not departmentally organized in arts and social studies".

There is no clear party line on small departments: but large segments of antagonism towards them exist in the profession as a whole as in the UFC, an unnecessary reflex and one we would counsel against. Whether or not a small department is untenable surely depends on the facts of the situation, and should not be governed by ideology.[15]

PART FOUR: FUTURE PLANS

National policies for the future governance of the university system have

---

[14] University College London for example does not see this as a problem.
[15] The UFC is expected to begin a new round of subject reviews after the 1992 selectivity exercise and rationalisation of departments will be the inevitable outcome.

been much debated; a number of ideas have achieved circulation, have even become conventional orthodoxy, without rigorous questioning. Yet they would change the essence of the university system as we know it. How therefore did our respondents feel about massification and increased participation; two year degrees and central planning: did they pay the customary homage to those idols of relevance and applicability?

One such idea is tripartheid, a controversial thought but one which found favour in many areas – the idea of concentrating resources was especially popular with those who stood to benefit most.

TRIPARTITE DIVISION

How do you react to the possibility of universities being divided into three divisions: full research; limited research; teaching only? What would be the implications of this for future funding?

> "I like the three division idea but am not clear about the implications for funding".
>
> "I do not think that the case for this tripartite division is anywhere near proven".
>
> "A 'teaching only' university would be a misnomer; without research it would cease to be a university. On the other hand no single institution could expect to excel in every subject and there is scope for rationalisation on a subject by subject rather than an institutional basis".
>
> "Totally unhelpful for the need for adaptability".

Thus in general this idea was disliked and regarded as disfunctional to what a university was trying to do.

Did they favour local universities, and could savings be redirected internally? Yes, thought the London college, though savings would be of a capital nature and not running costs; do not exaggerate the costs of the 'boarding' fee (Oxbridge college); yes (Rich college); already one third of students are local (Small technological).

PARTICIPATION

Did they view the participation rate in U.K. higher education as too low and would raising it necessarily lead to a drop in standards: how would they raise participation rates? They were uniform in their belief that participation rates were much too low, "and if a drop in standards means a drop in....ability among students, so be it". Another felt that there need not necessarily be a decline in standards, another that they would "but not pro-rata?"

As a means of raising participation rates, ideas were many and varied, such as diversifying the range of higher education institutions: "there is too great a uniformity of institution, concentrating on the standard three year degree programme. The concept of the two year generalist degree bears further re-examination, honours degrees could be pursued subsequently for a smaller proportion of the population".[16] Another commended student fee increases, which would give institutions incentives. For the Rich Oxbridge college "if I knew the answer to your second question I should long ago have gone to the House of Lords either as a reward or a way of muzzling me. But my guess is that this is connected with a fee-led system. Additional state funding in higher education should, wherever possible, come via fees paid by the student. But behind this there looms a much larger problem, that of changing a whole national culture". Here therefore are recognitions, at least at the formal level, that universities should and would expand numbers.

Would your university teach significantly more undergraduates than at present without a significant increase in staff numbers? The London college could manage 6% more. Much depended on the subject chosen – according to one Oxbridge college, larger subjects could not expand without destroying the tutorial system. The small technological university answered simply "no". Therefore hopes of simply doubling numbers without increasing finances are misplaced, since at least according to the universities' own account, there is little excess capacity both in terms of personnel and of plant utilization.[17]

How deleterious is central control of planning over numbers of undergraduate recruits?

> "I would like to see institutions of higher education given greater incentives (by fee changes) to expand student numbers".

---

[16] This view is in sharp contrast with the egalitarian ethos of the 1991 White Paper and deserves emphasis – we are in danger of producing uniform institutions without any clear analysis of how this will improve educational output. Diversity has been recognised elsewhere as the essential dynamic of a responsive system of higher education.

[17] Again this contrasts with current events and must lead to doubts about the quality of mass provision. Variety of provision is the only sensible answer to expansion.

> "Only marginal in many instances in that marginally qualified students can attend polytechnics or Further Education Colleges. Those hardest hit are likely to be students of professional specialisms for example in veterinary science, medicine, architecture, pharmacy where they might be forced into a second choice. In some of these subjects the professions themselves do not wish to see an over-production of graduates".
>
> "Very".

On the subject of the abolition of UCCA, nobody declared themselves in favour.

What role do mature students play now and what role do you anticipate them playing in the future? The London college saw little role for "those older students not qualified in conventional ways", but everyone welcomed qualified students and those on postgraduate professional courses and so on.

Clearly rhetoric about getting in more mature and less conventionally qualified students will be tested by the extreme scepticism of the universities.

Would you favour richer, if less bright, students having access to universities through higher fees, or would you regard this as unethical? Several regarded the notion with abhorrence; the wealthy Oxbridge college would "not regard this as unethical", and the small technological university said that "we balance ability to study and to pay". This was a deliberately provocative question, however, we felt the principle of meritocracy had already been abandoned vis à vis the overseas student market. Higher education had often faced during the nineteen eighties a choice of evils, and we believe that allowing money some influence is perhaps not as bad as making academics redundant, or preventing them being employed in the first place. What is surprising is that several heads were prepared to tolerate the idea – not an admission they would once have made.

What was their employment record? "Second to none" was one reply, and the others echoed it.

If current trends continue what is your prognosis for the institution up to 2000 A.D.?

> "My college will still be here in 2000 A.D., probably taking a larger proportion of graduates than now and with some further movement of its tutorial provision towards science based subjects".

"Any objective answer must say it depends on external factors over which we have little control. I do not expect the nineties to be as rough as the eighties have been".

"The prosperity of my college depends largely on the success with which the investment of its endowments (and trust funds) is handled. I see no reason why it should not be flourishing in A.D. 2000. The need for systematic study of our economic, social and political arrangements is, and will remain, very great".

"Decreasing reliance on the state but not necessarily achieving a satisfactory equilibrium between our ambitions and the wherewithal to meet them".

Responses here were somewhat vague. Neither hope nor fear for the future, but the expectation of surviving efficiently, but perhaps unglamourously.

CHAPTER NINE

MINERVA AND THE MARKET PLACE: A SURVEY OF INDUSTRY.

"A man or a group of men can make the decisions for very large-scale organisations if their activities are relatively simple, like manufacturing washing powder or selling merchandise, or if their activities are complex but their goals well-defined, like placing a man on the moon. If however, goals are ill defined or indefinable and activities are complex, the problem of centralised decision-making and the working of large scale system are so enormous that the probability of finding mere men able to perform the miracle is small".
Managing Director,
One of *The Times Top 1000* companies.

"Higher education is vital to industry on two main counts. First, it is a source of the able well-qualified young people which industry needs in order to progress and adapt in response to the changing economic, social and political climate. Secondly, universities and polytechnics play a most important part in providing the basic knowledge in science and engineering on which the economic success of this country depends".
Sir Denis Rooke,
Cambridge Review, 1989.

"Companies wish to see neither a reduction in the overall science base nor a shift by universities towards applied research. Companies value pure and curiosity-led research as the seed-bed from which their applied work can develop marketable products and technologies. They attach importance to the development of an effective partnership with universities".
The Council for Industry and Higher Education,
Cambridge Review, 1989.

"If then a practical end must be assigned to a University course, I say it is that of training good members of society. Its art is the art of social life, and its end is fitness for the world. It neither confines its view to particular professions on the one hand, nor creates heroes or inspires genius on the other".

J.H. Newman,
The Idea of a University, New York, 1959.

"Then there is how I should solve the fallacy, for so I must call it, by which Locke and his disciples would frighten us from cultivating the intellect, under the notion that no education is useful which does not teach us some temporal calling, or some mechanical art, or some physical secret. I say that a cultivated intellect, because it is a good in itself, brings a power and a grace to every work and occupation which it undertakes, and enables us to be more useful, and to a greater number".

J.H. Newman,
The Idea of a University, New York, 1959.

INTRODUCTION

What does business really want from universities; is it satisfied with what it gets; and how far is it prepared to fund institutions from which it derives such benefit? In our recent survey we sought answers to these and other questions and in particular to test some of the stereotypes and popular orthodoxies that float about in the media and in Parliament, and weigh heavily therefore on the shaping of public policy. Much of this policy is speculative since its assumptions are apparently untested – beliefs about how far business (forgetting the other pulls on its charity) is willing to fund universities or the presumption that what it really wants are technicians. We wish to lend rigour to such a debate by asking elementary questions of those best placed to answer them.

Thus a common assumption would appear to be that universities are remote from the market-place such that there is little they can teach industry; they exist not as a social necessity but a socialite indulgence: and that industry, were we only to ask it, would be willing to sustain more of the burden of their support, and so fashion them as more 'relevant', Academies of Useful Knowledge.

None of this is true. The picture that emerges is complex: industry never speaks with one voice, nowhere – except on the importance to them of graduates – is there consensus. Broadly speaking industry is satisfied with universities and wants the government to go on running them: but with qualifications, basically summarised by the notion of better management. Clearly there are differences between business and academic criteria of how we measure value, and it would be erroneous to imagine monolithic industrial opinion – especially where we choose to believe industry's self-appointed spokesman. In March 1990 the Director of the Institute of Directors cited (predictably) universities among a list of factors in Britain's decline: it is questionable how far real industrialists believed him.[1]

We received 120 replies to our questionnaire, usually from the managing director himself, to whom it was addressed. The firms were often household names, and included ICI, British Shipbuilders, B.P., I.B.M., Anglian Water, Courtaulds, Rolls-Royce, but all were offered anonymity to ensure the fullest possible response. The group – distinguished and influential – was fifty per cent of the total (250): clearly then everything

---

[1] Quoted in P. Augur, "Funding Universities", *op cit.*, p.17.

we say attracts the criticism of being unrepresentative and therefore speculative. The answer to this – and it is not very scientific – is that those who did reply were the large and more eminent organisations, so that a greater legitimacy should attach to our extant responses than a strict viewing of the statistics would suggest.[2]

Our survey has other obvious limitations. The managing director will enunciate lofty and socially worthy sentiments that his subordinates may well fail to share; nor does the survey cover small and medium businesses, which would exhibit less bureaucratic styles of leadership. But in general there is a surprising degree of satisfaction with the product – more than the universities' more ignorant critics (the Institute of Directors?) would have us believe: but there is no room for complacency.

Many of these results were what one would have expected, indeed stereotypical, but they are no less important for that, since they yield proof of what had been popularly suspected. Other results however gave us genuine cause for surprise and should be noted by policy makers. These responses are also important for another reason, since though the function of a university is to prepare the intellectual foundations for all of life, and this includes leisure and retirement, business remains one of the constituencies that has a core interest by the very nature of the fact that graduates spend so much of their lives therein.

We also discovered that almost all of the firms were highly alarmed by the shrinkage in the UK science base, and this indeed was one of the few areas where there was a consensus, for industry perceives this as a threat to its future ability to perform effectively.[3] On the subject of research funding, the number of non-investors startled us and should give rise to searching questions. There was a general sense that the universities need to exhibit more professionalism in their dealings with industry. Nevertheless the degree of satisfaction registered was not bad, and sometimes very good.

---

[2] The 250 companies were chosen at random from *The Times Top 1000* companies with the only criteria for inclusion being company size. We deliberately chose from large companies having a turnover in excess of £500m.

[3] One example can suffice to show the importance of the subject and comes from a major electronics company:
"British firms have failed to become leaders in most fields of semi-conductors or other electronic computers and electronic instruments. The declining international competitiveness of the United Kingdom electronics industry is reflected in a trade surplus of £106 million in 1963 being replaced by a deficit of £876 million in 1983; only in electronic capital goods, which are dominated by military electronic equipment, is there still a trade surplus''.

Moreover there were different kinds of permutation to research funding: some firms wanted the conventional project structure but others sought new kinds of relationships – funding research students for example.

INDUSTRY SUPPORT FOR BASIC RESEARCH

Our first major theme was the willingness of industry to purchase research, and support basic research, in the light of increased state parsimony. By 1987, according to the DES, universities earned 2.5% of their total income from industrial sources; the Committee of Vice Chancellors and Principals (CVCP) pointed out that in the previous four years, universities had doubled their income from external sources and some universities – Warwick, Salford and City – could now claim that over half their total income came from private sources.[4] Elsewhere the CVCP argued that greater influence could be exerted by industry in identifying potentially fruitful lines for basic and strategic research. By co-operating with universities in such work and helping financially they can more easily identify opportunities for applied research and development.[5] Nevertheless, the generally very low levels of support from business cannot be good enough. It must be the case that the skills and location of universities have a higher market value than this – that, in fact, they simply are not marketed.

Large companies, national and multinational, were the main sources of income. However, the newer growth industries made significant contributions, since basic research had proved highly instrumental to new product development. Especially weak contributors to universities were industries that were themselves dependent on the Exchequer for research and development funds, aerospace and electronics in particular. Some individual companies were giving amounts which seem in themselves large, but were actually a tiny fraction of their research expenditure; Shell contributed £1 million in grants, and also purchased substantial amounts in commissioned research, but its total 1984 research budget was £400 million. Such industrial disinterest may reflect the absence of a university-trained management tradition in British industry, as much as inertia on the part of universities themselves: clearly there is need for some

---

[4] DES, *Science and Public Expenditure, A Report to the Secretary of State for Education and Science from ABRC*, 1987.
[5] Evidence of CVCP to House of Lords Select Committee on Science and Technology, *Civil Research and Development, Ibid.*, Volume Three, p.83.

kind of brokerage system, some mediating force that can interpret the two cultures to each other. The government needs to play its part too, for companies giving evidence to the House of Lords Select Committee on Science and Technology, *Civil Research and Development*, claimed that *ad hoc* giving was emerging because there had been a failure to develop a coherent policy of public support for research and development. Such a policy would enable industry to respond in a generous and constructive way rather than piecemeal and unco-ordinated as is presently the case.[6] Some companies, however, are setting new standards for university/industry collaboration, and British Telecom is a good example, where each institution undertaking research has a liason officer in the company to act as a focal point for contact.[7]

RESEARCH FUNDING

We found that most major companies have at some stage commissioned research from universities, or intend to do so. But still, the number who had not, 52, is telling: we would have hoped that every one of them had at some stage commissioned research. Why, for example, should a major oil company anticipate no future commission, or a big electrical company/defence contractor say that it had never solicited any research from universities? But some firms, not necessarily the best known, had ordered substantial work from universities over the years: one for example currently had 50 projects in 18 universities and others supplied us with detailed lists of projects. Most worked with a few universities on the ground that concentration of funding could achieve more significant results and also satisfied the need for commercial confidentiality.

There were marked preferences in the objects of funding: a major public utility liked to fund teaching rather than research, another preferred specific projects with local universities, a brewery sponsored a centre of study, another funded studentships and research associates, others supported basic research.

As to the degree of satisfaction with their research contracts, a mere six regarded them as very successful; fifty however found them successful, and fifty-four acceptable, while eighteen said they were not very successful

---

[6] Cf. *Ibid.*, Volume Three, p.49.
[7] *Ibid.*, Volume Three, p.64.

and eight were unsuccessful. So, there had been few failures, and much that was satisfactory.

The most common complaint was that universities were so slow in completing the projects – they lacked the industrialist's sense of urgency. Others had found the experience a highly variable one. A major utility perceived great differences between institutions, and a chemical company pointed to the importance of university commitment and the quality of the staff concerned. The most frequent point made was the need for close management of contracts, with monitoring and supervision. Nevertheless there were many optimistic comments from satisfied customers.

Few firms would be committed to long term research – twenty all in all, eighteen of whom were also interested in shorter spans of research.

Fifty six would be committed to medium term funding, 72 to short term funding and 26 to none at all. This picture suggests that business would be a poor source of funding for long term and often basic research since it does not conceive this as being instrumental to its goals; a major aircraft firm pointed out that their research funding was "always a straight commercial decision". A pharmaceutical company would be unwilling to invest unless they could see profits arising directly – meaning in the short term.

Nor were universities accorded an exclusive monopoly on research. In reply to our question "Are there other institutions of higher education which are more suitable for research contracts than universities?", 52 said no. But 28 said "yes", 46 said "polytechnics" and 12 referred to Business School Colleges. One organisation, claiming a higher success rate with CNAA colleges, commented: "They are more committed to it and perform more like Research Institutions in the commercial sense". Another preferred independent research establishments and commented "in our experience polytechnics have been found generally more suitable through their closer understanding of market practicalities". Most (82) were against putting contracted research out to tender among universities, but a substantial number liked the idea.[8] Those arguing against especially stressed the importance of the local university, and also an intimate

---

[8] Tendering for research was also favoured by companies responding to the House of Lords Select Committee on Science and Technology and several suggested that the Research Councils might also put research out to tender, *Ibid.*, Volume One, p.18.

knowledge of a university, the requirements of quality and confidentiality, the need for long term relationships, the importance of reputation and the limited number of university operators in a given field.[9]

ON THE U.K. SCIENCE BASE

How anxious was industry itself at all the chatter about a shrinkage of the science base, which by that point was reaching a crescendo? In fact many companies claimed deep concern, although fifty-four regarded it as not very serious, twenty-eight felt it was not serious, and ten did not know. One firm believed it to be "very serious indeed from a research perspective and on the longer term likely to threaten the viability of high technology enterprises in the U.K." Others made remarks to the effect that the future of British technological competition was at stake, one claiming that "a science base in universities is the essential foundation for industrial research and for training scientists to work in industry". Industry, said one of the oil companies, should do everything possible to maintain the science base; a drug company claimed that research in pharmaceuticals was at risk, a construction firm said that there was too little emphasis on science and engineering and the applications from existing research were dwindling. One drew the distinction between shrinkage in facilities, which had occurred, and shrinkage in ability, which had not.

Again, though, there was a significant group of sceptics. Another major oil company felt that there was too much emphasis on the quantity and not sufficient on the quality of research; a computer firm identified the key problem as one of failure to exploit research findings. Others saw merit in the shrinkage, though they disagreed as to its nature: a cosmetics firm perceived increased concentration in research areas as overdue, other organisations felt that the reduction in funds would lead the direction away from pure research to a wider range of projects. Others seemed to believe that research was primarily the responsibility of companies, it was up to them to keep ahead in the field and industry should do everything possible to maintain the science base. There is some evidence to suggest that industry itself must shoulder some of the blame for the negative attitude to research. For the institutionalisation of British industry has given financial

---

[9] Since 1988 the Council for Industry and Higher Education has been attempting to encourage industry to develop a strategy towards higher education – research and teaching: *Towards a Partnership*, 1987 and *Towards a Partnership: The Company Report, 1988*.

management and organisational skills greater prominence in the boardroom than technical management and innovation.[10]

WHO PAYS?

Nevertheless those who viewed the decline in the science base seriously constituted a very heavy majority. The corollary of concern might have been commitment. If industry perceives the science base as so instrumental to its well-being, one might imagine it would be willing to contribute substantially to its sustenance. The contribution, as we found, was largely at the rhetorical level.

Yet such reluctance should not surprise us. The first duty of business is to its shareholders, and their perspective is naturally dominated by year's end figures: there is a will to do good but the law has to reinforce it, for industrial support, as distinct from supportive rhetoric, is contingent on some sort of tangible return: seldom are motives purely altruistic and commercial criteria predominate.

Herein lies a conundrum. The government thinks industrial support ought to play a bigger role and has cut university funds on that assumption. Business may not want to. Government policy is predicated on the assumption that business will give because, under an ideological schemata, it ought to, but the real world does not mirror the urbane contours of ideology and the consequence is a widening void in university funding, precipitating many institutions into large deficits with, for some, the spectre of bankruptcy.[11]

The lack of interest in long term research is not surprising, but the implications for government policy are far-reaching: state funding, or a graduate charge, are the only substantial sources of long term research revenue (other sources of external research funding may include alumni, but given the inertia of the universities the extent of their potential support remains mysterious).[12]

---

[10] Evidence of Whitbread PLC to House of Lords Select Committee on Science and Technology, *Ibid.*, Volume Three, p.89.
[11] Committee of Public Accounts, 36th Report, *Restructuring and Finances of Universities*, London, HMSO, 1990.
[12] The Rothschild Principle of customer/contractor relationship and its ramifications did not receive a mention amongst the respondents, *A Framework for Government Research and Rothschild Development*, London, HMSO, Cmnd. 4814, 1971.

More generally, if the government wishes to achieve its objective of variegated financing, in education or in the arts, it must modify the tax system to make contributions more attractive for companies: in the US, the real extent of state support is marked via the tax system. Such gifts, when made, are never really gifts: they are viewed as investments from which some form of dividend is gained. Other sources, as a minister claimed recently, may be 'wealthy' individuals. But will they give to universities in preference to other objects of their charity? And are they rich in the ostentatious forms of their American counterparts? And do they feel that such support of higher education is part of their responsibilities? In this connection the local university is important, since proximity leads to closeness of interaction.

IS INDEPENDENCE AN OPTION?

Our former interest in the possibility of an independent university system being carved out of the state system may already have become apparent. We sought to test this idea with the industrialists, particularly in relation to their willingness to fund it and the question of whether academic freedom and breadth, standards and pure research would therefore be compromised.

If some universities became privatised, would industrialists be prepared to contribute to the endowment fund? This is perhaps a rather odd question. The notion that a few universities might be offered the equivalent of five years' recurrent grant together with their independence from the state, fortified by increments from our proposed graduate levy and provided that their agreement was voluntary, was originally advocated by us in a pamphlet in January 1987. Professor Elie Kedourie amplified the ideas later that year in his pamphlet *Diamonds into Glass* for the Centre for Policy Studies.[13]

INDEPENDENCE

Under the scheme we then advocated, fees generated from the graduate levy would progressively build up endowments, and universities would become increasingly independent, one day even completely so, especially were industry and government to contribute to endowments. Yet there was

---

[13] N.F.B. Allington and N.J. O'Shaughnessy, *Ibid.*, and E Kedourie, *Ibid.*

very little support here from industrialists, showing perhaps how misleading it is to predicate social policy on the existence of some monolithic 'industrial opinion', for often, as is the case here, it simply reflects orthodoxies of the larger society from whose ranks they were drawn: indeed, it would be surprising were this not so.

Most respondents, 58, said they would not be prepared to endow universities if they became independent; but sixteen said yes, and a further eighteen said neither. Opponents were often very critical of the concept: one Japanese manufacturer said "this would undermine the academic independence of the universities", another firm "university education is an issue of vital national importance and they should remain in the state sector", while others could think of better alternatives – "privatisation no, but accountability yes" and "an industry levy would be more appropriate".

Those in favour expressed their support in very cautious terms indeed, and wanted to know more detail. A number specified that they would want some commercial benefit in return for contributing to an endowment fund – encouraging recruitment, or some other 'tangible return'. Several would only contribute to specific, not general, research. The prevailing mood was expressed in such comments as "we would not want to be the first investor" and "decision and amount of funding would very much depend on the ability of the university to convince that it, or rather its staff, were flexible enough to respond to changing national needs".

Our next question was: "Would privately funded universities teach and conduct research over a wide range of subjects, or would specialisation relevant to the endowing company be expected?" Only 26 thought such universities would be generalist; 66 saw them more as specialised and eighteen said neither. Many of their comments saw the broad, generalised education as highly desirable, but specialisation and the pursuit of commercial returns was seen as the likely issue of endowment; the paradox was summarised by a major public utility: "A broad base of training is seen to be desirable both in regard to scholarship and applications. However, specialisation relevant to the endowing companies would be desirable in the interests of the employees and shareholders of the company". Others endorsed the point about the likelihood of specialisation attracting sponsors.

Many were critical of the notion of commercial pressures dictating to universities: one said that "such specialisation would be damaging to the role of universities in maintaining a breadth of academic research", another that "commercial pressure should be avoided in the interests of academic standards", another that exclusive commercial ties "would inhibit free expression in many areas of their work", and yet another that "universities need to retain the capability of long term fundamental research without being tied to industry".

Breadth was perceived by companies as important: "in the national interest universities should maintain a wide range of teaching and research interests ... specialisation relevant to company interests can take place in company research and development departments, and independent research institutes". And another: "the exposure of students to a centre of learning, providing teaching and conducting research, over a wide range of subjects, must be the ideal". Only one was in favour of linking teaching and research to individual companies; at the other end of the spectrum a company felt that more state support was required to ensure frontier education.

Thirty two companies believed that 'privatisation' would give universities greater freedom: seventy two however did not, and people pointed out that greater freedom from government would only lead to control by the companies. Fifty four respondents thought that privatisation would merely lead to universities becoming extensions of the R & D departments of large companies, twenty six did not, and only thirty perceived any merit in the idea, with fifty-nine against. Respondents stressed the need to preserve academic standards, that the teaching function would suffer and that indeed the question misunderstood the purpose of a university. The threat to independence was the most often quoted objection, closely followed by the belief that breadth and generality would suffer in the pursuit of profitable areas, and that pure research and scientific innovation would be affected, as would the university's ability to "generate new ideas and solutions to old problems". The fact that so many companies explicitly cited these factors suggests they regard them as important. Other comments were that only the richest universities would win, that such patronage would be 'divisive'; a major medical corporation pointed out that the R & D function was so different from research in universities that there was little chance of an extension.[14]

Others however were more convinced: universities might become more aware of the needs of their customers; they would beneficially work much more closely with industry, they would focus more on the nation's needs; there might be some joint venture companies and competition between university and company. One suggested the need for an overarching body like the Independent Broadcasting Authority.

Surprisingly perhaps, a slight majority, 62 to 54, felt that more market driven universities would not threaten standards, and a further fourteen firms declared themselves to be indifferent. Still, plenty of comments amplified fears – that undergraduate standards might decline; that universities should be scholarship and not market driven and that speculative research as well as the 'depth and spread' of universities would be curtailed; a construction firm felt that academic freedom would suffer. And an oil company remarked: "you put blinkers on racehorses so that they reach the finishing post! Judgements will be made too soon and on the basis of prejudice not facts".

Other were more sceptical. One suspected that while standards in generalised subjects might be damaged, standards in more mediocre universities might be sharpened, and a drinks firm suspected that they were already 'pretty elastic' and several companies believed that output would become 'more relevant'. Another commented that in many areas industry was far ahead of universities so that the latter needed to catch up. Others again made perhaps more constructive remarks – universities would have to educate industry on the appropriate standards, there could be more direction to university research but their ability to carry out strategic research must not be impaired.

In answer to our next question, "Would you restrict such support to a few or most universities and on what basis would the decision be made?", 64 supported specialisation, fourteen would make their support general and twenty replied neither. Many cited 'excellence' and 'expertise' as their criteria, others efficiency and value for money; but many others cited some sort of commercial return or relevance, with recruitment being a major

---

[14] Clearly there are many counter examples in the medical world, for example, Upjohn's support for research at Oxford University.

factor, while often the local university was the prime if not the exclusive candidate for largésse. The ambiguity was expressed in the projected policy of one firm which promised a limited contribution to the endowment of chairs and up to say 30% of total research spending, with the rest geared to industrial requirements.

We wondered whether a more creative tax regime might induce a greater measure of corporate generosity towards the funding of research. The answer was very clearly yes; present tax arrangements being seen as inimical to giving, especially in comparison with those applying in the U.S.A. Thus seventy-two firms felt that changes in the present tax structure would incline them towards a greater contribution to university endowments, and thirty-four said that none would be sufficient. For the highest number – fifty-four – such an endowment should be set off against tax; six felt that the endowment should be treated as charity; sixteen that the DES should make a matching contribution. One Japanese firm asked for double tax allowances, another company thought that part of corporation tax should be nominated for university funding; a brewery wanted tax relief plus an extra incentive of X%; someone suggested a percentage of profits tax for higher education,[15] and other points included:

Companies already contribute through tax paid, but perhaps they could retain this and distribute it to better advantage;

Funding to be set off against corporation tax for up to an agreed percentage.

Contributions to be totally set against tax as well as control of the research programme.[16]

---

[15] A scheme successfully operated in France.

[16] The importance of tax incentives permeated the whole of the House of Lords Select Committee on Science and Technology with company after company pleading for some help in this area, *Ibid.*, Volume One, pp.53-54. The government rejected this plea on the grounds that incentives were already provided and that tax relief would further erode the tax base. The Committee retorted that:
"Everything possible must be done to persuade industry of the need for, and advantages of R & D. For an interim period at least, the Government could help create that new climate by incentives to R & D through the tax system, though this should not be regarded as a substitute for selective support. If the American system is unacceptable, the Committee recommend that the Treasury examine constructively the feasibility of other tax measures to stimulate private R & D. Consideration should in particular be given to the new scheme introduced by the Australian Government, which for six years provides a 150 per cent tax incentive for expenditure on R & D carried out in Australia: this scheme is designed to make Australian industry more innovative and competitive and to create stronger links between research institutions and industry". Cf. *Ibid.*, Volume Three, pp.6, 114, 283.

The House of Lords Select Committee on Science and Technology also found evidence of support for the idea of research clubs whereby a central fund accumulates money from an industrial levy determined as a percentage of turnover: such a system offers continuity of funding and the presence of the fund is widely known.[17]

Not surprisingly, industrialists were interested in tangible returns over and above the celestial rewards of altruism unalloyed. They did not see commercial pressures as destructive, but nor did they like the idea of private universities. But the beliefs of businessmen are coloured like those of any other members of the community, by the culture in which they participate, and a tenet of that culture is that education should be free.

While therefore there is some material support for independence, there is no deep enthusiasm, and a reluctance to fund long term research. They believe that a broad education can only be provided by the state, since with business support comes specificity in both what is researched and what is taught – a notion inimical to traditional ideas about universities. Privatisation is regarded as a fundamental abuse of a university's function and a threat to freedom. But, a minority perception exists that privatisation would make universities consumer oriented (that is to the business community), together with a preparedness to back the idea financially. However, there could be benefits in privatisation if vigorous local industries existed; they may be interested in supporting the local university.

BUSINESS AND THE SCIENCE BASE

When universities warned of the dangers of contraction of the science base, government gave the impression that it regarded this as just special pleading. Yet this survey furnished some evidence that such contraction is regarded by industry as a threat to its future operation: though this does not appear to translate into any great wish to succour the science base, so strongly is the view entrenched in the UK that education support is the exclusive prerogative of the state. This will be difficult to change since we are not only changing belief, but the cultural system underpinning that belief, and the common assumption is that the government should create enabling and contextual conditions, of which higher education is one. Industry's perspectives are also short term, even though the future is by its

---

[17] *Ibid.*, Volume Three, p.130.

own admission partially governed by the health of the science base, and though industrial R and D often depends on PhD's and researchers recruited from university programmes.

PERSONNEL:

STAFF TRAINING

Our third major theme was the impact of universities on corporate personnel, their education, their training, their horizons, not only in the 'production' of graduates, but also the mutual benefit to be derived from staff exchange and the intellectual development of managers later in their career. Clearly staff training represents a major market universities could exploit. There is a thirst for accreditation as management becomes more professional, international firms demand it, and unqualified, under-educated managers increasingly seek the legitimacy a university course conveys.

Many companies also saw an evolving role for universities in retraining existing staff or improving managerial/industrial skills, 96 as against 40. A number regarded this area as in-house – one major electronics firm for example had its own management college, others used consultancy firms or specialist management colleges, one replying that "universities are for education, other institutions are for training". Other comments were that universities appeared too remote, that there were doubts as to whether universities could put sufficient resources into projects, that they would be relevant only if lecturers could maintain a portfolio of industrial skills. Yet others were more open to the idea, one feeling that short courses would be useful, another that such retraining would become very much more the norm, another that what would be desirable would be "periods for industrialists to draw breath".

On the subject of teaching companies in universities, far too many companies, including the really big names, did not understand what was meant by a teaching company.[18] Sixty firms claimed to value them, actually or potentially, as against forty-six who did not. One company complained

---

[18] The Teaching Company Scheme enables young graduates to obtain industrial training, with oversight from their academic institutions, through project work relevant to the company's needs. Recent developments suggest there is scope for such schemes in public sector organisations and the service industries, as well as in manufacturing. Over 70% of trainees remain with their company or move elsewhere in industry.

of the problem of finding appropriate students, another about properly trained staff; one major firm said "we do not see them in universities", another praised the excellence of the government teaching company schemes.

Many companies, 78 in fact, favoured an interchange of staff between universities and industry "where appropriate" as against fifty-four who did not and eight who were indifferent.[19] One firm felt some of its staff would make good academics, but confessed to doubting whether the reverse was true; another, that the scope for interchange was limited unless university staff had some industrial experience, others that benefit to both would be limited and that there were too many differences to make this work. One saw more value in "an interchange with secondary education". Others made stipulations that there would have to be a clear transfer of technology, industry alone could not bear the cost, there would have to be an agreed series of objectives and programmes. But many firms became more enthusiastic – a major electronics company confessed to having five visiting Professors; one organisation suggested sabbaticals for academics to work in industry, another said that it was actively seeking academics to work there.[20]

GRADUATE DEMAND

Graduates are the principal and certainly most tangible 'product' of a university. Do universities produce enough of them and how many does industry think it will need? Certainly companies saw university education as important (96) or very important (30); only six saw it as not very important. Most, 88, usually or even always found the right graduates; 42 did sometimes, six never. Several firms pointed to the problem of retaining good graduates, one pointing to the competition of large salaries in the service sector; another complained of not being able to find the right graduates in sufficient numbers, and an electronics firm expressed its fears about a drop in desirable graduates over the next seven years. There were particular comments about the difficulty of getting suitable scientists and

---

[19] Responding to the House of Lords Select Committee on Science and Technology, companies supporting staff interchange demanded improved visitors' accommodation for interactive research and short training courses, *Ibid.*, Volume Three, p.18.
[20] CASE awards were also mentioned in connection with staff interchange whereby industrial support is given for research studentships held in universities. The MRC and SERC operate such schemes.

engineers, and also management specialists in the building industry. One firm regretted a lack of 'sparkle' amongst recent graduate recruits.

Companies were evenly divided on the matter of favouring particular universities (yes 66, no 62). Thirty six cited specialised courses as their reason, twelve gave the local location, four cited business studies programmes and four mentioned polytechnic sandwich courses.

Companies definitely saw themselves as benefiting from the employment of graduates (84) or strongly benefiting (34); only eighteen perceived graduates as only 'moderately' beneficial. Eighty four expected employment of graduates to increase over the next 10-20 years, and fourteen saw this as remaining constant. One firm claimed that they found no correlation between level of education and performance: but this view was certainly unique. An electronics firm said that it needed 250 graduates a year just to survive in the market place, and another that it employed 20,000 graduates; one oil company expected all middle and senior managers to be graduates in future, but another firm was at pains to stress that graduate status was not enough – there was a need for "style, business sense and determination", and a lot mentioned the importance of creativity. One firm stressed that future recruitment would be among generalists.

Companies do regard graduates as very necessary to their operations: they worry about getting people of the right calibre. They stress the importance of a supply of quality graduates: that status and label are not enough.[21]

Employers have their own ideas as to which are the good universities: and often they differ markedly from the UGC rankings. For example they list Hull, which had been threatened with closure on the grounds of its weakness, tenth; and the much-punished Salford they place tenth in science. Views diverge significantly between industrialists and heads of department in law and materials science, geology, civil engineering and business studies. This should not necessarily alarm since commercial and academic criteria are different. However, it does suggest that the views of commerce, as legitimate stakeholders, should be taken into account when the future of university departments are under discussion. Of course, if the

---

[21] A report from Sussex University's Institute of Manpower Studies, suggests undergraduate sponsorship has increased in importance. In 1983, 200 employers were taking part but in 1991 the figure was 650 with many in non-engineering and technology fields. The Institute expects 200 more firms to join in sponsorship over the next three years: *Should Employers Fund Undergraduates?* 1991.

state ceased to possess a monopoly of university education, the errors of centralised 'planning' – which the absurdity of excluding the industrialists' view reinforces – would be diminished.

PARTICIPATION

It is a commonplace in Britain that we are good at educating élites: it is the averagely able we neglect, with serious economic consequences arising from a dearth of technically and vocationally trained workers (a historical problem, as Corelli Barnett laboriously pointed out when he wrote that it took three times as long to build a Spitfire as a Messerschmitt).[22]

Most of the industrialists viewed the participation rate in U.K. higher education as too low (82 as against 30) and did not believe that raising it would necessarily lower standards (64 as against 20). However, individual comments on an appropriate public policy for this area varied very greatly. A number of major corporations placed the onus on better secondary education, one of them also asking for more scientists and better training of technicians, others suggesting better grants for a higher level of participation and non-honours degrees for the less able mature students. Still there were some powerful dissenting voices: one organisation wanted to see more resources for the top 5% ability group, another for high quality graduates as a priority; interestingly an oil company remarked that the drive towards vocational subjects was disturbing, with fundamentals being ignored. As with some of the other answers, views here do not suggest a specifically 'industrial' opinion, in that the views taken would be similar to those of any group of civilised individuals.

CONCLUSION

In general then there is a need for more reliability in the delivery of research – variability of quality must end, with a more widespread recognition of norms and standards: business ought to know what to expect from their universities, and this implies a need for better communication. So there remains on the evidence of the survey clear scope for improvement by the universities themselves: one has the impression of great talent, but with a

---

[22] C. Barnett, *The Audit of War*, 1987.

weak focus on pragmatic aspects. In particular, research contracts should be more effectively managed, and more initiative-led, which may mean changes in their internal reward system; there is surely, for example, scope for a brokerage house to arbiter between the skills of universities and the demands of commerce.

Nevertheless, our survey returns probably gave a better image of universities than is commonly imagined. Generally business desires much closer links, they want more of their staff to be trained by universities on the job, and some exchanges of personnel. But do the universities perceive this need, and will they then rise to the challenge? The two communities certainly need to better understand each other, and the fault is not only with the universities; nor should their future relationship be an unequal one since the universities have something very tangible to offer, not only graduates but the frontiers of knowledge itself. However, industrial/commercial opinion should be sought more often on the formulation of public higher education policy: they have perceptive insights and should be considered as major stakeholders, though not the only ones.

What however is so remarkable about so many of the replies is that their perspectives are not so different from those of the Oxbridge high table. So we can, in 1992, speak of an establishment opinion that would apparently still incorporate the industrial élites. In particular: the importance they attach to standards and independence; the belief that pure research is a necessary basis for innovation; fear of the distorting effects of commercial pressure; the significance of exposing students to practitioners of fundamental research.

It is interesting that the majority are against independence measures, indeed reject them very firmly, and that so many of the comments made against 'privatisation' were on academic grounds. Many directors had a clear idea of what a university ought to be, one very different from the narrow and 'applied' biases that caricature would attribute to them: they felt that privatisation would be inimical to the breadth, depth and intellectual liberty they regarded as integral to the idea of a university, and this welcome stress on higher education as a mental training rather than induction in a specific set of applied skills was a refrain we heard often.

Table 9:1.1 summarises the position with respect to research and development performed by British industry over a ten year period. Table

9:1.2 provides a more detailed breakdown of manufacturing R and D over the same period and, finally, Table 9:1.3 gives the source of funds for industrial R and D.

TABLE 9:1.1 RESEARCH AND DEVELOPMENT PERFORMED BY BRITISH INDUSTRY

R and D Performed in Industry (£ billion at 1985 Prices)

	1978	1981	1983	1985	1986	1987	1988
Manufacturing	4.226	4.394	4..28	4.674	4.895	4.949	5.084
Non-Manufacturing	0.213	0.351	0.325	0.448	0.85	0.888	0.856

TABLE 9:1.2 R and D PERFORMED IN MANUFACTURING INDUSTRY (£ million 1985 Prices).

	1978	1981	1983	1985	1986	1987	1988
1.	193	151	130	126	147	131	127
2.	333	293	276	263	259	263	261
3.	248	226	265	372	381	415	406
4.	635	452	370	395	423	427	428
5.	811	955	796	818	801	803	705
6.	753	773	813	942	1002	1201	1362
7.	1254	1546	1630	1759	1882	1709	1787

KEY

1. Other electrical engineering

2. Mechanical engineering

3. Motor vehicles

4. Other manufactured products

5. Aerospace

6. Chemicals

7. Electronics

TABLE 9:1.3
SOURCES OF FUNDS FOR INDUSTRIALLY PERFORMED R AND D (%)

	1981	1983	1985	1986	1987	1988
Overseas Funds	9	7	11	12	12	12
Government Funds	30	30	23	23	20	17
Mainly Own Funds	61	63	66	65	68	71

CHAPTER TEN

PROMETHEUS UNBOUND: AN ALTERNATIVE FUNDING MECHANISM

"Works indeed of genius fall under no art; heroic minds come under no rule; a University is not a birthplace of poets or of immortal authors, of founders of schools, leaders of colonies, or conquerors of nations. It does not promise a generation of Aristotles or Newtons, of Napoleons or Washingtons, of Raphaels or Shakespeares, though such miracles of nature it has before now contained within its precincts. Nor is it content on the other hand with forming the critic or the experimentalist, the economist or the engineer, though such too it includes within its scope. But a University training is the great ordinary means to a great but ordinary end; it aims at raising the intellectual tone of society, at cultivating the public mind, at purifying the national taste, at supplying true principles to popular enthusiasm and fixed aims to popular aspiration, at giving enlargement and sobriety to the ideas of the age, at facilitating the exercise of political power, and refining the intercourse of private life".

J.H. Newman,
The Idea of a University, New York, 1959.

INTRODUCTION

The economic performance of Britain depends, increasingly, on a flexible and dynamic workforce. It is a truism that the future of a nation's economy is essentially determined by the quality of its human capital: and in the United Kingdom this is underdeveloped, predestining us to a role that mixes giant theme parks with assembly plants for multinationals. Universities are only one among a number of institutions that could prove critical in avoiding that end, in leveraging for Britain a competitive advantage among nations, but their contribution to that end is distinctive.[1] While university education provides first a mental training that is only secondarily vocational, the intent of such a training is to create an openness to a life-long learning process, so that its economic benefits are real even though hard to quantify.[2] While the plans of South Korea, forty years ago a ravaged peasant nation, to send 80% of the age cohort to university are quixotic, the (Confucian) values that inform such eccentricity are ones we could honourably and usefully annexe.

It would be foolish, however, to expect government to fund the expansion of higher education. These are stronger political constituencies making competing demands on finite resources. Conservatives still aspire to cut personal and corporate taxation and reduce public sector expenditure, and at the same time both parties promise to improve the health and welfare of an ageing population. There is also the problem of low participation of 16-18 year olds in education, a priority which would preoccupy Labour and will increasingly concern this government; indeed attention to that is a prerequisite for building up higher education. So while the government proclaims a massified system, increasing numbers in higher education to one third of the age group, it offers no promise of increased resources. It is a measure of the administration's assessment of the universities that it can believe there exists so much lethargy in the system.

In Britain, we have what has become virtually a hereditary higher education system. Many undergraduates are the children of 'sixties graduates, and most are middle class, and by having a method of total state tuition support, with some living cost help, high per capita costs have been created such that places are rationed. Rationing also favours the best educated which is

---

[1] M.E. Porter, *Competitive Advantage of Nations*, Harvard, 1990.
[2] M. Blaug, *The Economics of Education and the Education of an Economist*, Edward Elgar, 1987.

not always the same thing as those with the best intellectual potential, so the working class is largely excluded, while there are, in addition, consequences for academic freedom in total state funding. We need, therefore, a system of university finance that allows students, parents, employers and government to make a contribution. Our belief is that the aim of making universities more prosperous and more independent is best sustained by variegated finance and our new charge mechanism proposes to do just that.

Australia provides an inspired example. To summarise their system: fees are differentiated by the cost of courses, in bands of 1,500, 2,000 and 3,000 Australian dollars: this adds an average of 2% on graduates' income tax and the revenue obtained is being used to fund universities' expansion. Australia had 415,000 university students in 1988: in 1990 it had 540,000. Graduates do not begin to start paying the tax until they are receiving above the average pay of A$21,500. Most pay within ten years. Twenty four per cent have been found to pay immediately and therefore obtain a 15% discount and the state has recouped A$300m through up-front and voluntary payments, plus repayments collected through the tax system.[3] Surely the import of such a tax to Britain would be no disincentive, especially when set against the tax benefits many graduates have enjoyed over the past decade, with progressive reductions in the highest rate of tax from 98% to 40%. What we are not saying is that there should cease to be significant state funding of universities: merely that other sources should be brought into play.

The system proposed should improve participation ratios amongst under-represented groups and allow universities to expand. What is advocated does not actually increase state funding in the longer run: rather, the state acts increasingly as administrative agency between producer and consumer.

In the remainder of this chapter, our new charge mechanism is explained in full, including illustrative costings, possible repayment scenarios, income generation accounts and revenue accounts if up-front payments are achieved. Following this, vouchers are examined as a method of funding higher education to create a more market driven, responsive, system.

---

[3] *Report of the Committee on Higher Education Funding*, (Wran Report), Australia Government Publishing Service, Canberra, 1988.

Existing grants and top-up loans receive critical attention and, finally, the philosophy behind the graduate tax is explained.

THE NEW CHARGE MECHANISM

The Higher Education Contribution Scheme (or Higher Education Users Payment Scheme – HEUPS), developed here by us, incorporates features of the Australian system, but has a unique repayment strategy to minimise student resistance. Its aims are manifold and include: widening access to higher education, raising the quality of buildings and equipment, better motivating those who work in it and enabling new recruitment into subjects which have become ossified as their teachers age. *A further, and perhaps more fundamental, aim will be to make universities less dependant on the state by creating a direct consumer-issued stream of financing.* The core idea will be that universities, the producers, receive direct funding from the government in the form of a voucher for each student, since many of the benefits of higher education are societal and not exclusively personal. But, because of the extensive element of individual benefit, most vouchers would not cover total tuition costs. The student-as-consumer would pay through the medium of subsequent enhanced tax appropriations, *but incur no interest payments*, marking this scheme out from most in Europe and that in America.[4]

The machinery will work like this: the universities will in future set full-cost fees for their degrees, which would reflect not only their differential costs but also premiums to incorporate the prestige, teaching and research profile of the college. Some funding for university research would be included in the full-cost fees, but the majority of research funding would in future come from the Research Councils (not a University Funding Council) with additional money from government departments, industry and charities as at present.

Next, student maintenance would be added to this, although students will have the option of going to the local university (and thus living at home) thereby effectively limiting the cost of a degree (maintenance is currently anywhere between 14% and 27% of the cost of a degree). Universities will

---

[4] The idea of government issued vouchers is not new of course, see for example: J. Kelly and G. Hills, "An Alternative Funding Scheme for Higher Education", Unpublished, 1989; A. Peacock, "Education Voucher Schemes, Strong or Weak?", *Journal of Economic Affairs*, 1983;

be able to reduce progressively the cost of degrees and/or expand the provision of places as endowment income builds up from fundraising activities advocated elsewhere in this volume.

Government must determine well in advance the value of vouchers for each cost centre, according to its perception of national need and manpower requirements, but universities have the option of recruiting as many additional students as they choose, although these would not be accompanied by a voucher. *The total cost to students of a degree would be full course costs (with or without maintenance) less the value of the voucher*, and such costs are then repayable through enhanced income tax. Such taxation in our examples would not exceed £1,500 per annum, and then only five years *after* graduation. Furthermore nothing would be payable until personal income rose above average earnings, currently £12,000 p.a. in Britain, so that ability to pay is taken fully into account. Hence it is unlikely that the student would be burdened in his or her first year at work.[5] To ensure maximum flexibility, however, there is no reason why those who choose to do so should not make accelerated payments, but this remains a matter of personal preference, not compulsion.

Categories of exemption can be designated, school teachers or clergy for example, or alternatively those spending the first few years after graduation working in socially useful areas could be exempted from the contribution.[6] While most would probably pay the charge after they had started work, some would wish to pay while still at university and thus become eligible for, say, a 10% or 20% discount on full cost. In Australia, one fifth of students have elected for that option. In all of this, parental or partner income becomes less relevant and plays no part in the motions of the system, though clearly those on higher earnings or with more parental assets will be able to make the repayment faster.[7] One possible alternative would be for a compulsory up-front payment from the top 30% of income earners, established by a means test of parents and/or students. Socialists would like this option though it would prove odious to all Tories, but such

---

[5] Confirmed by a survey of graduates' earnings conducted by Sussex University's Manpower Studies Group, 1990.

[6] Those gaining first class honours could also be exempted, a considerable incentive to do well.

[7] Students studying for professional examinations in law and medicine already have very valuable loans at cheap rates of interest made available to them, with repayments deducted from monthly salary. Thus the concept of 'user payment' is neither unknown, nor particularly burdensome where it already operates.

a measure would imply the benefit of an immediate and lavish windfall for the university system.

Faster repayment should also be possible. Some with the necessary resources would wish to pre-empt the tax and they should not be inhibited from so doing. Overseas students on the other hand will continue to be charged full-cost fees as they presently are, payable in advance, but since EC students must be treated as home students a system of safeguards and precautions is needed to guarantee their payments.[8]

As the scheme matures, several things will occur. Payments will be phased so that the impact on the marginal rate of tax is minimised. Charge scales will be indexed for inflation so the real value of the cost of the degree will be maintained, and the income level at which payments commence will rise as average incomes rise. The scheme would be tidily maintained and adjusted, but since it charts a new demesne there can always be modifications as problems invisible in the theoretic design arise in practical application.

Postgraduate funding however will continue as now. Postgraduates would not of course pay the charge but be fully funded through state scholarships with realistic fees. Taught courses would be at full cost as now and probably not attract scholarship support, but scholarships will continue to benefit postgraduates doing M.Phil and PhD research.

THE CHARGE MECHANISM AND REPAYMENT SCENARIOS

Table 10:1 gives a seven point outline of the HEUPS and Chart 10:1 demonstrates the geography of the scheme, including the flow of funds. (1) The government funds the Research Councils, and the latter fund university research; (2) industry provides the universities with endowments and research contracts (with the possibility of recruitment fees?); (3) the universities recruit undergraduates directly, and signify the full cost of a degree (with maintenance where appropriate) to the student; (4) any such maintenance is administered by the universities themselves, but universities are advanced the full value of the vouchers, the HEUP and

---

[8] For a Pan-European vision of the HEUPS, see N.F.B. Allington, "A Strategy for the Development of an Integrated European University System", *European Access*, forthcoming, April, 1992.

maintenance where appropriate as an up-front payment at the beginning of the academic year; (5) upon graduation, the university notifies the Inland Revenue that the course has terminated and arrangements are made to collect the HEUP. Whilst the government will be required to put more funds into the university sector, over time its share of the costs of higher education is reduced with all the benefits that flow from this, though its funding appropriations remain at the future monetary equivalent of their current level.

As we have said, the government will issue vouchers to cover part of the cost of courses (in consultation with the universities, who will set full cost fees plus maintenance charges). The value of such vouchers will be higher in the case of expensive courses and those deemed socially or economically desirable but unpopular. So government's major inputs will be: (1) the value of the voucher; (2) research funding; (3) postgraduate scholarships; (4) some capital expenditure on buildings and equipment, although there is no reason why depreciation allowances should not be included in full cost fees.

The value of the vouchers would generally be much lower than the sum of full cost fees plus maintenance: this difference would be attributable ultimately to the student, though initially the government would pay, subsequently recouping its investment through the HEUPS.

TABLE 10:1 THE HEUPS IN OUTLINE

(1) **FUNDING OF UNIVERSITIES:**

    (a) TEACHING – via endowments, government issued vouchers, user payment advances, up-front payments.

    (b) RESEARCH – via Research Councils, charities, government departments, industry, EC.

(2) **ROLE OF ENDOWMENTS**

    These are built up through contributions from alumni, industry, charities, donors and government and reduce the cost of courses and/or fund research.

(3) **ROLE OF VOUCHER**

Issued by government and reduces the cost of university degrees. The subjects for which they are issued and the number/value will be determined according to governments' perception of national need.

(4) **MAINTENANCE**

Advanced by the government to the university only where students choose to live away from home and thus require support.

(5) **TOTAL COST OF UNIVERSITY DEGREE**

Full course costs plus maintenance where appropriate, less the value of any voucher. Universities are free to recruit as many students as they wish at full-cost without a voucher.

(6) **HEUPS**

The repayable component of the degree is collected through enhanced income tax when earnings exceed the national average, by:

(a) Supplement on income tax, variable but set at a maximum of £1,500 per annum.

(b) A discount for up-front payment of 10-20%.

(c) The possibility of a compulsory up-front payment for the top 20-30% of income earners via a means test.

(d) Employers, parents or others could make a total repayment of this charge on behalf of the graduate and receive a discount.

(7) **OVERSEAS STUDENTS**

Will pay full-cost fees in advance for undergraduate and taught post-graduate courses.

(8) **POSTGRADUATE RESEARCH**

Home students receive scholarships or bursaries as at present, overseas students pay full-cost in advance.

CHART 10:1 GEOGRAPHY OF THE HEUP SCHEME.

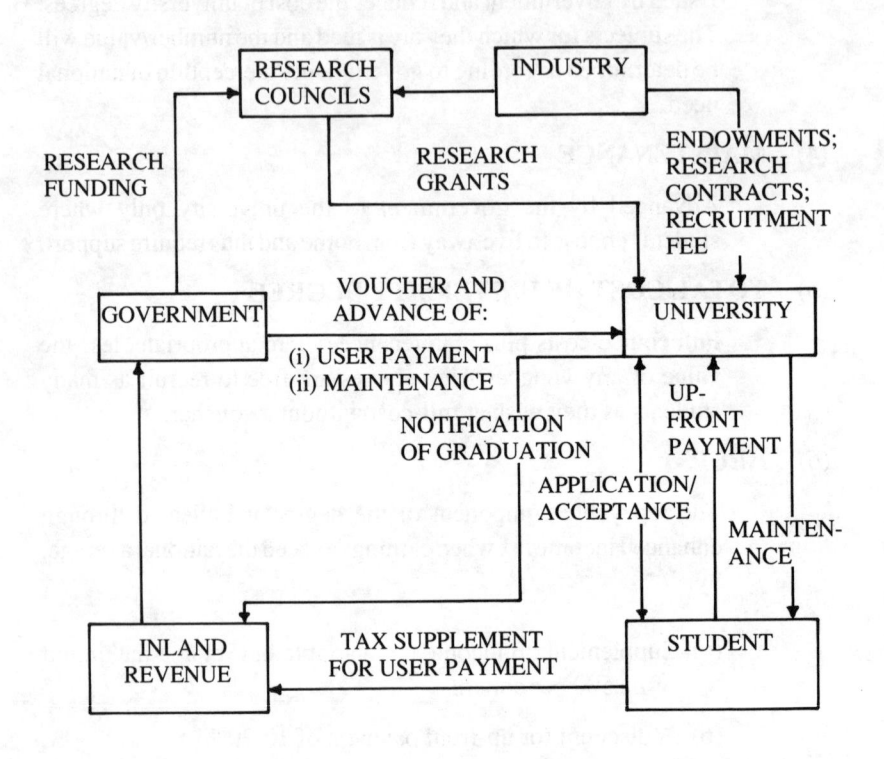

```
                    RESEARCH          INDUSTRY
                    COUNCILS
                                                    ENDOWMENTS;
   RESEARCH          RESEARCH                       RESEARCH
   FUNDING           GRANTS                         CONTRACTS;
                                                    RECRUITMENT
                                                    FEE

                    VOUCHER AND
   GOVERNMENT       ADVANCE OF:        UNIVERSITY
                    (i) USER PAYMENT
                    (ii) MAINTENANCE
                                              UP-
                    NOTIFICATION              FRONT
                    OF GRADUATION             PAYMENT
                              APPLICATION/
                              ACCEPTANCE
                                                    MAINTEN-
                                                    ANCE
   INLAND           TAX SUPPLEMENT      STUDENT
   REVENUE          FOR USER PAYMENT
```

SOME ILLUSTRATIVE COSTINGS

Some illustrative costings are provided in what follows, identifying the start-up costs and then projections for revenue generation. Firstly, Table 10:2 gives details of university student numbers from 1990/91 to 2000 based on Department of Education and Science estimates, with a 19% participation rate from 1993/94 onwards. In line with current trends, the participation of women in university education rises steadily to nearly 50% by 2000, from 44% in 1990/91. Next, Table 10:3 shows total enrolment by cost centre and this is sub-divided into home student numbers for individual centres in order that the projections in Table 10:4 for the years 1990/91 to 2000 can be undertaken. For simplicity, the distribution of students is assumed to be frozen at the 1988/89 pattern.

Secondly, Table 10:5 provides a breakdown of the full cost of courses in 1990/91 and gauges maintenance on the basis of the duration of the course. Average course costs equal £4,220 per annum or £14,092 for the entire degree, but with maintenance calculated at the average of the London plus outside London figures, *the average total costs for a degree at a British university amount to £21,592.* (Course costs are based on contract prices and course duration is taken from the *University Statistical Record*).

The up-front costs to the Exchequer are shown in Table 10:6 and cover two possible options: the first is a low cost, phased switch to HEUPS, in which only first year students pay full-cost fees and receive vouchers, with second and third years supported as before. The second is a higher cost scheme under which all three years switch to the new régime simultaneously. The estimates reflect the maximum possible costs in each case, since full-costs for the cost centres have not been reduced by any conceivable endowment or other income an individual university might have and every student is assumed to draw the full maintenance allowance. Low start-up costs are £1.8 billion and complete start-up costs are £5.4 billion, rising to £6.3 billion by 2000 at 1990/91 prices.

Under existing financial arrangements, the cost of university education to the Exchequer was £2.7 billion in 1990/91 (estimated at £3 billion for 1992/93) taking into account recurrent grant, student fees, student loans and maintenance. This represents half the cost of our high cost option, in which all three undergraduate years switch to HEUPS simultaneously. Nevertheless, we feel that this temporary increase in expenditure is a small price to pay for the provision of a first class, dynamic university sector, upon which the future of the country depends in no small measure. Furthermore, whilst present arrangements entail enhanced expenditure over time, even if inadequate to sustain the system, and only minor returns, our scheme yields substantial revenue amounting to 1 billion pounds after fifteen years. At this point in time the whole scheme becomes self-sustaining given student numbers.

TABLE 10:2 PROJECTED UNIVERSITY STUDENT NUMBERS TO 2000AD

GLOBAL	STUDENT NUMBERS IN 000s	WOMEN %	NUMBER
1990/91	277[1]	44[3]	121.88
1991/92	284[1]	44.5	126.38
1992/93	287[1,2]	45	129.15
1993/94	290[3]	45.5	131.95
1994/95	295	46	135.7
1995/96	300	46.5	139.5
1996/97	305	47	143.35
1997/98	310	47.5	147.25
1998/99	315	48	151.2
1999/2000	320	48.5	155.2

1. DES estimates.
2. Yields 19% participation rate.
3. Steady growth projections thereafter.

TABLE 10:3 TOTAL ENROLMENT AND HOME STUDENTS 1988/89

	COST CENTRE	TOTAL	%	HOME	%
1.	Pre-clinical medicine	8289	3.2	7759	3.2
2.	Pre-clinical dentistry	1077	0.4	1010	0.4
3.	Medicine	10823	4.2	10325	4.3
4.	Dentistry	2643	1.0	2530	1.0
5.	Studies Allied to Medicine	6818	2.6	6403	2.6
6.	Biological Science	17472	6.7	17056	7.1
7.	Veterinary Science	1686	0.65	1603	0.7
8.	Agriculture	2954	1.1	2785	1.2
9.	Physical Sciences	20162	7.7	19772	8.2
10.	Mathematics and Statistics	10221	3.9	9691	4.0
11.	Computer Studies	5968	2.3	5276	2.2
12.	Metallurgy	342	0.1	336	0.1
13.	Engineering and Technology	32401	12.4	27964	11.6
14.	Architecture	3848	1.5	3337	1.4
15.	Economics etc.	14788	5.7	13562	5.6
16.	Applied Social Work	3664	1.4	3558	1.5
17.	Politics, Law	19502	7.5	17283	7.2
18.	Business Administration	11542	4.4	10014	4.1
19.	Librarianship, Communication	233	0.08	218	0.09
20.	Languages	28590	11.0	27847	11.5
21.	Archaeology	887	0.3	857	0.35
22.	Humanities	14508	5.6	14104	5.8
23.	Creative Arts	4245	1.6	4139	1.7
24.	Education	3130	1.2	2828	1.2
25.	Multidisciplinary	34884	13.4	31383	13.0
TOTAL		260684		241640	

TABLE 10:4 STUDENT NUMBER PROJECTIONS BY COST CENTRE TO 2000AD[1]

		1990/91	1991/92	1992/93	1993/94	1994/95	1995/96	1996/97	1997/98	1998/99	1999/2000
1.	Pre-clinical medicine	8864	9088	9184	9280	9440	9600	9760	9920	10080	10240
2.	Pre-clinical dentistry	1108	1136	1148	1160	1180	1200	1220	1240	1260	1280
3.	Medicine	11911	12212	12343	12470	12685	12900	13115	13330	13545	13760
4.	Dentistry	2770	2840	2870	2900	2950	3000	3050	3100	3150	3200
5.	Studies Allied to Medicine	7202	7384	7462	7540	7670	7800	7930	8060	8190	8320
6.	Biological Science	19667	20164	20377	20590	20945	21300	21655	22010	22365	22720
7.	Veterinary Science	1939	1988	2009	2030	2065	2100	2135	2170	2205	2240
8.	Agriculture	3324	3408	3444	3480	3540	3600	3660	3720	3780	3840
9.	Physical Sciences	22714	23288	23534	23780	24190	24600	25010	25420	25830	26240
10.	Mathematics & Statistics	11080	11360	11480	11600	11800	12000	12200	12400	12600	12800
11.	Computer Studies	6094	6248	6314	6380	6490	6600	6710	6820	6930	7040
12.	Metallurgy	277	284	287	290	295	300	305	310	315	320
13.	Engineering & Technology	32132	32944	33292	33640	34220	34800	35380	35960	36540	37120
14.	Architecture	3878	3976	4018	4060	4130	4200	4270	4340	4410	4480
15.	Economics etc.	15512	15904	16072	16240	16520	16800	17080	17360	17640	17920
16.	Applied Social Work	4155	4260	4305	4350	4425	4500	4575	4650	4725	4800
17.	Politics, Law	19944	20448	20664	20880	21240	21600	21960	22320	22680	23040
18.	Business Administration	11357	11644	11767	11890	12095	12300	12505	12710	12915	13120
19.	Librarianship, Communication	249	256	258	261	265	270	274	279	283	288
20.	Languages	31855	32660	33005	33350	33925	34500	35075	35650	36225	36800
21.	Archaeology	969	994	1004	1015	1032	1050	1067	1085	1102	1120
22.	Humanities	16066	16472	16646	16820	17110	17400	17690	17980	18270	18560
23.	Creative Arts	4709	4828	4879	4930	5015	5100	5185	5270	5355	5440
24.	Education	3324	3408	3444	3480	3540	3600	3660	3720	3780	3840
25.	Multidisciplinary	36010	36920	37310	37700	38350	39000	39650	40300	40950	41600

1. It is assumed that the distribution of students by subject remains the same each year.

TABLE 10:5 COST OF COURSES AND MAINTENANCE AT 1990 PRICES

		COST[1]	YEARS[2]	COST OF COURSE(A)	MAINTENANCE AT £2500p.a.[3]	TOTAL COST (B)
1.	Pre-clinical medicine	4600	x 3	13800	7500	21300
2.	Pre-clinical dentistry	5200	x 3	15600	7500	23100
3.	Medicine	8500	x 5	42500	12500	50000
4.	Dentistry	9400	x 5	47000	12500	54500
5.	Studies Allied to Medicine	4000	x 3	12000	7500	19500
6.	Biological Science	4300	x 3	12900	7500	20400
7.	Veterinary Science	8100	x 3	24300	7500	31800
8.	Agriculture	4200	x 3	12600	7500	20100
9.	Physical Sciences	4600	x 3	13800	7500	21300
10.	Mathematics	2700	x 3	8100	7500	15600
11.	Computer Studies	3500	x 3	10500	7500	18000
12.	Metallurgy	5400	x 3	16200	7500	23700
13.	Engineering & Technology	4600	x 3	13800	7500	21300
14.	Architecture	3700	x 3	11100	7500	18600
15.	Economics etc.	3400	x 3	10200	7500	17700
16.	Applied Social Work	2700	x 3	8100	7500	15600
17.	Politics, Law	2200	x 3	6600	7500	14100
18.	Business Administration	2800	x 3	8400	7500	15900
19.	Librarianship, Communication	2900	x 3	8700	7500	16200
20.	Languages	2900	x 3	8700	7500	16200
21.	Archaeology	3400	x 3	10200	7500	17700
22.	Humanities	2800	x 3	8400	7500	15900
23.	Creative Arts	3300	x 3	9900	7500	17400
24.	Education	3500	x 3	10500	7500	18000
25.	Multidisciplinary	2800	x 3	8400	7500	15900
	Average cost p.a.:	£4,220		Average cost of course: £14,092	Average total cost including maintenance:	£21,592

1. Based on contract prices.
2. Taken from *University Statistical Record*.
3. Based on the average of 1990/91 London and Outside London Maintenance Awards: £2,848 and £2,265 respectively.

309

TABLE 10:6 COST TO EXCHEQUER[1]
(£000)

		1990/91	LOW START YEAR I	1991/92	LOW START YEAR II	1992/93
1.	Pre-clinical medicine	188,803	62,914	19,3574	139,049	195,619
2.	Pre-clinical dentistry	25,594	8,531	26,241	17,494	26,518
3.	Medicine	595,550	198,516	610,600	407,066	617,050
4.	Dentistry	150,965	50,321	154,780	103,186	156,415
5.	Studies Allied to Medicine	140,439	46,813	143,988	95,992	145,509
6.	Biological Science	401,206	133,735	411,345	274,230	415,690
7.	Veterinary Science	61,660	20,553	63,218	42,145	63,886
8.	Agriculture	66,812	22,270	68,500	45,666	69,224
9.	Physical Sciences	483,808	161,269	496,034	330,689	501,274
10.	Mathematics and Statistics	172,848	57,616	177,216	118,144	179,088
11.	Computer Studies	109,692	36,564	112,664	74,976	113,652
12.	Metallurgy	6,564	2,188	6,730	4,486	6,801
13.	Engineering & Technology	684,411	228,137	701,707	467,804	709,119
14.	Architecture	72,130	24,043	73,953	49,302	74,734
15.	Economics etc.	274,562	91,520	281,500	187,666	284,474
16.	Applied Social Work	64,818	21,606	66,456	44,304	67,158
17.	Politics, Law	281,210	93,736	288,316	192,210	291,362
18.	Business Administration	180,576	60,192	185,139	123,426	187,095
19.	Librarianship, Communication	4,033	1,344	4,147	2,764	4,179
20.	Languages	516,051	172,017	529,092	352,729	534,681
21.	Archaeology	17,151	5,717	17,593	11,728	17,770
22.	Humanities	255,449	85,149	261,904	174,602	264,671
23.	Creative Arts	81,936	27,312	84,007	56,004	84,894
24.	Education	59,832	19,944	61,344	40,896	61,992
25.	Multidisciplinary	572,559	190,853	587,028	39,135	593,229
Total		5,468,659	1,822,880	5,606,876	3,385,69	5,666,084

1. These figures assume no reduction in costs through endowments and do not take into account those not drawing maintenance or electing to pay up-front. Hence these are maximum cost figures.

TABLE 10:6 COST TO EXCHEQUER (CONTINUED)
(£000)

		1993/94	1994/95	1995/96
1.	Pre-clinical medicine	197,664	201,072	204,480
2.	Pre-clinical dentistry	27,258	27,720	28,182
3.	Medicine	623,500	634,250	645,000
4.	Dentistry	158,050	160,775	163,500
5.	Studies Allied to Medicine	147,030	149,565	152,100
6.	Biological Science	420,036	427,278	434,520
7.	Veterinary Science	64,554	65,667	66,780
8.	Agriculture	69,948	71,154	72,360
9.	Physical Sciences	506,514	515,247	523,980
10.	Mathematics and Statistics	180,960	184,080	187,200
11.	Computer Studies	114,840	116,820	118,800
12.	Metallurgy	6,873	6,991	7,110
13.	Engineering & Technology	716,523	728,886	741,240
14.	Architecture	75,516	76,818	78,120
15.	Economics etc.	287,448	292,404	297,360
16.	Applied Social Work	67,860	69,030	70,200
17.	Politics, Law	294,408	299,484	304,560
18.	Business Administration	189,051	192,310	195,570
19.	Librarianship, Communication	4,228	4,293	4,374
20.	Languages	549,270	549,584	558,900
21.	Archaeology	17,965	18,266	18,585
22.	Humanities	267,438	272,049	276,660
23.	Creative Arts	85,782	87,261	88,740
24.	Education	62,640	63,720	64,800
25.	Multidisciplinary	599,430	609,765	620,100
	Total	5,725,795	5,824,489	5,9923,221

TABLE 10:6 COST TO EXCHEQUER (CONTINUED)
(£000)

		1996/97	1997/98	1998/99	1999/2000
1.	Pre-clinical medicine	207,888	211,296	214,704	218,112
2.	Pre-clinical dentistry	28,644	28,644	29,106	29,568
3.	Medicine	655,750	666,500	672,250	688,000
4.	Dentistry	166,225	168,950	171,675	174,400
5.	Studies Allied to Medicine	154,685	157,170	159,705	162,240
6.	Biological Science	441,762	449,044	456,246	463,488
7.	Veterinary Science	67,893	69,006	70,119	71,232
8.	Agriculture	73,566	74,772	75,978	77,184
9.	Physical Sciences	532,713	541,446	550,179	558,912
10.	Mathematics and Statistics	190,320	193,440	196,560	199,680
11.	Computer Studies	120,780	122,760	124,740	126,720
12.	Metallurgy	7,228	7,347	7,465	7,584
13.	Engineering & Technology	753,594	765,948	778,302	790,656
14.	Architecture	79,422	80,724	82,026	83,328
15.	Economics etc.	302,316	307,2723	12,228	317,184
16.	Applied Social Work	71,370	72,540	73,710	74,880
17.	Politics, Law	309,636	314,712	319,788	324,864
18.	Business Administration	198,829	202,089	205,348	208,608
19.	Librarianship, Communication	4,438	4,519	4,584	4,665
20.	Languages	568,215	577,530	586,845	596,160
21.	Archaeology	18,885	19,204	19,505	19,824
22.	Humanities	281,271	285,882	290,493	295,104
23.	Creative Arts	90,219	91,698	93,177	94,656
24.	Education	65,880	66,960	68,040	69,120
25.	Multidisciplinary	630,435	640,770	651,105	661,440
Total		6,021,914	6,120,183	6,218,878	6,317,609

Thirdly, Table 10:7 gives a breakdown of student enrolment by year to establish graduation figures for the years 1990/91 through to 1999/2000 and these are instrumental in working out income generation figures. Before proceeding to that task, Table 10:8 presents various repayment scenarios, with annual repayments never exceeding a maximum of £1,500 per annum and with the longest repayment period 31.5 years after graduation.

TABLE 10:7 NUMBER GRADUATING, CONTINUING AND ENTERING UNIVERSITIES 1990/91 – 1999/2000

YEAR	TOTAL STUDENTS	GRADUATING	CONTINUING
1990/91	277,000 1st Year intake 92,333	92,333	184,667
1991/92	284,000 1st Year intake 99,333	92,333	191,667
1992/93	287,000 1st Year intake 95,333	92,333	194,667
1993/94	295,000 1st Year intake 95,333	99,333	190,667
1994/95	295,000 1st Year intake 104,333	95,333	199,667
1995/96	300,000 1st Year intake 100,333	95,333	204,667
1996/97	305,000 1st Year intake 100,333	104,333	200,667
1997/98	310,000 1st Year intake 105,333	100,333	209,667
1999/2000	320,000 1st Year intake 105,333	109,333	210,667

TABLE 10:8 – POSSIBLE REPAYMENT SCENARIOS

(A) Full average cost of degree plus maintenance equals £21,500.
No voucher, therefore cost equals £21,500.

Initial Repayments:	Year 1	£250
	2	£500
	3	£750
	4	£1,000
	5	£1,500

Total after 5 years   £4,000
To pay: £21,500 – 4,000 = £17,500 @ £1,500 per annum.
Total repayment period 5 years plus 11.6 years
     = *16.6 years.*

(B) Full average cost of degree plus maintenance equals £21,500.
50% voucher, therefore cost equals £14,500.

Initial Repayment:	Year 1	£125
	2	£125
	3	£250
	4	£250
	5	£500
	6	£500

Total after 6 years   £1,750
To pay: £14,500 – 1,750 = £12,750 @ £500 per annum.
Total repayment period 6 years plus 25.5 years
     = *31.5 years.*

(C) Full average cost of degree plus maintenance equals £21,500.
50% voucher, therefore cost equals £14,500.
Initial Repayments: Year 1 £125
2 £250
3 £500
4 £750
Total after 4 years £1,625
To pay: £14,500 − 1,625 = £12,875 @ £750 per annum.
Total repayment period 4 years plus 17.2 years
= *21.2 years.*

(D) Full average cost of degree plus maintenance equals £21,500.
75% voucher, therefore cost equals £10,500.
Initial Repayments: Year 1 £125
2 £125
3 £250
4 £250
5 £500
6 £500
Total after 6 years £1,750
To pay: £10,500 − 1,750 = £8,750 @ £500 per annum.
Total repayment period 6 years plus 17.3 years
= *23.3* years.

(E) Full average cost of degree plus maintenance equals £21,500.
75% voucher, therefore cost equals £10,500.
Initial Repayments: Year 1 £125
2 £250
3 £500
4 £750
Total after 4 years £1,625
To pay: £10,500 − 1,625 = £8,875 @ £750 per annum.
Total repayment period 4 years plus 11.8 years
= *15.8* years.

(F) Full average cost of degree only, no maintenance, equals £14,000.
50% voucher, therefore cost equals £7,000.

Initial Repayments: Year 1 £125
                          2 £125
                          3 £250
                          4 £250
                          5 £500
                          6 £500

Total after 6 years   £1,750
To pay: £7,000 − 1,750 = £5,240 @ £500 per annum.
Total repayment period 6 years plus 10.5 years
        = *16.5 years.*

(G) Full average cost of degree only, no maintenance, equals £14,000.
50% voucher, therefore cost equals £7,000.

Initial Repayments: Year 1 £125
                          2 £250
                          3 £500
                          4 £750

Total after 4 years   £1,625
To pay: £7,000 − 1,625 = £5,375 @ £750 per annum.
Total repayment period 4 years plus 7 years
        = *13 years.*

(H) Full average cost of degree only, no maintenance, equals £14,000.
75% voucher, therefore cost equals £3,500.

Initial Repayments: Year 1 £125
2 £125
3 £250
4 £250
5 £500
6 £500

Total after 6 years £1,750
To pay: £3,500 − 1,750 = £1,750 @ £500 per annum.
Total repayment period 6 years plus 3.5 years
= 9.5 years.

(I) Full average cost of degree only, no maintenance, equals £14,000.
75% voucher, therefore cost equals £3,500.

Initial Repayments: Year 1 £125
2 £250
3 £500
4 £750

Total after 4 years £1,625
To pay: £3,500 − 1,625 = £1,875 @ £750 per annum.
Total repayment period 4 years plus 2.5 years
= 6.5 years.

Table 10.9 provides revenue generation accounts for scenario (B), that is, full average degree costs plus maintenance but with a 50% voucher and also for (C), the same scenario, but with a different repayment régime. These revenues are calculated on the basis that 20% of graduates are initially unemployed or in further higher education, and that 50% of these return to the workforce after 3 years. The rest, including the unemployed, women raising families, those possibly still in education and those earning below average income, are left out of the assessment.

In the case of the lower repayments (£500 p.a.), income in 1991/92 would start at £9.2 million and reach a maximum annual generation of £1.02 billion in the year 2015/16. With the higher repayments (£750 p.a.), income in 1991/92 again starts at £9.2 million, since all repayments commence at £125, but reaches maximum annual income generation of £1.2 billion much earlier, in 2006/7. Future revenue generation is obviously based on course costs, maintenance and vouchers at the time.

Finally, Tables 10:10 and 10:11 indicate accelerated revenue generation if respectively 20% or 10% elect to pay up-front, assuming a 20% discount on full average course costs and maintenance. Annual revenue rises from £319 million to £368.4 million over a ten year period with 20% paying up-front, and from £159.5 million to £184.2 million over a similar period if 10% pay up-front.

TABLE 10:9 REVENUE GENERATED FROM TWO POSSIBLE SCENARIOS[1]

YEAR	STUDENTS				REVENUE GENERATED (£M) WITH 50% VOUCHER	
	TOTAL	20%	REMAIN-ING 80%	RETURNING	SCENARIO B	SCENARIO C
1990/91	92,333	18,466	73,867		-	-
1991/92	92,333	18,466	73,867		9.2[2]	9.2[3]
1992/93	92,333	18,466	73,867	+ 9,233	18.4	28.9
1993/94	99,333	19,866	79,467	+ 9,233	40.9	106.5
1994/95	95,333	19,066	76,267	+ 9,233	58.3	129.8
1995/96	95,333	19,066	76,267	+ 9,933	98.7	194.3
1996/97	104,333	20,866	83,467	+ 9,533	138.2	260.2
1997/98	100,333	20,066	80,267	+ 9,533	181.4	326.0
1998/99	100,333	20,066	80,267	+ 10,433	225.6	393.4
1999/2000	109,333	21,866	87,467	+ 10,433	272.2	462.6
2000/2001	109,333	21,866	87,467	+ 10,433	321.5	532.3
2001/2002	109,333	21,866	87,467	+ 10.933	366.8	604.0
2002/2003	109,333	21,866	87,467	+ 10,933	415.9	677.5
2003/2004	109,333	21,866	87,467	+ 10,933	467.0	751.1
2004/2005	109,333	21,866	87,467	+ 10,933	517.0	824.9
2005/2006						972.5
2006/2007					-	1225.0[4]
2014/2015					1007.0	
2015/2016					1019.1[4]	

1. Assumes 20% of graduates are initially unemployed or in further higher education; 50% of those return after 3 years with the rest comprising those still in education and women raising a family.

2. Assumes full average costs and maintenance but with 50% voucher.

3. Assumes same as (2) but accelerated repayment scenario.

4. Year of peak income generation.

TABLE 10:10 REVENUE IF 20% PAY UP-FRONT

Assume 20% Pay Up-Front with 20% discount on fees and maintenance.

YEAR	NUMBER	80% AVERAGE COST	REVENUE (£m)
1990/91	55,400	5,759	319.0
1991/92	56,800	5,759	327.0
1992/93	57,400	5,759	330.4
1993/94	58,000	5,759	334.0
1994/95	59,000	5,759	339.6
1995/96	60,000	5,759	345.4
1996/97	61,000	5,759	351.2
1997/98	62,000	5,759	357.0
1998/99	63,000	5,759	362.8
1999/2000	64,000	5,759	368.4

TABLE 10:11 REVENUE IF 10% PAY UP-FRONT

Assume 10% pay up-front with a 20% discount on fees and maintenance.

YEAR	NUMBER	80% AVERAGE COST	REVENUE (£m)
1990/91	27,700	5,759	159.5
1991/92	28,400	5,759	163.5
1992/93	28,700	5,759	165.2
1993/94	29,000	5,759	167.0
1994/95	29,500	5,759	169.8
1995/96	30,000	5,759	172.7
1996/97	30,500	5,759	175.6
1997/98	31,000	5,759	178.5
1998/99	31,500	5,759	181.4
1999/2000	32,000	5,759	184.2

WHY A VOUCHER?

The voucher scheme illustrated here will increase competition between universities for students and make them more market oriented; but 'market' must never imply diminution of standards, for they are sacrosanct and the glory of the British system. Academic integrity should ensure that standards are maintained, but such a view may be complacent, and if necessary the system should be policed using the Academic Audit Unit.

With such a voucher plan, students will enjoy much more flexibility in the choice of universities than the present UCCA system, with its lottery element, permits them. Since the voucher under this scheme has an allocative and not primarily a remunerative function, the objections normally associated with voucher proposals – that they restrict access, bear no relationship to the ability to pay, and raise little revenue – do not apply. The vouchers can however be used for fine tuning by subject, sector, region, course, gender/ethnic or social group.

Differential full cost fees are also permissible under this system, say $\pm 15\%$ of the contract price. Thus a university can capitalise on its prestige, environment and academic credentials. So it ought. Those going to the best universities enjoy greatly enhanced salary and career opportunities, while the institutions that train them usually have to sustain higher costs through their more individualized teaching methods, geographic location and higher research profile. It is only right that their beneficiaries should pay more for more privilege. Again, this will enhance competitiveness and raise efficiency in the provision of services. Our schemata also avoids all the problems associated with loans – rate of interest problems, defaults and long pay-back periods.

The scheme would be administered by the universities. An offer to the student will be signalled to the DES as a commitment to recruit if an appropriate qualification is obtained. The voucher's value would be agreed in advance: government may alternatively give an overall value for each department in a university, with any over-spend absorbed by that university (the difference between endowment plus voucher minus full-cost fees and maintenance will be covered by a special disbursement). If a student is drawing maintenance, it will be channelled to him or her from the government through the university administration and into their bank account. If the student is resident at home no maintenance is claimed and there will be positive incentive to do this. At the beginning of the student's final year, the university administration will inform the Inland Revenue of the size of the user-payment: the Inland Revenue will tag the student and collect a tax supplement as appropriate. This is a simple matter in a computerised tax collection system.

University revenue will be boosted by the repayments – an expansion of numbers and the reduction in course costs will be a concomitant, since revenue is linked directly to students. A recruitment fee could also be added: but employers may avoid this by not using university careers offices. However, if a fee of £1,000 per graduate were taken, an income of £70 million would have been generated in 1988 given the 70,000 who were graduating in that year.

It may however take time for income to flow from the scheme. A slow start scheme is one alternative, with the first year in our hypothetical illustration as the 1990/91 entry, and year 2 and 3 supported as before. Here there would be no revenue until at the earliest year four from the beginning of the scheme, with full revenue generation after year six. Alternatively there could be a more politically unpopular quick start, where all three years switched to the new scheme in 1990/91. Here, revenue would arise from year two of the scheme, with full revenue generation after year four.[9]

GRANTS AND LOANS

Before 1955, when the Anderson Committee reported favourably on student grants, local authorities had total discretion in the award of grants. After Anderson, living expenses were to be paid to all students with two A levels and a university place. But the means test and parental contributions were not scrapped, although the parental contribution scale was reassessed in 1962 so that 40% of the student population became eligible for grants. In 1961 the cost of awards amounted to £35m and by 1965 this had risen to £88m (for 307,261 grants).

---

[9] The Barr and Barnes scheme has a slow build-up to revenue generation and the more recent Barr/CVCP scheme envisages graduates paying back over forty years. N. Barr and J. Barnes, *Strategies for Higher Education : The Alternative White Paper*, Aberdeen University Press for the David Hume Institute and the Suntory-Toyota International Centre for Economics and Related Disciplines, London School of Economics, 1988. Cf. N. Barr "Student Loans : the Next Step", in S. Sexton (editor), *Funding and Management of Higher Education*, Institute of Economic Affairs, 1989, pp.89-103.

There have been numerous changes to grants since their inception, the major ones being:

(a) 1977 – a series of increases agreed to restore the real value of the grant;

(b) 1984 – minimum award of £50 scrapped;

(c) 1985 – supplementary grants for travel ended;

(d) 1985 – Keith Joseph attempts to cut grant and make parents contribute to tuition fees;

(e) 1986 – supplementary grants for special equipment ceased;

(f) 1988 – end of tax relief on covenants;

(g) 1990 – grants frozen and top-up loans offered to students. Students cease to be eligible for housing benefits.[10]

Table 10:12 shows the real change in mandatory student awards between 1962/63 and 1987/88. During the period, student numbers rose 277% to 393,000, but the government, with grant costs at £504m, wanted to cut public expenditure and perceived student grants as a soft option: top-up loans will accelerate the process of reducing state support. Returning to the table, over the 25 years the net grant fell 39% when total costs rose 131%; the parental contribution rose on average 54%, in total a 480% rise equivalent to £325m; the gross award fell 20%, but in total the bill rose 201% to £829m. In 1962/63 the net grant/parental ratio stood at 80:20, but by 1987/88 at 61:39, the parental share had risen 19%, the state's share had fallen by a similar amount.

Viewed another way, the rise in the average parental contribution increased the gross award by 11% in real terms, but the fall in the average government contribution cut it by 31%, giving rise to a net fall of 20%.

The White Paper, *Top-up Loans for Students*, published in 1988, aimed to increase resources available to students so that the real value of the grant returned to its 1978/79 level (the average for the 1970's). However, the withdrawal of social security benefits, that were actually well targeted and rather modest, had the effect of reducing the increase by 7%, 11% rather

---

[10] The government saved a paltry £65m in 1990/91 as a result of social security changes out of a total budget of £48 billion.

than 18%. In fact, 40% of the value of top-up loans in 1990/91 was removed by the change in social security provisions. Table 10:13 indicates how the burden of provision would change between 1990/91 and 2007/8. The parental contribution and net grant were frozen in cash terms from 1990/91. Assuming inflation averages 3% per annum, (highly unlikely of course), both will fall in real terms and loans will assume greater importance, 15% of total finance in 1990/91, but 49% in 2007/8. The net grant represents 29% of total support and the parental contribution 22% (falls of 40% in real terms for both for the average student). Thus student numbers can rise, but parents and government will both spend less. 'Top-up' thus becomes a misnomer, this represents a fully fledged loan scheme with none of the safeguards our scheme offers.

TABLE 10:12
MANDATORY STUDENT AWARDS (ENGLAND AND WALES): REAL TERMS CHANGES 1962/63 TO 1987/88.

		Increase	1987/8 figure
Student numbers		277%	393,000
Net grant-	Average	-39%	£1282
	Total	131%	£504m
Parental contribution-	Average	54%	£827
	Total	480%	£325m*
Gross award-	Average	-20%	£2109
	Total	201%	£829m
Shares of gross award		1962/3	1987/88
Net grant		80%	61%
Parental contribution		20%	39%
Contributions to change in gross award			
Average- Net grant		(-39 x 0.80)% =	-31%
Parental contribution		(54 x 0.20)% =	11%
			-20%
Total- Net grant		(131 x 0.80)%=	105%
Parental contribution		(480 x 0.20)% =	96%
			201%

* includes £6m assessed contributions by students and spouses.

SOURCE:White Paper, *Top-up Loans for Students*, 1988.

TABLE 10:13
DEPARTMENT OF EDUCATION PLANS FOR STUDENT AWARDS
(In 1990/1 prices – academic years)

	1990/91 £	%	CHANGE %	2007/8 £	%
Student Loan (SL)	420	15	+229	1380	49
Parental contribution (PC)	1019	36	-40	607	22
Government Grant (GG)	1356	49	-40	808	29
Total Award	2795	100	0	2795	100

Note: The figures are for students living away from home elsewhere than in London.

SOURCE: White Paper, *Top-up Loans for Students*, 1988.

Top-up loans were initiated because of the serious fall in the real value of grants – in the ten years after 1979 their real value fell 20%.[11] Thus in 1989 it was estimated that the income of 10% of students fell below the long term supplementary benefit level and parents were expected to make a greater contribution. Between 1979 and 1989 the parental contribution actually rose 209%, but some 40% were failing to make their full contribution. In 1989 the cost of grants to the government had risen to £761m and with the impending rise in student numbers this figure would have escalated.

In 1992, the government agreed to raise top-up loans to £715 in a full year for students outside London and to £830 for those studying in London. Grants remain frozen at £2,845 in London and £2,265 elsewhere. The minimum and maximum parental contributions remain at £45 and £58 respectively – hence parents earning residual income of £15,630 to £17,419 contribute £1 for every £11 of grant; those earning residual income of £17,420 to £25,599 contribute £1 for every £6.30 of grant.

Top-up loans attracted general hostility from the student body and the commercial banks asked to operate them considered them too expensive to administer, and the whole concept damaging to their image amongst students. In the event the government had to establish a separate company to organise them and until recently, when student indebtedness has soared

---

[11] *Top-up Loans for Students*, London, HMSO, Cmnd. 520, 1988.

to new levels, they have not proved popular. Now need, rather than acceptance, ensures greater levels of take-up. Our own scheme demolishes both maintenance grants and loans, so that parents are no longer expected to provide maintenance support for their children. Those electing to study away from home are automatically eligible for a full maintenance payment, indexed for inflation, and repayable after graduation as a manageable addition to income tax.

How is the current government student loan scheme perceived? Now a loan creates a perception of debt, while in the case of the mortgage analogy usually cited in its defence the individual generally has equity, since property prices usually rise over time. But the return on a degree is much less certain by comparison. While it is true that the United States system is operated on a loan basis, there exists in that country a culturally-conditioned willingness to pay for education, higher salaries to pay back debt; richer parents; greater opportunities for part time work and vacation work; vocational degrees eagerly sought to guarantee pay-back. Subjects are selected not according to what you want to do but to guarantee that you can pay back your loan, and quickly, to universities that become in turn mediums of training and not education. Moreover, in the United Kingdom loans could be a burden to anyone working in the lower paid public sector and hence a discentive to work there.

In contrast our scheme is more saleable politically, since a tax is perceived more favourably than a debt by consumers. The constructors of political programmes must not only look at the abstract merits of what is proposed, they must also look to the practical saleability of schemes. Nor is there any nonsense in our plan about no return until circa 2025 as there would be with Barr and Barnes. Our scheme generates swift returns to the state. But the loan scheme is a triumph of dogma over sense.

The problems associated with the present loan scheme can be summarised as follows:

(1) Inadequate support for students;

(2) Does not generate significant new funds;

(3) Lengthy transition from grants to loans;

(4) Parental contribution continues;

(5) Restricted eligibility;

(6) Administratively complex;

(7) High cost to tax-payer;

(8) Borrower/lender function invoked, and

(9) Rejected by banks, and not simply for political reasons.

Alternatively, the benefits of our scheme are quite clear:

(1) Adequate and adjustable support;

(2) Grant or voucher given through university not LEA;

(3) No parental contribution;

(4) Single collection through Inland Revenue;

(5) Unlike CVCP scheme, HEUPS related directly to cost;

(6) Following from (5), repayment related to cost;

(7) Just and simple;

(8) Finite repayment period, and

(9) Generates substantial new funds.

THE GRADUATE TAX AND IDEOLOGICAL RECTITUDE

The benefits of higher education are private as well as public: therefore there should be some kind of personal payment while seeking to avoid the negative clutter associated with the idea of debt. Graduates in general have better jobs, less unemployment, higher average incomes (those in their twenties earn incomes equal to those of non-graduates in their thirties), personal fulfilment, and enhanced promotion prospects.[12] Their comparative polish and ability to articulate means that they ascend to all kinds of positions of social, business and political leadership: though it may be fanciful to suggest they enjoy life more through greater awareness of its possibilities (they may also suffer from greater philosophic angst), they undoubtedly live lives which are different in texture to those of their contemporaries. Of course there are also costs to the individual in studying for a university degree – the opportunity cost of income foregone. It is our

---

[12] Survey of graduates, Sussex University Manpower Studies Group, 1990.

submission that those costs are low. Although the student forgoes income, he or she gains much at university which peers in work will not have – more cosmopolitan acquaintance and experience, sporting and other opportunities, an enhanced social life, freedom from many of the constraints of working life.

Employers, the other 'customers' of the universities, also gain – a skilled and adaptive workforce, access to university research, lower training costs, management capable of absorbing new ideas faster and conscious of broader horizons, the possibilities of in-house R and D. In France and Hong Kong by comparison education and training levies give industry a more benevolent attitude to higher education, such levies being an addition to the wages bill and not based on profits. There is also support for training programmes for employees through unions and so on, government provided matching funds for joint industry/university courses, and tax off-sets of up to 100%, particularly for equipment donated by industry. While British industry does pay taxes already, many enterprises pay comparatively little corporation tax: there is, in fact, no correlation between those that pay and those that employ graduates.

At present the tax-payer sustains nearly all of the costs of universities: the block grant, fees and maintenance. He or she receives few of the benefits: most are not privileged members of society and do not participate in higher education, and since there has up until now been no expansion, with level funding in real terms between 1979 and 1989, larger numbers have not until recently been recruited. There is currently no concept of the user costs that are essential to our scheme, and while there are solid benefits from universities – they provide training for engineering and many of the professions – such a contribution is often difficult to quantify, and this is at the root of the universities' dilemma.

Under present funding arrangements the future that awaits universities is mediocre indeed, partly because the funder, the British government, itself suffers ideological confusion – between contracts and per capita funding, between the tensions of market dynamics as against central planning. The one neglected support source is the future wealth of students themselves: their compulsory contribution could save the universities from quiet but inexorable decline.

CONCLUSION

Currently the attempt is to create retail mass higher education, costlessly. Our proposals would permit a populist system without destroying the ethos and quality of higher education, because it would enable the substantial expansion envisaged to be properly financed; though, for these authors, the question will always remain as to whether such money would be better committed to a more rigorous secondary education.

It is axiomatic of the thinking of what came to be known in America as the 'New Right' that 'throwing money' at problems will not solve them: that for example, good pay does not invariably equate with good performance. In our advocacy of better financed universities we also welcome moves to increase their efficiency. If universities are to sustain the respect of the tax-payer who remains their primary funder, the effectiveness of their self-stewardship must be made manifest. At the same time, there are physical limitations to capacity. There also comes a point where good management ends and parsimony begins: the scope for efficiency gains is not limitless, and it is a perception of many in universities that such a point was reached some time ago. Moreover, the mechanism we advocate has long term dividends but short term costs; a balance of demands which always contrives to offend the Treasury.

All the international models of universities are seriously flawed. In the United States the well-being of the middle class has been sabotaged by uncontrolled medical and higher education costs. Higher education is also a burden on individual states as they struggle with other social commitments. In Japan, private higher education pressures parents and ensures that the salaryman's strenuous labours will receive limited reward. In Europe, the slow-burning mixture of work and study is the optimally inefficient combination, ensuring that the least intelligent labour is performed by the most intelligent with a consequent postponement of tax yields until graduates start serious work in their late twenties or even early thirties. Yet all of these bogus models are those which the British with their contemporary sense of inferiority have, at various times, been exhorted to emulate. The distinction of our domestic alternative design is that it achieves what their systems achieve without the ridiculous costs.

British higher education represents a unique transfer of resources from the state to the individual. The only legitimate comparison is with major surgery such as a heart transplant, a contingency that is accidental and neither foreseeable nor universal, or likewise a long period of confinement in state care. Our scheme establishes a more equitable balance of responsibility between funder and consumer: the benefits of universities to most of the population are currently too abstract to justify their monopoly of the funding burden. The current government is anyway unwilling to spend more on higher education. Unless we have a more courageous and strategically determined approach to public spending priorities, robustly economising in some areas the better to finance those that contribute to national competitive advantage, or increased taxation, the only hope for the universities is either to charge their 'customers' or benefit from some scheme similar to our own. Ours is probably not the perfect answer, practice would probably modify it: but conceptually it is surely a potential solution.

The consequences flowing from underfunding universities are not dramatic. These are institutions where personnel change only gradually, and that is true anywhere in the world. And, since the consequences are not dramatic, they are not dramatisable – reductions in expenditure tend to have a delayed impact, one that eludes precise quantification.

Long-term however, there will be consequences. What we have described as the cycle of mediocrity, the confinement of recruitment to little bits of the century, will be merely perpetuated. What then, apart from theatre, will remain for the British to claim an international level of excellence? What are the trading consequences for a country from which the global community thinks it can learn nothing: what image will its products have in the international markets?

Indeed, we are withdrawing from research for the wrong reason – that it has not proved instrumental to economic success, at the moment when others are beginning to recognise the material utility of pure research. While the free-rider argument is beguiling and has seriously undermined the public credibility of British universities, research remains part of our national thrust, our core set of competences, one not easily emulated: the need is to improve those mechanisms by which intangible theory is transmuted into tangible product forms, and to achieve this before the sceptical gaze of a public which legitimately expects demonstratable benefits from all areas of high public expenditure. For the tax-payer is increasingly aware of rights as consumer as well as duties as funder.

CHAPTER ELEVEN

THESE RUINS ARE INHABITED: EPILOGUE

"The Government has no special hostility to the universities. It has a special hostility to public spending".
Professor Earl Russell,
The Times, 18 November, 1988.

..."the bottom line is what universities have been able to buy with the public expenditure made available to them. It has been the experience of most that they can buy less and less. It is there in their accounts. The cuts cannot be made to disappear".

And

"This is a know-nothing government whose philistinism is dangerous to the economic and cultural health of the nation".
Martin Jacques,
Sunday Times, 27 November, 1987.

INTRODUCTION

A vulgarian land teeming with individuals with jobs to work in, houses to return to and money in their pockets may not be an inspiring social vision, but there are worse. The story of the twentieth century should have cured us of our fondness for utopian ideals. Indeed, were education merely about cultural evangelism its advocates would certainly be ignored.

But the quality of the education system is intimately bound up with our economic future, even if the relationship eludes precise numerical quantification.[1] The sclerosis of the universities is part of a broader decadence. The innovativeness of our industry, the skill of its personnel and the insight and flexibility of its leaders depend intimately on a quality higher education as well as on better schooling. Our competitors are educating more and more highly: are we so right and they so wrong? What is the inner meaning of next month's trade figures? Poor economic results tell us not only about government's fiscal or monetary ineptitude: for they are merely the surface articulation of an underlying reality that a nation is sub-educated, overspent and undermotivated.

THE ROLE OF GOVERNMENT

History may judge the failure of government – and academics write history! – to have lain in its educational policies, and many otherwise loyal Tories find themselves perplexed. The government's response to the crisis in universities is often to deny it exists, on the logic that since its critics come from within the system they must be biased, self-interested special pleaders.

But the politics of emotion is no substitute for strategy. Government policy towards higher education suffers a fundamental *tension* between centralist and decentralist impulses: strategy must be cogently thought out, possibly through the medium of a Royal Commission. Policy is incoherent, piecemeal and sometimes contradictory, with confusion about objectives and means. There is a failure to specify what the system is to deliver, and fundamentally, a failure to appreciate what a university is for.

Without doubt universities are one of the few areas of national activity where the U.K. is a key global competitor. Global pre-eminence – at

---

[1] M. Blaug, The Economics of Education and the Education of an Economist, Edward Elgar, 1987.

anything – should not be surrendered frivolously. The lesson some purport to draw from South-East Asia – that pure research is irrelevant to growth – is misleading since countries, like strategically focussed companies, should build on what they already possess, on core thrust: applied in this case, that would mean a role for government in improving the flow of knowlege from academe to industry and assisting in those processes that would give it tangible product form, creating that is the contexts for interchange.[2]

The task of great political leadership is essentially the one that the ethos of a democracy most forcibly frustrates: to save the nation from itself. Every country, as will be apparent to the seasoned traveller, has its own familiar vices, its inbred modes, forms of perversity that are unique to it; great leadership must hold a mirror to the nation, that it might see itself as others see it. In the case of England this vice is an eccentric cultural reflex that fails to see the instrumentality of education or its meaning for ordinary men and women.

What is needed is no less than a revolution in the funding and management of British higher education. The government expects universities to become more efficient; the universities claim that they have cut from the fat down to the muscle and that the state into whose hands, for historical reasons, they voluntarily forfeited the fragile vessel of their sovereignty, has neglected them to the extent that they find it increasingly difficult to maintain their core functions.

OUR MECHANISM

Our overall aim is for the government to provide a smaller proportion of the totality of funding without reducing its current *level* of support, because other funders would assume greater significance. In spite of positive evidence of the growth of private funding, it has not proved nearly sufficient to cover the diminution of state support, so the need is therefore for an entirely new kind of funding: from the beneficiaries of knowledge themselves, either individual or corporate.

Under such a programme, students would be required to reimburse part of their tuition costs and all of their living costs via a graduate charge,

---

[2] C. Ball, "The Problem of Research", Higher Education Quarterly, 3, 1989, p.207.

expressed as a surcharge on income tax once income had exceeded average earnings, and the students would expect to pay this charge for the first part of their working lives. This would integrate with a voucher system, whereby the government would also provide vouchers for students that would cover some, or in selected areas most, of tuition costs: both the extent of provision and the subjects covered would be the decision of government in consultation with universities and employer organisations. This then is the principle of our policy.

The extra money thus created would be reinvested in the university system, the better to fund research, increase salaries, import younger talent, improve buildings and equipment and to expand the system. We emphasise that we do not therefore propose that the state contribution should diminish in absolute terms, merely that new funding sources should be incorporated and that, proportionately not absolutely, the state contribution will decline in the future.

Students could pay the charge as an up-front payment, hence creating a windfall for the universities, or if not they would pay through the medium of enhanced tax, a burden which could be shared jointly with employers or even assumed entirely by them. Currently employers enjoy the free receipt of well-educated personnel, many with a high level of technical training in the specific professions – for example, law, medicine and engineering - without paying a penny beyond amorphous corporation tax. Under these proposals also – and at this point they are particularly distinguished from the Australian scheme – differentiated levies would be charged: some subjects would cost more than others, reflecting the true cost position. This is not unjust, since the costlier subjects are usually the more vocationally oriented ones that generally offer better paying jobs to graduates at the end.

It is certainly a principle of our system that the university personally receives the money owed by the students, and that it does not, as in Australia, go into some amorphous central fund. This consequent build-up of endowments may one day put some universities progressively beyond the control of the state, a desirable end. It is not our purpose to finish with state direct investment, that is neither feasible nor desirable, but progressively to make it the junior partner. And we offer an important caveat. For while we look forward to the demise of central 'planning' and to the emergence of a 'market' system to enable responsiveness, short-termism and myopia implicit in any complete market system should be guarded against, so that areas that would suffer greatly from a market dynamic would be conserved.

OUR DEFENCE

Such a scheme, when described as a graduate tax, is unacceptable to the Tories. Ministers themselves have rejected a graduate tax. In politics, labels and symbols are everything. In the modern Tory party higher taxation is equated with socialism and is anathema. But we would urge Conservatives to reflect carefully on the nature of these proposals. What we are advocating is not a tax but a user payment that is administered through the tax system for the sake of political and social saleability, since ideology cannot be considered without reference to the way it is articulated, and efficient policies must not therefore be dreamed up in isolation from their communicability.

So we advocate a charge on the consumers that will reflect some of the costs incurred by the state, since benefits are personal as well as social. This is not nearly the same thing as increasing tax for socially redistributive purposes. It should connect comfortably with central streams in modern Conservative thought: but apparently it has not up till now, because its label conveys a different – and negative – set of associations. All of this is unfortunate. To have a loan system which was external to the tax system would undoubtedly deter people from entering universities, something no politician wants, for a non-tax integrated loan system creates a perception of personal debt and a whole negative clutter of fear and reluctance.

What we propose may be the salvation of our universities: might wrest them from the mediocrity which is ordained for them. Duplicated in the polytechnics qua universities it will indeed create the great swelling of higher education's cohorts that politicians demand, and the twenty-first century economy will need. The alternatives are tedious indeed. Chaotic and confused official policy will continue to thwart institutional attempts at planning and will be reciprocated by demoralisation and inertia in the universities: they will remain a rusting artefact of the nineteen sixties, a centrally planned and tawdry collective isolated from the ethos of the late twentieth century that roars past them.

Universities have no public constituency. They are ill served by any political party and their future is best assisted by putting them beyond the aegis and hegemony of the British state. It is clear that politicians of all parties place a limited value on the independence and intellectual freedom of universities; sometimes they appear to view them principally as machines for social and economic engineering. (Spending here is in fact low compared with other areas of public excess, for example The Rhine Army costs £3.5 billion a year; company cars have represented nearly three billion annually in revenues foregone, and mortgage tax relief stands at about eight billion).

Many academics in their disenchantment with what appears to be Tory underfunding, look towards the Labour Party. Labour would have continued with the idea of everything for nothing if history repeats itself: it believes in large, entirely free grants to the individual student, it would have attempted to increase access without any dilution of the concept of free tuition. The costs of this can well be imagined and would probably preclude either a better pay deal for academics or the recruitment of more academics. In addition, Labour's anti-élitism would involve some interesting permutations as far as universities are concerned.

If however the government remains oblivious to any calls from the universities for tuition charges, they will have to impose them themselves, and unilaterally. Poorer students might be helped as in the United States by *ad hoc* arrangements and cross-subsidy. Such proposals may appear anti-meritocratic, but if forced to choose between equal opportunities and the universities' fundamental mission, that of enhancing intellectual culture in the United Kingdom, the kind of choice they must make is clear. Our best universities should seriously consider whether they could stand a further decade of attrition without, at some stage, ceasing to be universities of international stature. The government uses the language of markets. The better universities could take them at their word. They could become largely postgraduate, and mainly foreign.

THE FUTURE, AND HOW TO AVOID IT

Educational policy is seldom an attractive area in which to make a political reputation, since its yields are long-term and politics is by its very essence short-term in focus. There is scant public gratitude to be harvested in this arena. But we have reached a point in the history of the nation when the assumptions that inform our educational system need to be modified or discarded. The combined attentions of liberal theorists, social engineers, Thatcherite budget cutters, public philistinism and parental ignorance and neglect have created a state secondary education system that is one of the worst in the western world, and a higher education system for which such a fate is also reserved in the absence of willed and radical change.

We are in danger of becoming a society that vaunts the second rate, in an age and time of unique cultural coarsening (although it is not clear that universities with their disciplinary myopia always uphold the values of high culture), a vision of England raucous and ignorant, the ill-kempt margin of Europe, its industries assembly shops for foreign firms, its academies mean and moribund: and how silly then they will look, defiant on the white cliffs of Dover, waving their £23 billion annual defence bill at increasingly invisible foes, strong of limb but vacant of mind, a tedious, delinquent tribe. There are alternatives. Many opportunities exist for the government to rescue its honour in education. The national curriculum was a beginning. Now let it wrest the initiative in higher education.

Ministers could begin by ceasing the carping and irritated tone they invariably adopt when addressing the subject of universities, and take a more upbeat approach. Generalised abuse is meaningless because it stigmatises the able as well as the lethargic, and does not relate the complaint to any systematic critical analysis. With every government policy initiative there should be an articulative as well as a legislative strategy: one which gives due weight to the symbolic power of public language and public gesture.

Politicians in a democracy, beset on all sides by articulate interests and powerful lobbies, will never act or think as consultants tell companies to act and think, that is, strategically. They will shrink from establishing a set of strategic priorities. They attempt to please everbody, so that finite resources are spread frugally, a thin diet for a queue of mendicants. Politicians must make the decision to curtail certain expensive constitutuencies (defence? mortgage tax relief?) in order properly to fund others: and a central choice criteria must be, does it contribute to the sustenance of national competitive advantage? Education, more than any other activity, does meet that criterion and should be the first beneficiary of economies made elsewhere.

University policy represents an opportunity for the Conservative Party to emerge as much more than a stern accountant, a Party committed to the defence of cultural values and disdainful of all trends that would lead us to a mindless materialism besotted with the imbecile worship of one moment in history. It is culture which, as much as technology, defines a civilisation and raises it above barbarism: and the belief of some of the younger Tories, that government is merely a colossal audit office, can only excite our contempt: for this is to deny any role of leadership in government and appeals to values, and fails to recognise the political truth, that in politics symbolic communications are often more important than austere facts. The great Conservatives of earlier generations understood this well: may they remain true to an honourable past.

SELECT BIBLIOGRAPHY

Advancing A Levels, *Report of Committee Appointed by the Secretary of State for Education and Science and Secretary of State for Wales*, (Higginson Report), London, HMSO, 1989.

Advisory Board for the Research Councils, *Report of Joint Working Party on the Support of University Scientific Research*, London, HMSO, Cmnd. 8567, 1982.

Advisory Board for the Research Councils, *The Support Given by the Research Councils for In-House and University Research*, 1983.

Advisory Board for the Research Councils, *Improving Research Links Between Higher Education and Industry*, London, HMSO, 1983.

Advisory Board for the Research Councils, *A Strategy for the Science Base*, 1987.

Advisory Council on Science and Technology, *The Impact of the Completion of the Single Market on UK Science and Technology*, 1991.

A.A. Alchian "Private Property and the Relative Costs of Tenure", in P.D. Bradley, *The Public Stake in Union Power*, University of Virginia Press, 1959.

N.F.B. Allington and N.J. O'Shaughnessy, *Learning Independence*, Adam Smith Institute, 1987.

N.F.B. Allington, "A Strategy for the Development of an Integrated European University System", *European Access*, (forthcoming April 1992).

N.F.B. Allington, "Funding Arrangements for Universities and Students in the European Community", *European Access*, 1991.

N.F.B. Allington and N.J. O'Shaughnessy, "Teachers and Traders: A Survey of Industry Attitudes to Universities", *Management Education and Development*, forthcoming.

M. Arnold, *School and Universities on the Continent*, 1868.

Association of University Teachers, "Saving British Science", *AUT Bulletin*, September 1989.

Association of University Teachers, "Academic Pay: An International Perspective", *AUT Bulletin*, February, 1991.

P. Augur, "Funding the Universities", *The Cambridge Review*, 1989.

K. Baker, "Higher Education: The Next 25 Years", *Policy Studies*, 1989.

C. Ball, "The Problem of Research", *Higher Education Quarterly*, 1989.

E. Barker, *The British University*, London, 1949.

C. Barnett, *The Audit of War*, 1987.

N. Barr and J. Barnes, *Strategies for Higher Education: The Alternative White Paper*, Aberdeen University Press, 1988.

N. Barr, "Student Loans: The Next Step", in S. Sexton, *The Management and Funding of Universities*, Institute of Economic Affairs, 1989.

M. Barrett, "The Buckingham Experience", in S. Sexton, *The Management and Funding of Universities*, Institute of Economic Affairs, 1989.

R.O. Berdahl, *British Universities and the State*, Cambridge, 1959.

M. Blaug, *The Economics of Education and the Education of An Economist*, Edward Elgar, 1987.

A. Bloom, *The Closing of American Mind*, London, 1988.

S. Bright and M. Sunkin, "Sponsoring Law Schools", *New Law Journal*, 1991.

E. Butler, *A Degree of Privacy*, Adam Smith Institute, 1987.

F.A. Cavenagh, *James and John Stuart Mill on Education*, Cambridge, 1931.

A. Chamberlain, "Centenary Commemoration of James Watt", *The Times*, 18, September 1919.

A.B. Cobham, *The Medieval Universities: Their Development and Organisation*, Methuen, London, 1975.

Committee on Scientific Manpower, (Barlow Report), London, HMSO, Cmnd. 6824, 1946.

Committee of Public Accounts, *36th Report, Restructuring and Finance of Universities*, London, HMSO, 1990.

Committee of Vice Chancellors and Principals, *Research in the Universities*, 1980.

Committee of Vice Chancellors and Principals, *Report of the Steering Committee for Efficiency Studies in Universities*, (Jarratt Report), London, 1985.

Conservative Party Headquarters, "Higher Education", *Politics Today*, 1989.

Council for Higher Education and Industry, *Towards A Partnership*, 1987.

Council for Higher Education and Industry, *Towards A Partnership: The Company Report*, 1988.

N. Crequer, "Lifting the Cloud Over Essex", *Times Higher Education Supplement*, 1989.

A.J. Culyer, "A Utility Maximising View of Universities", *Scottish Journal of Political Economy*, 1970.

H.C. Dent, *British Education*, 1949.

Department of Education and Science, *Accounts and Papers (Education)*, Volumes LXVI and LXVIII.

Department of Education and Science, *Higher Education Into the 1990's*, 1978.

Department of Education and Science, *Changes in the Structure and National Planning for Higher Education*, 1987.

Department of Education and Science, *Science and Public Expenditure, A Report to the Secretary of State for Education and Science from ABRC*, 1989.

B. Disraeli, Speech in House of Commons, 11 March, 1873.

Education Reform Act, London, HMSO, 1988.

H.S. Fearns, "How Much Freedom for Universities", Institute of Economic Affairs Occasional Paper, 65, 1968.

J. Fielden and G. Lockwood, *Planning and Management in Universities*, London, 1973.

A. Flexner, *Universities American, English, German*, Oxford, 1930.

E. Gibbon, *Memoirs of My Life*, edited by G.A. Bonnard, Nelson, 1966.

R.G. Grant, *The University of St. Andrew's*, Edinburgh, 1946.

J.A. Griffith, "The Threat to Higher Education", *The Political Quarterly*, 1989.

J.A. Griffith, *Universities and the State: The Next Steps*, Council for Academic Freedom, 1989.

M. Heseltine, *The Challenge of Europe*, London, 1990.

Higher Education: A New Framework, London, HMSO, Cmnd. 1541, 1991.

Higher Education, (Report of the Committee appointed by the Prime Minister under the Chairmanship of Lord Robbins, 1961-63), Robbins Report, London, HMSO, Cmnd. 2154, 1963.

G. Himmelfarb, *New History and The Old*, Boston, 1987.

House of Lords Select Committee on Science and Technology, *Civil Research and Development*, London, HMSO, Cmnd. HL20 I, II, III, 1986.

T.L. Humberstone, *University Reform in London*, 1926.

Institute of Manpower Studies, Sussex University, *Should Employers Fund Undergraduates?* 1991.

T. Kealey, "Science Fiction: and the true way to save British Science", *Centre for Policy Studies*, 1989.

E. Kedourie, "Diamonds Into Glass: The Government and the Universities", *Centre for Policy Studies*, 1987.

J. Kelly and G. Hills, "An Alternative Funding Scheme for Higher Education", Unpublished, 1989.

J. Kerr, *Scottish Education, School and University from Early Times to 1908*, Edinburgh, 1910.

M. Kogan and D. Kogan, *The Attack on Higher Education*, London, 1983.

R. Marris, "The Problem of Research", Paper Given at St. George's House Conference, 1989.

G. Maston, "Researching the Last Chord", *Times Higher Educational Supplement*, 1989.

R. Middlehurst, "Management and Leadership Development in Universities: What's Happening and Where Are We Going", H. Eggins (editor), *Restructuring Higher Education*, Society for Research into Higher Education, 1987.

A. Morris, "Flexibility and the Tenured Academic", *Higher Education Review*, 1974.

J.H.Newman, *The Idea of a University*, New York, 1959.

J. O'Leary, "Britain Turns to Euro-Millions", *Times Higher Educational Supplement*, 1989.

Organisation for Economic Co-operation and Development, *Changing Patterns of Finance in Higher Education*, Country Studies, 1989.

A. Oswald, "The Cream Goes West", *The Guardian*, 13 June 1989.

T. Owen, "The University Grants Committee", *Oxford Review of Education*, 1980.

E. Parkes, Address to Committee of Vice Chancellors and Principals, October, 1980.

A. Peacock, "Education Voucher Schemes, Strong or Weak?", *Journal of Economic Affairs*, 1983.

H. Peisert and G. Framheim, *System of Higher Education, Federal Republic of Germany*, New York, 1978.

H. Perkins, "The Academic Profession in the United Kingdom", in B.R. Clarke, *The Academic Profession: National, Disciplinary and Institutional Setting*, University of California Press, 1987.

Public Expenditure White Paper, London, HMSO, Cmnd. 9189, 1984.

H. Rashdal, *Universities of Europe in the Middle Ages*, Oxford, 1936.

Report of the Committee on Higher Education Funding (Wran Report), Australian Government Publishing Service, Canberra, 1988.

Review of the University Grants Committee, (The Croham Report), London, HMSO, Cmnd. 81, 1987.

W.A. Robson, "las universidades britanicas y el estado", *Nuestro Tiempo*, 1956.

B. Russell, *History of Western Philosophy*, Allen and Unwin, London, 1961.

J. Sandback, "The Universities Funding Inheritance", *Public Finance and Accountancy*, April 1989.

J.E. Schuitz, "Academic Employment as Day Labour: The Dual Labour Market in Higher Education", *Journal of Higher Education*, 1982.

P. Scott, "The Government and Universities", *The Cambridge Review*, 1989.

Select Committee on Miscellaneous Expenditure, 1848.

M. Shattock and R. Berdahl, "The British University Grants Committee 1919-1983: Changing Relationships with Government and Universities", *Higher Education*, 1984.

A. Smith, *An Inquiry into the Nature and Causes of the Wealth of Nations*, Glasgow Edition, Oxford, 1976.

A. Smith, *Correspondence of Adam Smith*, edited by E.C. Mossner and I.S. Ross, Oxford, 1987.

L. Southwick, "The University as a Firm", *Carnegie Review*, 1967.

P. Swinnerton-Dyer, Speech to the Committee of Vice Chancellors and Principals, September, 1987.

J. Taylor and I. Johnes, *Measuring the Performance of Universities*, London, 1991.

The Development of Higher Education Into the 1990's, London, HMSO, Cmnd. 9524, 1985.

University Funding Council, *Report on the 1989 Research Assessment Exercise*, 1989.

University Funding Council, "Statement on Research Policy", Circular Letter 22/89, 1989.

University Grants Committee, *Returns from Universities and University Colleges in Receipt of Treasury Grant*, HMSO, various volumes.

University Grants Committee, *University Development, 1957-1962*, 1962.

University Grants Committee, *University Development, 1962-1967*, 1968.

University Grants Committee, *A Strategy for Higher Education in the 1990's*, 1984.

University Grants Committee, "Planning for the late 1980's", Circular Letter, 12/85, 1985.

University Grants Committee, Circular Letter 5/85, 1985.

University Grants Committee, *Strengthening University Earth Sciences*, (Oxburgh Report), 1987.

University Grants Committee, *The Next Research Selectivety Exercise*, 1988.

University Statistical Record, Various Volumes.

L. Wagner, (editor) *Agenda for Change in Higher Education*, Leverhulme Programme for Study into Future of Higher Education, 1982.

C. Warnock, *Universities: Knowing Our Mind*, Chatto and Windus, London, 1989.

C. Williams, "Salford's Standards Restored to Pre-1981", *Times Higher Educational Supplement*, 1989.

G. Williams, *The Academic Labour Market*, Elsevier, Amsterdam, 1974.

G. Williams, *Universities Under Stringency*, OECD, 1989.

J.G. Williams, "The Historical Background of the University of Wales", *Final Report of the Working Group on Powers and Functions*, (Daniels Report), 1989.

R.J.P. Williams, "Time to Grade the Research Councils", *The Times*, 21 August 1989.

P. Wilsher, "Putting the Punch Into Research", *The Sunday Times*, 2 August, 1987.

D.A. Winstanley, *The University of Cambridge in the Eighteenth Century*, Cambridge University Press, 1922.

D.A. Winstanley, *Early Victorian Cambridge*, Cambridge University Press, 1940.

NAME INDEX

Alchian, A.A.	118	Kelly, J.	299
Allington, N.F.B.	124,264,283,301	Kerr, J.	37
Arnold, M.	42	Marris, R.	100
Angur, P.	81,276	Mason, J.	43
Barker, E.	53	Maston, G.	195
Baker, K.	80, 114, 125	Middlehurst, R.	115
Baker, W.	43	Mill, J.S.	27
Ball, C.	104, 131, 332	Morgan, G.	45
Barnes, J.	179	Morris, A.	118
Barnett, C.	99,292	Murray, K.	64
Barr, N.	179	Newman, J.H.	10,11,28,111,131, 200,201,275,296
Barratt, M.	51, 52		
Lord Beloff	75	Newman's *Idea of*	
Bentham, J.	40	*a University*	30-32,95
Berdahl, R.	32,42,45,64,70	O'Casey, S.	12
Blaug, M.	297,331	O'Leary, J.	149
Bloom, A.	105, 123	Oswald, A.	178
Boot, J.	45	Owen, H.	45
Bradley, P.D.	118	Owen, J.	42
Brougham, H.	40	Owen, T.	59
Burke, J.	22	Parkes, E.	73
Butler, E.	254	Peacock, A.	299
Campbell, T.	40	Peisart, H.	27
Carpenter, W.	43	Perkins, H.	98
Cavenagh, F.A.	27	Phillips, D.	165
Chamberlain, A.	65	Place, F.	40
Chamberlain, J.	58	Porter, M.E.	13,297
Clarke, B.R.	98	Presley, E.	21
Clarke, K.	109	Price, C.	184
Cobham, A.B.	33	Rashdal, H.	32
Crequer, N.	140	Raleigh, T.	46
Culyer, A.J.	121	Richmond, M.	148
Dent, H.C.	42	Roberts, D.	110
Disraeli, B.	12	Robson, W.A.	32
Drucker, H.	114	Rooke, D.	274
Eggins, H.	115	Russell, B.	32
Firth, M.	43	Earl Russel,(Prof)	330
Flexner, A.	48	Salisbury, E.	45
Framheim, G.	27	Sandback, J.	141
Fry, L.	43	Schuitz, J.E.	118
Galbraith, J.K.	184	Scott, P.	81,82
Gibbon, E.	35	Sexton, S.	179
Grant, R.G.	38	Shattock, M.	70
Griffith, J.A.G.	99,101,158,159,160	Simon, E.	47
Haldane, R.B.	58,59	Sloman, A.	140
Halsey, A.H.	167	Smith, Adam	35
Heseltine, M.	131	Smith, Andrew	75
Hills, G.	299	Snow, C.P.	122
Himmelfarb, G.	123	Southwick, L.	113
Humberstone, T.L.	40	Swinnerton-Dyer, P.	16,76
Humboldt, W. von	27	Taylor, J.	101,105
Hume, J.	40	Walker, D.A.	266
Jackson, R.	15,75,117,177	Webb, S.	58
Jacques, M.	330	Williams, C.	149
Jenkins, R.	118	Williams, G.	185
Joseph, K.	19	Williams, J.G.	45,46
Kedourie, E.	263, 264	Williams, R.J.P.	156,161
Kealey, T.	47	Wilsher, P.	138
		Winstanley, D.A.	35,36

SUBJECT INDEX

Aberdare Committee	46,54
Aberdeen University	39
Academic audit unit	91
emigration	177-8
freedom	121,123
personnel	116-8
Accelerated repayments	300
Access	95-6
1705 Act of Scottish Parliament	53
Administration	269
Administrative reform	114,115
Advisory Board for the Research Councils	78,104,105, 133,137,138, 140,153, 161,165,176, 180,181, 183,197
Allocation of resources 1990/91	83-85
1991/92	85-7
1992/93	88
Allocation of teaching and research funding 1992/93	88-90
Alumni fundraising	81,260
Anderson Committee	321
Assessment by students	123
Aston University	88
Australian graduate levy system of finance	298 16-17
Award of grant to Oxbridge	36
Basic research	140,174-5
and industry	278
Barlow Report	47
Bidding	77,91
Birmingham University	43,45
Bradford University	80
British Petroleum	150
British Technology Group	128,137
Bryce Commission	42
Buckingham University	50-53,110, 262,263
Cambridge University	23,83,88, 136,167
CASE awards	290
Church of England	54
Chronology of Funding arrangements	23-26
Citations	139
City University	88,278
Civic Universities	42-44
Colleges of Advanced Technology	50
Committee of Vice Chancellors and Principals	47,65,100, 102,126, 136,258, 278,299
Competitive bidding	19
Contracts	19
(research)	126,157
Council for Higher Education and Industry	128
Cost to Exchequer	311-3
Council for Industry and Higher Education	281
Course costs and maintenance	310
Croham Report	125,157
1981 Cuts	255
Denmark	
higher education	228
revenue	228
student support	229
Department of Education and Science	70,71,72,74, 120,157,162
Drop-out-rate	
Australia	22
France	22
Dual funding	140,162,174
Dundee University	77,88
Durham University	39,41,54,77, 88
Early retirement scheme	73
Economic and Social Research Council	162
Edinburgh University	39,83,114, 142,167
Education Act 1870	42
1944	47,66
1988	118,154
Education	
commercial success	13
its role	13
Endowments	59
Entry blockage	121
Fees-only students	77,90,92
Financial forecasts for universities	144-6
Finland	
higher education	233
revenue	234
student support	235
France	
higher education	219
revenue	221
student support	222
French Revolution	22
Fundraising	18
by subject 1992/93	90
Gates Committee	67
German academics	13
Germany	
higher education	215
revenue	215
student support	216
Glasgow University	38,77,88,102
Governance of Universities	20
Graduates demand for	290
Graduate tax	17,326-7,334

347

Greece			National Union of Students	18
higher education	239		Netherlands	
revenue	239		higher education	224
student support	240		revenue	225
Harvard University	19		student support	226
HEUPS in outline	302-3		New-blood Scheme	20,74,80
HEUPS geography	304		New universities	47-49
Higginson Report	77,96		Northumberland Committee	68
Higher Education:			Norway	
A New Framework	77,93,106-7, 154, 173-4		higher education	230
			revenue	231
Higher Education, Spending on	17		student support	232
			Nottingham University	44
Higher Education Contribution Scheme	299,301,305		Open University	124
			Owen's College	42
House of Lords Select Committee on Science and Technology,	133,256, 260,264		Oxburgh Report	78,103,104
			Oxford University	83,88,135, 150,167, 261,286
Civil Research and Development	279,280		Oxford and Cambridge	32-37,41,42, 44,45,49,54
Hull University	291		1897 Parliamentary Grant	56
Imperial College London	102,167		Participation rate	270
Independence	261,283		Patents	139
Industrial funding	259		Pay	116,117n, 119, 132,267
Interdisciplinary degrees	122			
International research comparisons:			comparative	
			Performance	
Australia	195-6		indicators	21
Denmark	189-90		Planning	125
Finland	189		Polytechnics	106,108,109, 127,174,176, 185,280
France	196-7			
Germany	188-9			
Greece	192			
Japan	197-9		Postgraduates	147
Netherlands	190		Privatisation	264,285
Norway	190-2		Proprietors of	
Spain	192-3		University of London	40
United States	193-5		Public Accounts	
Isis Innnovation Ltd	135		Committee	66,67,72,142
Japan			Public Expenditure	
higher education	211		Select Committee	71
revenue	212		Public relations	129
student support	214		Quinquennial grants	68,72
Jarratt Report	100		Reading University	44,88
Keele University	45,69,88		Religious tests	36
Kendrew Report	105		Repayment scenarios	314-7
Kent University	49		Research	109,134,137
King's College London	39,40		defence	141
Lancaster University	49		civilian	141
Latin Renaissance	32		Research Councils	96,102,128, 140,141,160, 165,174,179, 183,280,299
Link scheme	128			
Local students	124			
London University	39,40,41, 44,45,53,83,88			
London School of Economics	82		concentration of awards	164
Mason Science College	43		Research income	148,149
Massification	19,107,110, 126,244,		from industry	149,150,151
			industry	
overseas	202,270		commissioned	279
Medical Research Council	10		Research/Teaching	
National Defence Student Loan Programme	97		split	19
			Revenue generation	317-8

348

Robbins Report	17,49,68,129
Rockfeller Foundation	41
Royal Commission	129,331
Royal Commission on Technical Education	54
Salary	
non-monetary incentives	21
regional variations	21
Salford University	149,153,162,278,291
Science base	256,281,288
Save British Science	141,176,260
Science and Engineering Policy Studies Unit	162
Science and Engineering Research Council	101,153,164
Science/arts balance	71,72,73
Science budget	181-3
Schools Enquiry Commission on Technical Instruction	42
Scottish Universities	37-39
Select Committee on Estimates	66,67
Select Committee on Estimates	66,67
Select Committee on Miscellaneous Expenditure	54
Selectivity Exercises	78,82,99-101,149,156,165-173
Single European Act	147
Sources of University funding 1960, 1980 and 1988	97
Sources of University Income	60-3,64
Spain	
higher education	236
revenue	237
student support	238
Squibb Corporation	150
St. David's College Lampeter	45,52,83,88
St. Andrew's University	38
Staff numbers	146
Staff/student ratios	143
Staff training	289
State funding of Universties	53-58
Student enrolment	306-7
maintenance	18,299,325,326
numbers	306
projections	307-9
Subject guide prices	93
Survey of industry	276
of vice chancellors	255
Swansea University College	46
Sweden	13
university research	
Switzerland	
university research	13
Tax incentives	260,283,287
Teaching Company Scheme	154,289
Teaching/Research split	82,155,158,174,180
Technical Instruction Act	44
Tenure	21,118,119,204
The Development of Higher Education Into 1990's	77,94
The Royal Society	141
Top-up loans	322,325
Treasury	55,58,59,64,66,67,70,72,269
Tuition costs	18,299
fees unilateral implementation	19
Two-year degrees	20
UCCA	125,272
University Funding Council	91,93,96,132,141,142,149,156,162,172,179,183,269
University funding governance	255, 268-9
United States of America	
higher education	205
revenue	206
student support	207
tenure	21
Universities and government	15
University Colleges	44
University entrance	17
statues and ordinances	17
their importance	14
University College Aberystwyth	45,54
University College Bristol	43,83,88,142
University College Cardiff	46,54
University of East Anglia	49
University of Essex	49,77,83
University College Exeter	41,45
University College Hull	41,45,102
University College Leicester	41,45,77,88
University College Liverpool	43
University College London	39,150,167
University of Manchester	45,54,148,167

University of Newcastle	77,88
University College of North Staffordshire	45
University College North Wales, Bangor	46,54
University of Paris	38
University of Sheffield	43
University College Southampton	41,45
University of Surrey	114
University College of Sussex	48
University of Wales	45-47
University of Wales, College of Cardiff	46
University Grants Committee	44,45,47,48, 50,64,65,66, 70,71,72, 73,79,96, 100,104,136, 142,148,166, 255,258,269
foundation	55,58,59
new terms of reference	66
planning	68
ranking	101
transfer to DES	67-8
Vice-chancellors	112-4
Vouchers	299,300, 320-1
Warwick University	49,83,167, 278
Welsh National School of Medicine	46
Wran Report	298
Yorkshire College of Science	43
York University	49,69,167